"Captivating! Once I started reading, I cou
Then They Won Gold is a great resource for
that intertwines biographical data with ma:

Lisa Baumann - AquaFit Masters Founder/Head Coach
Metropolitan LMSC Swimming President

* * *

"Chuck Warner has picked up the mantle of America's Swimming Historian
from Coach Peter Daland. If *...And Then They Won Gold* started out as a cook-
book, it ended up as a masterful history of modern swimming. In these biographies, the common themes of what it takes to excel at the highest levels unfold
repeatedly. The 'recipes' become self-evident.

"Perhaps most important, these champions did not take a mythic, linear progression to the top. Coach Warner captures their humanity in the struggles,
failures and detours on the road to Gold.

"Many people say that the best parts of clinics are the conversations in hallways
or over meals. Chuck has pulled our chair up to these tables and has let us
listen in to the conversations and 'war stories' about the winding, but essential,
path to the podium. It is a path for which we should prepare all of our athletes
and their families."

George Block - CEO Haven For Hope
President World Swim Coaches Association

* * *

"When you read Chuck Warner's *...And Then They Won Gold,* you immediately
become immersed in the lives of 8 great Olympic Champions. There is attention to detail that the swimmer or coach can use as a framework for effective
training. More importantly, there are broad themes of motivation, discipline,
leadership ... that transcend the sport of swimming and provide a recipe of success for coaches, athletes and parents, regardless of the sport. Congratulations
to Chuck Warner for writing this thoughtful and motivational book."

Ben Bucca, Jr. - Women's Tennis Coach
Rutgers University

"...*And Then They Won Gold* offers a unique insight into the personal journey and growth of some of the United States most decorated swimmers. Chuck chronicles the path of individuals to Olympic greatness while enabling the reader to connect with the human side of great Olympians."

Frank Busch - USA National Swim Team Director

* * *

"It is important to have the facts as we analyze, interpret and learn from the past and use it for the future. This, meticulously, Chuck Warner has made possible with his painstaking research. The swimming community owes him a hearty vote of thanks for what he has found for us."

Forbes Carlile, Owner of Carlile Swimming & Swim Schools, Sydney, Australia, 1976 Inducted into International Swimming Hall of Fame

* * *

"I love the way Warner has brought these amazing stories to life—stories replete with colorful character portraits, psychological insights and rivalries from our greatest swimmers of all time. This should be required reading for swimmers of all ages hoping to attain their goals!"

Kristin Gary
Masters World Record Holder
Executive Director, Trident Swim Foundation

* * *

"Parents, coaches, swimmers and fans all crave information on this great sport of ours.

"Knowledge is power!

"What better way to absorb knowledge than learn from the greats. Chuck painstakingly shares the stories of many great champions. We become engrossed in their incredible journeys that will not only motivate future competitors but educate and entertain parents and fans… Well done Chuck!"

Laurie Lawrence - Six Time Australian Olympic Swimming Coach/Advisor
Owner of Laurie Lawrence Swim School
1996 Inducted into the International Swimming Hall of Fame

"One of the most difficult things to understand in modern swimming is the difference between 'what they do as mature swimmers' and 'what they did as age groupers to get there'. Coach Warner does a spectacular job of creating that differential understanding. This book should be considered must reading by every head coach who dreams of developing the next generation of great swimmers. Well done Coach Warner!"

John Leonard - Executive Director
American Swimming Coaches Association
The World Swimming Coaches Association

* * *

"...*And Then They Won Gold* opens up a coach's eyes to view and see things a bit differently. It is great for new coaches and swimmers as well as the ones who have been around forever."

Kate Lundsten - Head Coach
Aqua Jets Swim Team, Minnesota

* * *

"...*And Then They Won Gold* serves as a close up look into the individual paths that these swimming Olympians travel in their quest not only for gold, but for personal greatness. These men each pursued their dreams, and although each road was different, they all made their way to the top. As a coach of athletes at this caliber, it is fascinating to read how deeply the inner circle of each athlete affects progress. Warner's book tells the story behind the man and behind the medal. We can all; parents, athletes, coaches and fans, learn from these riveting accounts of greatness."

Teri McKeever - 2012 USA Head Coach Women's Swimming
Head Coach Cal Berkeley 2011 & 2012 - NCAA Champions

* * *

"We have a great deal to learn from the history and tradition of our sport. This much needed and well written book serves the dual purpose of providing well deserved recognition for our champions of the past, and motivating our champions of the future. The building blocks of success are clearly delineated in an entertaining and inspiring way through the personal stories of these past champions. Thank you Chuck Warner for this invaluable contribution to our sport and the values it promotes."

Denny Pursley - Great Britain National Team Director

"...*And Then They Won Gold* is the type of reading that is good not only for athletes but especially for the support cast. It can aid family members, age group coaches, senior coaches, and associated friends with exactly how many factors contribute to the athletes' success. This should be required reading for swimmers who have these lofty goals. It will help ground them and allow them to prepare better."

Gregg Troy - 2012 Head Coach USA Men's Olympic Team
Head Coach University of Florida
2010 NCAA Champions

* * *

"Want to know how to make an Olympic Champion? Start here. Read and savor these eight athletic biographies; distill out the common ingredients; mix and blend them in just the right amounts and just the right stage in life; and you will begin to create what Chuck Warner calls a 'recipe' for what Olympic Champions did to win a Gold Medal. Delicious! Bon Appetite."

Tim Welsh - Head Men's Swimming Coach
Notre Dame University
Former President ASCA

* * *

"With his latest book, ...*And Then They Won Gold*, coach and author Chuck Warner solidifies his position as the John C. Maxwell and Malcolm Gladwell of Swimming, by explaining success and emphasizing the importance of the idea that talent alone is never enough."

Bruce Wigo - Chief Executive Director
International Swimming Hall of Fame

CHUCK WARNER

Florian,
Thanks for coming to the
Arete Swim Camp. You are
a great student of swimming
and it will take you far.
I hope these stories help
you get fast! Chuck Warner

...AND THEN THEY WON G🏅LD

STEPPING STONES
TO SWIMMING EXCELLENCE

www.areteswim.com

ISBN-13: 978-0-9853928-0-2

Cover Design by   www.thephidesignstudio.com
Layout by   www.delaney-designs.com

Printed in the United States of America

ACKNOWLEDGEMENTS

The idea for this book came from Coach Eddie Reese and Coach George Block. The concept began with the thought of a recipe book of what great swimmers did to get to the top of the sport. It has evolved from that concept into a combination of a series of narratives with training spotlights that intend to give coaches, athletes and parents a concise view of what is entailed in an athlete becoming the very best in the world.

It is unlikely this book would have ever been written without the support and friendship of Jim Wood. Many know Jim as the first coach to serve as president of the national governing body of USA Swimming and also as the owner of the Berkeley Aquatic Club. Experiencing Jim's personal friendship and loyalty is a very special gift. Thank you, Jim.

It is also important for me to acknowledge the support of Diane Bonanno, the executive director of Rutgers University Recreation. Diane's friendship, influence and support have been very important to my professional career for more than 15 years and very critical to being able to produce this work.

Swimming World Magazine and publisher Brent Rutemiller are an invaluable part of holding on to our swimming history. Brent's granting of the use of all their archives is yet another demonstration of the company's gifts to swimming, which keep on giving. John Leonard and the American Swimming Coaches Association have permitted use of their archives and clinic books to compile various aspects of the book. Thank you, John and ASCA. Thanks also to Ben Nanna and Jessie Pogogeff for the research help.

The great minds of Terry Warner, Dana Abbott, Ira Klein and Kevin Johnson, acting as my "kitchen cabinet," have all been very helpful to bring this idea forward. The editing skills and immense work from Terry, Dana and Kevin have to be recognized. The resource of a great writer, editor and thinker in Todd Kemmerling comes through all over this book. I constantly go back to Todd for ideas and he always delivers his help and encouragement.

If you have read this far, please read a little more: These eight great athletes have given much to make this book happen. Thank you, Matt, Dave, Mike, Josh, Lenny, Ian and Aaron. Also great thanks to Denis Cotterell and Ian Pope for helping us peek into Grant Hackett's amazing swimming career. Many others of note are in the "interview section" in the "sources" section. Thank you all for allowing all of us to learn from your experiences so that children, families and coaches can benefit in the future.

Finally, a number of us went round and round about what to name this book. The source of the final result was Dave Reilly and an appropriate one at that. The first time I ever saw Dave was when we were 12-year-olds competing in the 100 individual medley for different summer clubs. His Woodbridge Swim Club had a seven-year winning streak on the line against our High Lane team. I needed to beat Dave to help us win. I looked underwater at the finish and what did I see ...

DEDICATION

This book is dedicated to:
Every young coach, parent or athlete that
is looking for the stepping stones to greatness.
They are there for you.

The legacy of these great eight athletes and people.
Their stories deserve to be preserved.

To my favorite person, my daughter Anne Rose Warner.
You are all gold to me.

TABLE OF CONTENTS

INTRODUCTION AND HOW TO READ THIS BOOK

An Olympic champion is the result of taking the entire world's population and filtering a sports competition to the point that the best athletes remain in the competition at the Olympic Games. The process continues at the Games with the battle to become a finalist and then on one day every four years, one person stands at the top of the award's podium as the best in the world. This book is written for the purpose of showing the process from the athlete's introduction into sports to the pinnacle of their experience as an Olympic champion.

The format is a short biography about eight Olympic swimming champions. Each story has these common elements:

- The individual development of the person.
- Coaching effectiveness and delivery of the sport to the athlete.
- Training progressions.
- Insight into the role of each athlete's parents and family.

The stories are presented in chronological order so that you may experience some of the changes and progressions in the sport of swimming over the span of twenty-five years. Each of the athlete's training is relevant today since each of them were so exceptional in their era that they would still be very competitive at the Olympic Games today.

Each biography has a slight emphasis on a quality that was special about that athlete's experience. Matt Biondi's career outlines his *process for excellence*. David Berkoff shows the value of being a creative and *innovative* athlete. To help understand the importance of *competitiveness*, Mike Barrowman's story is very illuminating. *Leadership* is one of Josh Davis' great qualities and comes through in the way he traversed his swimming career while positively influencing others. Lenny Krayzelburg *survived* so many challenges that he leaves an example of resilience for all of us to admire. If you are involved in a sport in which the opportunity seems limited, you can understand why Ian Crocker truly was the *underdog*. Grant Hackett displays the commitment and attention to detail to become *the greatest trainer in the world*.

The human mind is the most important part of anyone's success in sports. The final story about Aaron Peirsol is a living testament to what the result can be if you are *a believer*, but also serves, in a small way, as a conclusive chapter to the book.

The three dots (...) in the title ... *And Then They Won Gold* are for the purpose of pointing out that there are many steps taken before ever winning a gold medal. The information from many age-group and developmental coaches to help identify these stepping stones is important. Equally important is to recognize how valuable those people have been in the athletes' lives when they were beginning to be exposed to sports.

In the book *Four Champions, One Gold Medal* we depicted a pyramid that applies to all great athletes. It looks like this:

CHAMPION

Out of Body

Training & Competing

Personal   **Hard Work**

Responsibility   **Self-Image**

Opportunity   **Talent**   **Competitiveness**

These qualities hold up very, very well in examining the subjects in Volume I of ... *And Then They Won Gold.* (We look forward to Volume II devoted to great women swimmers.) Each stage of the pyramid leads to the following stage. For example, the critical aspect of a very positive self-image in one's sport ignites the athlete in accepting personal responsibility for their successes and their failures, and working hard to become a champion.

HOW TO READ THIS BOOK

Each story is written as a narrative. Training details and technique notes are segmented out, shaded and placed in a box. You may want to skip over those boxes when you first read about the individual. If you're a coach or a swimmer, you may want to come back to the highlighted training later.

TIME LINE HEADINGS: Since so many years are covered so quickly, there are headings like the "How to Read This Book" heading above to distinguish time periods. Generally, the author has used headings to segment a time line or key event from the remainder of the story. The opening story is unique because of the headings for the process of excellence that Matt Biondi develops. Those headings that indicated his process are in a different font called "engraving" which looks like THIS.

TRANING NOTES: It has been quite a challenge to reproduce training details from as much as 30 years ago. Thus there are times when the training notes are detailed and times when they aren't based upon the success of our research. We hope that coaches and swimmers will find that information very useful.

POOL COURSES: The sport of competitive swimming can be conducted in three distinct pool courses. The three distances in order of speed traveled are: 50-meter pools "long course" (the slowest speed), 25-meter pools short course (the middle range speed traveled - primarily referred to in the Hackett story), and finally 25-yard long pools are "short course." The Olympics are always swum in long-course meter pools. They are always depicted at the beginning of describing a competition, but after that point the events are only referred to by the distance swum. So an example in the section about the Olympics is that the first event might be written as 400-meter freestyle. Thereafter, the events will be only listed as 200 free, 100 butterfly, etc.

VIDEO LIBRARY: By going to www.areteswim.com and accessing the drop down menu on books/media, you can find a video library of most of the performances of these swimmers at the Olympic Games. Enjoy seeing their amazing career highlights and bringing the stories further to light.

Glossary of terms that may help you understand the book:

ASCA: American Swimming Coaches Association

Broken Swims: A term used in swim training to describe taking a complete distance and swimming it in parts, with rest between each part. Once completed, the total of the parts can be added up to a time for the total distance.

Comfort Zone: Describes the corresponding area of performance or feeling that one has to his/her self-image. It is the area, or zone, within which one feels at home, or at ease.

Dry-land: Non-aquatic training for swimming such as running, weight training, calisthenics, etc.

FINA: Fédération Internationale de Natation Amateur. The international governing body for swimming.

IM: Individual Medley. This is an event that is swum in equal quarters of butterfly, backstroke, breaststroke and freestyle.

Semi-finals: They were added to the Olympic Trials and the Olympic Games in 2000. The primary motivation was increasing the television exposure for the sport of swimming at the Olympics.

Taper: A reduction of overall work to recover from a season of preparation for peak performance.

US Swimming: The governing body for competitive swimming in the United States, which is now known as USA Swimming, Inc.

MATT BIONDI

October 8, 1965

A PROCESS FOR EXCELLENCE

circa 1978

The development of a personal process for excellence can be the most valuable product of an athlete's experience in sports. When an individual is competitive, has talent and is provided with opportunity, the results of that process can be magnificent. The pinnacle measure of athletic excellence in most every sport is the performance results at the Olympic Games. Because of the quadrennial buildup and timing of the Games an athlete is not only challenged to excel, but also to excel on a chosen day and time.

This is the story of a boy who created a system of unifying principles that led him to the brink of the greatest achievement in Olympic history.

* * *

The San Francisco Bay area is a magnet for people who love the outdoors. The temperate climate with its cool mornings and bright sunny days offers a nearly perfect setting for athletic enterprise. Outdoor swimming pools are abundant throughout the Bay area. Many have heated water and can be used throughout the year. Some of the pools are located at universities, many in high schools, and others are operated by municipalities. Beyond that, there are also pools in neighborhoods that require memberships and offer summer recreation programs. The Moraga Valley Pool (MVP) was such a site.

Located in the east bay of San Francisco, the rolling hills of the area formed a natural bowl around the club, which consisted of a Z-shaped out-door pool and four tennis courts. The club served 300 families who lived in the local area, and one of those families was the Biondis. Nick, the father, was an insurance salesman and his wife Lucille maintained the home. By 1970 the Biondis had three children: Ann Marie age 8, Matt age 5 and Mike age 3. Each year, from the middle of April until Labor Day, the Moraga Valley Club was the epicenter of their family's recreation life. The two young parents enjoyed athletics as a recreational experience and they passed it on to their children.

While in graduate school at San Jose State University, Nick's roommate happened to be Bill Walsh, the Hall of Fame football coach who guided the San Francisco 49ers to three Super Bowl victories. Nick and Bill maintained a friendship, but neither Nick nor Lucille aspired to see their children pursue professional sports. They did, however, provide a perspective that utilized sports as part of the developmental process that would lead to personal excellence in life. That process began when they encouraged their children to take personal responsibility for both their successes and failures as athletes.

This first foundation stone of personal responsibility is uncommon as all too often young swimmers begin by performing primarily for their parents and secondarily for their coach. As a result of this early imprinting, many competitive swimmers never completely experience the fulfillment that comes from the internal drive to excel for oneself.

When Matt's older sister Ann Marie decided to join the swim team at Moraga Valley her younger brother decided he should join too. Five-year-old Matt was eager to show what he could do in the pool, but in his first race he false-started twice and then his bathing suit fell down. Although he had an awkward beginning Matt had a talent for swimming, and even at such a young age he possessed an internal desire to improve. As a result, 12 months later Matt swam to a league record in the six-and-younger 25-yard butterfly with a time of 19 seconds. The record stood for 22 years.

TURNING ON THE LIGHT

In 1976, a critical event occurred that put in place the second foundation stone in helping Matt Biondi develop his process for excellence. This foundation stone might be called "turning on the light." The concept can be understood using a light bulb as an analogy. The bulb itself is useless without energy flowing into it. When it's connected to the appropriate source, it lights up. Without that source it is only metal, filament and a thin piece of glass. There was nothing more important with regard to turning on Matt's light than MVP's hiring of their new and enthusiastic coach, Stu Kahn.

Stu swam at Chico State University under renowned Coach Ernie Maglischo. Ernie was conducting a variety of research at Chico in preparation for writing three large volumes on the sport of swimming entitled *Swimming Faster, Swimming Even Faster*, and the follow-up *Swimming Fastest*. In his research, he filmed Stu and his teammates with underwater photography against a background grid that allowed him to measure the distance each swimmer traveled in a single stroke.

Coach Maglischo worked with Stu and his teammates on maximizing their "distance per stroke" with sweeping or sculling motions they often referred to as "blading." After his collegiate swimming career Stu worked for a year as an assistant coach at Chico State. Ernie told his protégé, "I'd love to see what would happen if you had a swim season that was all sprint 50s and 25-yard training." Stu took that idea and molded his coaching around it.

The Moraga Club competed in the Orinda Moraga Pool Association. They set up time trials to organize their team in mid-June and the championships were held Labor Day weekend, making the season about 12 weeks in length. The MVP team had placed seventh at the league championships the previous season. At the first team meeting, Coach Kahn told the team that he expected improvement. He asked each swimmer on the team to tell him their goal for the season and how they would contribute to the team's success. He and Matt sat down to discuss his goals.

"What would you like to do this season, Matt?"

"Well, I thought the team ...," Matt started in.

Stu cut him off. "Matt, tell me what *you* want to do. I want your goal to be personal, not your mom's, not the team's or mine."

Matt thought for a minute. "Well, I'd like to improve my time in the 50 freestyle."

Stu quickly said, "Good job! That's what I'm looking for. If you can get faster, the team will be better. Now let's get specific about your times."

For Matt, walking through the gates of the Moraga Valley Pool for swim practice with Stu felt like walking through the gates of Disneyland. Stu loved the sport, loved teaching and was passionate about conveying the skills to get faster to his swimmers. Practice included the same friends that Matt socialized with in his neighborhood. The coach walked along the side of the pool with the lifeguard's "shepherds crook" covered in Styrofoam (taken from a pull-buoy). He tapped on Matt and his teammate's arms to help guide their limbs into the correct movement patterns.

After a skill instruction period, he challenged Matt's and his teammates' with racing nearly the entire remaining portion of practice. The only equipment they ever used was a kickboard. They did speed-kicking face to face with teammates at the center of the pool, trying to push each other to the opposite end. They raced laying on top of the kick boards like surf boards, sculling and paddling down the pool. They practiced holding their breath while swimming as fast they could.

Matt Biondi Developmental Progression Moraga Valley Swim Team – Coach Stu Kahn

9-10 Years Old Training

Mid-June to Labor Day Championships

Saturday dual meets, alternate week invitationals on Sunday.

60 minutes – five per week – 11:30-12:30 pm

Warm-up:	10 minutes
Drill Set:	Catch-up freestyle with Coach using pull buoy on a shepherds crook
Teaching Set:	Sculling, fist swimming, kick board under chest (surfing)
	Emphasis on thumb-first entry, scull around belly button, little finger exit
	Armpit open at the beginning of stroke and closed at the end
Kick Set:	Tombstone kicking, wall kicks, challenge sets pushing each other physically against teammate
Sprint Set:	Start blocks, high RPMs, breath control work

11-12 Years Old Training

90 minutes – five times per week 10-11:30 am

Similar training as above but for a slightly longer duration

13 Years Old Training

Mid-June to Labor Day Championships

AAU Water Polo

90 minutes – five times per week 10-11:30 am

Stu's energy and enthusiasm for learning was contagious to the team. One day the coach was trying to teach them how to dive into the water through a small hole rather than slap the water with their chest or legs. In order to do it correctly, the swimmers had to lift their hips and legs at the proper moment. There was a spirit of freedom of expression amid many creative trials, but even so, the kids tried and failed over and over. Finally they heard Stu scream, "That's the one! Paul Berkowitz, that's the one!" Everyone looked at Paul to see what he was doing. Using his demonstration they saw how he entered the water with minimal splash and seemed to accelerate underwater as if someone was pushing him forward from behind. It wasn't long before young Matt was able to mimic the same exact dive.

In the summer of 1977, Coach Kahn's second season, the Moraga Valley Swim Club moved from third to first in the league championships. The 1976 Olympic year was still fresh in everyone's mind. John Naber, a local swimmer, won four gold medals at the Olympics in Montreal. Peter Rocca, another swimmer from nearby Cal Berkeley, captured a silver medal. At the annual team banquet Matt won swimmer of the year for his 11-12 year old age group. Coach Kahn commented that "just like John Naber and Peter Rocca, some day Matt Biondi can swim in the Olympics." Before Matt had turned 12 years old, Stu Kahn had connected with him in such a way that Stu had provided the energy source to turn Matt's light on. With his singular bold statement, Stu had planted a seed deep within Matt.

PERSONAL RESPONSIBILITY

Nick and Lucille Biondi coached life. They let their children's athletic leaders coach sports. A big part of their parental expectation was for their children to learn manners and live a healthy lifestyle. At the dinner table there was a "no thank you" rule. The rule meant that even if you didn't want to eat something and said "No thank you," one scoop was placed on your plate to try. Vegetables and healthy foods were always a part of the family eating plan. As a result of Matt's continual exposure to good nutrition, he eventually learned to enjoy eating in a healthy fashion.

The Biondis also viewed sports as an opportunity to learn good sportsmanship while having fun and being physically fit. The lessons of sportsmanship were especially important for Matt because he was such a fierce competitor. He never let younger brother Mike beat him at anything, even if it meant cheating at Monopoly. While Matt swam for Moraga in the summertime, the remainder of the year Nick and Lucille exposed him to as many sports and activities as possible.

Matt tried soccer. The good players were on offense, the weaker players were on defense, and the worst players watched from the sidelines. Matt found himself first on defense and then eventually watching. Soccer wasn't going to be a place to prove himself. He played the drums for a little bit. He followed Ann Marie into singing. She was very good, but it just wasn't what he was looking for. He loved playing basketball and pursued it for several years. He was so thin his coach told him, "If you turn sideways, you'll disappear." He did display some ability at basketball, but it didn't seem to him to be something in which he could excel in the long run.

In the sport of tennis it was a common sight during televised professional matches to see the players display temper tantrums and slam their rackets. Matt gave tennis a try, and during a match he became frustrated and slammed his racket on the court. His mother didn't say a word to him, but his match was over. Lucille walked out onto the court, grabbed Matt by the ear, pulled him to the car and drove him home. Matt's exploration into choosing a sport might be his own, but the way he conducted himself as a sportsman was fully under the guidance of his parents.

SKILL DEVELOPMENT - BASIC

Matt abhorred disappointing his mother and longed for her approval in whatever he did. At this time swimming was only a summer sport for Matt, but when he swam he felt he had a special ability to succeed. He was meticulous about listening to Coach Kahn and trying to perfect his stroke by controlling the water with his hands and arms. The summer program never demanded a lot of endurance training. It was centered on skill development and racing. Stu used what he had learned from Coach Maglischo to develop Matt's and his teammates' ability to increase their "range" or distance traveled down the pool with each stroke. Stu taught Matt to scull or sweep, especially in his weaker areas of freestyle. This happened most often when he anchored or began to control water on his entry as well as when his hands moved under his hips and exited.

As a 12-year-old he had another record-breaking summer season, but when he aged up to 13 he was competing with the older boys (13–14). This proved to be a challenge at first. Stu started each summer swim season with "time trials." The results provided him with specific information he could then use to divide his team into an "A" and "B" squad. The B squad swam their dual meets on Wednesday nights in the dark, while the A squad swam in the sunshine on Saturday mornings. Matt finished the time trials as the fifth fastest swimmer in his 13–14 age group and was therefore relegated to the B squad.

Stu didn't feel that Matt gave his full effort and told him so. Matt responded, "It will never happen again." Matt's words to his coach were indicative of the personal responsibility he accepted for his swimming success or failures. He went to work to earn his way up to the A squad.

As a gangly 13-year-old, Matt struggled with a long, thin, immature body that couldn't keep up with the early maturing boys who were growing faster in terms of strength gain. Even his attention to the detail of his stroke technique wasn't enough for him to keep up with them. He decided that maybe if he developed his kick it might help him keep up. Whenever the team kicked in practice, he worked to beat everyone. Before long his effort paid off and he could beat everyone on kicking sets—everyone except his friend and top-ranked national age-grouper, Tom Kafka.

Next he worked to add his kick into his full stroke. Matt gradually improved his kick and initiated the development of a great weapon when his body matured. In the short term his strengthened kick earned him a spot on the A squad and with it the opportunity to swim on Saturday mornings with the best swimmers.

Neil Sornsen, a year older than Matt, was a neighbor who had become involved in water polo. The summer before Matt entered high school, Neil invited him to join a summer water polo league. Since the game incorporated swimming with Matt's basketball skills of ball handling and team strategy, it was a perfect fit. Matt immediately loved water polo and quickly became adept at it.

1979 CAMPOLINDO HIGH SCHOOL

In the fall of '79 Matt entered Campolindo High School and the school's water polo program. He immediately had an advantage over the other boys who were being introduced to water polo for the first time. Although he played on the freshman-sophomore team, because of his quick introduction to water polo only weeks earlier, Matt's skills had become advanced enough for him to be invited to practice with the varsity squad. The competition he encountered with the older, more experienced players quickly prepared him to star on the "frosh-soph" team.

In California, the high school water polo season took place in the fall and the high school swim season took place in the spring months of February to May. Water polo offered Matt a new arena for competition and would also provide an ideal opportunity to build fitness for the spring swim season.

In the spring of his freshman year Matt's swim team coach, Ron

Richardson, immediately noticed his long smooth freestyle stroke and his tall thin body. As a result, Coach Richardson decided to place his young swimmer in the 200 and 500-yard freestyle events. Matt readily complied, and he spent the entire season working diligently each day to improve.

At season's end, Matt had failed to qualify for the North Coast High School Swimming Championships (NCS).

In the spring of 1980, Coach Richardson decided to focus just on water polo and stop coaching the swim team. When the boys on the swim team learned of Coach Richardson's decision, Neil Sornsen went straight to the school principal, Walter Hoy, and offered a suggestion for who should become the school's new swim team coach. Why not hire Stu Kahn? After listening to Neil's reasoning, Principal Hoy agreed.

The following summer of 1980 was another season of learning and racing at the Moraga Valley Pool. Matt was busy with water polo in the fall and the high school swim team in the spring, but his other training opportunity was in the summer recreation program. This also happened to be the summer that Coach Kahn was getting married, and while he had a great relationship with his swimmers it just wasn't practical to invite them all to his wedding. He ultimately decided to select one girl and one boy to represent all the other team members, and the boy he selected was Matt Biondi. Many years later Matt returned the invitation to Stu.

Stu looked forward with great anticipation to the spring of 1981 and the implementation of his plan to develop a sprint program at Campolindo High School. From the start, he brought enthusiasm and creativity to practice each day.

One example of his creativity was on full display in his first season when the school decided to keep the pool's heater off for the first month due to a national energy shortage. Stu discovered that one of the boys knew how to ride a unicycle and juggle at the same time. Since the kids couldn't swim for very long each day, he decided everyone should learn this unique way to improve their balance and hand-eye coordination. The Campolindo High School boys' swim team all became adept at juggling, some even doing so while riding a unicycle.

As the season progressed, and the water warmed, each week of practice was geared around sprinting. To motivate the team, Stu erected a huge thermometer-style chart poolside to show the team's progress toward success on goal sets. Every Tuesday afternoon they did a "breakthrough" set consisting of 10 x 100 yard swims on three minutes. The goal was to improve your best average each week in order to break through to a new level of swimming. If as an individual, you could average better than 50 seconds for the 10 x 100s doing freestyle, then Stu promised the car of your choice! The one caveat was that the cars were Hot Wheels, the miniature version. Stu hunted through toy shop after toy shop to find the exact car the swimmer had requested ahead of time so it would be on hand for those who accomplished this very impressive feat. Sometimes the smallest "rewards" can instill some large motivation.

The Campolindo High School Training Schedule

Mon, Wed, Fri:	90 minutes in the morning – about 4000 yards
Monday - Friday:	2 hrs. in the afternoon – about 6000 yards A lot of recorded timed sets looking for breakthroughs
Tuesdays:	10 x 100s on 3 min – goal to average under 50 seconds
Thursdays:	"Ideals" – 4 x 50s fast – progress through the season from 40 seconds rest to 10 one week prior to championships One "hell week" each year:
Afternoons of	M - 6,000 yds, Tu - 7,000 yds, W - 8,000 yds, Th - 9,000 yds, F - 10,000 yds, S - games

COMMITMENT

Matt was making some progress in swimming, but he was very shy in school and as a whole he didn't feel like he fit in very well. He wasn't invited to many parties or sleepovers. The thought of talking to a girl was virtually out of the question. On the other hand, with little in the way of social distractions, Matt continued to work at his craft of choice—swimming. He committed himself to mastering the small yet important steps of skill development. He wasn't strong enough to pull his body over the water so he worked on maximizing his leverage points, especially where his hand entered and exited the water. Each day he attempted to swim more efficiently and increased his capacity to repeat fast swimming.

Despite Stu's orientation toward sprint training, Matt was so thin that the coach kept him in the longer races (200 and 500 frees). At 16, Matt was 6' 1", but weighed only 135 pounds. Yet for the first time he qualified for the North Coast High School Championships when he swam his best time in the 200-yard freestyle (1:49.1). At the Championships, however, he swam a bit slower in the 200 (1:50.6) and 500 freestyles (5:04), which left him short of qualifying for the finals; therefore, he didn't contribute any individual points to his team.

Nonetheless, his mother and father enjoyed his improvement, and Matt's performance provided him with enough positive feedback to affirm his advancement in competitive swimming.

Going into the final of the 400 free relay at the North Coast Championships Campolindo's fastest four swimmers best times in the 100-yard freestyle were 46, 47, 48 and 51. Matt's was the one with a 51. The team was going to swim next to Terra Linda High School, their top competition for winning the race. Stu knew that Matt was a great competitor and put him last. Matt swam to an incredible split of 48+ on that anchor leg, but it wasn't quite fast enough to pull out the victory. Terra Linda won the race by just seven-hundredths of a second (3:10.22 to 3:10.29). The skinny sophomore stayed in the pool for nearly 10 minutes hanging on the gutter in disappointment. Finally, Matt pulled himself out and walked over to his coach and sternly said, "Stu, that will never happen again."

Matt was a man of his word.

In the summer between Matt's sophomore and junior years of high school he once again trained under Stu's guidance at the Moraga Valley Pool. The following fall he played water polo and became a star on the varsity team. On top of that, the repetitions of sprinting and of ball control were strengthening each arm in a way that Matt hardly noticed. He loved the competition of water polo and the immediate feedback of each play and each game.

Following the water polo season, the swim team started strength work in January, which led into the start of swim practice in February. The school elected to continue the policy of keeping the pool heater off until March. As a result, Stu built their dry-land program around a unique staple—juggling. This motor skill development of limbs, hand position and body balance, made learning technical swimming skills much easier when they returned to the water.

Matt had grown more than an inch in the last year and added valuable strength to his frame. He continued his diligent effort of attending morning practice three times per week and practice after school every weekday. At the start of the high school swim season, Matt was swimming faster than ever, so Stu made a commitment to move him to the sprint events. Matt responded very well. His split on the relay of 48 seconds at the end of the previous season was a time he was now performing with consistency in dual meets at the beginning of the new season.

MENTAL POWER I – DREAMING

Matt was introverted and given to thought. He also liked to dream. At times his mind wandered to winning on the largest stages, but now his thoughts were becoming increasingly specific. He started formulating an image of what he might achieve in swimming over the long term.

In April of 1982 *Swimming World Magazine* pictured Robin Leamy—at that time the fastest swimmer in the world—on its cover. Leamy held the American record in the 50-yard freestyle at 19.3 seconds, as well as the world record at 50-meters in 22.5. Matt cut that cover off the magazine and taped it on his bedroom wall. He took moments away from his homework and gazed at Robin. Before he went to sleep he studied Robin. He ingrained in himself the position of the script writing on Robin's blue "baseball cap" (UCLA Swimming) and the detail of his smile. When he woke up in the morning, the first thing he did was see the picture of Robin Leamy. In essence, that photo of Robin Leamy, and the position he held as the world's top sprinter, became Matt's Mona Lisa. Matt began to dream about beating Robin Leamy and becoming the fastest swimmer in the world.

The high school season culminated at the North Coast Championships that spring. Matt warmed up with his long, slow strokes that he had been refining. He liked swimming very slow in warm-up and feeling each body movement carefully. Little did he know someone was watching every stroke he took down the pool.

The competition was an opportunity for college coaches to see most of the best swimmers in the San Francisco area. Cal Berkeley Coach Nort Thornton watched Matt's long thin body cruising from one end of the pool to the other with enormous efficiency. He had seen Matt as an 11-year-old swim in a summer league meet. He had recognized back then that the young Biondi boy had some ability, but what he was watching now stunned him. He got out of his seat and walked down to the side of the pool to get a closer look. Nort was amazed at the control Matt held over the water with his long arms, and he began to envision him competing for Cal.

Matt's first event of the high school championship was the 50-yard freestyle. The excitement of competing turned to panic just before he stepped onto the starting blocks. He rushed to prepare his goggles and they filled with water. Consequently he couldn't see clearly and misjudged his turn. Despite catching up and passing four swimmers on the second length, he was very disappointed with his finish. Matt climbed from the pool and went to talk with Coach Kahn. "Stu, that will never happen again," Matt told him. From then on Matt always prepared himself early behind the blocks and adjusted his goggles in as perfect a position as possible.

Fortunately for Matt the goggle incident was only a minor setback as Campolindo proceeded to win their first North Coast Championship by overcoming a huge point deficit to the previous year's meet champion San Ramon High School. Matt's finals time of 21.0 in the 50-yard freestyle and 45.8 in the 100-yard freestyle ranked him among the top 15 high school swimmers in the country.

Tom Kafka was one of Matt's high school teammates. He had devoted a great deal of time to swimming as an age-grouper and become a national record-setter when he was 14 years old. In the summer after his junior year of high school, Matt followed his teammate to the Walnut Creek Aquabears United States Swimming Club Team. His commitment to water polo meant that he only attended swim practice sporadically. His membership on the Aquabears enabled him to enter the US Swimming competitions, and in particular gave him his first experience competing in long-course meets (50-meter pool). That summer he recorded long course times of 24.2 in the 50-meter freestyle and 53.2 in the 100, both of which earned him national rankings in the US Swimming top-16 time's program.

The college selection process is difficult for any high school senior. When you're an athlete it becomes more complicated, and when you're an athlete in two sports it's more complicated still! Water polo was only offered at 52 schools in the entire country, so Matt searched for those schools where he could both swim and play water polo. In his final season of high school polo, he earned all-American honors, which helped to generate interest in him. His first two college choices were Stanford and UCLA. Cal Berkeley was too close to home for his liking, but it would serve as a good backup.

When he went to Stanford on a recruiting visit, there was no one there to meet him at the appointed time and place to start the visit. He waited and waited, yet even after an hour there was no sign of a coach or even a student host. Finally the team came out of a meeting and an assistant coach approached him.

"Can I help you?"

"My name is Matt Biondi. Coach Kenney told me this was a good weekend to come on a recruiting visit."

Matt joined the group for the recruiting weekend and enjoyed his visit very much. He liked the campus and the team, and he enjoyed the coaches. However, in an individual meeting Coach Kenney told Matt, "I really don't think you have what it takes to swim at this level." It may be that Skip, the coach, was challenging Matt, but there was no scholarship offer forthcoming and Matt eliminated Stanford from his college list.

UCLA coach Ron Ballatore really impressed Matt. Matt very much enjoyed his recruiting trip to the UCLA campus. His host for his visit to the school was a freshman swimmer named Tom Jager. While watching the team practice, Matt took immediate notice of the spirit and energy that Coach Ballatore and his swimmers shared. Matt was sold on going to UCLA and becoming a Bruin. It was also where Robin Leamy went to college, plus it had a great swimming *and* water polo program. Unfortunately Matt's calls to water polo Coach Bob Horn went unreturned.

The only school choice he had left on his list was Cal.

In Matt's senior year at Campolindo High (1983) he had reached 6' 4" and weighed about 165 pounds. His transformation over the past two years was one of growth, added strength, meticulous skill refinement and improved conditioning. He had worked his way through the tough times of his freshman and sophomore years and was now one of the strongest swimmers on the team. He earned his Hot Wheels car for the second year by swimming all 10 x 100s on 3:00 under 50 seconds.

High school swimming in the Bay area was exciting and highly competitive. Bellarmine and Campolindo were two of the top teams that year. The Bellarmine star was Pablo Morales, and Matt Biondi was the star of Campolindo. The two teams were so good that in a dual meet, held at the neutral site of Cal Berkeley, the swimmers turned in 14 high school all-American times. Unfortunately for Matt and his teammates, Bellarmine came out on top. Later that season Campolindo went on to successfully defend their North Coast Championship and developed into one of the best high school teams in the country. At season's end Matt's 100-yard freestyle improved to 45.2, and he had established a new national high school record in the 50 freestyle with a time of 20.40.

Coach Kahn's "sprint city" mentality was so effective that in 1984, the year after Matt Biondi had graduated, Campolindo won the *Swimming World Magazine* Mythical High School Championship over distance-oriented Mission Viejo by one point. Campolindo had only one swimmer on the scoring team that trained for swimming year round. Coach Kahn had put together a marvelous squad of water polo players and boys that swam in the summer recreation program.

SKILL DEVELOPMENT II - SKILL ENDURANCE - Water Polo

In the summer prior to starting college Matt spent several weeks touring Europe with the National Junior Water Polo Team. They traveled to Germany and then to Madrid, Spain, where they competed in a tournament against the best 18-and-under players in the world. At the end of the competition Matt was selected to the all-tournament team, making him one of the top 12 junior players in the world. The importance of water polo to Matt's competitive swimming development cannot be overstated. In a game that spans more than an hour of sprinting, defending, hand-eye coordination and split-second decision-making, Matt's fitness level grew beyond what he could attain from standard swim training alone. The tremendous number of repetitions of the high elbow-low hand recovery water polo sprinting was increasing his muscular endurance for sprinting.

When Matt returned from the water polo tour, he once again competed for the Aquabears USS team, his focus meet for the summer being the Junior National Championships. In the 100-meter freestyle he swam in lane eight, missed his turn and was so disappointed with his poor performance that he considered quitting swimming altogether and focusing only on water polo.

1983 CAL BERKELEY

Coach Steve Heaston was one of the coaches on the Junior Team water polo tour and also an assistant coach for Cal's water polo team. This seemed as though it should help Matt's transition to Cal. Steve had been a part of the recruiting effort to convince Matt to attend Cal. Coach Heaston had been out for pizza with Matt and Cal's head coach for water polo, Pete Cutino, during Matt's recruiting trip. Coach Cutino had experienced tremendous success at Cal. His teams had already won four national championships, and he'd twice been named NCAA Water Polo "Coach of the Year." Pete was a huge, intimidating man standing over six feet tall and weighing approximately 320 pounds. On top of that, Pete had shaved his head well before Michael Jordan and other basketball stars made such a look fashionable.

The first day of water polo practice, Matt discovered he might have as challenging an adjustment to beginning the water polo program as he had meeting girls when he entered high school. He stopped to use a urinal in the bathroom before going to the pool. The bathroom was empty with a long line of porcelain options on the wall beside him. Coach Cutino walked into the room. He chose the space immediately next to Matt and scowled, "Get your ?#? in the pool right now, you ??#??. Your ??#?? is mine!"

Matt had been excited to leave home for college until now. He was so scared at that moment, he wanted to run home and jump into his mother's arms! The surprise meeting in the men's room served as the beginning of an intense process at Cal that would see him mature from a tall, skinny boy into a grown man.

Coach Cutino had established a system of challenging freshmen to first become a trusted contributor to the team, and only then could they earn the team's unconditional support. This was a part of his mastery as a coach. Matt's first season, daunting though it was at the outset, concluded on Thanksgiving weekend with Cal's national championship at the 1983 NCAA Water Polo Tournament in Long Beach, California. As a result of his play at the tournament Matt Biondi was voted onto the all-American water polo team.

1984 CAL BERKELEY SWIMMING

The swim season at Cal began in September. Matt missed at least the first three months of the swim team's endurance and technique work because he played water polo. Matt and the men's swim team coach, Nort Thornton, discussed an appropriate start date to begin swimming following the NCAA water polo tournament. They compromised to the date of January 1, 1984, although it was understood that Matt would help if needed at competitions in the month of December.

By his freshman year at Cal, Matt was well along the path of creating his own process for excellence. Coach Nort Thornton had his own process for success, one that he'd been developing over the 10-year period he'd been at the helm of the Cal men's swim team. Nort believed the greatest possible motivation came from an internal force deep inside the athlete to excel. His coaching philosophy centered on drawing each athlete's self-reliance to the surface. Fortunately for Matt, Nort's philosophy meshed beautifully with Matt's own personality as well as his personal process for excellence.

Nort's program was so effective that in 1979 the Bears had won the NCAA Men's Team Championship. Nort was a tremendous student of the sport, and through dedicated reading, coupled with experience, he had developed a system that prioritized his categories of focus as:
- Mental Training
- Power Development
- Range of Motion
- Technique
- Training/Conditioning
- Team Building

Coach Thornton had a well thought out, detailed approach to develop each category. For example, he believed that power was more specific to the need of a swimmer than strength. He devised a power circuit that Matt and his teammates did after practice each day. Matt only weighed about 170 pounds, and Nort knew that Matt's strength development would take years. Nort's overall training plan was for Matt to meet his potential gradually over time; therefore, for the first two years Matt worked only with bio-kinetic machines and light weights.

When Matt joined swim practice in January of 1984 he had goose bumps when he looked around the pool at the swimmers. There was superstar Dave Wilson who excelled in backstroke and butterfly, not to mention two swimmers he'd be training with—Swedish Olympians Bengt Baron and Thomas Ledstrom. The standard commitment on the swim team was much like water polo. Every team member attended each practice, and the history of the program was so strong that Matt dutifully complied. For the first time in his life, his daily performance was going to be easy to compare to some of the best swimmers in the world, and whether he was feeling 100 percent or not, he was always at practice.

Matt was eager to get back to swim training. In order to try and make up for some of the endurance training he had missed in the fall during water polo season, he agreed with Nort's plan for him to begin training for races longer than the races that were most important to him. This meant working with the middle-distance swimmers that prepared for the 200 to 500-yard events. In the middle of February Nort's plan called for Matt to shift his training focus more toward the sprints of the 100 and 50 freestyles.

The large volume of training was a huge difference from what Matt was accustomed to in high school, so Nort adjusted his program by rotating in a low volume of sprinting every Wednesday and Saturday. This program helped Matt improve his 200 freestyle by adding volume while the strength program and high intensity workouts helped his sprinting.

CAL MIDDLE DISTANCE/SPRINT GROUP TRAINING 1984-1988

– Coach Nort Thornton

September – December 1 (Thanksgiving)
Water Polo and Power Circuit

January 1 - August 20
Swimming

Monday AM Long Course: 7-7,500 – General Aerobic (Fartlek, kick w/fins 2,000, Pull with paddles)
         PM Short course: 7-8,000 – Over distance

Tuesday AM Long Course: 7-7,500 – (same as Monday)
         PM Short course: 5,000 – Technique emphasis

Wed   AM Long Course: 7-7,500 – (same as Monday)
         PM Short course: 3-4,000 – Speed
             Example: "Ideals" 10 x 50s on 1:30 strive for 200 to 100 pace (23.5)
             10 weeks out do 10, 9 weeks 9 x 50s and drop interval 5 seconds,
             Continue until 2 weeks out 3-4 x 50s 5-10 seconds rest 23.5 to 22.0

Thurs   AM Long Course: 7-8,000 – (same as Monday)
         PM Short course: 7-7,500 Over distance

Friday   AM Long course: 7-8,000 – (same as Monday)
         PM Short course: 5,000 – Technique emphasis

Saturday AM Short course: 3-4,000 Speed

Courtesy of Nort Thornton

At the 1984 Pac 10 (Pacific 10 Conference) Championships, Matt swam the 50, 100 and 200-yard freestyle events. As a result of his performances at the conference meet, Matt qualified to swim those events as well as relays at the NCAA Championships. Many considered the NCAAs to be the most competitive and, therefore, most exciting swim meet in the world that was conducted on an annual basis. It brought together many of the best swimmers from all over the world who yearned to earn a scholarship at an American university. Participating as a freshman was a significant achievement for Matt.

The 1984 NCAA Championships were held at Cleveland State University, a very deep and, therefore, very fast pool. During the first day's preliminaries, Matt qualified to swim in the consolation finals of the 50-yard freestyle (a heat of six) by finishing ninth. He improved his time to 20.1 that night. In the next two days he continued to adjust positively to the new environment. He won the consolation finals in the 200 freestyle (1:36.56) from the outside lane and also the consolation final of the 100 freestyle (44.06). Coach Thornton was very pleased with Matt's performance and the surprisingly strong point contribution the freshman made to the Cal team. As the swimmers and coaches walked out of the Cleveland State Natatorium at the close of the meet on Saturday night Matt casually said to Nort, "Coach, next year I'm going to own this meet." Nort thought to himself, *Is this kid crazy?*

MENTAL POWER II – GOALS

Matt's experience at the NCAA Championship turned his dreaming into specific goals. As he daydreamed about his expectations for the following year, thinking of the times it would take to win his events became inevitable. Even the American records in short course swimming in the 50 (19.4), 100 (42.6), and 200-yard freestyles (1:33.8) events, might be objectives to work for.

1984 was an Olympic year, and the USA Team Trials were to be held in Indianapolis at the beautiful new Indiana University–Purdue University (IUPUI) Natatorium. They were scheduled for June 25–29. Even though Matt's best time in his best event at that time, the 100-meter freestyle, was not even ranked in the top 140 times in the world, Coach Thornton thought Matt was improving so fast that it would be good experience for him to compete in the Trials. If things went beyond expectations, Matt might surprise people.

Matt's only experience in a US National competition was at the Junior Nationals the prior summer. In order to better prepare him for the Olympic Trials he swam in his first US National competition in March and qualified for the Trials with long course times in the 100 and 200-meter freestyles. When he swam the 200-meter freestyle on the first day of the Olympic Trials and finished 18th (1:52.64), it was just a warm-up for the excitement to come.

The 100 freestyle was two days later. The selection format for the Olympic Team was that the top two swimmers made the Olympic Team and swam individually. In the 100 freestyle, however, the top six swimmers make the team because there is a 4 x 100 freestyle relay. At the Olympics, the fastest four of the six are selected to swim the finals of the 400 freestyle relay.

For a swimmer to compete for an Olympic Team berth in his first national swim meet was unheard of. In the preliminaries of the 100 freestyle, Matt swam a lifetime best time of 50.6 and qualified sixth for the eight-swimmer final later that night. The qualities in Matt that put him in position to succeed in what many perceived of as pressure were simple: He didn't measure his worth by his swimming performance because his parents never had. First and foremost, his standard of success was displaying the qualities of good sportsmanship and being a fine person. Win or lose he could live with the results.

Matt readied for the start of the fastest field of eight 100 freestyle swimmers ever assembled. Mounting the starting blocks that night were Tom Jager in lane 3, veteran world record holder Rowdy Gaines in lane 4, and Mike Heath in lane 5. Robin Leamy, Matt's "Mona Lisa," took to the block in lane 6. Matt stepped up onto the block in lane 7 next to Robin. Matt had been a great racer from the time he was a little boy, and he continuously developed an approach to racing that served him well in the current moment. He thought, *I have my own lane to swim in. Unlike water polo or basketball, no one can play defense against me or affect my performance. Swim fast.*

Matt swam fast. The leader at the turn (50 meters) was Tom Jager, whose split time was 23.7. Matt found himself in the middle of the field (split time of 24.2). On the second 50 Matt increased the thunderous kick generated from his 14-inch feet and he practically flew down the pool to the eighth fastest time of all time (50.23). He placed fourth. Matt Biondi surprised just about everyone and made the United States Olympic Swim Team as at least an alternate for the 400 freestyle relay. Unfortunately his idol, Robin Leamy, placed seventh and missed making the Team by one place.

When first seeing the list of swimmers that qualified to swim the relay, Rowdy Gaines, the oldest swimmer on the 1984 Olympic Team, asked, "Matt who?"

There was a four-week training camp in preparation for the Games, which were held in Los Angeles. Tom Jager was one of those assigned to room with the Cal Berkeley freshman. Tom, who had just finished his sophomore year at UCLA, had won the previous two NCAA short course championships in the 100-yard freestyle and added the 50-yard freestyle to his title list in 1984. Although born one year later than Matt, their birthdays were nearly identical—Matt October 8, 1965 and Tom October 6, 1964. Unbeknownst to them at the time, the pair would become linked for years to come as competitors, as ambassadors for the sport and as friends.

1984 LOS ANGELES OLYMPICS

The Los Angeles Olympics was a surreal experience for Matt as well as a training ground for his future. He studied how his veteran and highly accomplished American teammates such as Tracy Caulkins and Steve Lundquist warmed up, composed themselves during the competition and dealt with the press. Then finally, on the fourth day of the Olympic swimming events,

August 2nd it was Matt's turn to race. The night before Lucille Biondi set him a note: "Tomorrow you will show the world what a good swimmer you are."

The US had never lost the men's 400-meter freestyle relay at the Olympics. In the preliminaries, the Australian team qualified first and the Americans second, leaving the finals crowd flush with anticipation of a historic race. Matt earned a spot on the evening relay by being one of the fastest two swimmers in the morning preliminaries. Matt Cavanaugh was the other. The two Matts joined Mike Heath and Rowdy Gaines on the evening relay. Mike and Rowdy had rested during the preliminaries of the relay because they were the top two swimmers at Trials and were also entered in the individual 100 freestyle event.

After Cavanaugh and Heath swam the first two legs, the US was behind the Australian team by one-tenth of a second. Matt swam third, trailed on the first 50-meter length, but then he built his kick, the pressure on his hands and on his arms to gain a half-second lead for Team USA's anchor, Rowdy Gaines. Rowdy held on for the win and a new world-record time of 3:19.03 to Australia's 3:19.68. That evening the tallest swimmer on the top step of the awards podium in Los Angeles was Matt Biondi. He had performed just as his mother had suggested and stood with an Olympic gold medal around his neck and a world record to show for it.

1984–1985

An unforgettable summer quickly ended when school started at Cal in the fall of 1984. The Bears repeated as NCAA water polo champions and Matt earned another spot on the all-American team. His body was growing closer to his final height of 6'6", and he was getting stronger. Once again he began his swim training on January 1, eager to continue his remarkable progress from the previous summer.

Coach Thornton was constantly learning and hoped to find new concepts to help his team's performance. At a practice in January of 1985, Nort implemented an experiment that he had arranged with some professors from the Cal Department of Psychology. The swimmers were placed in groups or heats to swim a series of 50s as fast as they could go. The coach emphasized to his athletes that this was a very important training series and insisted that everyone give their very best effort. Unknown to the swimmers, Coach Thornton's assignment from the Department of Psychology was to provide pre-determined feedback regardless of how fast the swimmer swam.

Coach Thornton gave one group positive feedback and told them they did well. A second group was told they did poorly and given slower times than they actually swam. Overall those that were given positive feedback continued to do well and swim as fast or faster. The group that was given scolding feedback and told they were swimming too slow, tended to do poorly; they eventually slowed down and gave up hope. Matt Biondi was placed in the second group and scolded for performing slowly. His reaction was unlike the others. He kept giving more and more effort to make amends for his poor performance.

The overall conclusion by Department of Psychology was that for most athletes optimism is a critical component to giving their best effort in training and in competition. However, Matt Biondi had developed the belief that he could accomplish nearly anything he set his mind to. He was very, very difficult to discourage and swam fast despite the negative feedback. He showed signs of an exceptionally strong internal will.

There were several ways that Matt focused his attention on performing on a select day he was visualizing. Two of those were the growth of facial and head hair for the months leading up to his peak performance. His mother felt that shaving your head was giving up your individualism, so when he did cut his hair he never went that far. The night before his championship swim meets he got a crew cut. Then he shaved his face the next morning. When Matt walked into the Texas Swimming Center on the morning of March 28 for the 1985 NCAA Swimming Championships, he was ready to channel all his experience and work into a performance that would change short course yard swimming standards in America for decades to come.

1985 NCAA CHAMPIONSHIPS – Austin, Texas

Matt's words a year earlier, "I will own this meet next year," were not idle chatter. He had "owned" his swimming for his entire life. His dreams had turned to specific goals. When he said those words, it was the beginning of building a vision in his mind that he could swim at a level that was superior to all his competitors at the NCAA Championships. It was the next step in the process he began by posting Robin Leamy's picture on his bedroom wall three years earlier.

In his swim the first morning, Matt broke Leamy's American record in the 50-yard freestyle by swimming faster than any human had ever swum it at 19.32. In the finals, he swam one-hundredth of a second faster, but Tom Jager out-touched Matt and eclipsed Matt's half-day old record with a blazing 19.24. The defeat was disappointing to Matt, but it didn't take long for him to make amends. He anchored the Cal 400 medley relay about an hour later and moved his team into second place. When he touched the wall, he looked at his excited teammates signaling to him from the side of the pool. They were smiling and holding up one and then two fingers. Matt thought, *I guess I went a 42*, which with the advantage of the relay start would be consistent with his goals and a good improvement from his best time of 44.0. His split was a 41.2. He had swum faster through water for 100 yards than any human in history.

On the next two nights Matt owned the 1985 NCAA Swimming Championships. In the 200 freestyle he broke Rowdy Gaines' American record by over half a second (1:33.22) in winning by nearly two seconds over Olympic medalist Mike Heath. It was Matt's personal best by over three seconds. He was euphoric with his victory and breakthrough time and followed it up that night with a 1:32.4 split on the Cal 800 free relay.

Tom Jager, however, was not to be outdone by his Olympic roommate. On that same second night of competition, Tom lowered the American record in the 100 backstroke to 48.2, and the stage was set for a great matchup the final night in the 100 freestyle.

In addition to the "Matt and Tom Show," after the second day of competition Stanford held a commanding lead and it appeared all but certain that the Cardinals would win their first championship during the Skip Kenney era. The coach had been very disappointed with a third-place finish for The Cardinals the year before. *Sports Illustrated Magazine* reported this scene on that (Saturday) morning: "It was clear on Friday night that—barring total disaster—Stanford had the championship locked up. At 4 a.m. Saturday, Kenney's wife, Debbie, was awakened by a noise in their motel room. 'I looked over,' she said, 'and there was Skip, sitting on the edge of the bed, sobbing. I got up and we must have talked for two hours about all the people who would be so happy we had won.'"

It was Saturday night, the third and last evening of the competition, and the pool area buzzed with a fever of anticipation. The 100 freestyle event final was called and eight swimmers stood at the ready behind the blocks. All eyes, however, were on Tom Jager and Matt Biondi.

Matt, displaying an almost surreal combination of power and technique, took it out from the start and hung close to Tom. Tom missed the 50 turn a bit and Matt lowered the American and US Open Record another half-second by posting a sizzling time of 41.87. He beat Tom by over a second. A little while later, Cal closed the meet with an American record performance in the 400 free relay with Matt coming from behind on the last leg for the win, splitting 41.3.

Following the relay, Matt noticed winning Coach Skip Kenney walking toward him. The newly crowned national champion coach would soon kiss the championship trophy and call the moment the highlight of his career. First Skip found Matt. He recognized the greatness in Biondi and had enough class to say so. He walked up to Matt and shook his hand. "I guess I was wrong about you not being able to swim at this level," Skip told him. "As a matter of fact, right now you are the best. Congratulations."

At the conclusion of NCAAs Matt looked ahead to the summer and his involvement in US Swimming in which up until now he'd hardly participated. At the time Matt was quoted as saying, "US Swimming is a great institution. I've always wanted to be a leader, and I think this meet has given me the chance to do that" (SW May 1985).

Cal Berkeley Training Program – Coach Nort Thornton

September- November Water Polo
Power Circuit
Morning Practice Long Course:

Warm Up:	800 IM Reverse Order Stroke Drill (25k-25 scull – 25 swim)
	KRLS (kick, right arm, left arm, swim): w/fins: 400 Fly on 6:30, 200 Fly on 3:15, on 400 Bk 6:30,
	200 Bk on 3:15, 400 Fr on 6, 200 Fr on 3
	SKPS (swim, kick, pull, swim)
	No fins: 400 Br 7:00, 2 x 200 3:45
Main Set:	5 x 300s on 4:45 Drag Suit breath by 50s every 5, 7, 9, 7, 5, 3
	800 IM on 14 min
	2 x 400s IM on 7
	3 x 200s IM on 3:45
Warm Down:	200
Total LC Meters:	7,300

Mid-Season Sprint Workout 1986:

Warm Up:	1000
Swim:	12 x 25s on :22
	200 Max DPS Drill on 3:00 (Distance per Stroke)
	3 x 100s Max DPS on 1:30
	20 x 25s Tempo on :30, 2 sets of 10, 12.5 fast, 12.5 easy
	10 x 50s Mini-Maxi on 1:00
Kick:	500 Moderate, then 5 x 100s on 1:45 (75 moderate/25 fast kick)
Swim:	6 x 100s on 3:00 Fast, Heart Rate 180 or higher
	200 easy
Pull:	10 x 150s on 2:00 breath by 50s every 7, 5, 3
Swim:	10 x 50s free on 1:00 very fast on 3, 5, 7, 10
Warm Down:	300
Total Yards:	6,900

Matt wasted no time in moving into that leadership position. At the 1985 Long Course US Nationals, held in Mission Viejo, California, Matt set his first world record in the 100-meter freestyle with a time of 48.9. He also beat Tom Jager in the 50 (22.7) and won the 200 freestyle with a five-second improvement from the Olympic Trials the summer before (1:47.8).

The top long course competition for the United States that summer of 1985 was the Pan Pacific Championships. The event was held in Tokyo, Japan, and involved the Pacific Rim countries, including Australia, Canada, and Japan. Many of Europe's top swimming countries attended the meet as well, which wasn't always the case. Matt not only qualified to swim for the United States Team but won the 50 freestyle (22.7), the 100 freestyle (49.1) and finished second to Mike Heath in the 200 freestyle in 1:50.1. He also anchored the American 400 medley and 400 freestyle relays, helping to stop the clock in world-record times for both events.

1985–1986

Water polo that fall gave Matt a much needed mental break from swim training. The last two summers had been a wonderful experience for him, but the international travel allowed for little time for a break from the summer swim season prior to the start of his junior year. However, water polo, like swimming, provides a training ground for life. For example, the process of being a successful water polo team includes solving problems and using logical reasoning to improve the team's chances for success. Coach Cutino wouldn't yell at his players for missing a shot, though he certainly would for taking the *wrong* shot. Matt and his teammates were honing their split-second judgment skills and increasing their likelihood of winning. Although they were not able to "three-peat" and win a third consecutive national team title, Matt was voted to the All-American team for the third straight year.

ADVANCED SKILL DEVELOPMENT – REDUCING BUBBLES

Even as a very young swimmer, Matt was intrigued with the feel of the water and how to minimize his resistance and maximize his propulsion. The best method to see underwater at the time was to have a window below the surface of the pool in order to either film or observe the crystal-clear image of a swimmer moving through the water. The trained eye could see the air bubbles around a hand that indicated the hand was slipping through the water, or check for the most balanced body position, or analyze any number of other potential areas for improvement.

The invention of a device called the "Coach Scope" offered a portable viewing and filming system to be utilized by coaches and swimmers. Matt loved trying to perfect his stroke. The Coach Scope offered a great addition to his awareness and, much like a person in need, he felt like an individual with poor eyesight putting on a pair of glasses for the first time. Matt worked closely with Coach Thornton to study the air bubbles around his hands. He then set out to eliminate them in his attempt to attain perfect traction in the water. One of his favorite drills to improve his body control and arm efficiency was a drill called single-arm swimming. Matt placed his non-working arm at his side, lifted his elbow on his working arm and carefully stuck his fingertips into the water. From there he focused on rolling high up onto his hip while extending the arm out forward as far as possible. With his fingertips tilting downward, he began to rotate his hip up on the working arm side. By controlling water with his hand and arm, the rotation helped him slide his body core forward.

Technique Notes:

Coach Thornton commented at the time: "At the 1985 NCAAs it was the first time Matt held his distance per stroke in the 50. He used to have a tendency to 'sprint' instead of 'swim' the 50. Matt has a lope in his stroke when he breathes. We're trying to get him to enter with his thumb pretty much down and his hand on a 45-degree angle. He also has a tendency to bury his head. I like the sprinters to have the water line between their eyebrows and hair line."

Matt's comments: "I tend to drop my right elbow when I breathe on my left side. You push against the water and the water pushes against you. My major emphasis has been to move through the water with as little resistance as possible." 1986 – *Swimming Technique Magazine*

The 1986 collegiate season culminated once again with the NCAA Championships, and Matt extended his individual NCAA title streak to five by winning the 50 (19.22), 200 (1:33.8) and 100-yard freestyle (42.0) events. Matt was reasonably happy with his performance, but by now he had his sights set on a bigger stage. The World Swimming Championships were scheduled for Madrid, Spain, later that summer and the US Team Trials for late June in Orlando, Florida. Matt was highly focused in training to prepare for his first opportunity to compete in an individual race against all of the best swimmers in the world.

The World Championship Team Trials were held long course and offered up another highly anticipated showdown between Matt and Tom Jager in the

50-meter freestyle. Once again Matt came away with a narrow victory while establishing a new world-record time of 22.3 (to Tom's 22.5). Matt was a bit more dominant in the 100 free, lowering the world standard to 48.7 (to Tom's 50.5). Matt also powered to the win in the 200 freestyle with a time of 1:49.0.

Matt also decided to add a new event to his lineup at this meet, the 100 butterfly. This was one of his first-ever performances in the event, and he pulled out another surprise by finishing second in 53.2 The swim qualified him for the US team and left him just four-tenths off Pablo Morales' world record.

The Long Course World Swimming Championships were established in 1973 as a competition for all the best swimmers in the world between the quadrennial Olympics Games. The format mimicked that of the Olympics except the number of days was shortened from eight to seven. In the seven-day format Matt, including individual events and relays, would be competing every day except the fourth. Before the competition started Matt showed his adjustment to the world stage when he told *Swimming World Magazine*, "There are so many great swimmers here that for me to say that I can win one gold medal for sure is a little far-fetched."

Matt's words seemed prophetic when the competition began on August 17. He was beaten handily in the 200-meter freestyle by Germany's Michael Gross, one of the stars of the 1984 Los Angeles Olympics. Although Matt was 6' 6" and had added 30 pounds to his frame since arriving at Cal, Gross was a bit taller and had a similar 7-foot-plus wingspan (the distance from fingertip to fingertip when arms are spread straight out). Gross easily won the race in 1:47.9 while Matt finished third at 1:49.4.

On the second day Matt swam his "new event," the 100 butterfly and finished second (53.5) to Pablo Morales in a 1-2 US Team finish. The men's 800 freestyle relay later that night wouldn't prove as satisfying for the Americans as they finished a distant third behind both the East and West German teams, despite Biondi's anchor leg time of 1:48.1.

Following his one day off from competition, Matt finally won the gold medal he sought, taking the 100 freestyle and just missing his world record with a time of 48.94. The evening ended with the United States bringing home the gold medal in the 400 free relay with Matt as anchor.

On the sixth day of competition it was Tom Jager who became a world champion as Tom captured the 50 freestyle with a time of 22.49. Matt finished a disappointing third (22.95).

On the final day, the world received a full display of America's new swimming leader. Despite a tremendous butterfly leg laid down by Pablo Morales

(52.3), the Americans were in fifth place as Matt left the block for the final freestyle leg of the men's 400 medley relay. With the crowd on its feet and roaring, Matt passed all four of the relay teams ahead of the US over the next 47.7 seconds while securing another American relay victory (3:41.2).

Matt walked away from Madrid carrying three gold (two from relays), one silver and two bronze medals. The first whispers began that Matt Biondi could be given serious consideration to duplicate Mark Spitz's feat of winning seven gold medals at the Munich Games in 1972.

1986–1987

Coach Thornton had a great relationship with Coach Cutino. They had known each other for many years before either had started working at Cal. Pete had once been Cal's swimming and water polo coach, but stepped down from swimming and had been instrumental in Nort replacing him as the Cal swim coach. So together, Pete, Nort and Matt planned the best possible environment to enhance Matt's opportunity for success at the 1988 Olympics. They all agreed that Matt would skip competing in water polo during the fall of 1986 and hold his final water polo season the fall prior to the Olympic year. This allowed Matt to have a more "normal" approach in the fall of 1987 leading up to the US Olympic Trials and presumably the Olympic Games. Although Matt practiced with the water polo team in the fall of 1986, he didn't compete. This made for a difficult fall as he couldn't experience the joy he felt in playing the kind of intense water polo that came only in the games.

The fall and winter came and went. For Matt it was full focus on swimming, and his first key meet of 1987 had quickly crested the horizon.

The 1987 NCAA Championships were back at the University of Texas and saw another string of records established by the senior Golden Bear. Tom Jager had graduated and that took away a bit of the drama from the 50 and 100-yard freestyle races, but Matt set a new American Record in the 50 (19.15) and won by over half a second. On the second day of competition the University of Florida's Troy Dalbey pushed Matt to a new American Record in the 200 freestyle (1:33.03). Rounding out his American Record-setting weekend, Matt easily won the 100 freestyle in 41.8. Matt put some icing on the cake when he finished off his collegiate career with another sizzling split of 41.02 to close Cal's come-from-behind win in the 400 freestyle relay.

All told, Matt's collegiate swimming career included eight individual and four relay titles at the NCAA Swimming Championships. In the process he had set or reset six individual American Records. He was recognized as the 1987 NCAA Swimmer of the Year and topped it off later that day when he was named the USOC (United States Olympic Committee) Sportsman of the Year. "I'm real happy and honored," he said of the USOC award. "I think it recognizes swimming and helps the sport. I love the sport and I'm happy I could do it. I can't tell you how many people have come up to me here and said, 'Great job.' And that's what's best, that people appreciate what I'm doing" (SW April 1987).

The past three years had been a whirl wind of worldwide travel for Matt at the end of each summer. As soon as he returned to school in September it was the start of water polo season. Even prior to entering Cal, he had been on the European tour with the US Junior Water Polo Team. Then in the spring of his freshman year he had left home to get "experience" at the 1984 Olympic Trials which led him straight to the Los Angeles Olympics. His one-month breaks in December between water polo and swimming were also loaded with school work. There was tremendous opportunity ahead in the Olympic year of 1988, and Matt knew it. He felt he needed a break during the summer of 1987, however, to gear up for the work to come in the Olympic year. Coach Thornton, on the other hand, knew from being an experienced and successful coach that the training of a swimmer the year before greatly affects the outcome a year later. The possibility existed for Matt to do something in the 1988 Olympics that would be extraordinary, and he wanted to help him get there.

Neither Nort nor Matt completely got what either wanted out of the summer of 1987. Matt stayed away from the pool at Cal and trained infrequently. When Matt did show up to train, Nort avoided him and walked the other way.

Despite his lack of sufficient training, Matt attended the 1987 Long Course US Nationals held that August in Clovis, California. The competition also served as the selection meet for both the Pan Pacific and the Pan American Games. Matt had plenty of speed and swam a world record in the 50-meter freestyle, nipping Tom Jager at the finish 22.33 to 22.4. He won the 100 freestyle (49.3) and finished second in the 100 butterfly (53.91), but his lack of conditioning showed most in the 200 freestyle in which he finished fourth with a time of 1:50.6, nearly three seconds slower than the previous summer.

Many of the top swimmers declined to attend the Pan Pacs to get ready for the Olympic year, but Matt felt obligated to go. Consistent with the Biondi family leadership philosophy Nick Biondi sent his son a letter on three small note pads that suggested there is always something to be gained from an experience. "Go on the trip," he told him. "You will meet new people and you can get out of it what you can."

The team traveled to Brisbane, Australia, for the competition. Tom Jager took back the world record in the 50 at 22.32 and Matt managed to win the

100 freestyle (49.7). His competitive will and his position as a leader of the US Team was never more evident than it was in the 400 medley relay. With the Canadians holding a commanding lead after the butterfly leg, Matt uncorked a 47.9 anchor leg to come from behind and win by four-tenths of a second. He had been true to his word to Stu Kahn in his sophomore year of high school. Matt Biondi had become the greatest relay swimmer in the world.

In 12 months' time, each relay contested at the Olympic Games offered not only an opportunity for a gold medal for the American men's squad, but also a chance for Matt Biondi to challenge Mark Spitz's amazing seven gold medal record performance in 1972.

1988 OLYMPIC YEAR

Cal won the NCAA Water Polo Championships in the fall of 1987 and Matt was named all-American for the fourth time in his four years of collegiate water polo. The now fifth-year senior had duly earned his position as a respected teammate and leader on the squad, and with that all the rights and respect granted from Coach Cutino. One day that fall, Matt sat in the coach's office with his feet up on the corner of the desk and his hands clasped behind his head while the two discussed good movies and girls. A freshman walked in and Coach Cutino raised his voice and summarily dismissed him. Moments later Matt and Pete resumed their conversation, a clear sign that the process transitioning another Cal water polo player from young man to a grown man had begun.

On January 1, 1988, preparation for the US Team Trials and Olympic Games began in earnest. Even though he was no longer eligible to compete for Cal during the collegiate season, Matt felt a part of the team because nearly all the swimmers that came to Berkeley in 1983 were still there training for their own country's Olympic Team or hoping to make the US Team. As we know, Coach Thornton was a great teacher of swimming and believed in making his swimmers self-reliant. That self-reliance included both training and competing. He taught Matt early on to "fake it until you make it." This meant get through your poor days at practice the best you can.

CONSISTENCY

Matt had grown to understand that "we define ourselves on our poor days, by doing what you should do even when you don't feel like it." Therefore, consistency had become a vital part of Matt's process for excellence. Each day that he came to the pool he made sure to improve his condition and nurture his technique. He fully understood the prize that awaited him that August in Seoul, South Korea. If he felt bad at the beginning of practice, he would "rip" a set, swimming as fast as he could while his inner voice coached him onward, *Just get through this set.* When he pushed through the discomfort, that one set would jump start him toward a good practice in which he could sustain his effort throughout.

Six and a half months remained until the Olympic Trials in Austin, eight until the Olympics in Seoul, and the coach and swimmer were back in sync. Each saw the opportunity to show the world what Matt Biondi could do, just as Matt's mother had encouraged in 1984. The shadow of Mark Spitz's seven gold medals and seven world records in 1972 had hung over every Olympics since 1972 and no one had come close to duplicating the feat. Matt had a real chance, and although swimming at his best was first and foremost in his mind, it was hard for him to ignore the questions from both the press and the people that followed swimming.

MENTAL POWER III - VISUALIZATIONS

Visualizing is a skill and a powerful one. When you have a college room-mate with a girlfriend, and you don't, you can spend a lot of time alone. Matt did that year, but the solitude translated into more time to visualize his goals. Matt actually saw himself in the pool, in the first person performing his swims in Seoul. The images were colored with emotion, with touch, with smell and even with taste. Matt had moved from dreaming of being the fastest swimmer in the world to visualizing his goals being achieved, in detail, in his mind's eye. When he walked across campus, he'd visualize his races over and over. Sometimes he beat Tom Jager. Sometimes Tom beat him, but he held images in his mind of Olympic success.

The 1988 US Olympic Trials were held at the University of Texas and Matt was in top form. In the preliminaries of the 200-meter freestyle he set a new American Record at 1:47.72. In the finals he intensified his kick after the midway point and was ahead of world-record pace at the 150 turn. The quick burst of energy hurt him on the last length, however, as he tired badly and was beaten by Troy Dalbey. But he did finish second, good enough to qualify him to swim the event in Seoul.

On the second day Matt swam the 100 butterfly for only his fourth time in major competition. He won the event with the fastest time in the world so far that year (53.08).

His strongest event, the 100 freestyle, was scheduled for the third day. The

Olympic coaching staff was selected by a point system, taking into account the performances of each coach's swimmers. The system included bonus points for swimmers, and thus their coaches, who set a world record. Matt wanted every possible advantage at the Olympic competition, and he knew that having Nort Thornton on the staff would certainly be an advantage. Matt went out that night and lowered his own world record in the 100 free to 48.42, in large part to help Nort secure a spot as one of the US Olympic Swim Team coaches.

In the finals of the 100 free, Tom Jager swam fast enough to make the American 400 free relay. Unfortunately for Rowdy Gaines, the popular and sentimental favorite and "old man" (at 29) of the US sprint corps, narrowly missed the relay by four-hundredths of a second.

In 1988, the Fédération Internationale de Natation Amateur (FINA) rules allowed for two false starts without a penalty. In the old FINA system, no swimmer could cause a third false start, even if that swimmer was not responsible for the first or second false start. If they did, they were disqualified. On the fifth day of the competition, in the finals of the 50 free, not one but two false starts had already been "charged to the field." The eight fastest swimmers climbed up onto the block for the third and final time. The anticipation ratcheted up to an incredible level and Tom Jager blazed his way down the pool to new world-record performance with a time of 22.2. Matt touched a distant second at 22.5.

Jager and Biondi had now faced each other 14 times in the 50 free, and with this Olympic Trials win, Tom was ahead of Matt 10–4.

Nonetheless, Matt left Austin having qualified for the US Olympic Team in seven events, his hopes of matching Mark Spitz's seven gold-medal performance in 1972 very much alive.

1988 OLYMPICS – Seoul, Korea

Matt was at or near the top of the world in four individual events, and the American men were always strong in the three relays. The same Rowdy Gaines that had asked, "Matt who?" four years before, observed, "Matt is not a human being. He's from another world. I'm confident he will win seven golds in a month. We need that, and he's the perfect person to do it because he leads by example" (SW September 1988).

Clearly, the Spitz comparison had come to the forefront of everyone's mind, not only in the swimming community but for all who held an interest in the Olympic Games.

Following the US Team's six-week Olympic Games training camp, they arrived in Seoul ready to go. And for Matt, his seven-race campaign was to begin on day one of the swimming competition with his weakest event, the 200-meter freestyle. Matt led for 195 meters, but as he faded toward the end of the race he was overtaken at the wall by Australia's Duncan Armstrong (who set a new world record at 1:47.25). His narrow loss took Spitz's record of seven gold medals off the table, but there still was the possibility Matt could win seven swimming medals. That was also a milestone achieved previously only by Mark Spitz.

On the second day Matt swam the 100 butterfly, now for the fifth time in major competition. This time he led for 99 meters, but he glided into his finish and was nipped by Suriname's (and US-trained) Anthony Nesty 53.00 to 53.01. Matt went graciously to the warm-down pool but was furious with himself. He thought, *Can't I fix this?* His application of effort and attention to detail, wrapped up in a "worker bees" mentality, had always worked for him before. Wasn't there a way to do this over? Of course there wasn't, and that is the magnificence of sport. His opportunity in the 100 butterfly had passed.

Coach Thornton's practice of making swimmers self-reliant served Matt well in this moment. At the Olympics, coaches aren't permitted on the pool deck during the competition. Matt needed to sort this out for himself and get ready for a very challenging relay coming up in a few minutes. As was his habit, he eased himself into the warm-down pool and swam very slowly and very easily, always applying as perfect a touch to the water as he could. As you know, a key element of Matt's process for excellence was visualization. It was now time to release his mind from the 100 butterfly and grasp the image of victory in the 800 freestyle relay. As he stroked up and down the warm-up/down pool his focus moved forward.

Although the Americans hadn't been beaten at the Olympics in the 800 free relay since 1956, they had finished third at the World Championships two years earlier. Matt Cetlinski (1:49.37) and Troy Dalbey (1:48.44) started for the USA with the first two legs. After Doug Gjertsen (1:48.26) swam third for the United States, they trailed East Germany by nearly a second. When Matt finished his anchor leg the Americans owned the new world record (7:12.51). Matt had turned in the fastest 200-meter freestyle split ever swum when he covered the distance in 1:46.44. "I was definitely tired of losing," said Biondi. "I was hurting the last 25. But all I was thinking of was I wanted to be on top of the awards stand." For Gjertsen, it was his only event at the Games and he was competing in his first international meet. "I'm just glad all three of us gave Matt the chance to win it. I think it helped that he had raced earlier.

I'm not saying I'm glad he only got the silver (in the 100 fly), but it did put fire in his eyes" (SW 1988).

That relay swim served as Matt's breakthrough; the pressure was off. Coming in he'd felt like the Olympics offered the opportunity to really show the world what he could do, and he finally felt like he was on his way to doing it.

The next day, prior to the 100 freestyle, he said to himself over and over, *100 fly, 100 fly, 100 fly,* a reminder to give 100 percent of his best. That night his best was good enough as he won the 100 free in an Olympic record time of 48.63 over teammate Chris Jacobs, who had a great swim of 49.0, as well in taking the silver medal.

On the following day the men swam the 400 freestyle relay. After Chris Jacob (49.63), Troy Dalbey (49.75), and Tom Jager's (49.34) completed 300 meters, the team held only a nine-hundredth of a second lead over the USSR. But Biondi swam a blazing 47.80 to cap off the win and help the relay set a world record (3:16.53).

On September 24th Tom Jager and Matt Biondi raced the 50 freestyle again, and this time for the Olympic gold medal. Typically in this race Tom got off to a fast start and Matt closed in on him toward the end. Throughout the training camp, Matt had been working with Coach Thornton on timing his breakouts (body first breaking the surface off the start) to make them as fast as possible. He also made sure that his first two strokes were long and full so that he established good traction in the water at the outset. As a result, when he burst to the surface, Matt was already in the lead. He held it all the way to the wall and swam to the gold medal with a new world record (22.14 to Jager's 22.36).

Matt and Tom visited the press room afterward and offered their view of the immediate future. Tom Jager was looking forward to his next Olympics when he said, "I'll be back in four years. I believe in myself and I have goals I haven't reached yet." Matt had planned to retire from swimming after the Games. When Matt was asked what it meant to have six Olympic medals he thought for a moment, then smiled and said, "It means I need one more" (SW November 1988).

The 400 medley relay was yet another world record for Matt and the Americans. David Berkoff led off, just missing his world record when he swam the second fastest 100 meters of backstroke of all time (54.56) to create a comfortable lead. With Rick Schroeder swimming breaststroke, Chris Jacob on the freestyle leg and Matt's second fastest all time split in butterfly

(52.3), their overall time put them well under the world-record mark. Matt's seven medals to tie Spitz for the most ever at a single Olympic Games was satisfying, but he was still having fun with his friends just like he did back at the Moraga Valley Pool when he was a young kid. "I love relays," he said. "If you could have seen us four hours before we swam tonight, you'd know why. We had some fun times. "This is the closest I've been to teammates, and that makes it more special" (SW November 1988).

There were many times when Matt might have quit swimming. Perhaps when his suit fell down in his first race, when he missed a turn at Junior Nationals or when he failed to score a point in his school championships in his sophomore year. There were times when people might have quit on him. Perhaps Coach Richardson when he couldn't qualify for the NCS Championships his freshman year at Campolindo High School. But they didn't and neither did Matt.

The opportunity to excel in a sport like swimming was always there for Matt, just as it is for everyone. He was granted the opportunity for personal responsibility for his success by his parents. He had the light turned on by Stu Kahn. Matt developed his own process for excellence, and because of it, his dreams became specific goals with detailed visualizations to match. He committed himself to consistent effort toward developing his skill to perfection and then trained to be in condition to fulfill his visualizations. He built his process for excellence to swim fast and because he did, he owned a process he could use in all facets of his life.

Matt Biondi retired from swimming after the 1988 Olympics, but continued to hold a passion for, and a curiosity about, playing international water polo. He played for the USA National Team in 1989 but disliked it. The veterans that made up the Olympic water polo team in 1988 were gone. The joy he had experienced playing at Cal was not there, and he decided not to continue to pursue water polo.

PROFESSIONAL SWIMMING – Building a New Generation

Matt hired Parks Brittain as his agent to help him take advantage of his Olympic success. Parks recognized the potential in this tall, handsome, articulate man and set up speaking engagements for him. Matt honed a 45-minute message that described how his process for excellence in swimming was a process for improving in other areas of life and in business. His reputation grew for being an entertaining, humorous and informative speaker, and at times he was on the road 25 out of 30 days of a month. He began to miss swimming and by June of 1989, he resumed the sport.

In August, Matt entered the US Long Course Nationals in Clovis but only in the 50-meter freestyle. Tom Jager continued his career and the matchup was the most anticipated race at the nationals for nearly every spectator. In a controversial call by an official, Tom was called for a third false start and disqualified. The crowd was incensed. Matt won the race (22.36), but the uproar reverberated all the way through the FINA Congress and the rule was changed to a "no false start" rule. This eliminated the gamesmanship that came with athletes trying to anticipate the starting signal. But other changes did not come so easily.

In 1989 the concept of professionalizing swimming was in its infancy, especially in the United States. For example, an international federation might invite Matt or Tom Jager to compete in their national championships and offer them a sum of money—perhaps $10,000. Matt and Tom would not only need to give their agent a portion of the payment but they also discovered that US Swimming was the biggest agent of all. They immediately took 40 percent as their fee. If Matt and Tom didn't comply, they could lose their right to compete for the US National Team and eventually lose their ability to swim in the Olympics. They were enraged when they realized the impact of the policy and sought to change it. "Tom and Matt were the only swimmers in the USA with stature enough to change the sport," recalled Olympic teammate and gold medalist David Berkoff. "I couldn't do it, but they could."

To the uninitiated viewer at the time, Matt Biondi and Tom Jager may have appeared selfish. They had a different view of the future of swimming, however, that few others could see. They envisioned swimming in the United States where athletes could retain all of their own earnings and have freedom to compete where they chose. They envisioned athletes being supported by US Swimming, not the reverse. They even envisioned a day in which professional swimmers representing the USA could earn an insurance program to help them with potential sport-related injuries. Much of their efforts to create these changes were selfless as were their actions in Europe the next winter.

In February of 1990, Biondi and Jager were competing in Paris and East Germany in major European competitions. They were there to earn income and support themselves in their profession as swimmers. Tom's family now included his wife Becky. The US National Junior Team was competing in the same competitions. The team was a collection of the top 16 years-and-younger girls and the top 18 years-and-younger boys in the United States. I was the head coach of the team and asked Matt and Tom if they would speak to the team about their careers, race preparation and their process for swimming excellence. Matt and Tom agreed to speak to the Junior Team.

In Paris one afternoon between prelims and finals they pulled themselves out of a nap and Tom and Matt sat on the floor of an upstairs elevator lobby with 54 eager teenagers. Sitting in a circle around the room were future Olympic gold medalists Josh Davis, Joe Hudepohl, Brad Bridgewater and Ashley Tappin. Packed into the small space were other Olympians and national-champions-to-be such as Peter Wright, Matt Hooper, Brian Retterer and Eric Diehl. The young swimmers listened to every word with bated breath.

"I see my swimming as a performance unto itself. Unlike other sports, no one can play defense on me," Matt Biondi explained. "I have my lane that's seven to nine feet wide..." and on he went. Tom Jager had been captain of many of the US National Teams since 1985, and in a sense he was leading as captain of that team in that moment. He was inspiring the Junior Team members to love the sport and embrace their development. One day they might be in the position of Matt and Tom and they should treat their role with integrity and respect, which were exactly the qualities that these two American swimming leaders were displaying.

At the evening finals there were few Junior National Team members swimming because they hadn't been fast enough to qualify high enough in the morning heats. The throng of youngsters raised the roof of the Piscine des Tourelles with roaring cheers of "Jager, Biondi, Jager, Biondi!" And when they successfully finished, "USA, USA, USA!" in support of their new friends and teammates. The youngsters became a more integral part of the American Swimming Team that day, both emotionally and practically as they supported their representatives on the blocks.

Tom and Matt traveled the world and saw different types of racing formats utilized by other countries to showcase swimming. In Australia, the City of Tassos Club conducted an annual "dash for cash" sprint race. US Swimming consented to organize a similar event in Nashville in March of 1990. The event was broadcast on national television.

The format started with eight swimmers racing the 50-meter freestyle. The seventh and eighth-place finishers were eliminated. Then six raced and two were eliminated. Then four raced and two were eliminated. All of the participants received some money regardless of their finish placement, but the winner would walk away with $10,000, and second place would earn $5,000. A world record was worth an additional $2,000.

Finally the race came down to a one-on-one matchup, and you guessed it ... Tom vs. Matt once again. It was another thrilling race in front of capacity crowd with Tom and Matt touching only four hundredths apart. Tom was victorious with a WR 21.81 to Matt's 21.85. Tom's world record stood for a decade until the great Russian, Alexander Popov, broke it in 2000.

Favorite Tom Jager Quality Training Set:

Eight weeks prior to the major competition

8000 Feet Altitude, New Mexico

> 10 x 50s every 8 minutes
>
> Dive, No Breathe on any 50
>
> Average short course 20.2, average long course 23.3

Over the next two years, Tom and Matt dominated sprint swimming throughout the world and led US teams. They battled each other in the pool and US Swimming out of it. Matt's suit sponsor was Arena and the sponsor for US Swimming was Speedo, which created conflicts. Their earnings from swimming were deposited in an account held by US Swimming. If Matt wanted to buy a car or Tom wanted to use money to put down on a house, they had to ask US Swimming for permission to access the funds.

On one trip Matt was being paid to compete in a meet in Bonn, Germany. He received a fax from US Swimming saying that if he competed he would lose his eligibility to compete for the United States and presumably swimming in the Olympics. He sat in the stands, stunned and disappointed, and watched the swim meet. Their fights went all the way to the floor of the House of Delegates at the US Swimming convention. Eventually they won a change to reduce the percentage of money taken from their earnings by US Swimming down to 10 percent. From their perspective that was the fee they were paying to represent the United States on the Olympic Team.

1992 OLYMPIC GAMES – Barcelona, Spain

By 1991 another Olympics was in sight. Matt was no longer feeling comfortable training at Cal. He was looking for someplace to make a home for the next year and a half in preparation for the US Olympic Trials and the Barcelona Olympics. He called Coach Eddie Reese at the University of Texas. Eddie's teams had won three straight NCAA Championships and over the past few years he had developed a plethora of US National Team members. He had also been named as an assistant coach for the 1992 Olympic Team. Matt told him that he would like to move to Austin, Texas, and train with him for the next year and a half. Eddie's response surprised him: "I have my own 100 freestyler, Shaun Jordan, and I'll need to talk with him about it." Eddie called Matt back and told him that he and Shaun had decided the answer was no.

Coach Reese's answer would likely be different today. But his success was derived in part from a great loyalty to his swimmers both as athletes and people. Shaun Jordan had been making huge improvements and could possibly challenge Matt Biondi as the top American 100 freestyler. Swimmers that continued after their college years were few and far between at that time. It was harder then than it might be today to know what the effect might be on the rest of the Texas team to have professional swimmers from other programs training with them. Matt hired his own personal coach, Tom Morin, and trained by himself in a lane made available by Rich Thornton, Nort's son, at the San Ramon Valley pool in California. At the World Championships in Perth, Australia, in January of 1991 Matt won three gold and one silver medal.

The Olympic Trials for the 1992 team were held in Indianapolis in March. The early trials were for the purpose of giving the team members more preparation time for the Barcelona Olympics to be held at the end of July. Matt missed the team on the first day in the 100 butterfly (54.2), won the 100 freestyle (49.31) and nipped Jager at the wall in the 50, 22.12 to 22.17. "I want a rematch with Matt," Jager proclaimed. "He took it to me at Seoul. I want a chance to get back at Matt" (SW April 1992).

There was no 200-meter freestyle in Matt Biondi's Olympic program, and his times weren't his best even though at 26, he was in his prime physical years to meet his swimming potential. American Swimming wasn't accustomed to post-collegiate graduates swimming at the time and struggled to support them, or even allow them to support themselves. Leading up to Seoul, Matt had strolled the Cal campus with images of Olympic success playing over and over in his mind.

From 1989 through 1992, victorious visualizations had been mixed with analyzing how to best change the American system to allow people such as he and Tom Jager to swim as a professional, support a family and extend their career. Matt had not just tried to be a great swimmer for the last four years, he had also tried to be an ambassador, a legislator, an entrepreneurial professional and a leader of the US Team.

The team in Barcelona was much more mature than the one in Seoul. Matt and Tom were back for a third Olympics and they were joined by Olympic veterans Pablo Morales, Mike Barrowman, David Berkoff, Jenny Thompson and Dara Torres. There was also firm leadership from the newly created position of National Team Director for the US Team, held by Denny Pursley. This created a tighter knit squad than Seoul.

The first day of competition was Matt's specialty the 100-meter freestyle. In the evening finals he led at the 50 turn but faded to fifth with a time of 49.53—over a second off his world record. A new up-and-coming swimmer from Russia named Alexander Popov won the race in 49.03. Entering the 50 freestyle, Matt and Tom had performed 24 out of the fastest 25 swims ever swum, but the Olympics are only about who is the fastest that day and it was Popov again. The Russian swam a time of 21.91, to Matt's 22.09 and Tom's 22.30.

Matt Biondi and Tom Jager were each still a gold medal away from becoming the first swimmer to ever win a gold medal in three Olympics. The United States had never lost the 400 freestyle relay in Olympic competition, but they came out of the morning heats qualified second for the finals behind the Unified Team (formerly the Soviet Union). Helping the morning relay qualify for finals were Shaun Jordan (49.9) and Joel Thomas (50.04). Matt and Tom were allowed to rest in the preliminaries and assigned to the evening relay. Alexander Popov also rested in the preliminaries and would be anchoring the Unified Team's relay. Two other swimmers qualified to swim on the evening relay for the United States by their performance in the morning heats. They were 18-year-old Joe Hudephol who led off in the preliminaries (49.76) and Jon Olsen who anchored (48.74) and was second in the individual race at the US Trials.

It is a fact that Matt Biondi and Tom Jager had done more to position themselves for victory that night than prepare just their own athletic performance. Joe Hudephol had sat on the floor with the Junior Team listening and learning from the two American standard bearers just two and half years before. Joe came out of the summer leagues in Cincinnati and had yet to begin college swimming. He was poised to do his part to bring America victory and etch another achievement in history for his teammates. Jon Olsen would soon enter the US Swimming "resident program," which would be a place for post-grad swimmers to train after college at the Olympic Training Center—a result, to some degree, of all the efforts Biondi and Jager had made to professionalize swimming in America.

Joe Hudephol led off in 50.05, which put the USA fourth but only one-tenth of a second behind the leaders. The US strategy was for Biondi to be second and get the team out front. "I wanted to do well for our team and for the good old USA back home." He said afterward, "I wanted to give Tom a lead" (SW September 1992). Matt (48.69) built a significant lead over the Unified Team of a full second and the Americans led the Germans by sixth-tenths of a second. Tom Jager (49.72) and Jon Olsen (48.28) held off Popov (47.8) and the Unified Team by seven-tenths of a second. The Americans won the gold medal, just missing the world record by two-tenths of a second (3:16.74).

Matt Biondi and Tom Jager became the first swimmers to ever win gold medals in three Olympics. They also became the only athletes in Olympic history to ever do so in the same event, the 400 freestyle relay. At first the pair had been rivals and then became friends. They enjoyed owning a ranch together in an area of Colorado aptly named the "Wet Mountains." They moved professional swimming forward in America so that athletes of the future could have a better means to earn a living by training and competing in a sport they love.

For many observers and fans of swimming, Matt Biondi was a super talent with the advantages of being nearly 6' 7' tall, having 14-inch feet and a long arm span. Those blessings shield an accurate view of his greatness as an athlete and as a person. His step-by-step process of improvement and attention to detail was the path he followed to success. Even when he was a weak and skinny 16-year-old that didn't feel comfortable in school, he continued to inch forward in the pool, by kicking when he couldn't pull, extending his stroke when he felt like shortening it, having faith that he would succeed over the long term.

As of this writing, Matt finally did retire with eight gold, two silver, and one bronze medal at the Olympic Games, becoming the most successful Olympic athlete of his era. He inspired millions of people around the world with his speed and grace in the pool and his thrilling relay anchor legs in which he always seemed to get his fingertips to the wall first—just like he promised Stu Kahn when he was a sophomore in high school.

Matt Biondi, Mark Spitz and Michael Phelps are the only athletes in any sport to ever win seven medals in a single Olympics.

Matt Biondi developed a process for achieving excellence that he has reproduced to transform all aspects of his life to realize his dreams. He is the proud father of Nate, Lucas, MacKenna and husband to Kristin Biondi. At this writing he is a fifth-grade teacher in Kona, Hawaii, as well as chairman of the school district's math department. He challenges his students through a curriculum that is success-based, rather than age or grade-based, to inch forward and find their own process for excellence.

Matt Biondi was inducted into the International Swimming Hall of Fame in 1997.

DAVID BERKOFF

November 30, 1966

THE INNOVATOR

circa 1978

Benjamin Franklin was one of the most prolific inventors in world history. Today we live more safely with Franklin's lightning rod and more alertly with his bifocals and we're warmed by his furnace stove. We change our clocks twice a year, in part because of Mr. Franklin's inspiration for the eventual invention of daylight savings time.

In the early 1720s, when Benjamin Franklin was a teenager, he liked to swim in Boston's Charles River. He swam primarily for fun and fitness, but he also wanted to swim faster. Being the natural innovator that he was, Ben set about finding a way to accomplish that goal. First he designed a pair of (wooden) flippers that he attached to his feet, and then he crafted a set of plates that he strapped to his hands. These incredible innovations enabled him to zoom through the water like never before. Soon thereafter the Boston-born American patriot moved south to Philadelphia.

This story is about another quite innovative young man who grew up in Philadelphia and then moved north to Boston at about the same age that Ben traveled south. It is the story of a person whose creative ability, like Ben's, also emerged at a young age. Yet for this young man it was up in Boston that he developed his own incredible innovation, an innovation that changed the sport of swimming in such dramatic fashion that it continues to affect every competitive swimmer in the world today.

* * *

The younger swimmers' practice at the cavernous Germantown Academy pool started precisely at 6:30 pm, and Head Coach Dick Shoulberg patrolled the pool deck. It was his domain, his classroom—every inch of it. His beard shielded his face from his swimmers' eyes. He could stare you down when he looked out of his glasses, but it was difficult for a swimmer to catch a clear look into his eyes. His voice could sound like a growl when he wanted it to. He let you know who was in charge, and when it was time to start practice, you were in the water or you heard his growl.

Hmmm ... let's see ... yes, the large red fiberglass starting block behind lane six was a perfect spot. David had used such a hiding place before at times just like now when he wasn't yet ready to take the plunge into the cool water. Even Coach Shoulberg couldn't outsmart him. David tucked himself into a small ball and cuddled up behind the side of the starting block near the corner of the pool.

"I want a 300 individual medley in reverse order," the coach barked. "First length is drill, second is swim and the third is kick. Go on the 57." Shoulberg liked innovation too. Why start on a round number? Anybody could do that.

The swimmers entered the water precisely on the 57 and every five seconds thereafter—that is all except for 11-year-old David Berkoff. David pressed his cheek and shoulder flat against the fiberglass block. His heart raced. He heard all the other swimmers turning and stroking but didn't move a muscle for fear it might expose him to the sight of his new coach. Beyond the normal sounds that accompanied a collective of swimmers moving through the water, David sensed a stillness, a silence-like sensation that roared in his ears.

Where was Coach Shoulberg?

Shoulberg saw a foot sticking out from the side of the red block number six? Quietly, he bent over and picked up two hard Styrofoam kickboards and then tiptoed over near the block. He slapped the two boards together with all his might. "WHAACK!" The crack sounded like lightning had struck the very spot David was hiding. David scrambled to his feet and raced down the pool deck in the opposite direction as fast he could.

"BERKOOOFF!!!" the coach screamed in his loudest growl. Underneath the beard he couldn't help but smile as he watched the chubby little boy scoot down the deck. "Berkoff, in the water noooow!!" David made a leaping dive into the pool and slithered into the group of swimmers.

Later that night Shoulberg met Judge Elaine Berkoff in the hall after her son's first session at Germantown. The coach relayed the events of the evening.

"He's a pistol," Elaine said.

"We'll look after him." And Dick Shoulberg did.

Charles and Elaine Berkoff had every right to smile at the thought of their 11-year-old running on the pool deck. There was a time they worried about him running at all. In kindergarten David had such trouble coordinating his limbs in such simple activities as skipping that the school suggested he stay back to develop some coordination. It wasn't that he was tall and gangly; as a matter of fact, he was short and quite chubby. At just a year old he weighed 17 pounds. The Berkoffs were a cerebral couple and David was a bright child. Charles had a Ph.D. and was an organic chemist who worked for a pharmaceutical company. Elaine had been an attorney and a district judge for 20 years. David seemed too bright to stay back in school just to gain some coordination.

Instead, the Berkoffs took their son to the family pediatrician with the hope that he could recommend some appropriate physical challenges. The doctor suggested finding a sport to help David develop physically. Soccer was convenient but out of the question because he simply couldn't kick a ball. The Berkoffs older son, Tim, was involved in swimming at their summer club. David seemed to enjoy the water, and if he could learn to swim, the summer pool seemed like a safe place for him to be.

So that summer his parents enrolled him in swimming lessons.

UPPER MORELAND SWIM CLUB

The Berkoffs were members of the Upper Moreland Swim Club near their home in suburban Philadelphia. The summer club was tucked away in a neighborhood, only visible to those who knew its whereabouts. With its expansive grass play areas surrounding two large pools and one baby pool, it was a wonderland for the more than 500 family members each summer. One pool was built purely for recreational use and included two diving boards, one board low (1 meter) and the other high (3 meter). Pool depth ranged from three feet in the shallow end to 12 feet in the diving well. Beyond that there was a third, six-lane, 25- meter pool built for both recreation and competitive swimming.

In the summer of 1971 the Berkoffs felt it was a good time for David to learn to swim. Younger brother Kevin, two years David's junior, was almost ready to learn as well. Debbie Pollack worked as a swim instructor, lifeguard and an older swimmer on the team. She helped David get started, using an approach founded on gentle, loving guidance. Once David did learn to swim, it became almost impossible to get him to stop—that is, once he finally got in the water. Debbie and the rest of the staff marveled at what they had launched: the Berkoff boys at sea!

From that point forward, every summer David and his friends played all day at the Upper Moreland Swim Club. The games and contests they invented were better than any video game could ever be. They moved from pool to pool and diving board to diving board. They learned how to do handstands on the bottom of the pool, swim through each other's legs and play sharks and minnows. They progressed to doing flips off the starting blocks, having somersault contests off the diving boards, going underwater and grabbing each other's ankles to twist each other around. Hundreds of game possibilities poured out of their imaginations.

The summer that David was eight years old, he joined the summer swim team. The coach needed a backstroker for the eight-and-under medley relay and placed David on the lead-off leg. It was his first backstroke race, and as he neared the finish he rolled over onto his stomach before he touched the wall. He was appropriately disqualified. His teammates gathered around him and told him, "Everyone rolls over on the finish the first time they do it." David appreciated their empathy, but he didn't like failing, and he was devastated. He began to listen to his coaches more in practice so he could improve and not be embarrassed again.

The Suburban Aquatic League was a collection of winter swim teams in the area. The local team was called the Upper Moreland Aquatic Club. When his parents saw how much David enjoyed swimming, they decided to register him for the team. He wouldn't be practicing every day, but it provided him a much needed physical activity and he began to develop more coordination.

When the Upper Moreland Summer Club opened the following spring, he (and now younger brother Kevin as well) was back on the summer swim team.

Upper Moreland Summer Club Practice Plan - Coach Bob Israel

7-9:00 am -   13 year old and older swimmers.
                     4-5,000 short course meters
9-10:30 am - 9-12 year old swimmers
                     3-3,500 short course meters
                     Warm-up with skill and technique drills including:
                     8 kick each side, progressing to single arm - working on full
                     extension and rotation
                     6 x 200s on 30 seconds rest
  OR
                     10 x 3 x 75s on 15 seconds rest (rotate 50 fly/25 bk, 50 bk/25
                     breast, 50 br/25 fr)
                     20 x 25 on 1 min rest, swim faster than 30 on each one
                     Relay starts and turns
10:30-11:30 - 8 year old and younger swimmers

In school and other activities David experienced the subjective nature of grading. For example, David felt like there was no way to really determine exactly how good someone's cursive writing might be, yet somehow the teacher decided upon a grade. David quickly discovered the objective nature of competitive swimming. It was simple: You either won or you lost. Your personal performance in each of the strokes and distances determined an exact time. There was no guessing involved.

When David was 10 he switched from the Upper Moreland winter team over to the Hatboro YMCA and a winter Y league. He became even more excited about swimming, in equal parts due to the charismatic nature of Coach Jim Nicholas and the success of the team. Coach Nicholas was always excited at practice and at meets, and for David it was fun to try and please him. As a result David improved rapidly and nearing the end of their season he was the third fastest 10-year-old on the team. The season culminated at the Pennsylvania YMCA State Championship meet where the 10/under 200-yard freestyle relay that David was a part of won the event with a time of 1:59. David was thrilled with the excitement of winning, and he began to think he might have a chance to become a good swimmer.

A typical path that many competitive swimmers take is to begin competitive swimming on a summer team and then, if the desire and a certain amount of talent are evident, take the step of joining a year-round team. It's not unusual to continue on the summer club for years, while practicing and competing with the winter club.

David Berkoff walked a different path. He was loyal to the Upper Moreland Swim Club in the summertime and always came back to practice and compete there as long as the rules of age limits allowed him to do so. When David was nearing his 12th birthday, he swam in the Suburban Aquatic League (SAL) in the fall, but it was only recreation racing without a US Swimming affiliation. In need of something more, David began to practice with the Germantown Academy Aquatic Club team. This offered him both a more experienced coaching staff and a team to compete with once the SAL season was complete.

David swam on three teams and the Berkoffs were innovating!

The Germantown practices were much more difficult than what he was used to with the recreation team or even at the Hatboro Y. Coach Shoulberg presented himself as a stern taskmaster, but underneath the gruff exterior he possessed a warmth and affection for children. Coach Shoulberg was busy with many responsibilities. He served as a swimming instructor outdoors in the summer, taught swim classes at Germantown Academy (GA) and coached both the prep school team during the school year and the club team year-round. The only person Coach Shoulberg enjoyed being around more than his swimmers was his wife Molly.

David liked racing much more than practicing, which presented a problem. The GA workouts were difficult for him because there wasn't much rest between repeats. Wednesday nights were the toughest nights at GA, when Coach Bob Jacobs filled in for Coach Shoulberg. Twelve-year-old David dreaded those practices most of all. His best time was only 1:00 in the 100-yard freestyle and therefore sets of 10 x 100s leaving every 1:15 were extremely painful. This intense set was for David nothing more than a test of survival. Some nights he hurt so much that tears trickled from his eyes.

When David began to compete in the United States Swimming (USS) meets, he encountered a level of competition much higher than what he was accustomed to. Some of the best 11-12-year-old male swimmers in America were training with and competing for Philadelphia-area USS clubs. David was used to winning races in the recreation and Y leagues, yet now he picked up the meet programs and read the names of Joey Regan, Blaise Matthews, Jeff Prior, Jeff Evans, and national age-group record holder Jamie Taylor. His first thought was that if he did *really* well he *might* be able to finish in the top six swimmers in the 100-yard backstroke, his best event! David's previous best in the 100 back was 1:05, while Jamie held the national record at 58. David was a smart kid and he knew he was far behind the top swimmers in his age group.

In the time between meets he did everything possible at practice to try and catch up.

During the summer the Berkoffs were back at the Upper Moreland Swim Club. David and his brother Kevin were inseparable there. They continued to practice with the swim team and then played, both in and out of the pool, all day long. The games became more sophisticated. There was a lot you could do with a ball and a diving board. Putting them together was even better. A good run off the diving board coupled with a nicely timed throw of a tennis ball, meant you might have to stretch out to catch the ball in the air. Sometimes the landing hurt, but the ability to coordinate it was an athletic feat. If you could throw the ball back before submerging underwater that was even better. But to be an aquatic "King of the Day," one had to do a somersault in the air, catch the ball *and* throw it back.

When David moved into his early teens, he practiced more with Germantown, but he still loved the summer club meets. The competition could be keen, particularly in the League Championship Meet. Over many years David and Kevin developed rivalries with swimmers like David Wharton from the Highlander Swim Club. Wharton was a top swimmer in the area and a swimmer who was also destined for great achievements in the sport.

1981-1984 HIGH SCHOOL YEARS

It was September of 1981 and, though only 14, David was preparing to enter the 10th grade. Though he had attended Germantown Academy in middle school, his parents decided to send him to the Penn Charter School for high school. Germantown and Penn Charter were high school sports rivals, which left David with an uncomfortable feeling as he was scheduled to train and compete with Germantown in club swimming, but he would be competing against them in high school/prep school meets. After a great deal of thought, David decided to look for another USS club team to join.

The high school season didn't start until November, so in the fall of 1980 David began practicing with the Abington Aquatic Club and once again competing in the Suburban Aquatic League (SAL). He wasn't going to move up to the 15-and-over age group until his birthday November 30th. Tami Hession was the coach at the Abington Aquatic Club and Tim Bracken was going to be his coach at Penn Charter. They each cornered David. Most coaches might be pleased to have a fine swimmer on their team but they pointedly told him, "You are too good for this team and too good for this league." David understood and appreciated their point. He started looking for a stronger club.

The Westchester Swim Club (WSC) had recently hired a new coach, Jack Simon, who came with an excellent reputation following a very successful stint at the Santa Barbara Swim Club in southern California. He had developed Paul Hartloff, who had made the 1976 US Olympic Team in the 1500-meter freestyle while still a high school student. Westchester also had some of the best swimmers around David's age in all of the greater Philadelphia area. For the Berkoffs the only downside was that Westchester was across town and that meant that with the Philadelphia traffic the drive to practice would be upwards of 45 minutes each way. All things considered, however, Westchester seemed like the best fit.

WSC trained in a 50-meter pool on multi-millionaire John DuPont's rustic Foxcatcher estate. It was one of the rare indoor 50-meter pools in the area at that time. The facility was only about 20 yards in width, therefore the team practiced long course (50 meters) all the time. The squad included many of the great swimmers that David had previously competed against in US Swimming—nationally ranked swimmers like Patti Gavin, Libby Kinkaid, Lisa McClain and Blaise Matthews were all very committed to the sport, as was their new coach. Their regular practice week included nine or ten pool sessions for each swimmer.

Jack was a taskmaster. If David had any inkling that leaving Germantown for WSC was going to mean an easier training regimen, he soon discovered that he was wrong. In the second week of practice Coach Simon directed his swimmers:" We are going to race for two hours. Count your meters!" David thought he was going to die. He completed 10,750 meters. Exhausted, he climbed from the pool and quietly asked the coach, "Do we do that often?"

Over the next two years David earned the nickname "taper man" from his teammates for several reasons. David didn't get to practice regularly because of the long drive to Foxcatcher and the intermittent dual meets for Penn Charter. He might be at WSC practice four or five times per week while his teammates were there for at least nine practices. Jack worked his swimmers very hard and when David did come to practice, his training mates were tired and he wasn't. In addition, he recognized that since he wasn't there as often as his teammates, he should work very hard when he was able to attend. This combination of factors resulted in him training well at Westchester and learning that he could call on a higher intensity level in training than he'd ever realized.

1982-1984 WESTCHESTER SWIM CLUB/FOXCATCHER–
Coach Jack Simon

In school: 5 evenings 2-2:15 min, 3-4 mornings 1.5-2 hrs, Total with dry-
land 24 hours per week

Out of school: 11 practices per week 2.5 hours each.
No practice on Wednesday evening
7,500-8000 long course meters per 2 hours

Favorite sets:

Pull: ⎸ 10 x 400s free on. 5:00 (Odd breath every 3, 5, 7, 9 stroke per
100, even 9, 7, 5, 3)

Swim: 10 x 200 IMs on 3:10, then drop 5 seconds on each 50 to finish
on 2:20

Swim: 3 x (4 x 200s back on 3:00 neg split, 2nd 100 should be 100 pace
of 200, 100 back on 1:20, 2nd 50 should be 2nd 50 time of 100, 2 x
50s on :40, easy 150 on 3:00)

Provided by Coach Jack Simon

David's unusual training schedule helped him improve his times dramatically. In his junior year of high school, having recently turned 16, he was
ranked in the top 20 nationally in his age group for three long course events.
He was third in the 100-meter backstroke (59.74), 13th in the 200 backstroke
(2:09.8), and fourth in the 200 individual medley (2:11.25). While his times
weren't world class for the amount of training he had done, he certainly
showed the potential for a bright future.

The decision of where David would attend college was an important one
for all the Berkoffs, though ultimately Dr. Berkoff and Judge Berkoff left the
final choice to David. The swimming program that any university would offer
was important, but the more important factor was the quality of academics.
After considerable thought and research, David narrowed his search to Cal
Berkeley, the University of Virginia, Yale, and Harvard. Unfortunately for
David, the process of college visits, combined with his training, overwhelmed
his health and in the fall of his senior year he succumbed to mononucleosis.

He returned to swimming later in the winter season and by this time
Westchester Swim Club had been renamed Foxcatcher to better acknowledge
Mr. DuPont's support of the swimming program.

In March of 1984 Foxcatcher was competing at the Middle Atlantic
Championships, held at the University of Pennsylvania, and David was

reunited with an old competitor from the area named Richard Hughes. Richard was a year older than David, and the previous year had gone to school and to swim at Stanford.

What's he doing in Pennsylvania? wondered David.

Richard told David that at Stanford he was about fifth on the team depth chart in the backstroke events and therefore he didn't receive much attention from the coaches. Because of that he didn't feel very important to the team. He had transferred to Princeton where he was more valuable to the team and enjoyed swimming with a fine coach, Rob Orr.

Richard's experience and explanation left a big impression on David.

Coach Simon had been giving him a nudge toward Cal Berkeley. Jack felt that both the swimming program and the coach, Nort Thornton, would be a good fit for Dave (Jack addressed him as Dave). But David's impression of Cal Swimming was that he needed to be 6' 5" tall and hail from California for the coach to show any serious interest in him, and David was only 5' 9".

It was on his trip to Harvard that David really clicked with the team. He figured that with both Richard Hughes and Dan Veatch swimming back-stroke for Princeton, he would have plenty of competition within the Ivy League. Of course, when it came to academics, how could he beat Harvard?

David's decision was made. He would go to Harvard and swim with the Crimson.

Despite enduring his bout with mono and all the college visits, David continued to improve and had an outstanding season of swimming his senior year of high school. Coach Simon encouraged him to train toward the 400 IM (Individual Medley), but David resisted. Jack believed he could set a world record at the longer distance, but David loved the shorter races and didn't enjoy the type of pain associated with training for and competing in the 400 IM. David recorded all best times in his strongest events that season in the 25-yard (short-course) pool: 100-yard backstroke (51.9), 100-yard backstroke (51.9), 200 IM (1:53), and he improved to 4:03 in the 400 IM.

1984 US SPRING NATIONALS – A Discovery

David qualified to swim in his first US Long Course National Championship meet that spring, which was held the last week of March in the beautiful and brand new IUPUI Natatorium in Indianapolis. It was billed as a final testing ground for swimmers hoping to make the United States Team for the Los Angeles Olympics. It was to be conducted the first week of August. Although it was uncommon for swimmers to compete beyond their collegiate years at that time, there was a large group of postgrad (beyond college) swimmers at the Nationals preparing for the Trials. This turn of events was a direct reaction to President Jimmy Carter's US boycott of the 1980 Games that were held in Moscow. Four years earlier the president's rationale had been that the boycott would be an effective way to protest the Soviet Union's invasion of their neighbor Afghanistan.

The boycott had robbed many swimmers of their opportunity to compete at their peak on the grandest of world stages, the Olympic Games. Swimming super-stars Sippy Woodhead, Tracy Caulkins, Mary T. Meagher, Craig Beardsley, Steve Lundquist, Rowdy Gaines and Bill Barrett were all hanging on to their swimming careers at the average age of about 23. Lundquist referred to them as the "gray beards."

On the opposite end of the spectrum, among the rising young stars at that spring's Nationals, was 16-year-old Dara Torres. Though she didn't swim as fast in the 50-meter freestyle as her world best from the previous year, her time of 25.88 was still good enough to win.

The Nationals were the highest level of competition that David Berkoff had ever attended, yet he handled the environment around the star-studded atmosphere well. He swam his best long course time in the 200-meter IM (2:09.5), and in the 100 backstroke (59.0) he qualified high enough in the preliminaries to earn a second swim at night in the consolation finals (ninth–16th in prelims), where he finished 14th.

Rick Carey, the world record holder in both backstrokes (55.38/1:58.93) was not in attendance, but David watched and learned from the others. The swimmer who most caught his eye was Jesse Vassallo. Jesse placed second in the 400 IM, and what David noticed was that he used three dolphin kicks while still underwater on his backstroke push-offs. Later in the meet Jesse won the 200 backstroke (2:01.6), and once again David noticed the three underwater dolphin kicks off each wall. It appeared to David that from using these kicks Jesse gained an advantage over the rest of the field. Ordinarily dolphin kicks were only performed in butterfly, yet evidently there wasn't a rule that prevented a swimmer from using them in backstroke. David replayed the flow of Jesse's movement over and over in his mind. Could he integrate what he saw into his own swimming?

Three months later, in the last week of June, Coach Simon brought his team back to Indianapolis for the US Olympic Team Trials. Jack had hoped that David would increase his training and be prepared to swim his best in the highly intense competition. That's what good swimmers tended to do. That's not what David did. He wanted a more relaxing summer before going off to college. He asked Coach Shoulberg if he could train periodically at Germantown Academy. GA was closer to home, which would save him time for other activities each day. The coach welcomed him back to GA, and David enjoyed his summer as he prepared to leave home for college.

1984-1985 HARVARD – Freshman Year

Harvard University attracts the best and the brightest from all over the world. Over time the Harvard community has come to appreciate excellence in every field, including athletics. The transition for any 17-year-old from high school to college can be a challenging one. For David, the transition included a required commitment to train more than he ever had before, while at the same time confronting the most challenging academic load of his life.

HARVARD TRAINING SCHEDULE – 1984-1989 – Coach Joe Bernal

Monday – Friday:	3- 5:00 pm Swim Training
Mon, Wed, Fri:	5:30-6:30 am Strength Training
	6:30-7:00 am Swim loosen up
Tues and Thurs:	5:30-7:00 am Swim Training

At that time the head swim coach at Harvard was Joe Bernal, a man whose background included being a Commander in the US Navy. Prior to his arrival at Harvard, Joe had been the coach at Fordham University in New York while at the same time building his own club team, Bernal's Gators. Leading up to the 1976 Olympics Joe had developed American distance swimming legend Bobby Hackett. (Hackett's amazing career is chronicled in the book *Four Champions, One Gold Medal*.) Joe's program was demanding, and if you were a member of the Harvard team, attendance at practice was required. His swimmers were expected to attend two practices per day, five days a week and one session on Saturday. For a swimmer like David, who had generally practiced five or six times per week, the difference was enormous. Compounding his challenge was the fact that his roommates were not swimmers and they were frequently up until 2 a.m. As a result, David spent much of his freshman year sick or run-down. When he was at the pool, practice was certainly interesting.

One day the team was doing short sprints and Coach Bernal was walking the deck, stalking every move they made. David and his teammate Jeff Peltier were playing around with finding various ways to go fast and race their teammates, much like David had done as a kid in the summer at the Upper Moreland Swim Club. In this case he was kicking underwater like he'd seen Jesse Vassallo do at Spring Nationals using dolphin kick.

"What are you doing, David?" the Coach yelled.

David smiled. "Just trying to keep up!"

"That looks pretty good. Let's time that!" Joe yelled.

Coach Bernal timed David's underwater dolphin kicking from the start to halfway down the pool. They found that David was faster kicking to the halfway point than he was when he swam. After the completion of the set Joe told David, "Hey, that was faster than your swimming. Let's work on that."

At each swim meet Coach Bernal insisted that David kick underwater on each of his starts in backstroke. The timing of when to come up was crude at that point, but he was clearly gaining an advantage. In workouts they continued to refine the number of kicks and the angle of trajectory of David's path to the surface of the water to breakout into swimming.

Despite his adjustment to college and the many practices he missed when he was sick, David qualified to swim in the NCAA Championships as a freshman. However, he walked to the beat of his own drummer. He had other experiences on his mind.

"Coach Bernal, spring break would be a great time to hike the Appalachian Trail. What would you think if I skipped the NCAAs? I'd really like to go hiking and camping that week?"

Coach Bernal was not pleased with the request, but he had an athlete to educate. "Look David, Harvard supports us as a program to represent the university at the highest level we can attain. It's an honor for you to go to the NCAAs and good exposure for Harvard."

David responded, "It's getting pretty nice outside, Coach. We've been indoors all winter and have no other breaks from school and training coming up except that week."

Joe created a small compromise. "Tell you what. Let me know some other weekend you want to go camping and you can miss practice on that Friday and Saturday to go."

After some thought David responded, "Sounds good!" He was proud of his small victory.

1985 NCAA CHAMPIONSHIPS – Austin, Texas

The 1985 NCAA Division I Swimming Championships were held in Austin, Texas. Traditionally the NCAA Championship Meet represents one of the most difficult competitions in the world to get into. It was the day before the start of the meet and David had just finished his warm-up. He was standing with Coach Bernal on the pool deck taking in the entire experience. Joe was greeting colleagues he hadn't seen since the summer nationals or perhaps even the previous year. Coach Nort Thornton from Cal stopped to say hello.

"Who's the German kid on your team?" Nort asked.

"We don't have any German kid."

Nort persisted. "Well, who's your backstroker named Berkoff? Isn't he German?"

David thought to himself, *He doesn't even remember me, and he recruited me just last year!*

David's performance of 50.2 in the 100-yard backstroke was an excellent improvement over the previous year. He placed 11th (third in consolation finals) and scored points for Harvard. His underwater dolphin kicking was in its infancy, but it still drew the attention of several other coaches.

"What, are you trying to do—kill that kid—Bernal?" was UCLA's Ron Ballatore's question to Joe after David swam.

It wasn't but a few minutes later that USC's coach Peter Daland offered Coach Bernal more cerebral advice. "Joe, he would be more efficient and have more energy to finish that race if he would stay underwater for a shorter period of time."

The entire competition opened David's eyes to swimming at a very fast speed and at a very high level. David was only 5' 10" tall and weighed about 155 pounds. It seemed to him that just about everyone in the meet was 6' 5" tall. His competitors were not only tall, they also tended to be much stronger and raced with enormous intensity. David overheard many of the comments from other coaches regarding his use of dolphin kicking.

Like any impressionable young man, he was having second thoughts about the direction Coach Bernal was taking him down. "I don't know about this, Coach. Do you really think trying to stay underwater so long is a good idea?" Joe reassured him, but it took a shower and a break for David to think it through.

David thought, *How can I catch up to these guys?* He came out of the locker room about half an hour later and reaffirmed with Joe the path they had started down made sense.

During the month of April, David continued to train regularly at Harvard prior to going home to Philadelphia for the summer. By that time, Jack Simon had left Foxcatcher Swim Club, so David rejoined the Germantown team and Coach Shoulberg. His training went well that summer, and before he knew it the time had come to taper down for the national championships to be held in Mission Viejo, California.

1985 Germantown Academy Training – Coach Richard Shoulberg

Early Season Afternoon

Warm up: 12 x 75s :52 (minus three normal strokes per length)

9 x 200s (100 back/100 breast) three rounds of:
Technique on 2:50, Negative Split each 100 on 2:40, Race on 2:30

Kicking: "Super 500," speed kicking: 25 on :30, 75 on 1:45, 50 on 1:00, 25 on
:30, 50 on :60, 50 on :60, 75 on 1:30, 25 on :30, 50 on :60, 25 on :30, 25
on :30

Main Sets: 1 x 2000 (22) 500 "6/6 turns" (six kicks on back, six kicks on side,
then swim) 500 race, 500 12/12 turns, 500 race

16 x 75s fly on 1:02, double circle, straight-arm recovery

9 x 250s on 3:25, descending by sets of three:

75 fly, 50 back, 75 breast, 50 free

50 fly, 75 back, 50 breast, 75 free

100 weak stroke, 75 second weakest, 50 next strongest,
25 strongest (IM order)

Speed: 5 x 50 on 1:00, 1) Fly/back, 2) Back/breast, 3) Breast/free,
4) Choice

Mid-Season Afternoon

Warm-up: 16 x 25s on :25, drop one second per 25 until failure, rest 10 seconds, begin again

Main Set: 12 x 50/150 (3 sets of 4)
50 on :45, one of each stroke, IM order within 3 seconds of life
time best.

150s: 1) Neg split on 2:00, 2) technique on 1:50, 3) build on 1:40,
4) race on 1:30

Quality Set: 1 x "Super 500": 25 fly, straight-arm recovery, 50 back/breast
(think turn), 75 any three strokes, IM order

Main Set II: 20 x 100s: Odd IM on 1:18, Even freestyle on 1:02 – fast!

Turns: 6 x 30 on 1:00, start five yards from wall, perfect stroke with
perfect transition turn, then sprint 25

Reprinted with permission from *Swimming World Magazine*/Technique –
November 1987-88

At the 1985 summer Long Course Nationals, US Swimming was selecting two teams for international meets based on placement. David finished fourth in the 100-meter backstroke (57.4), which put him into contention for the US team trip to Japan. Charlie Siroky finished ahead of David and had the prerogative to go on two trips or just one. If he turned one down, then David would be headed for Japan. The US Swimming staff asked David if his passport was in order. Passport? He didn't have a passport. To David's dismay, without a passport, attending an international meet as a part of US Swimming was not an option.

With the passport issue weighing heavy on his mind, David was entered in the 200-meter IM the following day. David swam well that next morning, qualifying in the consolation finals that night. The only time available for David to get a passport was between the prelims and finals, and the only location for him to obtain a passport was in Los Angeles. The trip by car, depending on traffic, was about an hour north of Mission Viejo.

There was another swimmer facing the same circumstances; fortunately the pair was able to enlist the help of a driver. They raced off to Los Angeles and the agency that issued passports. The line was long and so was the processing time. The hours passed and they became more and more worried about missing their event in the finals.

Finally, with passports in hand, David and his cohort jumped back in the car and raced through the streets of Los Angeles. As they checked the time and the traffic, the inevitable was facing them: To save time they would need to make a "car change." They slipped off their clothes and into their racing suits. The driver raced from the Santa Ana freeway through the hills of Mission Viejo. By the time they turned onto Marguerite Parkway, each had a hand on a door handle ready to run.

Coach Shoulberg recognized the situation, even in this pre-cell phone era, and had an assistant coach waiting at the gated entrance to the pool. David leapt from the car, ran to the warm-up pool where he sneaked in a short 200 warm-up prior to the start of the 200 IM. David made it through the swim okay, but after all that had happened in the previous 24 hours, Charlie Siroky decided to accept both trips.

David would have to wait another year (or more) to use his new passport. He was angry that he had come so close to making the trip to Japan only to miss out due to a decision that was out of his hands. David didn't want to face this situation again. He asked himself how he could catch up to the very best American backstrokers and thought, *I can do it if I develop better use of the underwater dolphin kick.*

1985–1986 HARVARD – Sophomore Year

Joe was a demanding coach and pushed David hard his sophomore year. Certainly Coach Bernal recognized the challenge that the academic load at Harvard presented, but there was simply no shortcut to becoming a world-class swimmer. One had to train at a very high level and Joe set out to cover every detail of helping his swimmers reach their potential. Coach Bernal worked on increasing the number of dolphin kicks David used on his start, as well as off of each turn. He also helped David improve in other areas.

The attainment of athletic excellence in any sport has consistent threads despite the differences in the sports themselves. One of the qualities necessary for every high-achieving athlete is the ability to develop the skill of visualization—learning how to see oneself in the mind's eye in the first person, present tense, oneself actually performing their sport. It's a method of programming the subconscious mind with an experience before it physically happens. Coach Bernal understood the importance of this process. Once every two weeks or so, he had the swimmers listen to a tape that took them through a relaxation exercise and then into visualization. David enjoyed the experience and took it a step further. He put on music in his dorm room and visualized his races over and over, further developing his imaging ability.

The H-Y-P (Harvard-Yale-Princeton) Tri-meet was always one of the biggest events on Harvard's schedule. The competition had grown so intense among the programs, Harvard and Princeton in particular, that in any given year either team or both tapered their training and shaved down for the two-day meet. Coach Bernal was a master team-builder and motivator, and a week before the meet Joe held a team meeting in the locker room. The coach asked each swimmer in the circle to share with their teammates his individual goals for the meet. The sharing rotated around the squad, and the excited team members reacted louder and louder to hearing their teammates' goals. Eventually it was David's turn. He knew he would race Richard Hughes leading off the medley relay against Princeton. His goal included getting his team off to a rousing start by beating Hughes.

David had a pad of paper with his goals written down and read them to the team: "100 backstroke, 22.79 at the 50 and I'm going 48.81!" He ripped the paper off the pad and slammed it on his locker. Then he took out a piece of tape and stuck it up there for him and all his teammates to see.

"And I want you to hold me to it!" he said.

The whispers started. "Don't you think you should go 49 before you go 48?"

By the time 1986 H-Y-P arrived a week later, David had visualized every detail of his 100 backstroke swim dozens of times. The first event of the meet was the 400 medley relay. The meet was held at Harvard, and one of the Harvard swimmers who wasn't competing that weekend was announcing the meet. His job was to broadcast the details of the races over the loudspeaker system. He knew David's goal times from the team meeting a week earlier.

David blasted off the start, utilized his underwater dolphin kicks and took a commanding lead on the first lap. When he turned at the 50 the scoreboard read 22.79—the exact time he had visualized. Amazed and without thinking, the announcer shouted into the microphone, "David Berkoff turns in 22.79 ... Holy s**t!" When David touched at the finish, his time was exactly 48.81.

For David the entire swim was like a dream. He could only remember the start and the finish; everything else had already been programmed into him from his numerous visualizations. Unfortunately, and despite a great team performance, Harvard lost the meet on the final relay. But afterwards teammates asked David, "Do you have any more paper from that magic pad?"

Given his performance in the H-Y-P meet, David reset his goals for the NCAA Championships. The American record was 48.2 and he just swam a 48.8, in a non-championship meet. He decided to set his goal—and mind—on winning the 100 backstroke at the NCAAs. The talk around the Harvard campus spread about David's swimming prowess. The school newspaper wrote an article about the potential of Harvard having its first NCAA swimming champion since Henry Dyer accomplished that feat in 1957.

Note: *Dyer was one of only three Harvard men to ever win an NCAA swimming title, and David's time in the 100 backstroke was already faster than Dyer's 49.4 winning 100-yard freestyle time.*

As the NCAAs at IUPUI approached, the pressure of expectation mounted on David.

The goal was alive in the preliminaries when Berkoff qualified second to SMU's Mark "Mook" Rhodenbaugh, just three-tenths of a second behind him. The prelim time of 49.1 was disappointing for David, and a third place finish in finals with a time of 48.87 devastated him. He had been faster in the H-Y-P meet. The objective information that swimming gave him said he hadn't performed at his best when it counted the most. David felt that he'd failed himself, and on top of that he'd let down the entire Harvard community.

David Berkoff had a strong opinion of what was right and what was wrong. Beyond that, he was an independent thinker. He came and went from club to club growing up, and he came and went from practices at Foxcatcher with Jack Simon. His actions weren't always on the traditional path that leads to swimming excellence, but he always followed his heart. In the spring of 1986, after his disappointing performance at NCAAs, his heart was not in swimming. There were also problems at home that he didn't want to confront. He discussed the matter with Coach Shoulberg who saw how down David had become. Shoulberg said, "Why don't you just go teach canoeing in Maine for the summer." David did.

CAMP ANDROSCOGGIN, MAINE

Driving with an ever-increasing sense of peace, David coiled his way through the hills of Maine, each passing mile putting increasing distance from both Philadelphia and Boston. His smile grew with each turn of the wheel, as did his anticipation of a summertime spent in the wilderness.

When David pulled into the parking lot at Camp Androscoggin he stepped from his car and was immediately overcome by the rich scent of pine and the symphony of sound created by the wind blowing through the trees. The deep green foliage seemed to wrap itself around him, eliciting feelings similar to those provided by the support of good teammates. The sun began to set and turned a deep orange color. The rays spilled across the western mountains and sparkled off the waters of Lake Androscoggin. He was drawn to the water's edge. He stood by the lake, feeling at home, anticipating that he and the great outdoors were about to spend a warm and adventurous summer together.

David spent a lot of time around the water that summer; he spent very little in it. He paced the camp's 200-foot dock along the 2,000-foot shoreline and tutored kids in swimming. He taught the "J" paddle stroke to campers in their canoes. He learned to love the large pitchers of juice in the dining hall and the family-style eating. He led crafts and helped teach basketball, soccer and baseball.

He also had teachers of his own. They were the smiles on the faces of the campers. Their joy reminded him of his own that he had always experienced while participating in sports.

The tug of a large-mouth bass on his fishing line was the greatest competitive thrill he required. Often at night he sat outside and stared up at what seemed like millions of stars bursting from the dark sky. That summer David discovered that nothing in his experience could challenge the vastness and glory of nature. He considered the enormity of the trees, the purity of the lakes and highest mountain peaks, a combined force so overwhelming that it put all of his life's challenges into perspective.

By August he felt renewed and invigorated in a way he'd not felt before. David Berkoff recognized that his own internal competitive flame was burning brighter than ever.

1986–1987 HARVARD – Junior Year

In the fall of 1986 David began his junior year out of shape for competitive swimming. Yet his focus and enjoyment regarding swimming had changed. He was eager for swim practice and focused on becoming the fastest 100-yard backstroker in the history of the sport. His season goal was to be the first swimmer ever to break 47 seconds.

David, his roommate Jeff Peltier, and Coach Bernal were developing a method of training with the underwater dolphin kick. They were adding sets with fins where they would stay underwater for a series of 25s. They kicked series of 50s underwater as well. Coach Bernal made underwater dolphin kicking a priority in the Harvard program, and he integrated it into the training regimen, as though it were another stroke.

TECHNIQUE TIP – UNDERWATER DOLPHIN KICK:

In David's words: "Watch the nose of a dolphin when it begins to move from a still position. The nose drops first then the body starts to move. Use your hands like the dolphin's nose. Begin your underwater dolphin kick by pressing slightly with the hands on the water. This will help initiate the action through the entire body."

Additional tips:

Arms are positioned overhead, with both hands flat on top of each other. The fingers are pointed. The thumb of the bottom hand is wrapped around the wrist of the top hand. The shoulders are squeezed together from the torque of the clasped hands. Arms are located slightly behind the ears toward the back of the head (the goal is a streamline flat back—no arch. The positioning of the arms may vary for individual differences in shoulder flexibility to flatten the back).

The dolphin action is performed from the lower ribs through the toes. Keep the up and down movement within a small sphere or amplitude (a number of inches about half your age). If your toes turn in a bit you're at an advantage. It's very important to kick evenly on the up and especially the down kick. There should be a constant whip and flowing motion. (The biggest mistake is kicking from the knee and stopping after each knee extension.)

At the 1987 Ivy League Championships, David lost three very close races to his friend Rich Hughes. Instead of being deflated by the losses, he decided to be more persistent than he'd ever been before and prove himself at the upcoming NCAA Championships.

1987 NCAA CHAMPIONSHIPS – Austin, Texas

On the first day of 1987 NCAAs, Harvard did not make the finals of the 400-yard medley relay. In the finals that night, Jay Mortensen led off the Stanford relay in a 100 backstroke time of 47.94 to become the first swimmer to ever best the 48 mark. David was upset because his goal of being the first to swim a 47 was gone. He sulked much of the night, but eventually he sat himself down for a talk. He decided that no one could control his outcome and likewise he couldn't control theirs. He told himself that he would come back the next day and do everything possible to win the individual 100 backstroke event.

The following morning David qualified third in the preliminaries with what he felt to be a moderate effort. Later that night, before David's race in the finals, Coach Bernal advised him, "Don't put so much pressure on yourself. Just go out and do that thing you do and have fun." To this point in their relationship Joe had almost continuously pushed David, but his relaxed approach was just what David needed to support his desired mind-set on this occasion. He won the race in 48.20. He had been in the finals of a national meet before but had never won. David was ecstatic.

For most accomplished swimmers the dream of swimming in the Olympics is never far from their thoughts. David, however, had never really thought much about it until now. It was a year and a half to the Seoul Olympics and about 15 months to the US Swimming Olympic Team Trials. David thought to himself that winning the NCAAs was a big accomplishment—and just maybe he had a legitimate chance to make the Olympic Team.

Following finals that evening Coach Bernal hosted a pizza party back at the hotel for the team. Everyone was excited about Harvard's first individual national champion in 30 years. As the celebration wound down, David took Coach Bernal aside and asked him, "What would you think about me taking next year off from college competition and instead focus all of my training toward the Trials?" David anticipated a backlash from the coach about the prospect of not representing Harvard the following year.

Coach Bernal said, "Are you sure you want to do that?"

"I don't want to have any doubts about investing my very best effort to make the Olympic Team," answered David. "If I swim for Harvard, there will be some rest for the Princeton meet, then NCAAs. I think that will take away from what I would do at Trials."

Joe thought a bit. "I'm willing to do that David."

Coach Bernal's statement surprised him.

Then Joe smiled and said, "But you're going to hate me every day."

David smiled, "I already do." The two laughed.

David's training regimen in the summer of 1987 split his time between Germantown and Harvard. Most importantly it was a summer of tremendous international race experience. David qualified to swim in the World University Games that were held in Zagreb, Yugoslavia, July 9–14.

On the first day he swam the 100-meter backstroke. His dolphin kicking off his start was now extending out to more than 25 meters in a long-course pool. When he broke through the surface, he was normally ahead and could get a glimpse back at the rest of the field. This time Japan's Daichi Suzuki broke out from underwater at precisely the same time. Suzuki won the race with a time of 56.5 to Berkoff's 57.2. David was struck by the fact that someone from the other side of the world was working on the same innovation as was he and at the very same time. He sought out Daichi in the warm-down pool. David's Japanese was no better than Dachi's English, but they acknowledged one another with smiles and the similarity in their mutual enterprise.

At the US Long Course Nationals in Clovis the last week of July, David swam the first sub-57 100-meter backstroke of his life when he finished fourth in 56.7. He didn't qualify for the US "A" team that competed in the Pan Pacific Games in Australia, but he did earn a position on the "B" squad that would compete at the Pan American Games in Indianapolis in about a week's time.

Both the World University Games and Pan Am Games were multi-sport competitions just like the Olympics. The opening ceremonies at the Indianapolis Motor Speedway included more than 100,000 spectators, and when the American Team was introduced just about every spectator chanted, "USA! USA!" David slipped on his start in the preliminaries of the 100 back but shrugged off the mishap with a smile. Later that night he finished second in the finals (57.3).

David enjoyed his two-week break that August, but as soon as it was over he readied himself with great anticipation for the Olympic swimming year.

1987–1988 OLYMPIC YEAR

The Olympic Trials were scheduled for August 9–13 in Austin, Texas. Coach Bernal established a separate training group for those focused on peak performance at Olympic Trials. The small squad consisted of seven high school swimmers along with Harvard swimmers Peter Egan and David Berkoff. During the upcoming year they would all represent Joe's US Swimming Club, Bernal's Gators.

The first practice was Monday September 12. Coach Bernal came strolling down the pool deck singing, "I love the Olympic year!" He was in great spirits and David and his teammates were excited to get started. Harvard's pool can be configured for short-course (25 yards) or long-course (50 meters) swimming, and in this case it was set for short-course.

The first swimming series for warm-up was 10 x 100s choice, leaving every 1 minute and 15 seconds. The group of nine swam relaxed. The next swim was a 500 butterfly. When they finished the butterfly, there was another series of 10 x 100s every 1:15, then a 1000 butterfly. David sensed a pattern developing and wasn't excited where it seemed to be going. The coach ordered another set of 10 x 100s every 1:15, then a 1500 butterfly, another set of 10 x 100s then finally a 2000 butterfly. Coach Bernal was making the point that the swimmers needed to be ready for anything during this year and the training would be very hard.

Joe wasn't finished.

The coach gave each swimmer in the group a goal time they had to beat for a 100 swim. When they did it, they could leave practice. It seemed to David that the goals for most swimmers were quite reachable, but not for him. He had to swim a 53-second 100-yard backstroke to leave practice. He was exhausted. In addition to the grueling first practice, he hadn't brought enough food or drink with him.

His first effort was a 1:06. The other swimmers were successful but not David. They got out of the pool and went home. His second swim was a 1:00. The coach said, "Not good enough." David tried harder, giving everything he thought he had and turned in a time of 56. He thought perhaps he could get out with that swim and began to try to exit the pool. Coach Bernal pushed him back in and said, "Not good enough." David was furious. He summoned every ounce of energy he could for another swim. When he finished, Joe said, "53. You can go."

David climbed from the pool irate and famished. He wanted food. The only location he thought of that might have it was Coach Bernal's office. He stormed into the office and yanked open the refrigerator door. The only food in it was a chocolate Easter bunny Joe's daughter had given him, perhaps two years ago. David ripped it open and bit off the bunny's head. He walked to the showers holding the body of the bunny in his fist like a trophy for the day. He stood in the steaming hot shower, with melting chocolate dripping down his face.

An assistant coach looked into the showers and asked David if he wanted a ride home. David bit from the dripping bunny and nodded. The Olympic year had begun.

Coach Bernal started each day with shouting across the pool deck "I love the Olympic year!" It became a little obnoxious to David after a while, but it was also a signal that his coach was present at practice, connected to the swimmers and committed to helping them bring the best out of themselves. The hardest swimming set David ever recalls doing in his life was a set of 50 x 100s that mixed in underwater kicking with fast swimming. At number 37 the coach noticed someone not following instructions and the group started over again.

The group of nine completed 87 x 100 that day.

Bernal's Gators/Harvard Training Set Highlights

Fins –   10 x 50s on 1:00 long course, on 45 short course
           – stay underwater entire time except turn for yards
Fins –   20 x 25s underwater dolphin kick on :20 seconds
           50– 87 x 100s yards on 1:15
           (David's hardest set ever – started over at number 37)
           25 underwater, 50 above, 25 underwater
           1) Recovery 2) 5 surface, 50 underwater, 25 surface
           3) Backstroke swim under 1:00 4. Recovery

The 1988 Long Course Spring Nationals were held in Orlando, Florida, in March. David had increased his dolphin kicks to 32 off the start so he could travel underwater about 35 meters before he surfaced. The start was becoming well known and the media referred to it as "The Berkoff Blastoff." The crowd made an "ooooh" sound in anticipation of the breakout, wondering how far David would go. It was magnificent theatre. When David pushed off the 50 turn, he kicked another seven to nine meters underwater. David was victorious in the 100-meter backstroke in his best time ever of 55.46. He also finished fifth in the 200 backstroke with a lifetime best of 2:03.49.

David knew he was on his way to a great year.

1988 OLYMPIC TRIALS – Austin, Texas

The 1988 US Swimming Olympic Team Trials were held August 9–14 at the beautiful University of Texas Swimming Center. The Olympic Trials are the most pressure-packed of any meet on the US Swimming quadrennial calendar. The top two finishers in each event from the evening finals make the team. If you finish third, unless you're swimming on a freestyle relay, you're out. There are four more years of waiting to try again. Those objective results that David Berkoff appreciated as a 10-year-old are unforgiving.

David had come into the Trials with a goal to swim faster than two minutes in the 200-meter backstroke and make the Olympic Team in both the 100 and 200 backstrokes. His first preliminary swim of the week was the 200. He swam a 2:03.5, not even his best time. David was extremely upset and asked himself, *Did I train the whole year for this?* He didn't feel good in the water. He didn't feel fast. By finishing eighth in the preliminaries he did qualify to swim in the finals, but he had a very poor swim (2:05.7) that night and placed seventh.

David had matured over the years and had become a better athlete. He fell back on the lessons he learned at the NCAA Championships in his junior year. He gave himself one night to sulk; then it was time to move on.

There was an off-day between the 200 and the 100 backstroke events, a welcome day for him to relax. Prior to Trials, David and Coach Bernal had been developing and perfecting a crossover backstroke turn to enhance the underwater dolphin kick. David utilized this innovation in the 200 back. The rule of the day required a hand touch on the wall. David was athletic enough to stay on his side while he reached for the wall, touch, push his head down, immediately roll to his stomach, spring off the wall and begin his dolphin kicks. This turning style is the same as the best swimmers of today (2012) utilize to transition from backstroke to breaststroke in the IM.

The Olympic Trials television coverage included cameras that were set up high in the swim center. When coaches observed David's turns in warm-ups prior to the 200-meter backstroke Coach Bernal was told, "We'll be watching." After the race more than one coach told him, "David cheated. That turn is illegal." After a video review, the same coaches came back and apologized, saying they were wrong. Texas Coach Eddie Reese's progressive observation was, "I'm teaching my whole team that turn next year."

On the morning of August 12, David went through his race-day ritual, which included Lucky Charms for breakfast. In the preliminaries of the 100 backstroke he still didn't feel fast. He was a little short on his number of kicks at 31, executed a poor turn but thought to himself while he was swimming, *You can swim a 56 and still have a chance to make the team.* He touched the wall and the crowd was going crazy. David thought to himself, *Someone had a great swim from an outside lane; who was it?* So he looked at the scoreboard and scanned from top to bottom. In his lane the scoreboard read, 54.95. He had just set a new world record! David thrust his fist into the air—*I knew it all the time!*—and acknowledged the crowd.

While he was warming down, the fulfillment of his decision to take the year off from college swimming hit him full on. It was easy to be pleased, of course, since he had broken the world record, but his perspective went deeper than that. There were times in his life when he walked a path that seemed a bit easier than some others took. He had relaxed the summer before going to Harvard and went to Maine when he was embarrassed about his performance at NCAAs his sophomore year. This time he stayed and it paid. David chose work and it worked. His commitment during the Olympic year had been at the highest level he could possibly imagine and Olympic Team or not, he was proud of himself.

David enjoyed his traditional major swim meet lunch of bean burritos and readied himself for finals.

The lore of the Olympic Trials is filled with stories about swimmers that broke world records in the preliminaries and never finished high enough to make the team in the finals. Kurt Krumpholtz had done it in 1972, nearly becoming the first person to ever break 4:00 in the 400-meter freestyle only to miss the team with a slower time at night and with his world record still standing. Others would suffer similar fates in the future, just as they had in the past. David knew the stories and wanted no part of that experience.

In the evening finals he had an even better swim. He broke his world record with a time of 54.91. He won by nearly a second and wore a "perma-smile" for the remainder of the competition. When *Swimming World Magazine* published their September issue in 1988 they had lots of choices of athletes to picture or collage together on the cover. They chose one picture and one picture only. It was of David Berkoff. The chubby kid from Upper Moreland Swim Club had grown up and had his fist thrust into the air, with the simple caption, "Berkoff Breaks Back Barrier." He was the first and only swimmer to ever swim a time faster than 55 in the 100-meter backstroke.

Just weeks after the Trials, *Swimming World Magazine* wrote a feature article on David Berkoff's sudden impact on the swimming world. His comment in it displays a lot about his gentleness and love of kids. It was also a reminder about his enjoyment of innovating. "You know, I think the advice is more to the older swimmers to never push away a younger swimmer and to always encourage them," he said. "And to the young ones, to never be afraid to try new and different techniques. It's the best way to learn."

1988 OLYMPICS – Seoul, Korea

The Olympic Games in Seoul were the launching pad for many relatively inexperienced swimmers for the US Team. Some, like Janet Evans, had wonderful success. Others did not. There were unexpected casualties at the US Trials, most notably Pablo Morales who had departed Austin as a reigning world record holder but not a member of the US Olympic Team. The US Team missed the quiet leadership of swimmers like Pablo.

There was also an effort to reshape the US Olympic staff. During an era that ran from the 1960s to 1984, the Olympic staff was always from the same core of coaches. George Haines and Don Gambril were on nearly every staff. The addition of coaching legends such as Doc Counsilman, Sherm Chavoor and Peter Daland tended to give a predominance of veteran leadership to every squad. Richard Quick was named national team coach and head Olympic coach although he was also the full-time coach of the Stanford women's team. It was an enormous honor, but in some respects an unenviable position since there was a large staff of coaches who were very strong and independent leaders in their own right.

David was disappointed with the way the US Team and staff handled themselves at the Olympic Games. His teams at Harvard, the Gators and Germantown were always very close, but it seemed to him that each individual on the US team did "their own thing." If the coaches said wear red shirts, some athletes wore blue. There were several swimmers who wore their college shirts rather than USA shirts. He noticed at times that the team members wouldn't sit together in the stands. Instead, some team members gravitated to their college friends—even if those friends were representing another country.

The 100-meter backstroke was the second to last day of the Olympic swimming competition. In the preliminaries David lowered his world record to 54.51. Before the finals there was a rumor swirling that the two Russian swimmers who had also made the finals planned a strategy to try and derail the world record-setter. The rules at the time allowed for two false starts that would be charged to the field, and then if anyone false-started a third time that individual would be disqualified.

The swimmers were called to their mark. The starting signal sounded and David hesitated, thinking a false start was likely. No one false-started. He was left behind on the blocks. He whipped underwater and by 35 meters he was in the lead, but not by much. His early effort to catch up tired him badly in the last five meters. His Japanese friend Daichi Suzuki nipped him at the touch pad 55.05 to David's 55.18.

Following the race, reporters were quick to look for David's reaction to the loss. They asked him how he felt being the world record-holder but only winning a silver medal. David responded, "If a year ago you told me that I would have won a silver medal at the Olympics, I would have been challenged to believe it. I'm very proud to win a silver medal."

David made amends, of sorts. On the 400 medley relay, he led off in 54.5 again, and the US was off to a world-record swim and a gold medal for Berkoff.

1988-1989 HARVARD – Senior Year

David's senior year at Harvard in 1988–89 was one of awards but seldom of smiles. Instead of being applauded for his great Olympic year, people in the swimming community began to challenge him as a cheater and questioned Harvard administrators regarding his legitimacy as a student.

At a Harvard social function for the men's and women's swim teams, the athletic director entered a conversation with David and Coach Bernal. "I question if someone can spend so much time training to become the best in the world in swimming if they're really having the 'Harvard experience.'"

David responded with courtesy, kindness and intelligence. "My Harvard experience has been centered around the library and the pool. It's been a great experience. I have friends who have placed drinking and late nights as their priority. I'm very pleased with where I've placed mine."

David whipped through that season's dual meets. In one 50-yard freestyle he stayed underwater and dolphin kicked nearly the entire distance to split 19 plus on his team's 200-yard freestyle relay. He was named Swimmer of the Year for the Ivy League, set a new American record in the 100-yard backstroke in winning the NCAAs (47.02), and swam his best 200-yard backstroke ever (1:45.88) at NCAAs to finish second. After his last swim at the NCAA Championships he said, "I've done everything I've wanted to do in swimming and more. I have no more goals so it's time to retire" (SW 1989).

On the outside David was gracious, but on the inside he was hurt and angry.

What hurt the most was the talk that he had cheated by utilizing the dolphin kicks to such a great advantage. There were whispers that without them he wasn't a great swimmer. One coach at the NCAA Championships was quoted as saying, "I don't think flipper was ever timed faster," referring to David as a dolphin. Perhaps worst of all, FINA, the international governing body, validated the talk by outlawing anyone from staying underwater more than 15 meters on a start or on a turn. The excuse they used was that it was dangerous. Strangely enough it took until 1998 for the organization to decide that staying underwater in butterfly was dangerous and make the same rule change for that stroke.

David had been an innovator and a creative entity unlike any competitive swimming had ever seen. He'd brought crowds to their feet in anxious anticipation of witnessing the Berkoff Blastoff. All of that was being turned upside down.

If David had a "perma-smile" after making the Olympic Team, he now wore a "perma-frown."

Swimming couldn't end soon enough his senior year. Following graduation that spring David went back to the mountains and went to work for the Forest Service in Montana. He spent the summer fishing, hiking and camping. He loved it. When the summer ended he returned to Boston to be with his girlfriend, who was still attending Harvard. Coach Bernal gave him a position as an age-group coach, which meant once again he'd be working with young kids.

David loved working with the young swimmers as much as he did during his summer at Camp Androscoggin. Each day at the pool he was greeted with their joyful smiles and a laughter that burst easily from each of them. The swimmers also asked him questions he had never asked himself about the sport of swimming.

"Coach David, why are we doing this set?" He didn't know.

David asked Coach Bernal, "What's this set for?" Joe explained the set's purpose and then he explained it to the swimmers.

The Olympic gold medalist never paid much attention to the various training aspects of the sport. As adept as he was at skill innovation, David hadn't appreciated the recipe of energy system requirements that was necessary to build the conditioning or development of a swimmer. In his work with Coach Bernal as a young coach himself, his appreciation for practice design and season planning grew steadily. By the winter of 1990 there was a hunger building within him. He enjoyed coaching, but David missed being able to measure the results of his own training by competing himself.

That summer David started to train again. He entered the Summer Nationals in the 200-meter individual medley just to see what he could do. His time of 2:04.7 was as fast as he had ever been. The thought began to enter his mind of proving to the world that he was a swimmer, not just a dolphin kicker.

1991 – The Comeback

David trained with Bernal's Gators during the winter of 1990–91 and entered the 1991 Spring Long Course Nationals held in Federal Way, Washington (just outside Seattle). US Swimming had decided to institute a funding program for any swimmer that had a time that was among the top four in the world in the Olympic events. If a swimmer achieved a top-four time, he or she received $1,500 per month as a training stipend up through the 1992 Olympic Trials, and the funds would be paid retroactively back to 1991. This was a result, in part, of the strong stand that Matt Biondi and Tom Jager had taken to support the concept of professionalism for those high-level swimmers who wished to continue swimming beyond their college years.

David's $400 share of rent for his apartment was soon due for April. He had $200 in the bank. He gave his roommates a check for $400 and said, "If I don't swim a 56.0 or better in the 100-meter backstroke, don't cash it." The 200-meter backstroke was on April 4th. He didn't swim it. He rested. On April 6th David swam a 55.91 and qualified first in the preliminaries. His roommates watched the results come in and cashed the check.

When David's girlfriend graduated from Harvard in the spring of 1991, they both wanted to get out of Boston and David wanted to try and make the 1992 Olympic Team. The US Swimming stipend of $1,500 per month helped, but it wasn't something they could live on. He asked Coach Shoulberg if he could return to Germantown. Shoulberg said yes, and Judge Berkoff allowed her son and his girlfriend to come live at their home.

Germantown had an elite group of swimmers gearing up for a run at the Olympics in Barcelona. Sean Killion, Trina Radke, Dave Wharton and Dan Jorgensen were all viable US Olympic Team contenders. Interestingly, David's life had come full circle. In the early days it was Coach Shoulberg clapping kick boards by his head and scaring the life out of him. Now he saw the coach as having mellowed. David was no longer the weak trainer of the group trying to stay up, but he was an established Olympian, world record-holder and he could train with nearly anyone. He knew Dick's system of distance training and asked the coach to let him have some control of his training after Thanksgiving of 1991. The coach readily agreed, and they went to work.

Like David, Coach Shoulberg was an innovator as well. One of the staples of Shoulberg's program was that he asked each of his athletes to do extra training unique to their needs. He wanted them so committed to success that together coach and athlete would design an additional challenge that separated each of them from other national-level swimmers.

For example, he might ask someone to always carry an extra weight at school to strengthen their legs while walking up and down stairs. Dick felt this was as important for developing mental strength as it was for physical development. David was devoted to his fitness and proving to the swimming world he was good enough to compete at the Olympics no matter what the rules. For David, his unique extra training was long bike-riding and running. On some days he rode his bike 26 miles to the practice at Foxcatcher. Following workout on those days a teammate put David's bike in the car and gave him a ride back to GA for their dry-land workout. On other days David ran a half-marathon (13.1 miles) after he swam practice.

Coach Shoulberg calculated that when David set his world records he was underwater dolphin kicking for approximately 35 meters on the start and eight on the turn. He totaled it up to 43 meters of kicking underwater and the swimming to 57 meters. If he maximized his dolphin kicks under the new rules and traveled 15 meters underwater off the start and the turn, he would have to swim 70 meters, only a 13-meter increase from Seoul. He devised a plan to help train David to do it.

Dick bought two long yellow ropes. He tied each end to a handle of the sliding glass doors that lined the Foxcatcher pool deck. He located them so they would cross the pool at exactly 17 meters from each end of the pool. Every day at practice he gave David a set in which he had to stay underwater and dolphin kick until surfacing at the yellow rope. The last three weeks prior to the Olympic Trials, he moved the yellow rope to 13 meters so that David practiced surfacing in time to meet the regulations that required him to break out onto the surface at the 15-meter distance.

1992 FOXCATCHER/GERMANTOWN PROGRAM –
Coach Dick Shoulberg

4 Short Course yards practices per week at Germantown 6-8:30 am
5 Long Course practices per week at Foxcatcher 12:30-2:30 pm
5 Drylands at Germantown 3:30-4:30 pm
1 Sat Foxcatcher 3 hrs and 2.5 hrs

Favorite Berkoff Yellow Rope Sets

Place two yellow ropes at the 17-meter mark at both ends
You must underwater water kick past the 17-meter mark at both ends
Three weeks before trials the yellow rope was placed at 13 meters at both ends
Example Sets: Long Course
8 x 200 on 3:00 Descend 1-4

3 x 800 on 11:30 -1) 200 MAX Back, 400 Mix Back Drills, 200 Build Back, 2) 125
Drill Back, 75 max Back, 3) 800 Max Race Back

12 x 100 on 1:40 1) Fly kick underwater 17 meters off both walls, 50 Back- Five
Strokes Right Arm. Five Strokes Left Arm. 50 Fast Back 2) Breakout past 17
meters. 50 Back- Five Strokes 20 kicks 50 Build Back 3) Race Back- Breakout
past the 17-meter mark.

20 x 50 on :55 Breakout past 17 meters

Note: We are an IM-based program and David Berkoff did a lot of IM training
with Dave Wharton that year.

Provided by Coach Richard Schoulberg

In the November of 1991 David Berkoff was a 25-year-old Harvard graduate and Olympic gold medalist. He was bright and confident. In December of
1991 Stanford's Brian Retterer broke David's American record in the 100-yard
backstroke. When David heard the news, he told Coach Shoulberg, "Well, I've
got him." He felt that if Brian was swimming that fast he couldn't be training
very hard and therefore wouldn't be competition for the Olympic Team at the
Trials in March.

Before leaving for an altitude training trip to Flagstaff, Arizona, David asked Shoulberg if he could take his bike along. The coach agreed. One morning David asked Shoulberg if he could miss the afternoon practice to ride his bike with some pro triathletes. Dick told him to go have fun.

Three and a half hours later, David walked into the pool with the pros from the bike ride "He's in the wrong sport!" they said. "He crushed us! He should be a triathlete." One of the proudest moments of David's swimming career was when Coach Shoulberg quietly told him, "Pound for pound, you are the hardest worker I've ever had." David wasn't just a dolphin kicker anymore; he was a swimmer and an athlete. The Olympic Trials were weeks away and the perfect place for him to prove it.

The camaraderie among the Germantown/Foxcatcher Team in 1992 was extraordinary. David Berkoff and Dave Wharton still enjoyed some of the bravado from their summer league rivalry. Wharton was one of the premiere IM swimmers in the world and the former world record-holder at 400 meters. Berkoff frequently verbally challenged him: "If I trained for the IM, I'd beat you and take your world record." Coach Simon might have enjoyed hearing that!

On a plane ride to The Charlotte Ultra Swim Meet, David Berkoff happened to be sitting next to a beautiful woman and enjoying a nice conversation with her. Dick insisted David play him at tic-tac-toe. He really didn't want to be bothered. The coach insisted, growling in his deep voice, "I've never lost a game in my life."

They played one game. Without Dick knowing it, David managed to set up a distraction for the coach during the game. When Dick was distracted, David made two moves. He won the game. Coach Shoulberg was enraged. "Play me again! Come on, you've got to give me a chance to redeem myself!" Though David laughed, he refused to revel in the joy of his Germantown teammates at the expense of the coach he once feared. A few minutes later Shoulberg walked down the aisle of the plane and once again spoiled his swimmer's interaction with the woman when he said to David, "Did you call your wife and kids before you left?"

1992 was the most fun year of any that David Berkoff enjoyed in swimming.

Several weeks prior to the March Trials, Coach Shoulberg told him, "I know how to train you and you're in great shape. But I have no idea how to taper you. You need to do that yourself and I'll help you."

1992 OLYMPIC TRIALS – Indianapolis, Indiana

The 1992 USA Olympic Team Trials turned out to be international swimming's deepest competition to date. The sport had improved beyond almost anyone's wildest imagination over the previous 20 years. The times that 50 years ago won the Olympics in the men's events wouldn't medal in the women's events in 1992. The US field in backstroke in particular was strong with a mix of veterans like Berkoff, Scot Johnson, Dan Veatch and Jeff Rouse along with youngsters developing quickly such as Tripp Schwenk, Derek Wetherford, Brad Bridgewater and Brian Retterer.

The 200-meter backstroke preceded the 100 back and David swam a lifetime best of 2:01.5. He felt ready. Schwenk and Royce Sharp, another backstroke newcomer, made the team in the 200 and therefore might not be quite as hungry in the 100. In the preliminaries of the 100 David qualified second with a time of 55.22, but there were four swimmers within five-tenths of a second of his time.

In the finals, David used his dolphin kicks precisely to the 15-meter maximum distance on the start. When he broke-out following the turn he saw his 50 split on the scoreboard and it read 26.5. He knew he was in the best condition of his life and could swim a great second 50. He roared home. He stuck his hand into the touch pad and looked at the scoreboard. He saw Jeff Rouse with a number "1" and the time of 54.07. David Berkoff number "2" with a time of 54.65. It was the best number two he had ever seen. David turned to mid-pool where he knew Coach Shoulberg always located himself so his athletes could find him. He saw something he had never seen before. His coach was doing a jig, dancing happily on the pool deck.

David pulled himself from the water. Coach Shoulberg finished his dance. David walked to the warm-down pool at the far end of the Indianapolis Natatorium. Coach Shoulberg walked to the far end of the Natatorium and out into the hall to a pay phone. David swam continuously for about 20 minutes. Friends tried to interrupt him to congratulate him, but he wouldn't stop. He didn't want his teammates and friends to see that he was crying.

Out in the hallway Coach Shoulberg dialed the phone, and he was crying as well. Dick Shoulberg spoke to his wife Molly on the phone: "I just want to let you know that David Berkoff made the Olympic Team. That gives Foxcatcher/GA the most club kids of any program in America on the team."

David Berkoff's tears finally subsided. He had proved to the swimming world that he wasn't a cheater, that he wasn't just a kicker; he was a swimmer and a two-time American Olympian.

1992 OLYMPICS – Barcelona, Spain

From David's perspective the differences between the 1992 Olympic Team and the squad from 1988 were remarkable. To begin with, there was a large contingent of men who had been on the team in Seoul and once again earned a position on the 1992 Team. There were strong leaders in Matt Biondi and Tom Jager. There were others who had missed out on the Olympics in 1988. They were determined to perform at their very best—American veterans like Mike Barrowman and Pablo Morales.

There was also a change in the American system of leadership. US Swimming had hired a full-time National Team Director who worked on all the logistical details of the Games preparation and trip. This allowed the coaches to focus only on coaching. US Swimming's first-ever National Team Director Dennis "Denny" Pursley would also insist on each team member's adherence to an agreed-upon set of rules.

Barcelona was the first Olympic Games that were open to acknowledged professional athletes. The steamy temperatures at the end of July, combined with the outdoor swimming venue, made it very warm for spectators. On the fourth day of competition David was sitting in the stands with his teammates when a huge man walked into the row and asked, "Would you mind if I sit here?" David recognized him as Evander Holyfield, the boxing heavyweight champion of the world.

David said, "Sure."

"I have a friend that will be here shortly. Can we make room for him, too?" Holyfield asked.

"Of course," David answered.

A few minutes later "the friend" appeared. It was New York Yankee owner George Steinbrenner. He sat down with David and the team.

"What are you doing here?" David asked Mr. Steinbrenner.

"Are you kidding? You guys are unbelievable! I've been watching the swim team perform on television and wow! If I had 10 players on the Yankees like any one of you, we'd never lose a game!"

David's pride in being a member of the 1992 US Olympic Swim Team became even greater. His 54.78 100-meter backstroke was good enough to win the bronze medal. He also won a gold medal by swimming the preliminary heats for the United States' winning 400 medley relay. He said later, "I would take a bronze medal from this team and this Olympics over a silver medal from Seoul. I was so proud of what this team accomplished."

David Berkoff and Joe Bernal's creativity and innovative actions changed the world of swimming. In every pool around the world that conducts the sport today, there is a mark on the lane lines at 15 meters. It sets limits because David Berkoff had none. It tells you how far you can go to do your own "Berkoff Blastoff."

Sure, someone else may have eventually pushed to the limit to see how fast they could travel underwater if David and Joe hadn't done it. But Olympic swimming has been conducted since 1896 and no one had pursued it before. Many swimmers today find it challenging just to kick underwater to the 15-meter limit. David trained himself to go consistently 35 meters off his start ... and he was *fast!*

As a boy David was forced to come out from hiding behind the starting block. As a man David took hold of that block and blasted off. He had first learned how to swim, and then how to play, and along the path to adulthood he proved himself to be a swimmer, an athlete, an innovator and a person so extraordinary that he forever revolutionized the sport.

David now lives in Missoula, Montana, with his wife Shirley Gustafson, his son Cale, and daughter Catharine. He splits his time between being an attorney and a part-time swim coach. At this writing he is also technical vice-president for USA Swimming Inc.

David Berkoff was inducted into the International Swimming Hall of Fame in 2005.

MIKE BARROWMAN

December 4, 1968

THE COMPETITOR

(L-R) Mike Barrowman, Coach Kevin Thornton 1982

The capital of the United States of America, Washington DC, is home to some of the most intense political competition in the world. In the American democratic system of government, the people with the most well-articulated proposals, coupled with the most persistent drive to see them come to fruition, tend to move upward within the massive political power structure. The drive to get to the top is intense. The cauldron of political competition can separate the good from the mediocre as well as the excellent from the good, just as a refiner's fire can separate gold from impurities. The hotter the fire, the purer the result.

In sports, a jungle gym of short-term goals dares the determined competitor to struggle and climb through an upward ascent not unlike the political struggles in DC. There are no direct, clear-cut paths to those short-term goals. Additionally, there are challenges with other athletes both in training and in competition that help motivate an athlete with a greater resolution to strive for victory. This competitive drive—this fire—is a core trait and seems to be inherent in every great athlete. Where it comes from is difficult to discern.

This story is not about a swimmer. It is the story of a competitor who happened to swim. His passion to get faster eventually made him so fast that when he left the sport of competitive swimming, his best was better than anyone else's best—for 13 years.

* * *

"Go Mike go! Go Mike go!"

Donna Barrowman had seen very few swim meets in her life, but she knew how to yell for her favorite in a race. And she loved to encourage her kids.

"Go Mike!"

Eight-year-old Mike Barrowman finished his first swimming race of his life. He went to see his mom. "How'd I do, Mom?" he asked, dripping wet and still panting from his effort.

"Uh, I'm not sure, but you looked great!" his mom answered. "Why don't you ask Coach Hall?"

"OK." Mike began his walk through the swimmers, parents and families on the pool deck of the Montgomery Square Copenhaver Swim Club.

His mother called after him, "You really looked great, Mike! I'm so proud of you!"

Mike walked from the starting end around the shallow play area of the pool and found Coach Burt Hall watching races and evaluating the swimmers.

"Coach, how'd I do?" Mike asked.

"Mike, I loved your effort. That's what counts the most right now," answered Burt.

"But how did I place?" Mike persisted.

"You were third on our team and sixth overall," the coach confessed.

"You mean I was last?" Mike asked.

"Yes."

Mike had been racing around the Montgomery Square Copenhaver Swim Club since he was four years old. He liked seeing if he could beat the bigger kids to the ladder and get out of the pool before they did. His grandmother Jean Albert instilled in him a belief in his abilities in water when she taught him to swim when he was 18 months old. He had attended swim clinics the previous winter at the Bethesda Y with Burt Sampson. The clinics helped prepare him for this, his first swim meet on Wednesday night in the Montgomery County Swim League (MCSL).

The next swim meet was on Saturday morning three days later. Mike swam the 25-yard freestyle again. He gave another great effort. He looked across the pool for the other swimmers when he finished. They all seemed to be at the wall before he was. But he knew what to do now. Go see Coach Hall.

His father was unable to attend his first meet on Wednesday night. He had been caught in the awful Washington DC traffic and just missed Mike's swim. Ray Barrowman was employed by a company that supplied information to the Department of Defense. The ride to and from Washington DC was treacherous during rush hour. He was excited to be there on Saturday and sought Mike's attention.

"Mike!" Mike saw him. "You did great, Son!"

Mike waved to his dad and continued his march to Coach Hall. "How'd I do coach?"

Coach Hall saw Mike coming. He appreciated the little boy's eagerness to learn from him. Mike had finished last again. But Burt Hall was a master at coaching. He had studied it through books and clinics and had learned from his own experience. Over his long tenure at the Montgomery Square Copenhaver Swim Club, he had helped swimmers get started into the sport, move to the local US Swimming clubs, and go all the way to Olympic Teams. Two of them were Dan Veatch and Clay Britt. Mike didn't have the natural strength or physical skills that Dan or Clay had. As a matter of fact, he was small and a bit chubby. The coach chose his words carefully. He knew his input could encourage or discourage a child for a very long time.

Coach Hall brightened up as Mike approached him. "Mike, you did your best time!"

"What?"

"You did your best time, Mike!" the coach said with excitement.

"What's that?"

"We time each swimmer for their races. On Wednesday night you swam a 22.3. Do you know what your time was tonight?" Burt asked him.

Mike could hardly contain his excitement as he read the look on his coach's face. His anticipation of this news that he had accomplished something of significance practically lifted him off the ground. He had no idea that swimming was more than a race but included a time too.

"What? What was it?"

"You swam a 21.6! That's nearly a full second faster than three days ago!" Burt was beaming, which was a reflection of the glow on Mike's face. "That's fantastic! Do you know where you're going to be if you keep doing that?"

"Where?" Mike was confused.

The coach was a bit confused too, but surely he could finish this conversation sensibly with this novice eight-year-old that just swam the second race of his life. "Well, eh, you're going to be great! You're on the way, Mike!"

The MCSL in Maryland consisted of 140 teams. This enormous organization gave thousands of families a portal into the sport of competitive swimming. There were so many swimmers that if you climbed to the top of the league, you had achieved a great deal.

It was the summer of 1976 and the last one for Coach Hall at the Montgomery Square Copenhaver Swim Club. He accepted a position at the highly successful Rockville-Montgomery Swim Club (RMSC) to coach their age-group swimmers. Mike wanted to continue to improve his swimming that winter, so his mother and father allowed him to join RMSC.

1976-1980 EARLY YEARS AT RMSC

Coach Hall was a student of the sport. Near the beginning of his coaching career, he read Doc Counsilman's famous book, *The Science of Swimming*. He regularly attended clinics conducted by the American Swimming Coaches Association (ASCA), but at RMSC he had another learning resource. The team included several national-level high-school-age swimmers. Two of those were his former summer club swimmers Clay Britt and Dan Veatch. Coach Hall made sure he watched them practice with Head Coach Jim Williams, so he could learn from them.

One of the most important aspects of becoming a fast swimmer is stroke efficiency, and Coach Hall recognized this. He saw it in Dan and Clay and attempted to ingrain it in the young swimmers he coached. Burt understood that his job was to increase the potential for speed in every swimmer he coached by striving to develop perfection in their fundamental technique and skills.

Mike began in the eight-and-under program. Practices were held five times a week, 45 minutes in length. He didn't attend every practice, but he was there as part of his regular routine. They swam one length at a time, learning proper technique from Coach Hall.

Mike had respect for authority and was very coachable. These were traits he learned at home. His father, Ray Barrowman, had grown up in a very small town in the southwest part of Virginia. He was a self-made man who worked his way up in his business. He was a senior executive for the Defense Mapping Agency in Washington. His company put together maps to help the Defense Department plan strategy for the covert and overt defense of the United States. Mike witnessed his father's work ethic and saw how his family benefited from the results of his work, including the lovely home they lived in. Donna Barrowman maintained the home and drove Mike and his younger sister Sophia to their various activities. She was an enthusiastic supporter of her children no matter what they participated in.

The RMSC program was well-organized with logical progressions from one group to the next. With each step the training load increased. When Mike turned nine he moved into the next level with the other nine- and ten-year-old swimmers. The practices increased to 75 minutes per session and were offered five times per week. Sixty swimmers were packed into the six-lane pool. The increased time and larger group size were difficult changes for Mike to adapt to. Even though Coach Hall added more challenges to their training, he always began their practice with him teaching them something about each of the four strokes. Overall they swam about two miles, or 3,500 yards.

Mike Barrowman Age-Group Developmental Progression:

8 and under: 3 x week
45 minutes each, skill work

9-10 years old: 4 x week
1:15 minutes, 3,500 yards mix of skill and conditioning

11-12 years old: 3 x week
1:45 minutes, 6,000 yards beginning conditioning
2 x week
1:15 minutes, 5,000 yards beginning conditioning &
30 minutes, dry-land training

13-14 years old: 5 x week, 1:45 minutes,
6,000 yards conditioning emphasis
1 x week
2.5-3 hours, 8-9,000 yards conditioning

The competition in the Washington DC area, or Potomac Valley Swimming (PVS), was fierce. There were many good clubs, including RMSC's major rival, the Curl-Burke Swim Club. Mike competed regularly in meets but seldom won a race. Even more important to him, he wasn't experiencing the type of time improvements that seemed to come so easily that first summer at the Montgomery Square Copenhaver Swim Club.

Mike was diligent at practice. He watched the pace clock on the wall and paid attention to how fast he was swimming. He listened to his coaches. He enjoyed the social experience each time he went to the pool. But he didn't have any special natural gifts. He wasn't tall, he wasn't strong, and he hadn't grown early. He became increasingly frustrated with not becoming more proficient at the sport.

Almost any game was of interest to Mike, and his parents saw value in exposing him to lots of them. He played softball, football and soccer. He was a Boy Scout too. He loved the competition in each sport and was competent in everything he tried. He wasn't sure which sport to focus on yet but continued to challenge his sister into matches of skill at home.

Sometimes breakfast at the Barrowmans included more than food. It could also be a contest.

"You want to race?" Mike asked Sophia.

Sophia matched Mike's snake-eyed stare. She wrapped her little fingers and hand around her orange juice glass just like her older brother.

At 10 years of age, Mike was a man of the world to Sophia. He held his glass up and touched hers.

"Go!" Mike yelled.

The two threw back their heads and guzzled their orange juice as fast as they could. "I won, I won!" Sophia leapt with excitement. "That's the first time I've won!"

"Come on, you two." Mom was referee again.

Mike sneered. "Soph, look."

"What? Look at what?" Sophia asked.

Her older brother matter-of-factly pointed out the truth while he shook his head, "You've still got drops of juice in your glass."

Sophia looked at the bottom of her glass in horror.

"Sorry, you lose, Sis."

There was a branch of Ray Barrowman's company in Providence, Rhode Island. It was failing and his boss asked him to go reorganize it. In the spring of 1980, the Barrowmans made a temporary corporate move to Rhode Island. The company rented out their Potomac, Maryland, home for them so that when Ray's project was completed they could return. They also found them a house to live in while they were in New England. To make the move more palatable, it was a home on a lake.

RHODE ISLAND

The house at the lake was an enormous change from their home in the Maryland suburbs. It was located 300 feet from the water with a lawn that sloped towards the lake to create a wonderful place to play. It looked like a vacation home to Sophia and Mike. It felt like it, too. Their grandfather gave them his fishing boat to use while they lived there. After school and on the weekends they were always down at the lake. The winter days were a countdown to spring when they could enjoy water skiing, fishing and swimming right outside their front door.

The local swim team was called the Cumberland Lincoln Boys Club Team (CLBC). The Barrowmans joined. It was coached by 26-year-old Kevin Thornton. He had served a valuable apprenticeship for Brown University's Coach Dave Roach. Kevin had a similar philosophy to RMSC. He wanted his swimmers to be well-rounded, so every swimmer trained in all four strokes. But there were also some significant differences. Many of the 15- through 17-year-old swimmers practiced with their high school teams during the winter. Therefore, for much of the winter Coach Thornton's oldest training group were 11- to 14-year-old boys and girls. Even though Mike was just turning 12, he was placed in the "senior" training squad.

Swim practice was a bubbling mix of adolescent energy. Whenever Mike had the option of lanes to swim in he followed Kristen LaChance and the other pretty 13- or 14-year-old girls to their lane. Since there were only five lanes in the pool, they couldn't go far. Coach Thornton met the social needs of the group beautifully and built a safe, productive playground for young teens while they learned how to excel in the sport of swimming.

Kevin studied the training that Coach Dick Jochums had been doing in Long Beach, California, with great success and copied much of it. Practices were one-hour, 45 minutes in length. The main training sets he gave Mike were a mile and a quarter in length (2,000 yards) and were repeated weekly. This gave Kevin a way to compare progress of the swimmers. Twice a week they reduced their swimming by 30 minutes to run, do calisthenics and push-ups.

1980-1982 CUMBERLAND LINCOLN BOYS CLUB
– Coach Kevin Thornton

11-13 Years Old

Monday, Wednesday, Friday:

Warm-up:	400 swim, 300 kick, 200 pull, 100
Swim:	5 X 200 IM on 3:00 descend 1-3, 4-5 5 faster than 3
Kick:	20 X 50 on :60 sets of 4 done (ez, fast, fast, ez, build, timed)
Main Set:	Pull - 10 X 100 on 1:20 - hold best average
Main Set:	10 X 100 on call - 75 drill/25 off the top timed
Total:	4,400 yards

Tuesday, Thursday, Saturday:

Warm-up:	3 X 600 on 9:00 neg split and descend
Swim:	12 X 100 on 1:45 stroke - 50 drill/50 race
Turns:	24 X 25 on :30 turns from the middle
Sprint:	12 X 50 on :60 25 drill/25 race
Swim:	800 IM – (8 x 100 IM's continuous/getting faster as you go)
Total:	5,000 yards

Dry-land was a circuit with stations around the pool or gym

25 push-ups/25 sit ups/15 burpees/20 squat jumps/30 mountain climbers/10 pull ups (or negative pull ups) done on a 1:10 for 24 minutes

Provided by Coach Kevin Thornton

The coach presented weekly and monthly goals to his young charges. For example, he might order a "get-out swim" to see how many swimmers could swim faster than 2:20 in the 200-yard individual medley at the end of practice. If enough of the group succeeded, then on Friday night they would be treated to a game of Marco Polo, sharks and minnows, water polo or a swim set of their choice.

Monthly goals for the group were presented by Kevin for attendance and practice performance. The ultimate reward for Mike and his teammates was to earn a meal with the coach at "Ted's Big Boy" up the street from the pool. This meant earning more time outside the water socializing. At Ted's the coach packed his award-winning group in a booth and they enjoyed the best burgers around, along with delightful conversation about the newest movies, best songs and latest music groups. When the bill came, Kevin paid it from his own earnings. Kevin Thornton was connected and committed to his swimmers and his swimmers to him. They were on a joyous ride, exploring their own potential and the sport of swimming.

The combination of moving into the older half of his 11–12 age group and moving into the weaker New England competition from the very strong Potomac Valley Swimming (PVS) program provided Mike a well-timed spark to his experience in the sport of swimming. His times and place of finish began to improve under Coach Thornton's guidance. He won races frequently through that winter and summer of 1981. Mike Barrowman loved the feeling of winning.

Mike had tried other sports but couldn't find any other competition that created the exact same conditions for each athlete at exactly the same time. For example, in football a pass might not be thrown right to you or someone might miss a block when you were running. In each instance your teammate's error limited your accomplishment. But in swimming, you knew when you did well and when you didn't. When Mike achieved a goal time or place he felt fulfilled. It felt like the spillway of a dam opening, the rush of water filling every nook of a previously dry riverbed downstream. He was enjoying swimming so much that he put all his time into it and dropped the other sports.

The Barrowmans found a summer club in Rhode Island similar to the Montgomery Square Copenhaver Swim Club. It was called the Sher-Le-Mon Swim Club. Mike and Sophia spent their summer vacation from school there from the first thing in the morning all the way until late afternoon. They swam and played tennis and baseball all day. But it was always great to go home to the lake. Mike sat on the boat reading, fishing. If he could find someone to drive the boat, he worked on his water skiing tricks.

The summer in Rhode Island on the lake was spectacular for the Barrowmans and for the CLBC. Mike's parents invited Coach Thornton and the swimmers to their home and a day on the lake. Mike had made an easy social transition into the group and so had his parents. The Barrowmans welcomed their new adopted swim team families. Mike and Sophia zipped around the lake on water skis, generating huge sprays of water and showing off their tricks and athletic ability.

Each day at practice Mike listened intently and worked hard. Even though he hadn't grown much, he began to show his ability especially when he swam individual medley, butterfly and breaststroke. The technique he had learned in breaststroke at RMSC was popularized by the success of Tracy Caulkins, one of the greatest woman swimmers in the world. It was a very high upward jutting of the head and shoulders when the swimmer took a breath. Coach Thornton tried to flatten out Mike's forward movement or limit his amplitude. But when he was left unattended, Mike began the high motions again.

Near the end of the season some team members were traveling to a meet called the Zone Championships. It was a higher level competition than the state championships. You had to achieve a special time standard to attend. The fastest swimmers in the Zone were rewarded with the opportunity to represent Rhode Island and compete against other states. When Mike was 13, he set his mind to join his friends and qualify for Zones. He swam fast enough to make the time standards in the 200 butterfly and 400 individual medley.

During his time at CLBC he had become more and more comfortable being uncomfortable. Pain was a welcome part of practice and of racing. Mike accepted it as a small price to pay for the achievement of a goal. Perhaps more importantly he could never know what he could accomplish unless he went through this pain-training process. He learned quickly that it was a sensation that didn't hold you back if you pushed yourself through it. Each time he did, it was easier to do it again.

At the Zone Championships Mike qualified to swim in the finals of the 400 individual medley. He was the seventh qualifier assigned to lane one. He took off on the first 100, using his strong butterfly to his advantage. He was in the lead. As he swam backstroke he recognized that he was ahead of everyone and fought to stay there. By the time he started his breaststroke leg he was slightly ahead and knew it was his strongest stroke. He increased his lead and raced as fast as he could to keep it in freestyle. He won the biggest victory of his life.

Mike went to see Coach Thornton after the race. Kevin knew that Mike wanted his evaluation of his swim and didn't wait for him to ask for it.

Kevin extended his hand to shake Mike's hand and shouted, "You're on the way, Mike!" Mike wore a huge smile. Kevin knew the sport and Mike Barrowman well enough to recognize his special aptitude for learning and for using competition to help him, not scare him. He knew the win was feeding a very hungry young man something even better than a Ted's Big Boy Burger. He knew that Mike was truly on his way toward great achievements in swimming.

1982 RETURN TO RMSC

In the summer of 1982 the Barrowmans received news that their time at the lake house had come to an end. After successfully reorganizing the Providence office, Mr. Barrowman was transferred back to Washington DC. Mike was about to enter ninth grade. As much as he loved living on the water, at least he could enter high school with his old friends.

He returned to the Rockville-Montgomery Swim Club and was assigned to train in the senior group with Coach Jim Williams. Practice sessions were offered for an hour and 45 minutes after school and another 90 minutes in the morning before school. The group had a longer practice on Saturday mornings for two and a half to three hours. As a 14 year-old, Mike was expected to attend six practices per week, but gradually increase to seven per week when he turned 15. Jim made the morning session more attractive by including a lot of technique work and swim sets with strokes other than freestyle.

The coach set up the six-lane pool in the evening with the girls on one half and the boys on the other half. The practice always included a hard freestyle set after warm-up, a kicking set as a break and then another challenging set of individual medley or specific stroke. The swimmers in the group were fast and Mike chased them every day and learned from them.

1982-1987 ROCKVILLE MUNICIAPAL SWIM CLUB – Coach Jim Williams

Training – 9 practices per week offered.
14-17 years old

Three mornings of 90 minutes
Five nights of 1:45 min and Saturday mornings of 2.5-3 hrs.
Sample:
Warm-up
Main Set:　　　20 x 150s Freestyle on 1:45 (averaging 1:30s)
　　　　or
　　　　　　　IM Set: Fly – 12 x 75s 3 all fly, 1 easy choice
　　　　　　　Then, 20 x 150s IM on 2:20 (50 back, 50 Breast, 50 Free)

Note: The IM set is split up this way to help six swimmers per lane get through fly with better technique.

Kick Set:　　　(details unavailable)
Second Main Set: 1500 yards (details unavailable)

Total:　　　　　6,000 yards in

Courtesy of Coach Jim Williams

During his first year back at RMSC, Mike noticed that the best swimmers were going to Junior Nationals or even Senior Nationals. Even though he was still 14, he saw no reason not to be a part of the Junior National squad. He told Coach Williams, "My goals this season is swim a 1:01.89 in the 100-yard breaststroke and qualify for Junior Nationals."

Jim laughed. "That's a long way to go from where you are Mike."

Jim had been familiar with Mike when he was in their age-group program, but he hadn't spent enough time with him to assess his mental strength as an athlete. As Jim worked with him each day in practice and then at swim meets, he noticed a difference in Mike's ability to review swims and analyze them for ways to improve. Despite just becoming a teenager, he had the concentration of a much older and mature athlete. Mike listened to his coach and learned fast.

Toward the end of the winter season, Mike swam a 1:01.89 and met his goal. The RMSC team arrived at the University of Alabama for the 1984 short course Junior Nationals. Mike looked at the paper with all the entered times on it, nicknamed the "psyche sheet." His 1:01.89 seeded him dead last. And that is where he placed. He quickly analyzed the situation and decided that he never again would he set a goal to just "qualify for a swim meet"—or so he thought.

Mike reset his goals for the summer. He told Coach Williams that his goal was to swim in the championship finals (top eight swimmers) in four events at the Junior Nationals in Ft. Lauderdale. Jim laughed again. Coach Williams saw the effort Mike put into reaching his goals. His laugh this time was out of delight in Mike's resolve to achieve what he set his mind to. Mike was anxious and willing to do the hard work necessary to swim that much faster. He applied himself to Coach William's recipe for success, which included a mix of speed and endurance. The workouts seldom required huge distance sets. He liked watching his swimmers swim fast in practice, not simply survive. Mike applied himself eagerly all spring and summer.

At the 1984 long course Junior Nationals in August he placed sixth in the 200-meter breaststroke (2:28.8), fifth in the 100 breaststroke (1:08.6) and 12th in the 200 individual medley (2:13.1). He didn't quite achieve his goal, but his improvement was amazing. Mike was eager for more.

When the swim season started in September, Mike entered 10th grade. He told Coach Williams that his goal for the season was to win four events at the next Junior Nationals. Jim laughed. He knew Mike loved a challenge. If he sensed his coach had any doubt in his ability to match his deeds to his words,

Jim's laughter would simply further embolden Mike's commitment to "own the goal." During that winter Mike climbed the ladder of practice competition at RMSC. He became one of the best male swimmers in spite of being only 16.

At the 1985 short course Junior Nationals in Syracuse, New York, in early April, he didn't win every event, but he did finish second in the 200-yard breaststroke the first night of finals (2:05.6). On the second night he won the 400-yard individual medley (3:59.85), which qualified him for that summer's US Olympic Swim Festival. His second-place finish in the 200-yard individual medley (1:53.2) and seventh-place finish in the 100-yard breaststroke (58.8) rounded out another tremendous season. It affirmed his ability to set goals and use them to move him forward in the sport. Mike Barrowman was shooting for the stars. He was undaunted by missing his exact target as long as he remained in orbit.

The US Olympic Festival was a way to introduce high-school-age swimmers to a multisport competition and inspire them to progress toward the Olympic Games. The American system of competition, with its freedom to excel, was very much at work for those that earned this introductory level of a national celebration of their ability, commitment and progress in their sport. All the swimmers traveled to Baton Rouge, Louisiana, for the Festival. The swimmers each represented a team from their geographical location such as North, South, East and West. The night before the competition began, all the teams gathered for an orientation meeting and they were addressed by an official.

"Welcome and congratulations for qualifying for this great event. I think you know that this is a finals-only competition. Each team will have two lanes assigned to them per event and you will use those lanes throughout the competition." She went on to explain more about the rules, then said something that caught Mike's attention.

"You may not believe this now, but one-fourth of the people in this room will be on the 1988 Olympic Team."

The competition was conducted in a 50-meter pool. Mike began the meet with a fourth-place finish in the 400-meter individual medley (4:39.3) for his North team. Two days later, on July 29th, he swam to third place in the 200 individual medley (2:10.5). A day later he finished last in the 200 breaststroke (2:31.1). One swimmer was disqualified, so Mike officially moved up to seventh. He was very disappointed in the way he finished the meet.

Mike was anxious to talk with Coach Williams and analyze what had happened. His progress had been consistent and rapid. But he couldn't get out of his mind the notion that one-fourth of the swimmers in the room would be on the 1988 Olympic Team.

The 1985 US Long Course Nationals were held in Mission Viejo, California, two weeks later. It was Mike's first opportunity to compete with the top swimmers in the United States. The answer to his questions about why his Olympic Festival 200-meter breaststroke wasn't faster seemed to be that he needed a little more rest to recover from his season of work. He placed 16th in the preliminaries (2:24.28) and earned himself a second swim in the consolation finals at night. He showed his racing mentality when he moved up to 11th in the finals and improved his best time to 2:23.34. He wasn't as successful in the 400 individual medley (4:34.35) in which he placed 28th. Nevertheless he had great experiences over the summer of racing swimmers at a higher level than ever before.

In the winter of 1986 Mike was reminded that there is more to success in swimming than setting goals, working hard and achieving them. A swimmer can stall or plateau for many reasons. There are a few worth mentioning here. One is that their body can go through natural physical changes that they need time to adjust to. Another may be that they need an additional challenge to their conditioning to advance a step. They may also be limited by their stroke efficiency, which can create increased resistance as they get stronger and more powerful. This might be understood as the application of Newton's law that "for every action there is an equal and opposite reaction." Their additional strength might start working against them. Working through plateaus is a part of any athlete's realization of their full potential.

The 1986 winter season culminated at the US Nationals the last week of March in Orlando, Florida. Despite training hard all season, he was more of a spectator than a competitor. His 400- yard individual medley (4:04.5) was five seconds slower than the previous year. His lone best time was in the 100-yard breaststroke (58.30) in which he finished 46th. He finished 33rd in the 200-yard breaststroke (2:06.2) and watched the finals.

One of Mike's former competitors from the Montgomery County Swim League was swimming in the finals. It was Bryan Nicosia who represented the Curl-Burke Swim Club. Mike cheered for him but became distracted by the swimmer winning the race. It was a Hungarian breaststroker, Jozsef Szabo. Szabo's technique had some odd stops and starts in it, but he seemed to be trying to do something different than everyone else with a wave trajectory through the water.

"We're going to have a new assistant coach helping us this spring. He's from Hungary and specializes in breaststroke," Coach Williams told him later.

The summer season began. At practice one day Mike noticed the pool deck wasn't exactly the same as usual. There was someone new there. He tried to swim as perfectly as possible to impress the visitor, regardless of who it was. The man walked around looking at the swimmers then stopped by Mike and with a heavy accent said, "Breaststroke. Strong!" His name was Jozsef Nagy.

1986 – COACH JOZSEF NAGY

Coach Nagy came to the US from Hungary with his wife Piroska. She was assigned a five-year tenure with the International Monetary Fund in Washington DC. He had applied for various jobs in the Washington DC area without any luck. By chance his wife was working with a woman whose child swam at RMSC and suggested he look there. The 34-year-old coach had been an international level breaststroke swimmer during his own career as an athlete. He had earned his degree in Physical Education, Pedagogy, Physiology and Psychology at the University of Budapest in Hungary. In 1979 he wrote his thesis on something he called the "Wave Breaststroke."

Coach Williams assigned Nagy a group of 14 swimmers to work with. Jo learned a few words of English to help his coaching but otherwise didn't know how to speak the language. He wrote the practice on a piece of paper and gave it to the swimmers to perform. Periodically he marched up and down the pool deck barking instructions.

"More longer!" he'd yell.

"More harder, more faster!"

Jozsef drew a wave line on a piece of paper to show the flow he was looking for in the breaststroke. Then he drew another one that was a sharper angle at each point showing how Mike and some of the others were swimming. Despite his limited English, he was trying very hard to teach and communicate. Mike strained to understand what he was saying. If the Hungarians were so good in breaststroke, he wanted to know why. During the first month, Mike learned as much Hungarian as he could to try and learn from his coach.

Coach Nagy's training sets were much more intense than Mike and his teammates had ever done before. For example, if they used to be able to swim moderately through 20 x 100s freestyle, Coach Nagy gave the group 5 x 200s butterfly. The new coach's attitude was "put out or get out."

After the first week, the group of 14 swimmers was down to seven.

After two weeks of nearly impossible practices, there was only one swimmer remaining—Mike Barrowman. The 16-year-old saw an opportunity to learn a new breaststroke from the coach even if he hardly understood a word of his Hungarian. In Mike's mind he would teach his coach how to speak English while his coach taught him *his* breaststroke.

"Where are you on the list?" Jozsef asked Mike one day.

"What list?" Mike thought he might be thinking of the wait list for an upcoming concert.

"World rankings?" Jo asked.

Mike had never thought about world rankings until now.

Jozsef had a picture in his mind of what breaststroke should look like and insisted it be done correctly. He motioned Mike out of the pool. On the deck he twisted and turned his limbs to put them in the places that he wanted them to be, no matter how much it hurt to put them there. Then he sent him back in the water, observed and taught.

"Quick," he'd yell at Mike and sweep his hands inward.

"High" to get his feet up toward his hips to catch water.

"Narrow!" as he lunged forward.

TECHNICAL NOTE: DESCRIPTION OF THE WAVE BREASTSTROKE

The goal of the technique was to create continuous forward movement, building momentum down the pool by attempting to eliminate any "deceleration" or slowing down. The instruction began with extended arms forward as far as Mike could reach. With the face down in the water, the hands pressed outward just past the shoulders, swept inward and his body would slide forward. A key element in the stroke was this slide. It meant that the water on his back would roll off gradually, rather than Mike lifting upward and wasting energy lifting it, which he had been doing for many years.

Coach Nagy emphasized the "lunge" as a critical aspect of the stroke. The lunge meant moving the hands and forearms from sweeping in to extending them forward. At the same time the feet were beginning to move toward the hips and prepare to anchor in the water. Mike struggled to learn the new concepts, but when he did them correctly, he would wait for his hands to sweep inward in front of his shoulders to lift his head to breathe.

Jozsef worked with Mike on falling on top of the water as he lunged so he would skim across the surface rather than sink below it. Just as the arms were completing their lunge, and the head would begin to follow them as the final submersion into the water, the feet would be pushing him forward at their maximum point of power. If the stroke was done to Jozsef's requested perfection, there would be a "wave" of the shoulders rolling forward over the water and subsequently a smaller wave of the hips rolling over and forward. On occasion Mike could feel the potential of the stroke as he began to feel its flow.

Within weeks Mike was ready to share his confidence in his new coach with his biggest fan. "Mom, Jozsef seems to really understand breaststroke ...I'm not sure where we're going but it's exciting."

"That's great Mike. Do you understand him better?"

"I'm working at it. I try to learn a new Hungarian word every day."

"This is quite an education."

"Do we have any plans for Saturday?" Mike asked. "He wants me to come over to his house—something about his dog. I think it might be sick and needs to be transported out of the country. I think he said to Siberia."

"I'll check with your father, but I don't see a problem."

Mike went to Coach Nagy's house on Saturday and was greatly relieved in two ways. The first was that Piroska Nagy spoke fluent English and translated the entire conversation for Mike and his new coach. The second was that it turned out his dog wasn't sick at all. In fact, the Nagys didn't even own a dog. The Coach had simply invited Mike to dinner. Throughout the meal, Piroska Nagy conveyed to Mike what Jo was trying to teach him. Personal relationships were very important to Mike and he delighted in spending the evening getting to know his coach and family. But that didn't make practice any easier at the pool.

The 1986 Long Course US Summer Nationals were held in the beautiful new Justus Aquatic Center in Orlando, Florida. The top American swimmers were competing at the World Championships and Goodwill Games, which weakened the competition. The 16-year-old took full advantage of the circumstances to finish fifth (2:21.09) in the 200-meter breaststroke. Three days later, his 100 was a miserable 1:07.0 for a 36th-place finish. But Mike had improvement in his 200, and this gave him the encouragement he was looking for to continue on his path.

1986–1987

In the fall, Jozsef and Mike went back to work. Mike used to come to six or seven practices per week. Jo wanted him there at every one of the nine practices plus two additional ones he personally added. He also added a dry-land program geared toward breaststroke.

"I want 10 jumps in 20 seconds," the coach ordered.

"That's impossible," Mike said.

"I do with you. I am old and if I do, you do. Squat all the way," Joszsef told him.

The two went jump for jump. Jozsef stopped at nine because his legs hurt so much. Mike continued to the 10th one. They continued through 10 sets of squat jumps and a 25-minute medicine ball routine that Jozsef taught him. For the next two days, the coach's legs were numb, but he never let Mike know. By the third day he moved through his house like a seal because his legs hurt so much. Fortunately a huge snowstorm hit and the pool was closed for a day so Mike couldn't see his pain. But it established a creed for the two of them: "If I can do it, you can do it."

At the US Open in December he had the highest national finish yet with a third place in the 200-meter breaststroke (2:20.81). But he also felt the unbending standard to be the best from his coach afterward. Jozsef told him, "You take that third place medal and sleep with it. You put it around your neck; you hold it and think of it because it is not anything. We are aiming for gold—nothing else."

By the middle of January Mike was exhausted and fed up with his driving coach. He still hadn't made the top 25 world-ranking list for the 200-meter breaststroke swimmers in the world. He began to ask himself. *Why am I doing this? I'm killing myself; I feel terrible and I don't know how far I'm getting.* Coach Nagy saw how upset he was at practice and handed him a piece of paper with "2:15.0" on it. That was faster than Steve Lundquist's American record. Mike understood that Jozsef was telling him he believed he could be the fastest 200 breaststroker in American history. Mike continued to work.

It was Mike's senior year of high school. He was visiting and considering different universities to attend the following year. He had long dreamed of attending Stanford. His college choice had come down to Stanford and Michigan. He had been offered a full scholarship by Michigan but not by Stanford. When he went to the spring Nationals he still wasn't sure which school to choose.

The Nationals in 1987 were in Boca Raton, Florida, and conducted in a 25-yard course. Mike nipped Brent Beedle by three-hundreths of a second at the finish to win the 200-yard breaststroke in a time of 1:58.36. The swim was a huge drop in time and beat his best from the prior year by seven seconds. It was also a time faster than world champion Jozsef Szabo's winning time from the previous year. Although many of the college swimmers were missing from this competition, Mike was improving his ranking among the elite American breaststrokers.

He still had his college decision to finalize. He was leaning toward Michigan, in part because of the full scholarship offer from Jon Urbanchek. That offer meant to Mike that Jon believed in him. After Mike became the 200-yard champion, Stanford coach Skip Kenney increased his offer to a full scholarship. Mike found Jon Urbanchek and asked when he could sign the letter of intent to attend Michigan. Mike's first priority was the coach's faith in him.

1987 HUNGARY

Returning home as a national champion helped Mike receive permission from his high school to travel with Coach Nagy to Hungary to train and do independent study for six weeks. His high school recognized that Mike was an outstanding student. With the Olympics just 16 months away, they wanted to support him by giving him every advantage possible to make the US Olympic Team.

When he and Coach Nagy boarded the plane to Hungary, Mike proudly wore his US National Team jacket from the Olympic Festival. Hungary was a country struggling for economic survival while its people lived in the economic Cold War behind the "Iron Curtain." They landed in Budapest. When Mike stepped off the plane, he was shocked at what he saw. There were armed guards carrying machine guns patrolling the airport, something unheard of in the free world during that era. (Armed security has become more common than it used to be since the September 11, 2001, attacks.) As he looked out the window of the terminal, Mike saw the guards on the streets as well. They weren't there to keep people out of their country. They were there to force them to stay. He immediately took off his USA jacket. The sight of the depressed and oppressed countryside made him sensitive to how they might feel about an American appearing to boast about his country.

To add to the irony, they stayed at the Communist School and walked across the frozen courtyard to the pool to train. The water was brown and there was green alga everywhere. Coach Nagy thought nothing of it and they started practice. When they entered the water it was worse. The water was exceptionally cold. Mike dove down deeper where the water was warmer. The only heat in the pool was coming from the hot springs underground. Mike's will was being revealed through the challenges of his coach. He saw the cold and green water as another contest to win. He was learning to do the same with Coach Nagy's practices. Whatever the coach gave him, he was determined to succeed at.

1987 USA SUMMER NATIONALS – Clovis, California

The best American swimmers converged on Clovis, California, for the 1987 USA Long Course Nationals. It was the year prior to the Seoul, Olympics and they were competing for places on the national "A" team, which would compete in the Pan Pacific Games. The second tier of swimmers would make the National "B" team and compete in the Pan American Games. Jozsef and Mike had no interest in second-tier teams or finishes. Mike planned to qualify for the Pan Pacific Team.

He improved his best time in the 200-meter breaststroke to 2:18.56, but finished fifth. He had only improved two seconds in eight months. Mike felt that he trained much harder and much faster than his time showed. His place qualified him to swim on the USA "B" Team for the Pan American Games. After his race he received nothing but a stern push from his coach: "Take that fifth place and think about it; wallow in it and be better next time."

Many swimmers may have reacted much differently to Jozsef's comments than Mike did. His coach believed he could be much faster, and Mike liked that. He was an athlete who wanted to dig as deeply into himself as he possibly could and find his ultimate speed. When the teams each went into a room for uniform outfitting, Mike was ushered out of the line for Pan Pacific A team. He simply never thought about being on the B team.

The Pan American Games were held in Indianapolis, Indiana. Despite the American site for the "international" competition, there were advantages to the Pan Ams. The Pan Pacific Games were only a swim meet. The Pan Ams were a multisport competition and therefore more closely resembled an Olympic setting than did the Pan Pacific Games. The teams from all the sports participated in opening ceremonies at the Indianapolis Motor Speedway, where more than 100,000 fans welcomed them. They were even treated to meeting baseball legend Mickey Mantle at the city's minor league ballpark.

In the 200-meter breaststroke, Mike finished second (2:19.2) behind American teammate Jeff Kubiak. His time was slower than his best and Kubiak beat him by more than 1.5 seconds when he set a new Pan Am Games Record of 2:17.6. Coach Nagy prodded Mike forward telling him, "You should sleep with that silver medal. You can achieve gold."

1987 MICHIGAN

In the fall of 1987, Mike entered the University of Michigan. The transition from home to college is challenging for most anyone, and it was for Mike. Both he and his freshman roommate Scott Ryan were very close to their families and the adjustment of being away was difficult. There were nights he missed his mother's cooking, his father's quiet reassurance and even games with Sophia.

At Michigan he was one athlete among a large team of outstanding swimmers competing in the NCAA arena that brought together some of the best swimmers from around the world. Michigan had a fine coach and proven program. Mike had all the best in facilities, good competition in practice and regular swim meets with other Big Ten Conference teams. But Mike was in transition. He had been on his own mission to climb the ladder toward the top of the world in breaststroke. He missed the near one-on-one coaching that Coach Nagy had provided him.

At the NCAA Championships in March he finished 32nd in the 200-yard individual medley (1:51.0) and placed 16th in the preliminaries of the 100 breaststroke (55.9). That earned him a swim in the consolation finals at night as the last qualifier. Despite swimming slower, he fought his way up to 11th that night. On the final day he managed a fourth-place finish in the 200 breaststroke (1:58.8). He hadn't improved at all in his first year at college. In April, Michigan recessed for the summer and Mike couldn't wait to get home.

1988 OLYMPIC SUMMER

Coach Nagy had worked wonderfully with Mike and a few other athletes at RMSC, but the club couldn't afford to have one coach work with just a few swimmers. The needs of the club and the desires of Coach Nagy didn't fit each other, so they made a choice to end the relationship. Rick Curl, owner of the Curl-Burke Swim Club, had built a huge club with a satellite system of pools and coaches around the Washington DC area that all competed under the Curl name. He hired Jozsef to coach at a new site they created especially for him and Mike.

Mike came home to RMSC. But after a week without Coach Nagy, Mike realized that it was Jozsef's knowledge of breaststroke and his driving approach to coaching that had been the key to his past success. He believed Coach Nagy was also critical to his hope for achieving his potential in the future. It was very hard for him to leave his long-time club. But he thanked Coach Williams and went to swim with Jozsef at Curl-Burke.

The site that Rick Curl had rented was the old University of Maryland pool. It was five lanes wide, 25 yards long and didn't have lane lines. It was better than the facility at the Communist School in Budapest but not a modern facility. Jozsef had more practice time, a little deck space to use for his dry-land program and a doorway into the basketball arena with hundreds of rows of steps.

The small Curl training group at the University of Maryland included Olympic Trial qualifier Mike Lambert and Tommy Sullivan. Jozsef gave Mike the exact program that he believed in with no compromises for other swimmers. Practices were held 11 times a week with about 60 percent of the time spent training for the breaststroke. The Nagy method was to separate the stroke into the components of pulling, kicking and sculling. He worked with Mike on improving his skill circuits for each area and his conditioning at the same time.

The coach gave his swimmers one skill to concentrate on for each "swimming set." An example was sculling on their back with their feet forward, which they called "the boat drill." The coach's instruction was "fast hands." That's all Mike thought about on that set. His forearms burned with pain through the set but his hands moved quickly. Then a switch was made to kicking or to pulling. In order to create the constant flow of the breaststroke, the swimmers were instructed to do flip turns on all breaststroke sets.

Coach Jozseph Nagys Training

Warm-up:	400 choice
	200 Breaststroke kick
	8 x 50s on 1:00 two of each stroke, IM order
	200 free, breathe every seven strokes
	100 easy
Swim:	8 x 50s on 1:00 breaststroke
	100 easy
Kick:	4 x 100s on 1:40
	2 x 200s on 3:15 breaststroke
	2 x 100s on 1:40
Swim:	100 easy
Pull:	100 easy
Main Set:	3 x 4 x 100s breaststroke on 1:40: 25 kick/25 pull/50swim, easy 50 after each set of 4 x 100s
	100 easy
	2 x 400s breaststroke on 30 sec rest: four strokes under water, four strokes above water
	100 easy
	400 easy kick with fins, freestyle/backstroke
	8 x 25s on: 45 underwater: 4 breast pull, 4 breast kick
Warm-down:	400, freestyle/backstroke

Reprinted with permission 1989 ASCA Clinic Book

In the middle of the summer, two of Coach Nagy's swimmers from Hungary came to train for four weeks. One was Tomas Debnar and the other was Peter Szabo. The Europeans had dominated the breaststroke events in recent years and Peter was one of the reasons. He was ranked 10th in the world with a best time of 2:16.5. Peter had worked with Coach Nagy in Hungary and had his own dreams of Olympic success.

Peter gave Mike new tangible competition goals for practice each day. One goal was to beat Peter on at least one of the swim sets. Another was to outperform him on their daily land program and jumping program. At 5:30 a.m. they went into the basketball arena and did full squat jumps up and down the steep aisles. The medicine ball routine was arduous and stretched their hips, knees and ankle joints. These were all qualities specific to moving them closer to their ultimate potential in breaststroke.

Mike zipped the medicine ball at Peter and Peter at Mike. The ball appeared to be on a rubber band bouncing back and forth. At 12 pounds it wasn't heavy at first, but as the minutes went by it felt heavier and heavier. In the middle of the routine were "supermans." Peter and Mike lay face to face on their stomachs and passed the ball back and forth over their heads. Sweat poured from their faces, making a small wet pool below their chins.

"This is what I need to make the Olympic Games," Peter grunted.

In that one statement, a light went off in Mike's mind. He had only been a fifth-place finisher at the summer nationals and second on the "B" team. But he thought to himself, *Peter is ranked 10th in the world and he is human just like me. He has his goals. If Peter believes what we're doing is what's necessary to compete at the Olympics, then I must be on a good path too.* Peter's words reinforced to Mike that Coach Nagy knew the training path necessary to compete at the Olympic Games.

Coach Nagy gave them a grueling practice that night. Peter and Mike were fighting to win each set. The entire little group was training fast. But Peter and Mike's performance was tremendous. When they finished, both of them were both exhausted and exhilarated. The coach very rarely praised his swimmers. But at that point Jozsef said to them, "Now that's what it will take to go 2:14!" That statement meant everything to Mike—they were on the way to a new American record.

There were a few occasions during a practice when Coach Nagy left the pool deck inexplicably. It might be for a phone call and other times for no reason discernible by the swimmers. At one practice Jozsef had to leave practice to pick up his wife. He wrote down the rest of practice and told them he would be back in about an hour.

As soon as the coach left, the Hungarian boys got out of the pool. They went out on the lawn next to the pool building and into the warm sun. They had a Frisbee. Mike and his teammates followed. They decided that if these guys had swum for Coach Nagy in Hungary, they couldn't be going too far astray with their actions. The small squad enjoyed a spirited game of ultimate Frisbee until they spotted their coach's car in the distance driving toward the pool. They sprinted for the door to get back into the pool building. It was locked. The athletic flock shimmied up a pole, climbed over the roof and into a window just in time to get back in the water before the coach walked in.

They were just a month away from the Olympic Trials in Austin, Texas, that started August 9. As the days counted down to Austin, Mike continued to improve his training. During the last few weeks prior to traveling, Jozseph had Mike swim more sets rather than pull, kick or scull. This was Coach Nagy's method of sharpening a swimmer's timing and bringing all the stroke segments together that they had worked so hard on.

1988 OLYMPIC TRIALS – Austin, Texas

Mike Barrowman entered the Trials ranked 17th in the world in 1987 in the 200-meter breaststroke. He was the sixth fastest in the United States. The American record was held by Steve Bentley (2:14.99) and was set at the Pan Pacific Games in 1987. Canadian Victor Davis held the world record since the 1984 Olympic Games in Los Angeles of 2:13.34. Jozseph Szabo was the world leader for the past year, with a time just off Davis' global standard of 2:13.87.

By the Trials a Barrowman-Nagy team had clearly been forged. It frequently functioned with Coach Nagy's knowledge and experience being presented through Mike's tenacious mind and body. Jozsef told Mike there was a perfect stroke tempo and technique for the 200-meter breaststroke. He explained that swimming the 100 compromised excellence in the 200 by speeding up his tempo and altering the technique efficiency he needed to be at his best in the 200. Mike's height was also just 5' 10". The 200 gave him a greater time swimming, rather than starting or turning, negating his height advantage to some degree. The 100 was swum on the first day of the Trials and Mike passed it by.

The fourth day was the 200. Mike was seeded sixth and swimming in lane five next to Jeff Kubiak, the Pan Am gold medalist from the prior summer. He followed the race plan that he and his coach had established by swimming as easy a first 50 as he could while maintaining a good flow of speed. He increased his effort ever so slightly on the second 50.

When Mike turned at 100 meters and surfaced, he heard the roar of the crowd. He had heard noise like this at big meets. It often came when a swimmer was ahead of the pace to break a record and the crowd screamed to support the athlete. The crowd's energy can actually vibrate into the swimmer's ears and helps fuel them to continue a great swim. Mike thought, *Jeff Kubiak must be having a great swim! Listen to the crowd cheer for him.* While Mike swam his third 50 he snuck a peek at Jeff to see where he was. He couldn't see him next to him. By the 150 Mike thought, *Holy cow, they're cheering for me!*

The final 50 was glorious! He increased his speed to the maximum level he could while maintaining the efficiency of his stroke. The wave technique was flowing beautifully. He touched in 2:13.74! He had been near world-record pace at the 100 and set a new American record by nearly 1.5 seconds. He swam the best time of his life by almost five seconds!

That night at the finals of the Olympic Trials, Mike Barrowman swam the identical time and won the race by nearly three seconds. With the help of his coaches, he had transformed himself into the fastest 200-meter breaststroker in the history of the United States of America. Mike talked about the swim and his coach afterward.

"I'm very surprised," he said. "I didn't expect any of this to happen. I expected everyone to do 2:14 or 2:15. But I put in a good summer of work. He [Coach Nagy] taught me how to think like a champion. He told me how to eat, sleep, what to swim, how hard to swim, how many hours a day, not to go out, just everything. He was like my father to me the whole summer," Mike said. But he also revealed his awe of Jozsef Szabo. "Szabo," Barrowman continued, "is nearly unbeatable. I'd like to think I can race him and have a chance. But he can go 2:12 if he's pushed. I don't think anyone can beat him, but I'm going to at least give it a shot" (SW 1988).

The last time an American had held the world record in the 200 was 1974, when John Hencken did it. The same year six-year-old Mike was scooting around the pool at Montgomery Square, chasing the big kids. He was a few ticks away from the world record, but could he accept his success and see himself winning the gold medal? The Olympics were just five weeks away.

1988 OLYMPICS – SEOUL, KOREA

The news hit the Washington DC area that local boy Mike Barrowman had broken the American record and made the Olympic Team. The media outlets also picked up the unique story of the Hungarian coach working with this American boy. The *Potomac Gazette* reported that Coach Nagy wasn't part of the American Olympic coaching staff and could not afford to go to Seoul for the Olympics. They set out on a fund-raising campaign in the Washington DC area and thousands of people contributed. When all the donations were counted, people had contributed more than $6,000 to a travel fund for Coach Nagy. NBC television solved the problem of the coach not having access to the pool deck to coach Mike. They issued Jozsef a press pass.

Coach Nagy had his own race to win. He wanted to show his colleagues in Hungary as well as the world of swimming that he could train Mike to an Olympic gold medal. But Mike's goal to make the Olympic team was similar to his goal to make his first Junior Nationals. He hadn't thought much about what he would do when he got to the Junior Nationals and he hadn't accepted that he could compete for an Olympic gold medal.

Barrowman qualified for the finals in Seoul. Then, for the first time in his life, he swam with fear for the first three quarters of the race. It was only after 150 meters, and in last place, that he sensed a great opportunity was slipping away. He hurried to catch up on his final length but finished fourth. He was out-touched for a medal by Spain's Sergio Lopez. Mike's time of 2:15.45 was slower than both his swims at the Trials. His best was only two-tenths away from Jozsef Szabo's winning time of 2:13.52. The reality of all that had been lost hit Mike hard. Not only had he failed his team, himself, and his coach, he felt he had let down all the people from his hometown area who had contributed their hopes and prayers as well as the money to his coach's travel fund.

The Hungarian national anthem played for Jozsef Szabo's gold-medal swim. Mike Barrowman sat under the bleachers alone, with his head down and listened.

Mike and Coach Nagy returned from Seoul, Korea, the last week of September. Mike had missed so much school already that he wasn't going to go to Michigan until the next semester. After a two-week break from swimming, Coach Nagy asked him, "Do you want to stand up or do you want to quit swimming?"

Without thinking, Mike quickly answered. "Stand up." But there was more time needed to ponder this important decision.

Mike's analytical character generated a conversation with Jim Williams, his coach at RMSC, as well. Jim gave Mike similar advice as that of Coach Nagy. "If you think you've done all you can do, then quit swimming. If you feel as though you have more to do, then get back to work." Coach Williams' willingness to advise Mike since he had left RMSC for a rival program might seem unusual, but not for this coach. "I respect hard work, commitment, and willpower. Those words define Mike Barrowman," Jim said later. "Whether he swims on our club or somewhere else, I support him."

Mike told Jozsef that not only did he have more to do in the sport of swimming, he also wanted to break the world record in the first meet he could compete in. He was ready to do whatever was necessary to prove himself and make all of the people that supported his coach in making the trip to Seoul proud of him. He immediately began training again.

1989 MICHIGAN

Mike returned to Michigan in January. He matured enough to enjoy his sophomore year of college life and his development as an independent young man. He also began to appreciate the difference in coaching styles from Coach Nagy's driving method to Coach Urbanchek's warmer approach. He saw in Jon the perfect college coach because he occasionally allowed a missed practice for academic or social reasons. He provided humor and friendship for his swimmers.

Michigan provided Mike a much stronger team atmosphere than training in Maryland, but it lacked the nearly one-on-one coach to swimmer ratio that he enjoyed with Coach Nagy. Jon had only one assistant coach and he needed to share his time with many swimmers. But Coach Urbanchek thought the next best way to ensure that Mike trained as hard as possible was to get him a training partner. He recruited one of the top breaststrokers in the country, Eric Wunderlich, who pushed Mike every day in practice.

Jon Urbanachek's Weekly Program from September to November

10 workouts/66,500 yards

Weights: T, Th, Sat

Dryland: M, W, F (Med Ball, Swim Bench, Jumps, Plyometrics, Breast Bench)

Reprinted with permission: ASCA World Clinic Program

	M	T	W	TH	F	S	SN
AM	Aerobic Pulling/Power Kick Hypoxic EN1-2 Total 6,000 yds	Recover Drills off Stroke Kick/ Power EN1-2 Total 6000 yds	Off	Recovery Pull/Power Speedplay Alactic EN1-2 Total 6,000 yds	Aerobic Kick/ Power Drills Hypoxic En1-2 Total 6,000 yds	Anaerobic Lactate Speed or Meet Spl-2 Total 6,500 yds	
PM	Anaerobic Threshold 3-4,000 yds EN2-3 Total 7,500 yds	Active Rest EN1-2 Total 7,000 yds	Anaerobic VO2 Max Lactate EN3/ SP1 Total 7000 yds	Threshold 3-4,000 yds EN2-3 Total 7,500 yds	Subjective (Go by feel) Active Rest Power H20 Speed Assist, Buckets, Cords EN1-2		

At the NCAA Championships in March, Mike finished second in the 100-yard breaststroke (54.2). On the final night of competition he won the 200-yard breaststroke (1:55.7) and Eric Wunderlich placed third. Mike had the will to prepare for winning but he was still in the process of forging the type of ironclad confidence to be the best in the world. His comments after the 200 win at the NCAAs demonstrated that. "I was still worried the whole time that someone was going to catch up with me, especially Kirk," he said after his 200 win. "I have the utmost respect for his 200 and I had no doubt he could stay up with me" (SW 1989 April).

The second-place finisher, Kirk Stackle, was over half of a body length behind him.

Mike recognized the importance of having a good training partner to push him daily to reach deeper inside himself to find his potential. Peter Szabo in Maryland and Eric Wunderlich at Michigan had both helped him tremendously. When he thought of swimmers he could recruit to the Nagy Group, Sergio Lopez came to mind. They were familiar with each other since Sergio swam at Big Ten rival Indiana University. Sergio had also beaten Mike at the Olympics by one place. Mike called him in Spain and asked him to come and train with the Nagy group in Maryland for the summer. Sergio agreed to do so.

Sergio had a very similar tenacity in competition and in training that Mike did. He didn't come to train with Mike to help Mike be the best in the world. He came to use Mike to help him become the best in the world. Practice became a daily battleground between the two of them. Each of them worked to outperform the other in the water and on land and also to prove to the other that they were the stronger one mentally. If Mike won a hard set he might look away, catch his breath and then look at Sergio and smile, suggesting he had outswum him on the set without completely exerting himself. Sergio was equally adept at shooting mental bullets at Mike.

Coach Nagy pushed them harder than ever. The only thing better than proving he could coach someone to become the best in the world would be to prove that he could coach two or three swimmers to be the best. He prodded them on. "More wider!" "More narrower!" "More faster!" Mike had always thought of his coach as using only clean language. But as his English improved so did Jozsef's knowledge of American curse words and some of those began to come out at practice for emphasis as well.

The 1989 US Long Course Nationals were held at the University of Southern California (USC) the first week of August. Many of the top swimmers in the world had taken an extended break after the Seoul Olympics and were not in top condition if they were competing at all. They might be looking ahead to the Barcelona Olympics in 1992 or the World Championships in 1990. But Mike Barrowman had something to prove and was in the top condition of his life.

John Hencken was the last American to hold the world record in the 200-meter breaststroke and that was in 1974 (2:18.21). In the preliminaries Mike swam faster than anyone in human history with a time of 2:12.90. His splitting of 31.1, 34.0, 33.8, and 33.9 was precisely the type of emphasis he and his coach put on performing well on the third quarter of the race. Coach Nagy almost never gave Mike a compliment, but afterward he smiled at Mike and said, "Pretty good!" The two hugged and Mike remembered something that his coach had told him. "If you break the world record you get to push the coach in the pool." So in they went—stopwatches and all.

The partnership had succeeded at the highest level and they were overjoyed. The world record consummated all their work together and affirmed to Mike his ability to use competition to better himself. He felt a degree of personal satisfaction like he had never felt before.

Another opportunity for the Olympic gold medal was three long years away. Mike's comments after the record indicated he still felt as though he had more to do. "I could have gone faster," he said matter-of-factly. "I felt this morning was not my best race. It was about 85-95 percent. There's more inside me." Mike sent a letter to the *Potomac Gazette* to apologize for his poor Olympic performance and said he was in the process of making amends to all those who had supported him and his coach.

Swimming World Magazine named him "World Swimmer of the Year" for 1989.

1990–1991

The 1990 collegiate season at Michigan was capped off with another great NCAA performance. As a junior, Mike battled Texas' Kirk Stackle again in the 200-yard breaststroke. Both swimmers broke Steve Lundquist's American record, but Barrowman buried Stackle on the last 50 to put the record (1:53.77) in a place that no one could touch for 11 more years. After the race, Texas coach Eddie Reese expressed his respect for the champion. "Mike's amazing. Part of his lifestyle is (geared) to train the breaststroke. When he sits, he sits with his knees in and his feet out. When he goes up steps, he puts his hands behind his head and hops up the steps" (SW April 1990).

In the summer months some of the best breaststroke swimmers from around the world came to Curl-Burke to train with Mike and Sergio. Roque

Santos joined and stayed, but no one else did. In they came by the dozens, but soon they left. The training intensity was extreme, the coaching was harsh and the core three swimmers were zealous in their desire to win everything they could each day. It was fun for them, but not for anyone else.

At the 1990 Goodwill Games in August, Mike dropped one and one-half seconds off his record to swim a 2:11.53. Again, he was honored as "World Swimmer of the Year" by *Swimming World*. But Sergio Lopez was right behind him with his best-ever time of 2:12.2, faster than Mike's world record from the summer of 1989.

In his final year of eligibility at Michigan, the college season was compromised by preparation for the 1991 World Championships held in January in Perth, Australia. Mike won his third consecutive NCAA title in the 200, but didn't match his record swim from the 1990 championships. He did make it three consecutive years with world records when he won the gold medal and set another global standard of 2:11.23 in Perth. Norbert Rosza from Hungary (2:12.03) and Nick Gillingham (2:13.12) from Great Britain were close behind.

1992 OLYMPICS – Barcelona, Spain

The overall American performance in the 1988 Seoul Olympics was disappointing. In 1992, US National Team Director Denny Pursley felt that by having the Olympic Trials 20 weeks ahead of the Games gave swimmers a full training cycle and the proper mental preparation time for the Olympics. Therefore, the US Olympic Trials were held the first week of March and the Games were the last week of July.

At the Trials, Roque Santos won the finals of the 200-meter breaststroke, beating Mike 2:13.50 to 2:13.54. It was the first time Barrowman had been beaten in a major race since the 1988 Olympics and Santos was shocked. But Roque was well off Mike's world record and the two of them were more than two seconds ahead of third place. Mike was delighted that his teammate had made the team and relieved that this step was over. He thought of Roque as such a nice person that he just didn't have the nasty mental attitude it would take to win the Olympic Games. In 1988 Mike was focused only on making the USA team, but in 1992 he had transferred that focus to his Olympic performance. "How can I be pleased with a performance three or four seconds slower than what I can do?" he asked, referring to his lackluster Trials swim. "This takes the pressure off. The only thing in my mind now is next summer, July 29th" (SW April 1992).

Thursday May 14, 1992 – 11 weeks to Olympic 200 Breaststroke

AM
60 minutes dry-land
Warm-up:	400 IM (25)
Main Set:	10 x 400s -30 seconds rest
Sprint Set:	16 x 25s Choice 95-100% every 2 25 no air on :35
Warm-down:	200
	5000

PM
Warm-up:	400 Choice
	200 breast kick 25, 1-1-2 (right, left, whole) 25 Regular
	200 Breast Pull 25 head-up, 25 4 underwater, 4 on surface
	4 x 100 IM on 1:30
	100 easy
Main Set:	4 x 75 (25 P, 25 K, 25 Swim) on 1:15
	4 x 100 (25, 25, 50) on 1:40
	10 x 150s (50, 50, 50) on 2:15
	4 x 100 (25, 25, 50) on 1:40
	4 x 75 (25 P, 25 K, 25 Swim) on 1:15
	100 easy
	400 Choice with fins
	2 x 100 (25, 25, 50) on 1:40
	2 x 150s (50, 50, 50) on 2:15
	2 x 300 (100, 100, 100) on 4:15
	2 x 150s (50, 50, 50) on 2:15
	2 x 100 (25, 25, 50) on 1:40
Speed Work:	4 x 50s breast on 1:00
Warm-down:	600 with fins, 25 underwater, 25 surface
	8,300 For the day

Reprinted with permission ASCA Clinic Book 1997

Tuesday July 21, 1992 - 8 Days to Olympic 200 Breaststroke

AM

Warm-up: 800 Warm Up
             800 Breast – 100 kick, 100 pull
             4 x 50 Breast on :50, 4 kick underwater,
             4 pull up on surface on 1:30 95-100% effort
             100 Easy
             2 x 200 IM on 3:00 (25 each stroke x 2)
             100 Easy
             4 x 25s Boat Drill on :30
             50 Easy
             4 x 100 Free on 1:30
             100 easy

Main Set: 8 x 50s on 1:00 (25 fly – no breath, 25 Back on 1:00)
             50 easy

Warm-down: 400 Choice
             3900

PM

Warm-Up: 400 Choice
             200 Fly 1-1-2
             400 Breast Kick 25 1-1-2, 25 Regular
             200 Back-Free (by 25s)

Main Set: 4 x 75 (25 P, 25 K, 25 Swim) on 1:15
             4 x 100 (25 P, 25 K, 50 S) on 1:40
             2 x 150s (50 P, 50 K, 50 S) on 2:15
             4 x 100 (25 P, 25 K, 50 S) on 1:40
             4 x 75 (25 P, 25 K, 25 Swim) on 1:15

Break: 100 easy
             400 choice with fins

Skill & Maintenance:
             8 x 50s breaststroke kick underwater – 25 breast pull on 1:00
             8 x 50s breast pull – 25 underwater – 25 regular pull on 1:00
             8 x 50s breast pull – 4 underwater, 4 on surface on 1:00
             200 easy

Speed work: 100 Breast (25 pull 4 underwater, 1 up/25 regular pull/25
              breast 4 underwater, 1 up/25 breast)

Warm-Down: 400-600
             5500 yards
             9400 for the day

Reprinted with permission ASCA Clinic Book 1997

The training through the spring and summer with Sergio, Roque and Mike was as intense as ever. However there was an extra bit of joy in knowing they were all going to compete on the grandest stage in sport, the Olympic Games. Tuesday and Thursday afternoons were the most difficult practice sessions. Jozsef tried to build their fatigue through lactate tolerance training and get them in the same state of pain they would experience on the third 50 of a 200-meter breaststroke. Then he demanded good technique from them while they continued to train hard. They always finished those practices with a set of 8 x 50s on 1:00 to test their progress.

With three weeks until the competition Coach Nagy reduced their training. The dry-land sessions dropped from five per week to twice per week and each land session from 45 minutes to 30 minutes. Jozsef even let them pick their own exercises. When they joined the US training camp on July 15th, the dry-land exercises were cut out completely. Coach Nagy's training for the 200 breaststroke did not include much sprinting, but as July 29th neared they sharpened their technique and performed pace 50s for their race. The last three days before competition were easy.

SATURDAY JULY 25, 1992 – Four days to 200 Breaststroke

AM

Warm-up:	400 Choice
	200 IM (25 kick, 25 pull), 200 Fly (1-1-2), 200 Breast Kick, 400 (75 Back easy, 25 Fly fast), 200 Breast Kick, 400 Free (75 Easy, 25 Fast), 200 Breast Kick
	8 x 25s Breast Pull Underwater

PM

Warm-up:	800 Warm-up
	400 Breast Kick (10 Kick easy, 5 Kick fast), 50 easy, 400 Breast Pull (10 Pull Easy, 5 Pull Fast), 200 Choice
Speed Work:	4 x 50s Breast (3 Kick, 1 Pull) on 1:15 95-100% effort
Loosen up:	400 Choice
Speed Work:	2 x 100 Breast (4 underwater, 4 Surface) on 2:00 90-95% effort
Warm-down:	400 Choice

Reprinted with permission ASCA World Clinic book 1997

1992 OLYMPIC GAMES – Barcelona, Spain

Mike Barrowman went to Barcelona to bring back the one prize that had eluded him and his coach in their swimming careers: an Olympic gold medal. Over the past four years he had reset the world record five times. He believed he had trained to swim a 2:09 or even a 2:08. But winning the gold medal was more important than his time.

In the preliminaries he was swimming in the lane next to one of the top-seeded swimmers, Norbert Rozsa from Hungary. In 1991, Rozsa was ranked second in the world (2:12.01) to Barrowman. Mike decided to try to destroy Norbert's confidence. When they dove in on the start Mike sprinted three or four strokes to get ahead of him. Then he let Rozsa catch up to him. Then he sprinted three or four strokes again. Then he let Rozsa catch up to him again. He continued this game for the first 150 meters of the race. On the final 50 Mike extended his lead and finished well ahead of the Hungarian (2:11.4 to 2:12.9). Just like he had done in his battles with Sergio Lopez in practice, he turned away from Norbert and took a few quick deep breaths. He didn't want to him to see any fatigue on his face. Then he turned back to Rozsa and smiled broadly, jumped out of the pool and walked away.

To say the finals were more of a coronation than a competition might seem to be excessive praise for Mike Barrowman. But when he sat in the ready room with the other seven finalists and gazed around the circle of the best swimmers in the world, each one of them turned his eyes away from him. Roque Santos had failed to make the final eight. Sergio Lopez had qualified eighth. The only athlete who could stop Mike Barrowman in the finals was Barrowman himself.

The swimmers were paraded to the starting blocks and were introduced to the crowd. Mike swam with little effort through the first 100 and turned at 1:03.91. He held a slight lead over Nick Gillingham (1:04.1) and Rozsa (1:04.4). On his underwater pullout Mike snuck a peek at his competition. When he saw that they were slightly behind him he thought to himself, *If these guys think they can keep up with me after that easy first 100, they better think again.* He smiled and began to laugh. (The picture caught on camera is one of his favorite in swimming.) He only stumbled for a second when he swallowed a little water during his laugh. Optimism is one of the strongest advantages an athlete can have, and Mike Barrowman was full of it.

His second 100 was the fastest second half of the 200-meter breaststroke in the history of the sport. He was a half-second behind his world-record pace at the halfway point and lowered the world record by a half-second when he touched. It took a second for the results to come up on the scoreboard. When it did, it read 2:10.16, new world record and Mike Barrowman Olympic champion!

Rosza (2:11.23) was second and Gillingham was third (2:11.29). Sergio Lopez made a gallant effort from lane eight moving up to finish fourth (2:13.29). Mike Barrowman had now swum seven of the top ten 200-meter breaststroke times of all time. He leaped into a seated position on the lane line, fired his arms over his head with clinched fists and exalted in victory. He was so overwhelmed with his emotional fulfillment that he functioned in a daze until after he received his Olympic gold medal.

Following the completion of the swimming events for the United States, Mike and Jozsef exited the swimming venue and went for a walk together. They sat on a beach and shared story after story about the road they took to their victory. They talked into the early hours of the next morning.

"You know when you left the pool deck to make a phone call?" Mike asked.

"Yes."

"We really slacked off," Mike confessed.

"Why do you think I left?"

They laughed. Jo was such an intense coach that he didn't want to watch easy swimming, but there were times he knew that his athletes needed a break from him.

Some swimming observers might think that Mike Barrowman's singular focus on winning the 200-meter breaststroke could have kept him from receiving the accolades that can come with winning multiple gold medals. To others he demonstrated purity in his mission to measure excellence in as exact an analysis as possible. Was Mike Barrowman good enough to have won the 100 breaststroke and add a third gold medal by swimming on the American 400 medley relay?

We will never know the answer to that question. But to put Mike Barrowman's superiority of preparation in perspective consider these facts: Nelson Deibel won the gold medal in the 100 breaststroke in a time of 1:01.5. When he did that he split 29.0 on the first 50 and 32.5 on the 50. In Barrowman's 200 win he split 33.1 on his third 50 and 33.0 on his fourth.

Hungary's Tamas Darnyi won the Olympic gold medal in the 200 individual medley with a time of 2:00.76. Mike Barrowman swam the 200 individual medley on March 6th, at the US Trials, since it was two days after the 200 breaststroke. He finished third with a time of 2:01.7 and missed the Olympic Team by 23-hundredths of a second. He improved 3.4 seconds in his

200 breaststroke from the Trials to the Games.

Hours of conversation drifted by on that night of the Olympic victory in Barcelona while Mike and Jozsef sat on the beach. They gazed out on the water, as though they were looking for another mountain to climb together.

"What do we do now, Jozsi?"

The coach responded, "I tore off the rest of my calendar after July 29. This is all I've been living for. I don't know."

Mike handed his coach his gold medal and said, "You sleep with this tonight."

For 13 years Mike Barrowman was the standard for the entire planet in the speed swim for the 200-meter breaststroke. It was one of the longest periods of domination by any swimmer in history. Japan's Kousuke Kitjama finally broke his world record in 2002. Mike's development and time improvements from the Montgomery Square Copenhaver Swim Club to the Barcelona Olympics didn't include great physical ability or significant advances in suit technology. Mike Barrowman became the best at what he did by winning every competition he could find, including the most important one, with his best self.

Following the Olympics Mike spent a brief time on the US Kayaking team, which was a path that was etched in part by chasing an attractive girl to California. Today he lives in the Cayman Islands with the two loves of his life, his wife Terri and his daughter Harper. He works as an executive in a bank, has written several manuscripts for fiction books but is still in search of his next challenge—a way to use his competitiveness to help the world.

Mike Barrowman was inducted into the International Swimming Hall of Fame in 1997.

JOSH DAVIS

September 1, 1972

FREE TO LEAD

OLYMPIAN JOSH DAVIS

JOSH AT AGE 11

L eadership has been thoughtfully described as social influence. One of the most committed leaders in American history was Colonel William Travis who drew a line in the sand at the Alamo in San Antonio, challenging his men to cross it and fight to the death with him for the freedom of Texas. This story is about another leader from San Antonio. His battles were at swimming pools. His victory would be won if he could find his ultimate speed inside himself, train to sustain it and also help his team be better than any other. His social influence was effective, but drawing a line in the sand was never his style. Like every great leader, he led by deeds first and words second. The result of his efforts changed him and many others around him. He was, and is, one of the great leaders in the history of American swimming.

* * *

THE EARLY YEARS – Finding Swimming

Thirteen-year-old Josh Davis was having a difficult time on his new swim team. Until now his only swim experience was on the Harmony Hills Cabana Club summer team. As he stroked up and down the pool, he kicked his legs as hard as he could and tried to stay up with the other kids in his group. He listened to the coaches and concentrated on transferring their words into his actions. The transition to this big year-round US Swimming Club was more demanding than he ever could have imagined. But if he was going to qualify to swim on the Churchill High School swim team he had to improve and do it quickly.

In all his experiences with sports, up until now other sports had come and gone. He played soccer for four years but lost interest when he was 10. In sixth grade he played basketball, but he wasn't an impact player. In seventh grade, he fell in love with gymnastics and pole-vaulting and pursued them with all his might. Although he showed some improvement in coordination and athleticism, his long skinny arms wouldn't put him anywhere close to making the high school team. Everyone seemed to have found a sport at Churchill High School and he desperately wanted one, too. It was tough enough to fit into school socially, but if you were an athlete it made it a lot easier.

Baseball didn't work out even though he was left-handed, which would have made playing first base easier, but his long, lanky body couldn't hit a pitched ball past the pitcher. So the previous summer, when he was 12 and starting to win some ribbons for the Cabana Club, he thought maybe swimming could be the sport he could use to be a varsity athlete at Churchill.

The big club coach was describing their next swimming set. "Listen up everyone. We're going 16 x 50s on 1 minute 10. The odd ones are kick and the even ones are stroke drill, two of each stroke in IM order. We're leaving on the top (when the pace clock sweep hand reached the 60 mark at the top of the big round clock)."

Josh thought to himself, *OK, I can do that, but I came here to learn breaststroke. I can't do the drills for breaststroke if I don't know how.*

The requirement to be admitted to the junior varsity swim team at Churchill High School was to be able to perform all four competitive swimming strokes legally. Josh had joined the big club to learn how to do breaststroke and qualify for the Churchill junior varsity team. He had been in the club for three months, but he still hadn't learned how to do the proper breaststroke kick. When his mother Joan came to pick him up from swim practice that night she went into the pool area and politely asked the coach for a moment of his time.

"How's he doing?"

"He tries hard. You have a wonderful son," the big club coach said.

Josh walked up and listened.

His mother gently asked, "He needs to learn the breaststroke to be eligible for the high school team. How's he doing with that?"

The coach said, "Not so well."

Josh interceded meekly. "I think I can get it, if someone will teach me."

The big club coach said, "We've been trying, Josh. You might want to consider another sport."

There was much at stake for Josh's social integration to high school; he needed to have a sport to play. Swimming was the last choice after all the other options. The big club coach's advice to try another sport obviously wasn't welcome.

Determined to find another solution, the Davises found another swim team and another coach.

Although Josh was beginning to develop a passion for swimming, the journey to this point of his life took him through many other athletic experiences. His mother and father had supported his various investigations into activities, even eight years earlier when he tried ballet.

As the music from the piano his mother played flew across the wooden dance floor, five-year-old Josh Davis attempted to twirl around the room. He didn't have a natural flow, but he tried. Occasionally he spun and flew to the piano to turn a page of music for his mother. Being with his mom was a safe place to be, but that class didn't last long. He was quickly moved down a level to learn with the four-year-olds and in an attempt to improve his behavior.

* * *

For Joan Davis, like her son, movement and activity were a part of her life. If she wasn't feeding her mind with a book she was teaching piano, cooking or actively supporting her four children in sports. She played the organ at church and when Josh was in fourth grade converted the family to "healthy meals." Out went the Lucky Charms and in came the Grape-Nuts. Gone were the heavy meats and in came lentil soup, pastas and fajita night.

Her husband Mike was active in and frequently contributed readings at church, a duty that came easily to him. He was a professional fund-raiser and his services were often engaged by large concerns like a local college or hospital. Their Irish Catholic heritage was proudly shared within their extended family in San Antonio, Texas. His large family and their activities would have a great influence in Josh's approach to his own family years later, as well as giving him leadership skills that he would use as a team leader in high school, college, and national team swim squads.

Three years after Josh was born the Davises added twin brothers, Sam and Will. Their daughter Tynan was born four years after the twins. While they were toddlers, Josh was getting an introduction into sports. Ballet was temporary. By the age of six he had left ballet behind and was playing soccer; the great Brazilian player Pelé became his hero.

In 1982 the Davis family moved to a new home a few blocks away from the Harmony Hills Cabana Swim and Tennis Club. The club was a spectacular place to play. It included two pools, with one- and three-meter diving boards, four tennis courts and volleyball courts. They held their grand opening activities on Memorial Day. It included greased watermelon relays and a variety of games. For ten-year-old Josh Davis it was a living heaven on earth. He rode his bike a few blocks in one direction to church and a few blocks in the other direction to Harmony Hills.

During the summer months Josh practically lived at the pool, arriving promptly at 11:00 a.m. when it opened. He stayed for five to six hours there on most days. When he found out there was a swim team practicing from 7:30–10:00 a.m. he became excited to join. Anything he could do to spend more time at the Cabana Club, Josh was more than willing to try. In the middle of June, he received permission from his parents to join the Harmony Hills Dolphins.

Fletcher Watson was a lifeguard at the pool, a student at Duke University, and also served as the swim coach. In his swimming career, he had been exposed to some programs that measured work by the volume of swimming. He rejected that approach. He believed that by practicing the finesse of swimming you could improve your fitness. Fletcher believed that technique could be varied to suit each individual swimmer, but he began with three key teaching points for freestyle: "Thumb by Thigh, Elbow High, Reach out Front." At practice he instructed Josh and his teammates to do a good start, then swim 10 to 15 good strokes and give a good strong finish to the wall. They swam one length at a time. If the swimmers became fatigued and began to get sloppy, he stopped them and made corrections. Then practice resumed.

Josh, age 10, was excited to swim his first race of that summer season. He gave it all he had, zigzagging down the pool like an errant pinball. Then he sought feedback from Coach Watson.

"What can I do better, Coach?" Josh asked, still huffing and puffing from the swim.

Fletcher thought to himself, *Everything.* But he selected his words thoughtfully "Why don't we start by swimming straight down that black line. You see that thing?"

Josh nodded with excitement. "OK!"

"One end to the other straight down the middle of that lane."

"Got it, Coach!" Josh began the process of learning how to become a faster swimmer and embraced it.

The young coach of the Cabana Club believed much of the endurance training needed for the summer league sprint races came from the endless games of "kick the can" kids played at that age. He felt their core strength developed from all the tree-climbing they did. They warmed up with jumping jacks, ran a half-mile run around the grounds, and then worked on good technique in the pool.

During the winter months Josh played other sports. In the summer he resumed his instruction from Coach Watson. As Josh grew older, the coach increased the skill training to 50s. Over their 10-week season, Fletcher gradually challenged the 11 and 12-year-olds to improve their conditioning. Toward the end of the summer they extended their workload by swimming heats of 100-yard individual medleys in reverse order so that the hardest stroke, butterfly, was last. Fletcher instructed them to swim the fourth length butterfly only if they could do it with good form. If they couldn't swim with good form they should swim freestyle. Josh always tried to do butterfly no matter how bad it looked. The coach marveled at the youngster's determination and fortitude.

Josh Davis Developmental Progression –
The Harmony Hills Cabana Club – Coach Fletcher Watson

Began swimming competitively in the summer only at age 10

Age 10-13:   10 weeks of training each year
              30 minutes of running, sit-ups and push-ups
              1 hour to 1:30 x 5 days per week
              Starts and 10-15 strokes done perfectly
              Progress 50s repeats
              Progress to 100s IM reverse order trying to hold technique.

Provided by Coach Fletcher Watson

As he progressed through elementary and middle school, sports and play were activities where Josh felt comfortable. He was a late bloomer and relatively new to his neighborhood. Consequently, Josh became introverted in the formal school setting. But when the bell rang for gym class or recess, he lit up with excitement and energy, racing out to the playground and bursting with joy. He showed his aggressive competitiveness trying to win a dodge ball game or excel at any other physical activity.

Josh yearned to be an athlete and when the big club coach told him to find a sport other than swimming, Josh didn't accept that advice. He had tried just about every sport there was, but he felt swimming could be "his" sport, so the Davises looked around some more. They discovered another small team in San Antonio not too far from their house. It was the Alamo Heights Aquatic Club and the head coach was Jim Yates.

The Davises contacted the club, made inquiries and Josh quickly joined. The assistant coaches helped him learn how to kick breaststroke legally. A little success in swimming whetted his appetite and encouraged Josh to achieve more. He was now eligible for the junior varsity team at Churchill, but most of his friends had been swimming competitively for a number of years and likely were going to make the varsity squad. Josh continued his eager approach to learning swimming skills and pestered Coach Yates for every tip he could get. For example, when they videotaped stroke technique, he asked to see it again and again. When they practiced turns, he stayed after practice and spent extra time to improve them.

An arrangement had been established between Jim and the high school coach that swimmers would be placed on the high school varsity or junior varsity squad based on their "tryout" in the club program. The endurance requirement to be on the varsity was to complete a set of 12 x 100-yard freestyle swims, leaving every one minute and 15 seconds. Josh worked and worked throughout the summer to improve his endurance. Eventually Jim Yates called the high school coach and said, "This may be hard to believe, but that kid Josh Davis made the 12 x 100s."

1986–1987 CHURCHILL HIGH SCHOOL – Ninth Grade

The high school program was coached by Al Marks. Coach Marks had grown up in the northeast part of the United States and developed an interest in coaching swimming. He applied for several jobs. He was offered a position with the Solotar Swim Club in Washington DC that became available when an assistant coach, Rick Curl, left to form his own team. But Al really liked the way Texas set up their school day to allow athletes to excel in their sport.

The high schools started at 9 a.m., but the swimmers were allowed to use their first period for athletics to practice and not start academic classes until 9:40. Al was hired as an economics teacher at Churchill High School and as their swim coach. He organized the high school team with varsity practice from 6:30-8 in the morning and then the junior varsity team right after school from 3-4 p.m. The varsity boys were encouraged to also be a member of a club that practiced after school.

Swim season started a few weeks into the school year and in 1986, extended all the way until March. By the second week of September Josh was a Churchill High School varsity athlete and living the corresponding lifestyle! At 5:45 a.m. his mom scratched his back. "It's time for practice. I've got a smoothie downstairs ready for you. I'll drive you to practice when you're ready." Joan wasn't always that nice because it wasn't easy to get up that early every morning. The Davis family believed in commitment, however, and Josh was ready to go to swim practice by 6:10 each morning.

Al Marks was very committed to being an effective swimming coach. He read and studied swimming and borrowed every idea he liked. His science background trained him to have strong analytical and statistical skills. He used those in his coaching. He created a system of standardized training sets to measure his swimmers' progress. He also gave the sets interesting names that helped his athletes appreciate their heritage.

The names of sets included "The Hungarian," "The Gauntlet," "The Mind Grinder," and "The Trojan Treat." The Trojan Treat came from the USC program. The swimmers also remembered the details of each set by its name. For example, everyone knew that The Gauntlet meant swimming all the high school events, from beginning to end, alternating an easy effort with a more intense effort. Whenever they swam one of the special sets, the coach recorded each swimmer's times then encouraged them to improve on their best average time when they did it again. Coach Marks liked to say, "You can't fool the numbers."

Coach Marks built a culture of hard work and goal achievement at Churchill High School. He called his fastest lane of swimmers "The Animal Lane," a phrase he took from the highly successful Mission Viejo program in California. The name suggested that those were the swimmers in the pool who were able to accept the most difficult challenges in a workout. This created motivation for Josh and his teammates to work hard enough to earn the right to swim in the special lane.

Josh soaked up the coaching, learning as fast as he could. But since he was only a ninth-grader, his enthusiasm wasn't always received warmly by the seniors. At times the older swimmers scoffed at his eagerness. If Josh had noticed, it might have bothered him, but he was busy acquiring every detail to help him swim faster and make a greater contribution to his team.

Coach Marks insisted that each swimmer learn how to accurately use the pace clock. It was an important part of his system of record-keeping and statistical analysis of their swimming. Eventually Josh learned the team practice of each swimmer subtracting and keeping track of the total number of seconds under his best average for each repeat. This simplified the calculations and made Coach Marks' recording process easier. Josh and his teammates strived for results in negative numbers from their previous best set. Josh enjoyed being with his friends and seeing his painful efforts translate into faster training times. He concluded that his body was changing, growing and strengthening.

Churchill High School Practice – Coach Al Marks

Tuesday November 28, 1989 6:30-8:00 am
HS Practice Monday, Tuesday, Wednesday, Friday mornings
These are workouts from Coach Marks log book for Josh's senior year when he swam 1:36.5 200-yard free.

	4-5,000 yards per practice
Warm-up:	3 Starts, 10 minute swim changing strokes each 25
	2:00 rest
	Swim 6 x 125s Free on 1:45 or 1:55 with fins
Sprint Set:	5 x (9 x 25s on :30, rest :30, 50 easy on 1:10, 75 fast on 1:00) –
	3 times free, 2 choice
	Pull – 2 x 200s free breath every 4 strokes

Hungarian Repeats (recorded test set two or three times each season):
Animal Lane intervals
2 x (8 x 50s on :35, timed 400 free on 4:30, 8 x 50s on :55)
Relay Practice   5,000 yards

Tuesday January 23, 1990
Warm-up:	5 x 200s on :10 rest (1. Free fins, 2. Back fins, 3. Breast, 4. Free fins, 5. IM Fins)
	6 x 100s IM on 1:30/1:40 alternating

Trojan Treat (once per season) lasted approximately 1 hr and 9 minutes
4 x 100s back on 1:30, 400 IM on 6:00, 4 x 100s free on 1:20, 400 free on 6:00
4 x 100s fly/fr on 1:30, 400 IM on 6:00, 4 x 100s free on 1:15, 400 free on 6:00
4 x 100s breast on 1:40, 400 IM on 6:00, 4 x 100s free on 1:10, 400 free
Descend the 400s IM, Descend the 400s free - Record 400s
Non-Animals alternate
100/75 on 100s, swim free for fly on IM
6,400 yards

Provided by Coach Al Marks

It was traditional that the seniors drove teammates to one of the year-round clubs after school. By 4:10 p.m. Josh and his teammates arrived outside the pool for the Alamo Heights practice. The three hours of swim training each day wasn't enough to burn off their energy. They jumped, slid, pushed and had a great time playing basketball each day before going into the pool for practice that started at 4:30. It lasted until 6:00 p.m.

The coordination between the Alamo Heights coach Jim Yates and Churchill High School coach Al Marks was one of the keys to the success of their swimmers. The coaches had worked together in town in the past and respected each other's different backgrounds and styles. Jim had attended Texas A&M where he played water polo. A transplant from California, he had swum at the Santa Clara Swim Club under George Haines, one of the most successful coaches in the history of swimming. Jim was very knowledgeable but had a relaxed style in his coaching approach. On Halloween, for example, he wore jeans, a vest and a cowboy hat just like Crocodile Dundee in that popular movie of the day. He looked exactly like the character.

Much of what he learned from Coach Haines gave Jim Yates a special set of strengths in his coaching. He understood how important technique was for a swimmer to reach his potential and develop his ultimate swimming speed. He saw the cumulative effect of adhering to specific details of nutrition, stretching, strength, technique and massage. He transferred his knowledge of the physical skills he valued so effectively to his swimmers that they took pride in having great relay starts, turns and individual starts. Jim had also introduced Josh and his teammates to strength training. For $30 per month the swimmers joined the Olympia Gym. After their swim practice, two or three times per week, they went to the gym and learned the proper way to strength train.

There were many other skills that Coach Yates taught the swimmers. One of the most important was the power of visualization and how to use it. The team would lay on the pool deck, close their eyes and release the tension from their bodies. Then they would visualize themselves in the first person, present tense, preparing for and swimming their races. Josh loved the experience. He practiced at home. In his mind's eye he saw perfection in his start, in his technique and in his finish. Josh may have been one of the weaker swimmers on the varsity, but he was excited about how much there was to learn about swimming and eager to improve.

Joan Davis became an official so she could have something to do during Josh's swim meets. Mike attended the meets when he could but there were sometimes conflicts with Sam's and Will's volleyball practices and games, as well as Tynan's singing. When Mike was able to attend a swim meet he was enthusiastic in his support of Josh.

"That was great, Son!" he often said after races.

Josh tried to educate his father. "But, Dad, that was three seconds off my best time."

"Did you give your best effort?" his father continued. Josh nodded and his father cheered and supported him. "I'm proud of you for giving it your best, Son."

Joan and Mike Davis supported the qualities of character that their son was developing: effort and a positive attitude. His parents provided Josh a safety net of love and support that would always be there for him if he stumbled or fell.

ALAMO HEIGHTS PRACTICE 4:30-6 – Jim Yates

Friday January 8, 1988

Warm-up:	Drill w/ fins - 6 x 100s on 1:30
	Kick w/fins - 6 x 50s on :55 (no board)
	Pull - 400 (breath 3/5 by 100s)
Main Set:	Pull - 8 x 100s on 1:45 (no. 1-4 breath, 1, 2, 3, 4, no. 5-8 breath 4, 3, 2, 1)
	Swim - 16 x 25s on :25 IM order (sub free for breaststroke)
	Easy 75
Quality Set:	Swim - 1 x 200 broken swim :10 at each 50 (Josh 1:39.5)
	Drill - 5 x 75s on 1:20
	Drill - 8 x 75s on 1:20 (25 catch-up fast legs, 25 DPS by 6 kicks, 25 fly kick on bk)
	375 swim - 60% effort
Time Trial:	100 best stroke (Josh 57.3 back)
	4,525 yards

Tuesday January 12, 1988

	Meeting - Goal-Setting
Warm-up:	Drill - 400 w/fins
	Pull - 500 (every 4th length breaststroke pull)
	Swim - 8 x 50s on :50 (DPS by 6 kicks, think legs pushing you along)
	Pull - 6 x 200s on 2:30 (buoy and paddles, negative split)
Main Sets:	2 x (4 x 25s on :45 no breath, 1 min rest, 1 x 50 on :45 no breath)
	500 broken swim, :10 rest at 100s (Josh 4:48, fastest on team)
	3,300 yards

Provided by Coach Jim Yates

The high school season and US Swimming club season all culminated with their championships in March. If you were fast enough in the Region Meet, you earned the opportunity to move on to the Texas High School Championships. They were held each year at The Texas Swimming Center at The University of Texas at Austin. The Swimming Center is one of the most attractive pools in the world, as well as one of the fastest. There are 2,100 orange seats placed so that every spectator has a clear view of the bright white walls accented with natural wood acoustic panels, the competition pool and the diving well. It also has deep gutters and deep water to help minimize surface turbulence, which helps an athlete swim faster.

Churchill had a chance to win the 1987 state title and Josh wanted to contribute. He managed to qualify for the championships as a ninth grader. The first individual event was the 200-yard freestyle. He swam a time of 1:44, which was amazing for someone in his first year of year-round swimming, but he finished 12th, scoring just one point for his team. He was so disappointed in his small contribution that he put his head on the edge of the gutter and cried. Fortunately, Churchill High School eventually won the state title that year.

The Cabana Club Swim Team was a part of the past by the summer of 1987. Josh trained all summer with Alamo Heights. Practice was for 90 minutes in the morning long course and 90 minutes in the afternoon short course. Josh earned a spot on a relay team for the Junior Nationals in Mission Viejo, California. The whole family went to support Josh and then visited Disneyland. The trip introduced a tradition of the family celebrating Josh's success at the major swim meets.

1987–1988 CHURCHILL HIGH SCHOOL – Sophomore Year

Josh completed his first full-year training cycle in the summer of 1987. It seemed that his constant bike riding and multisport participation for the years leading up to eighth grade had paid off. He appeared to have a surprising and strong foundation to be a very successful high school swimmer.

In his sophomore year of high school, Josh and a teammate embarked on two traditions. One was that Churchill was in the running for the state title again. The common goal drew the team together and overwhelmed the swimmers' interest in club competition during the winter season.

The second tradition became known as the "Texas Dump." When Josh and his best friend Murray Easton arrived at the Texas Swimming Center for the 1988 Texas State High School Championships, they got out of the car after their one-hour drive, went into the Swim Center and looked at the spectacular pool setting. They were so excited they became very nervous and went to the bathroom. When they reappeared on the pool deck they were ready to swim fast. The tradition continued for the next two years.

The best 200-yard freestyle swimmer in Texas High School swimming in 1988 was Jack Kosharek from Dallas Adams High School. But Jack misjudged his effort in the preliminaries of the event and failed to qualify as one of the final six swimmers to compete in the "championship final." Although Jack swam faster in the consolation finals than Josh did in the championship finals, Josh was the official winner with a time of 1:40.08. He touched the wall, looked up at the huge timing board, saw his time and the number 1 by it. He thought to himself, *Holy cow, I won something! This is great!* He wanted more.

The team of Davis, Todd Laurie, Scott Schumaker and Kit Patterson won the 400 free relay with a time of 3:06.43 to close out the meet. It was the top high school 400 free relay time in the country. But no sooner than they'd celebrated, Coach Marks helped them reset their goals for the next year.

"Boys, the national record is held by Mercersburg and it's 3:02.61. You can do that next year."

"You think so, Coach?"

Coach Marks broke the improvement down for them. "Each of you needs to improve just one second. You have 364 days to do it. That's three-one-thousandths of a second per day."

Josh smiled. "We can do that!"

The boys went off to the locker room eager for their coming year.

At the end of that summer the Olympics were held in Seoul, Korea, and the star of the Games was swimmer Matt Biondi. His performance earning five gold medals, two silver, and one bronze had only been exceeded in the sport by Mark Spitz in 1972. The Davis' VCR recorded each of Matt's races and Josh watched them over and over, dreaming that perhaps one day he too could swim in the Olympic Games like Matt Biondi.

1988–1989 CHURCHILL HIGH SCHOOL – Eleventh Grade

The passion Josh had for learning about swimming was infectious because his teammates witnessed how it translated into his improved performance. He and his teammates worked through the summer and into the next high school season. During his junior year he became someone the team not only counted on for team points, but also someone they admired for the example he set in his work ethic.

In order for the swimmers to achieve top performance at the Texas High School Championships, Coach Yates balanced his training with Coach Marks during the final few weeks leading up to the championships. Jim checked each day with the boys about what they had done in practice that morning. He was careful never to add quality swimming to a day when they had already trained that way in the morning. At this time of year the two coaches communicated more than at any other time, carefully coordinating their reduction of training for peak performance.

By the time the 1989 Texas High School Championships arrived in March the Churchill High School team was ready for a great meet. Josh won the 200-yard freestyle in 1:38.99 and finished second in the 100-yard freestyle (45.02). Churchill was running away with the team championship, but they wanted the national relay record.

Josh loved relays most of all because of the team element. He and his teammates tried to grab the record in the preliminaries to take some pressure off them. They missed by two-tenths of a second when they swam the time of 3:02.81. Rather than become frustrated, they refocused their energy on everyone getting just a little bit faster. The four of them warmed up together, sat together and quietly unified their energy. In the finals Murray led off in 45.8, Josh swam second (44.4), Todd Laurie swam second (46.0), and Kit Patterson anchored (45.3) to establish the new mark. It was the first of many record-setting relays for Josh, as well as initiating a love for swimming in the second position.

The record stood for 19 years. In the summer, *Swimming World Magazine* named Churchill High School swim team the Boys Public School Mythical National Champions.

1990 USA NATIONAL JUNIOR TEAM – (Team Captain)

In the summer of 1989, the major meet for the Alamo Heights team was in Tempe, Arizona. Josh swam his best time of 1:53 in the 200-meter freestyle. He was excited about his big improvement in time. Shortly thereafter Josh noticed in a newspaper that an Italian swimmer named Giorgio Lamberti had set a new world record in the event of 1:46.69. That time put a new perspective on Josh's performance but the swim earned him a great opportunity through US Swimming.

US Swimming and National Team Director Denny Pursley developed the concept of the National Junior Team. The top 18-and-younger boys and 16-and-younger girls from the United States were selected for the squad. They were invited to a training camp in the fall and then to compete in Paris and East Germany at the end of January. Josh qualified for the team.

The fall of 1989 was also the beginning of his senior year of high school.

He was fielding phone calls from college coaches, training and getting ready for a great season. Then he discovered he had contracted mononucleosis. He wasn't allowed to swim at all for 30 days and that included the training camp at the Olympic Training Center in Colorado Springs.

Since his mono wasn't contagious, he was permitted to attend the training camp, attend meetings, observe and learn. He flew to Colorado Springs, unloaded his bags in the dorm and went to the meeting with the team. When he walked into the room at the training center, he saw flags hanging from the ceiling that represented many countries around the world. But the Olympic and American flags were the ones that caught and kept his attention. He felt a deep sense of pride inside him to be a part of another team: "The American Swimming Team." From that moment forward, his favorite team color became red, white and blue. The members of the Junior Team sat down for their first meeting.

National Team Director Denny Pursley addressed the team. "Congratulations on being a part of your first US National Team." Josh tried to lock onto Denny's words but was distracted by the banners. He thought to himself, *From the Harmony Hills Cabana Club to this?*

Denny went on. "We hope there will be many more." Josh thought to himself, *So do I!* That moment opened his mind to the possibility of other opportunities to represent the United States of America as a part of its national swimming program.

Josh's mono presented a huge problem. He couldn't get in the pool and show what he could do. He thought, *How am I going to help this team this weekend? What can I do for them?* He decided to get to know every single name of every swimmer on the team. As they rode the bus to and from some of the training sessions at the Air Force Academy, Josh found someone new to sit with and get to know them. During practice sessions he walked the pool deck and cheered for his new teammates. At the end of the camp the team voted for captains. He and his female counterpart from North Carolina, Heather Blackman, were elected.

By the time the team met in New York in late January Josh was healthy. They competed in Paris first. The team ate dinner in the Eiffel Tower and saw some sights. The competition included the best Europeans, which made it very difficult for Josh and his young teammates to place high enough in the morning preliminaries to swim in the evening finals. Instead they found two USA Team representatives to cheer for.

Matt Biondi and Tom Jager were competing as professional swimmers from the USA. Each night during the finals the young team filled the Piscine des Tourelles with noise for Matt and Tom, as well as any of their teammates who had made it into the evening competition. Eventually, the meet referee's whistle quieted the cheering for the start. National high school record-holder Eric Diehl screamed above the uproar, "I'm cheering so much I'm sweating through my shirt! What a workout!" The French administrators smiled and shook their heads in admiration for the American Team celebrating their great sporting experience.

The US head coach asked Matt and Tom if they would meet with the Junior Team to discuss developing their swimming careers and how to achieve swimming excellence. They agreed. One afternoon they ended their rest period early and sat in the upstairs elevator lobby with the 40 teenagers. You could have heard a pin drop. Josh and his teammates were mesmerized by these two icons of swimming. Josh thought, *Maybe someday I can give back to swimming and be a leader like Matt and Tom.*

The team's travels continued to the stark surroundings of East Berlin. A visit to the Berlin Wall was a high point, but a low point was a gastrointestinal bug suspected to have come from eating the "mystery meat." It left many of the swimmers disabled or unable to perform at a high level in the final competition. However, it was a launching pad for international experience for many of the squad, six of whom went on to swim for the US in the Olympics. Josh was hungry for more.

1990 CHURCHILL HIGH SCHOOL – Twelfth Grade (Team Captain)

The 1990 US Nationals were in Nashville, Tennessee, during the same week as the Texas High School Championships. Josh decided to compete in both. The week began with the nationals and he swam his best times in the 500-yard freestyle (4:25) and the 200-yard freestyle (1:36.5). But by the end of the week he was running out of energy.

Josh had been elected team captain for the Churchill High School swim team. He had developed into a fierce competitor with a high level of expectation for winning races. His mind was set on leading his team to a fourth consecutive state title and closing out his prep career in glorious fashion. But in the 200-yard freestyle he was out-touched by Jason Fink (1:36.8 to 1:37.2). He was terribly upset to be beaten. Adding to his disappointment was the fact that his time from Nashville would have won. But during the awards ceremony he stood on the second-place award platform next to Jason, smiled and waved to the crowd and congratulated the victor. There may have been a dent in his image as a winner, but he demonstrated great sportsmanship.

The Davis family safety net was always present, but Josh appreciated it more than ever that night. He had established a tradition to take a quick trip into the stands to see them after his high school races and give them his award. For the first time since his freshman year he carried the silver plaque for the 200-yard freestyle rather than gold. His mother greeted him with tears streaming down her face.

"I've never been so proud of you, Josh," she wept.

Josh handed her his award and gave her a hug.

"You showed wonderful sportsmanship the way you congratulated the winner."

Mike and Joan Davis taught their son that character was more important than performance.

Despite a poor third turn, and a second place in the 100-yard freestyle (44.8) Josh and Churchill won the 400 freestyle relay and walked away with another team title.

It was late March and Josh still had not committed to a college or university. In the fall he visited Cal. Even though it was the alma mater of his hero Matt Biondi, it just didn't seem like the right fit. It was one week after a huge earthquake and the prospect of swimming outside in cold California winters didn't appeal to him. There weren't enough attractions for him to decide to leave Texas.

He scheduled four straight recruiting weekends during the month of April. The first was to Iowa. Among other things it was also too cold. The second trip was to Tennessee. His ego was growing with his swimming improvements and he concluded he was too fast to go there.

The next was Stanford. He and his teammate Brian Retterer from the Junior Team had a plan. They would both visit Stanford for fun, then the next weekend do their final visits and then both commit to Texas. On the trip to Stanford they were very impressed. They met the women's team and some of their great stars such as Janet Evans and Summer Sanders. They enjoyed the beautiful spring weather and parties. They loved everything about Stanford, so what would they do now?

Josh Davis was 17 years old, hopscotching the country from school to school and party to party, and seeing beautiful college girls. He loved the experience. The following weekend he visited Texas while Brian visited the University of North Carolina. Brian's home was in Nevada and he decided to commit to Stanford. This change in their mutual plans was perplexing; Josh couldn't decide what to do.

Every night Josh knew he was going to get two phone calls—one from

Jeff Rouse who attended Stanford and the other from his old high school teammate Kit Patterson who swam at Texas. Each urged him to come to their school. This went on for two weeks as Josh weighed a full scholarship offer from Stanford (valued at $100,000 in 1990) with a full scholarship in-state offer from Texas (valued at $20,000 in 1990). Josh couldn't decide. He finally asked his parents for help.

"We think Eddie Reese and Kris Kubik would be great mentors for you, Josh," his father told him.

There are many reasons that Eddie Reese has enjoyed recognition as one of the world's finest and most successful swim coaches. There are a record number of team championships, Olympic medals, and fast times. But at the core of his legacy is a man who has modeled living a life of joy and affection for those around him, especially his family and swimmers.

"We love watching you swim, Josh, and having Texas just an hour drive up the highway would be wonderful," pitched in his mom. Texas had also just won three consecutive NCAA team championships. Josh committed to the University of Texas.

The spring travel, the missed training and the parties began to catch up with Josh. He swam poorly in the summer championships and became sick in August before going off to college.

1990–1991 THE UNIVERSITY OF TEXAS – Freshman Year

The Texas program was a substantial increase in Josh's training load. There were nine swim sessions per week, three strength sessions and two dry-land sessions. All the training was done with great competition and the kind of consistent effort that characterized one of the most successful college programs in history. During the first year he grew an inch to 6' 2" and gained 20 pounds, now tipping the scales at 185.

The University of Texas Training Program Overview

6:30-8 am –   Water Training – M-W-F
              Major emphasis on worst stroke for individual medley
              swimmers – Josh breaststroke
1:45-2:45 pm – Land Training
              M-W-F Heavy weight training
              T-Th- Dry-land training: Rope Climb, running stadium steps, "wheels"
3-5:00 pm –   M-Fr Water Training
              Occasional distance work, but primarily middle distance group
8-10:00 am – Sat Water training

The team was in pursuit of their fourth consecutive NCAA Championship. The team captain was Shaun Jordan. Shaun had learned a great deal about how to train, how to compete, and how to develop your personal independence from Doug Gjertsen, Kirk Stackle and other seniors when he came to UT. They had learned it from Kris Kirchner and Scott Spann before them. Texas had built a legacy of perpetual leadership by passing on important experience from one class of leaders to the next.

The team embraced the freshman and Shaun began to mentor Josh. The captain made sure he felt comfortable within the team, invited him to his house, gave him a bed to sleep in as needed and helped teach him about college life. The "invisible training" done away from the pool was critical to adapt to their training program so they monitored their sleep and limited their alcohol and participation in parties as they prepared for the March championships.

Josh earned the nick name "The Otter" from Eddie Reese because Josh always seemed to want to be at the pool. He arrived 20–30 minutes before afternoon practice, just to say hello and see his teammates and coaches. After practice he stayed in the water, like an otter. He fiddled with his hand pitch and did some extra turns. He was constantly exploring ways to get faster. Recreation swimming began shortly after the varsity. At times the lifeguards had to ask him to move out of the way for the recreation swimmers. He may have been only a freshman, but he was a wonderful leader by example of loving the sport of swimming and working toward achieving your potential.

Practice was very competitive. Coach Reese often gave the swimmers times to achieve or heart rates to control, but frequently Josh and his teammates were so competitive they raced with greater intensity than what Eddie asked for. When it came time to taper down for the conference and NCAA Championships, Shaun counseled Josh, "Once the hard work is done, swim pretty. Don't go fast unless Eddie tells you to. It takes confidence to rest." The freshman complied.

By the time the third and final day of the NCAA Championships arrived Josh Davis was totally a part of and engaged with his team. The team points' competition was close with Stanford; there was another NCAA title on the line. The Longhorns enjoyed a home pool advantage, which included the marching band assembled behind the starting blocks, ready to launch into the Texas fight song. Josh prepared to lead off the final event, the 400-yard freestyle relay, to clinch the championship. Shaun Jordan admonished the freshman, "Don't mess up this relay, Davis!" Josh's lead-off leg was 44.0 and the team won the championship.

After the season, the team had a two-week training break but hosted recruits. The weekend visits included a large amount of time and energy, try-ing to attract the best swimmers in the country to Texas to continue the run of national team titles. By the time school recessed in May, Josh was exhausted from the academics, training and especially the parties. He planned to train at Texas over the summer but went home for a two-week break. He went to Alamo Heights practice and tried to swim but was completely drained of en-ergy. The boy who couldn't stop moving and rode his bike everywhere around the neighborhood was gone. Instead was an 18year-old young man, shattered from running his body into the ground. For two weeks Josh was sick in bed.

Joan Davis saw the life her son was moving toward. He was compromis-ing himself and his values to please others. He wasn't free to be his true self. He was following the crowd, not following his own path.

She entered his bedroom.

Josh rolled over.

"Josh, I really think you have a gift," his mother began.

Josh not only loved his mother, but he also respected her deeply. He saw the warm intensity in her eyes. He listened carefully.

"You won't be able to live that gift if you treat yourself this way. We raised you in faith that God is your creator and that your path should be to use the special qualities that you're blessed with to follow Him. But any faith you do have, or can have, is not the faith of your parents, it is yours."

Josh had the most important epiphany of his life that day: that he truly didn't know how to live life to the fullest and even if he did know, he didn't have the power to do it anyway. His mother's concern caused him to take a deep look at his life. *Why was I here on earth? What's my purpose? How am I supposed to live life to the fullest?* A part of his answer came from a passage he read by C.S. Lewis who said about hard times, "God whispers to us in our pleasures, speaks to us in our conscience, but shouts in our pains: It is His megaphone to rouse a deaf world."

Even though Josh had experienced much swimming success in a few short years it left him empty inside. The pain and frustration he felt lying in his bed that week led him to a posture of humility, a place of attentiveness to listen with his heart and not just his head about how much God loves us and wants the best for us. Although he went to church his whole life a major transformation took place quickly.

He accepted his mother's words and realized that his faith was his own. He had to make his own choices in his life. His first choice was to acknowl-edge Jesus Christ as his new "head coach" and adopt the Bible as his manual for how to live his life.

Josh began to read the Bible more frequently and found a passage (Ephesians 4:29) that said, "Let only wholesome words come out of your mouth." He stopped cursing and using profanity. He read another passage (Ephesians 5:18), "Don't be drunk with wine...instead... be drunk with the Spirit of God." He stopped drinking alcohol. His favorite movie became the story of athletes and their passion for excellence chronicled in the "Chariots Of Fire." He loved the climax of the movie when Jackson Shultz hands Eric Liddel a note saying "He who honors me I will also honor." Josh felt that God had given him a gift to not only swim fast, but the gift of forgiveness and eternal life. He felt that to give his life to God was the least he could do since Jesus had given His life for Josh.

Josh returned to Austin with a firm code for living that was articulated by his continued reading of the Bible and following its teachings. His swimming improved in relation to his lifestyle changes. Despite his poor spring training, he got back on his feet for the summer season and competed for the USA at the 1991 World University Games in Sheffield, England. His times in the 100-meter freestyle (51.5) and 200-meter freestyle (1:51.4) showed improvement, but to qualify for the 1992 Olympic Team he would need to become much faster.

1991–1992 THE UNIVERSITY OF TEXAS – Sophomore Year

When the freshman class of swimmers arrived in Austin in the fall, the vast majority of them had been positively impressed by Josh Davis' capacity to find and enjoy parties on their recruiting trip the previous year. They looked forward to Josh leading them to more of the same during the school year, but were surprised to find that he now had other interests. Josh was at a Bible study each night, rotating among the Fellowship of Christian Athletes and other groups. On the weekends he sought more religious education in the social atmosphere of the Baptist church group. Josh stuck to his new path even if his teammates didn't understand it.

There was an enormous difference between the coaching of Al Marks and Eddie Reese. While Al used his system of recording sets to help his swimmers improve, Eddie relied on his intuition. He had been a fine swimmer himself at the University of Florida. He learned about physiology in graduate school and began to refine his coaching as an assistant coach for the Gators. Eddie came to practice with a plan to develop endurance early in the season and speed late in the season. But he blended some of each type of work into each part of the season. He never wrote down a practice ahead of time. His right-brain, left-handed instincts were more effective in assessing the team each day and providing them with a difficult but productive workload. His art, or perhaps his genius, was to be able to read the bodies and minds of two to three dozen college men on a daily basis and provide them step-by-step adaptation.

The 1992 Olympic Trials were held the first week of March in Indianapolis. The IUPUI Natatorium was packed with swimmers and tension, characteristic of the most competitive swim meets in the world. There was competition from post-graduate swimmers who had put life on hold to make the team. The very best American collegiate swimmers were all there and one also had to contend with the talented and hungry horde of young club swimmers. The electric atmosphere was more than Josh could handle. His performance was tense with an element of fear and he showed little improvement in his best times from the previous summer (51.0 and 1:51.2). But his renewed faith accepted the experience as an opportunity to learn. He studied the swimmers who made the team and how they handled themselves. Josh prepared himself for the future.

The NCAAs followed 10 days later at Texas. After the long emotional experience in Indianapolis, the results were disappointing. Stanford ran away with what was their first of three titles in a row. They had a stellar sophomore class including Josh's National Junior Team teammates Brian Retterer and Joe Hudepohl.

1993 THE UNIVERSITY OF TEXAS – Junior Year

Since Josh wasn't on the Olympic Team, he devoted his summer to hard work and preparation for the 1993 winter season. His personal changes began to pay off for him during his junior year. At the NCAA Championships he won the 200-yard freestyle (1:34.25) and finished third in the 200 individual medley (1:45.6). His performance helped him move into a leadership role on the team. Josh became one of the team's best swimmers while living a lifestyle that his teammates were growing to respect.

In the summer he began spending a little time training with Craig Harriman in Colorado as part of a Christian organization called Athletes in Action. Josh chose to promote the group and be public about his faith by competing under the team name Athletes in Action, although he did most of his training at Texas. At the national championships he qualified for the US "A" squad to compete in the Pan Pacific Games in Kobe, Japan. There he won the 200-meter freestyle in his best time of 1:48.5, which was the third fastest time in the world. He also anchored the victorious American 800 freestyle relay. Suddenly Josh Davis was one of America's outstanding swimmers.

1994 THE UNIVERSITY OF TEXAS – Senior Year (Team Captain)

Eddie Reese wanted team captains who could help him move the team where he wanted it to go. Texas had a legacy of team captains who did this well. For 1994 Josh Davis was honored to be the University of Texas captain. But more than an honor, it was an affirmation that he was valuable to the team. Whether he was on the US National team or leading the Longhorns, Josh sought ways to serve his team. He did this by embracing each individual and searching for their needs. Generally all that was needed was a kind word, but the experience he offered the freshmen was invaluable.

At the 1994 NCAAs Josh contributed three top-five individual swims, but he wasn't quite as fast as the previous year. He did conclude his college eligibility swimming second again on the Texas 400 yard freestyle relay. The result was a new American Record (Fink 43.4, Davis 42.1, Eckerman 43.3 and Gary Hall Jr. 42.1) in a time of 2:51.07. Stanford came out on top of the team standings and Josh looked ahead to his postgraduate career.

A major event took place in Josh's life that year which led him to a wonderful transformation in his life. He had noticed Shantel Cornelius in the university dining hall, who was a sophomore on the volleyball team. They quickly became best friends and fell in love. Josh and Shantel planned to be married in May of 1995.

The relationship added another important part of life to balance with swimming and school. Josh had completed his eligibility to swim for Texas and would receive only one more year of scholarship assistance while he completed his studies. He had begun to pursue swimming at a late age and loved its active lifestyle and the process of getting faster. He longed to make the Olympic Team and represent the United States in Atlanta, but that was two and a half years in the future.

The 1994 US Long Course National Championship meet was the qualification for the World Championships in Rome. If you proved yourself in the Trials, you advanced to the world's biggest swimming stage other than the Olympics. In the preliminaries of the 200-meter freestyle his time of 1:49.3 was fast enough for an individual berth on the team. But in the finals, his swim was sixth place. He also placed sixth in the 100 freestyle (50.5). He swam to fourth place in the 400 freestyle (3:52.7) and as well as in the 200 individual medley (2:03.). He showed versatility and a solid performance, but he missed the chance to compete individually at the World Championships.

Josh's placement at nationals did qualify him to make the trip to Rome but just to swim the preliminaries of the relays. He sought ways to learn from this experience, just as he had at others. World record-holder Giorgio

Lamberti was there in his home country, working for a public relations firm and making a paid appearance. Josh found him.

He enthusiastically introduced himself. "You're the great Lamberti who holds the world record in the 200 freestyle?"

Giorgio smiled. "Yes, I am."

Josh continued, "My name is Josh Davis and I swim the 200 freestyle."

"Nice to meet you."

Josh said, "1:46.6 is so fast! I've always wanted to meet you!"

The Italian was gracious. "You can swim that fast, too."

Josh thought to himself, *What a crazy Italian. How do you drop 2 seconds after college? But what if he's right? If this 5'11" guy can do it maybe I can too?*

1995 THE UNIVERSITY OF TEXAS – Fifth Year

US Swimming offered a small monthly stipend (about $1,200 per month) for any swimmer with a time in the top four in the world. If Josh could swim fast enough to earn it, he would have the means to help pay his rent, provide food, and fund his travel to swim meets. The major post-graduate swimming competition that winter was the Pan American Games in Mar del Plata, Argentina. He swam terribly. His time of 1:51.92 in the 200-meter freestyle was his slowest since high school. He won the 400 freestyle but with a mediocre time of 3:55.9. He was moving in the wrong direction. He began to ask himself, *Do I really want to do this? Am I going to get married and train the next year only to miss making the Olympic Team?*

Since Eddie Reese has coached at the University of Texas, Kris Kubik has been his assistant coach each year except a short hiatus in the early 1980s. Coach Kubik works in many capacities. One is to shadow Eddie and provide support wherever he needs it. An additional part of Kris's role is to be a caregiver and a teacher to the athletes on the team. Kris witnessed the life challenges that Josh was facing. He noticed Josh losing hope to fulfill his potential and perform on the 1996 Olympic Team. One day at practice Kris approached Josh.

"Josh, I found this picture of a gold medal that will be awarded at the Atlanta Olympics. I laminated it for you. It's just the right size for your wallet." Kris had cut the image out of a publication and handed it to Josh. "You're the best 200 freestyler we've got and next summer you're going to win your own gold medal, Josh. When you win yours, give me back this one."

Josh and Shantel married on May 27th and moved into a 600-square foot garage apartment without air conditioning or heat. The price was right at

$295 per month and added to their monthly bills that totaled exactly $1,200. Fortunately Shantel had one more year remaining on her volleyball scholarship, but Josh needed a job. He found one as a secretary in a balloon factory.

He trained from 7–9:00 a.m. Then he went to work from 9:30–3 and answered the phone and took orders. As the hours passed, he became more and more tired and more and more hungry. He was back training from 3:30–5:30 p.m. Josh liked to be busy, but living this way wasn't conducive to being a world-class athlete. After four days he made a decision. *I can't make my goals this way*, he thought to himself. *I will trust in God to provide for us in this time of need.*

Josh came home and told Shantel of his desire to leave his first job. There were two reasons she could accept Josh's wishes. One was she too trusted that God would help them put food on their table and keep their little apartment even though it wasn't clear where the funds would come from to do so. Her second reason was she held in her heart unconditional love and support for her new young husband. With her encouragement to focus on his strengths and his goal of making the Olympics, Josh's courage grew stronger.

Josh quit his job and trained full time.

Shantel and Josh worked out a good deal at the dining hall to eat and Josh trained through the summer with growing optimism. He frequently reminded himself of the gold medal in his wallet, the faith of his coaches in him, his faith in them, as well as in God. He tackled training sets with the attitude that he was an Olympic gold medalist. He was taking one step at a time, one set at a time and moving forward.

By the 1995 US Long Course Nationals at the Rose Bowl pool in Pasadena, California, he had invested a great deal of work and was ready to perform. His eyes were set on making the United States "A" squad. They would compete in the Pan Pacific Games at the newly constructed Olympic pool in Atlanta, home for the Olympics themselves in a year's time. It would be the perfect preparation for his second goal: to win an individual Olympic medal.

His time in the 200-meter freestyle (1:51.13) was 10th. His 400 freestyle (3:54.52) and 100 freestyle (50. 31) times had improved from the winter, but he finished fifth. There was no invitation to the Pan Pac team. His choice was go to Fukuoka, Japan, for the World University Games with the "B" squad or go home. Many of the other Olympic hopefuls had elected to go home and begin preparation for the big Olympic-year push. Josh placed his trust in God and thought to himself, *Maybe God has a plan for me that is in Japan.* He agreed to go with the "B" team.

Training Samples University of Texas

Long Course:

Warm-up:	4 x (100 free, 100 back) 10 seconds rest
Swim:	8 x 100s on 1:40
Kick/Drill:	8 x 50s on 1:00
Swim:	100 easy on 2:00
Swim:	4 x 400 free on 5:00, descend 1-4
	100 easy on 2:00
	4 x 300s back on 4:30, descend 1-4
	100 easy on 2:00
	4 x 200s free on 2:30, descend 1-4
	100 easy on 2:00
	4 x 100 back on 1:30, descend 1-4
	100 easy on 2:00
Warm-Down:	6 x 100s stroke drill, easy
Total:	6,300 meters

Short Course:

Warm-up:	400 free, rest :10
	2 x 300s IM, rest :10
	Pull 3 x 200s free, rest :10
	Kick 4 x 100s stroke, rest :10
Sprint:	20 x 50s (odds free on :40, events stroke on :45)
Swim:	300 easy on 5:00
Sprint:	20 x 100s free on 2:00 (Josh average :51)
Swim:	200 easy on 5:00
Kick:	800 on 13:00, moderate pace
Pull:	500 on 7:00, moderate pace
Total:	6,800 yards

Reprinted with permission *Swimming World Magazine* July 1998

The 1995 World University Games team was nearly completely made up of swimmers who had yet to achieve success at the two premiere international competitions: the Olympics and the World Championships. The same was true of the coaches. The men's squad was led by Coach Don Wagner, an assistant coach at USC and the women's squad by Coach Ira Klein, an assistant coach at Auburn University. The swimmers and the coaches were unpretentious and had a great deal left to prove in their sport.

Josh Davis was elected captain of the men's team. His joyous participation in training and the team's preparation was a great example for all to follow. He showed no sign of disappointment in not being on the "A" team. Although time was running short to get his ship back on course toward the Olympics, his faith comforted him. He put into practice and lived what he read, to be "drunk with the joy of life." Josh made his team better and in the process bettered himself.

One of the traditions in swimming for the USA National Team was that first-time members must demonstrate some type of talent to the other team members in a show just before the competition began. The entertainment took place in a stark, windowless room. The 54-member squad, plus coaches and staff squeezed into the room, which was barely big enough to hold them. Josh and his teammates received the efforts of the performers with hysterical laughter. The dramatic skit of a magician and his dense assistant who was confused over whether to fold and prepare a not 'banana" or a "bandana" to blindfold his boss for their performance brought down the house when the assistant smeared the mauled banana across the magician's eyes.

The highlight of the talent show was the final act. Coach Todd Kemmerling entered the makeshift stage as a crippled old wise man from the Far East. He sat in a chair and read the story of the "USA Tribe." Todd's writing skills were masterful, and each team member's name was plugged into the story but used with an altered meaning to tell the tale. For example, Sarah Anderson and Beth Jackson heard their names as "and-her-son" and "Jack's son." Josh and his teammates leaned in silence together toward Todd. Not a word was uttered or even a slight movement made for fear of missing the moment when their names would be used to tell the story of this team of swimmers that came from America for victory in Japan.

Josh's tenth-place performance at the nationals in the 200 didn't earn him an individual swim in the 200-meter freestyle in Fukuoka. However, he did qualify to swim on the 800 freestyle relay. He asked Coach Wagner if he could lead off the relay in order to perform an official individual time. Perhaps if Josh swam fast enough he could earn a monthly support stipend from US Swimming. Even more importantly, he needed an opportunity to restore a trajectory toward his Olympic dream. The coach agreed.

On the second evening of the competition Josh Davis led off the American 800-meter freestyle relay in the time of 1:48.1. It was the fastest 200-meter freestyle in the world for 1995. He had improved his time from the nationals by three seconds. Later in the meet he won the 400 freestyle in his lifetime best time of 3:51.9 and swam his best-ever 100 freestyle (50.3) to finish third.

Josh Davis was swimming faster than any time of his life and the Olympic Games in Atlanta were just 12 short months away.

1996 OLYMPIC YEAR

Josh trained through the fall of 1995 with renewed optimism but living a Spartan financial existence with his new bride. US Swimming had a policy that relay lead-off times didn't count for financial support. This kept Josh from receiving a training stipend from the national organization. Nevertheless, each night he and Shantel shared the highlights of their day together in their little apartment. She was in the final year of her volleyball scholarship at Texas, which gave them a small subsistence. Although they were poor, their faith kept them optimistic about the future. Each day Josh continued to care for his UT brethren as though he were still captain of the team, looking for places to serve with a smile or gentle advice.

During the winter break from school, the Texas team went to the Hickory Street all-you-could-eat salad bar after practice. Each team member was given meal money from the University since the dining halls were closed and the athletes were still required to stay at school and train. Josh Davis went with them to the restaurant. When they sat down to eat, Josh held only a bottle of water.

"Aren't you going to eat?" Kris Kubik asked.

Josh smile and said, "Money is pretty tight."

Kris knew that US Swimming was funding a program called the "Resident Team." Some of them were not ranked among the top-10 swimmers in the world in any swimming event. At the same moment those swimmers were in Hawaii training and living in a nice hotel presumably with no financial concerns. He was upset that the number-one ranked swimmer in the world in the 200-meter freestyle couldn't afford a meal.

The next day Kris wrote out on a piece of paper in as large writing as would fit: "NUMBER 1 RANKED SWIMMER IN THE WORLD CAN'T AFFORD FOOD!" He faxed it to the US Swimming main fax number, with an additional explanation about Josh's plight. Shortly thereafter the policy was amended and Josh was given a stipend of $1,200 a month.

JOSH DAVIS – In his words Starts and Turns

Starts - Grip and Rip It (Be Steady but Ready): Grip hands over the front of block with taut arms. Lean back just a millimeter. When the horn sounds pull yourself forward and try to rip the top of the block off! Enter your whole body through the hole that your hands make with a perfect streamline. Swim your first few strokes when you breakout to maintain the maximum momentum from your start.

Turns: Put your feet on the wall with your back flat in a streamline position. If you had a box under your knees it would fit perfectly. Your shins will be up higher than your trunk. Drive yourself off the wall past the flags. Just like your start, use your momentum from your push off by swimming (not breathing) your first few strokes when you break out from the turn.

The 1996 Olympic Trials were set in the same location and same time as the 1992 Trials. It was early March and in Indianapolis. This time Josh had carved out a comfort zone based on three years of international and NCAA experience. He had experienced many ups and downs but had refined his physical and mental preparation. Josh continued to compete under the banner of Athletes in Action, promoting his faith on his cap.

The first day was the 200-meter freestyle. Josh placed first in the preliminaries (1:49.34). He managed the pressure well enough in the finals to finish second (1:49.29) and he was on the team! Josh was overjoyed and pulled himself from the pool and went to celebrate with his Texas team. Craig Harriman from Athletes in Action grabbed him and spun him around with delight. Eddie Reese and Kris Kubik stood quietly off to the side, enjoying the excitement.

During the trials Josh also finished in a tie for third in the 100 freestyle (49.97), putting himself in position to earn a spot on the 400-meter free relay in Atlanta. He focused on winning an individual medal and relay gold. For the next six months he lived and trained like an Olympian, aided by the funding support. Josh loved the life of a full time swimmer and he was finally able to afford to live it.

1996 OLYMPICS GAMES – Atlanta, Georgia – USA

By the time Muhammad Ali jogged into the Olympic stadium for opening ceremonies in Atlanta, the US government had spent 1.8 billion dollars to stage the event. The city had spent 500 million dollars more for infrastructure to support the mass influx of spectators from around the world. The improvements transformed Atlanta into a spectacular setting for this international quadrennial celebration of sport, which also was the highlight every four years for the sport of swimming.

The 200-meter freestyle was the first day in the Olympic program. In the morning heats Josh swam the third fastest time of 1:48.63. The field was very tight together—only one second separated first, Sweden's Anders Holmertz, and eighth, Britain's Paul Palmer (1:49.05). Josh swam faster in the finals (1:48.54) but so did most everyone else. His seventh-place finish was disappointing. He missed his goal of winning an individual medal.

The competition in the United States to make an Olympic swim team is always the greatest of any country in the world in nearly every event. But if you do make the US team and swim the appropriate events, the American depth almost always gives a swimmer the chance of winning a relay gold medal. The 100 and 200-meter freestyles offer the most opportunity for relays. The reason is that there is both a 4 x 100-meter freestyle relay and a 4 x 200-meter freestyle relay, each of which require four relay members and two alternates.

The second day of swimming was the 800 freestyle relay. It had once been an event that the United States dominated. It tends to represent a country's collective work ethic in swimming, since it is the longest relay in the Games. In 1992 the United States finished third. At the World Championships in Rome in 1994 they fared worse, finishing fourth. To add to the challenge in Atlanta, John Piersma, the top US 200 freestyle finisher at the US Trials, swam so poorly he was pulled from the relay. Brad Schumacher, with a history primarily as a water polo player was a late substitution, getting the nod just a few hours before the start of the relay.

The US strategy was to put their fastest man first and compete for the gold as long as possible. Josh Davis led off. He bettered his individual performance by five-tenths of a second with an awesome time of 1:48.0 and put the USA into the lead by a full second. Anchorman Ryan Berube sat by the warm-up pool swishing his feet back and forth, saving his valuable energy and tried to relax until it was his turn to swim. Joe Hudepohl, a veteran from the '92 team held a narrow lead with a 1:49.2 split. Brad Schumacher swam third. Australian Michael Klim closed in on him (1:48.0) as did Sweden when

Anders Holmertz split 1:47.0 to move his team from seventh to third. Only four-one-hundredths of a second separated the three teams. The USA was second. The crowd was on its feet seemingly trying to will the home team to victory.

Ryan Berube dove into the pool for the American anchor leg with the stadium noise at a deafening pitch. An American victory seemed improbable before the event, but in Olympic swimming, emotions and excellent preparation creates shocking performances. Gradually Ryan inched forward and the Aussies and Swedes lagged behind. Josh, Joe and Brad were going crazy at pool side. If it was possible for a human to orbit the facility without wings they might have done it. Josh Davis had been excited for the Harmony Cabana Club races. Churchill High School was even better and once upon a time the University of Texas relays seemed as though they were the pinnacle of a swimmer's existence. But nothing matched the heart-pounding race for the United States and Olympic gold. Berube extend his lead on the third length and buried the field on his last 50. He touched the wall first (1:48.4) and the USA had won the gold medal!

The foursome was still sky high when they entered the press tent a few minutes later. They sat side by side. Ryan Berube said, "Tonight I left the nervous part to Josh. I sat with my feet in the diving well to relax and not let the adrenaline start pumping. I'm certainly not the one who won (the race). There are three guys sitting beside me who are just as big a part of it" (*Swimming World Magazine* September 1996).

Joe Hudephol finished up. "This is the one I've been working toward since '92. No one expected us to be here, and I know I'm speaking for all of us when I say this is one of the greatest moments in our lives."

Josh got ready for the 400-meter freestyle relay. It was scheduled for the day after next.

America's legacy in the 400 relay was even stronger than the 800. The US had never lost the race in any major international competition. On the third day of the Olympics, Alexander Popov nicknamed "the Russian Rocket" had successfully defended his 100-meter freestyle title from 1992. He was in top form and had just missed his world record time. His Russian team was strong and there was talk that his squad might be able to upset the Americans for the first time in Olympic history. Qualifying right behind the Americans in the heats was the German team.

Gary Hall was the silver medalist in the 100 and he was going to anchor the American relay. Team captain Jon Olsen was going to lead off. But the other two swimmers were determined by the fastest legs swum in them morning heats. Dave Fox (50.46), Scott Tucker (49.68), Brad Schumacher (49.19) and Josh Davis (49.07) swam in the preliminaries. Brad and Josh earned the other two legs for the finals.

Based on the morning swims the Russians were in lane two, Brazil in three, the USA in four and Germany in lane five. The starter called for quiet and the hushed silence roared in the swimmers' ears. The horn sounded, the crowd exploded and eight swimmers flew off the start. Olson's lead-off split of 49.94 left the US in fourth behind Brazil, Germany and Australia, and only one-hundredth of a second ahead of the Russians. Popov swam second for Russia and Josh also was in his favorite second place spot for the US. Josh's task was to keep the race close enough for the American's to come from behind on the finals leg. Popov opened a large lead over the field with his stellar 47.88 split, but Josh kept the Americans just behind the Germans when he split 49.00 and within striking distance of the Russians. Brad Schumacher (49.02) caught up a half-second on the Russians, but the US still trailed in third behind them and the Germans.

Gary Hall blasted off the block on the final leg for the American team. Josh was one of thousands cheering wildly and watching the glorious sight of Gary slicing through the water, quickly closing the gap on the Russians for the USA. Gary turned at 50 meters in stunning speed, splitting 21.8 and by the time he was at the 35-meter mark he was in the lead. His split of 47.45 was the fastest of all time, and the USA and Josh Davis won another gold medal in Olympic record time (3:15.41).

There was only a .02 seconds difference between the 400 freestyle relay splits of Josh Davis and Brad Schumacher. Perhaps being an otter and working on the technical details of his strokes during his career made the difference for Josh? Surely it did. Consequently when it was time to pick a freestyle swimmer for the preliminaries of the 400 medley relay he received the assignment from the coaches. The USA easily won the gold in the finals and Josh his third Olympic gold medal.

When all the Olympic sports were completed, the male athlete with the most gold medals from the Atlanta Games was Josh Davis with three. He had lived a spectacular Olympic experience and looked forward to advancing his career in his sport—that is, if he could earn a living at the same time.

PROFESSIONAL SWIMMING

Professional swimming was building in America slowly but steadily. Josh was enjoying swimming more than at any time of his life, but he was faced with the task of figuring out how to make a living at it. He had three relay gold medals, but he didn't have any for his own individual performance. The four months immediately after the Olympics seemed like the most opportune time to set up sponsorships and endorsements for the future.

Shantel was pregnant, so the joys of their imminent family were coupled with quickly devising a family financial plan. Josh made an agreement with sports agent Billy Stapleton to help him. Billy had the perfect credentials. He was a Texas swimmer who competed in the 1988 Olympics in Seoul. He had proven himself as the agent for Lance Armstrong, the world's greatest cyclist, and had an office in a beautiful high-rise building in downtown Austin.

Several weeks went by and there were no calls from Billy's office. Finally one day the phone rang and Josh was hired for his first appearance. His assignment was to go to a car show and Coke was going to pay him $300 to promote their product and sign autographs. Josh drove to Waco for the show, but no one greeted him. He found a piece of cardboard and wrote out a sign that said, "Come see an Olympic Gold Medalist" and signed autographs for anyone who appeared.

In February he was offered a second appearance. There was a huge hot-tub show in the area and Josh was hired by a hot-tub company to sit in the tub and sign autographs for two days. He lingered in the tub and smiled and waved at the people passing by. If they stopped, he signed autographs and chatted. During his breaks he walked from booth to booth shamelessly asking for free handouts of power bars, towels or anything that the various hot-tub sponsors would give him. There was an engaging young man working at a shoe booth and they struck up a conversation. His name was Evan Morgenstein. When Josh continued on his way, Evan followed him and they exchanged their contact information. A few days later Evan called Josh on the phone: "I've got three deals for you." He listed off the deals for Josh, which amounted to more work than from all the time he had spent with Billy Stapleton's firm.

Josh Davis was poor and hungry for a means to make a living and swim. But he was also very loyal. He wrestled with the idea of accepting work with Evan or waiting for it from Billy. Finally, he called his father for advice.

"Dad, I'm really torn. I made a commitment to Billy Stapleton and his firm to work with them. But I'm not getting any work," Josh told him. "I have the chance to work with another agent with some opportunities that seem promising."

Mike Davis told his son, "You're responsible for your family now, Josh. You need to provide for them and if there's work you should take it."

Josh called Billy Stapleton, apologized for leaving his company but explained that he could get work through Evan Morgenstein and needed to accept it.

Josh and Evan immediately began a clinic company and set up dates for Josh to visit local clubs. The concept wasn't new, but Josh's love of teaching, children and superb public speaking skills produced a budding product that would serve swimming and his family wonderfully for years to come. Josh found through the clinics that he was more than just a great teammate, but an inspirational leader of thousands of young swimmers throughout the country.

He also signed small contracts with Brooks Shoes and the Home Shopping Network. In return for appearing on a billboard for a new apartment complex, he and Shantel were able to move into a new apartment for free. The competition was growing between the swimsuit companies. Speedo, Nike, TYR and Arena were all competing to get the most high-profile athletes wearing their suits. Speedo rewrote Josh's contract and increased their sponsorship dollars. Despite having never met his goal of earning an individual medal, he was earning an aggregate income in excess of $100,000. There was no school to contend with, just swimming and speaking. Josh Davis was living a dream!

1997–1998

The balance between swimming and professional appearances was challenging, but in the summer of 1997 Josh won the 200-meter freestyle (1:49.0) at the World Trials in Nashville. He was recognized for his passion for individual and team achievement when the "A" team elected him captain for the World Championship team.

Josh Davis had been team captain for his high school, university, National Junior Team, and now the USA National "A" Team. He never drew a line in the sand and asked a team to cross it with him. But he did walk a line of a wholesome lifestyle and modeled behavior that was responsible, loving and joyful. Numerous teammates admired him and therefore leaned toward his spirit to learn more. At his heart was the conviction as a man of faith who felt free to be himself in virtually any circumstance. Coupled with a passion to swim fast, his example reflected the consummate team captain.

The 1998 World Championships were hosted by Australia in Perth. The star was the Aussie's Michael Klim. His performance started in the 200-meter freestyle on the first night when he nearly broke the world record. By the time he finished he had seven medals, four of which were gold. Australia nearly beat the USA in total medal count. The best Josh placed was ninth in the 200 freestyle. He did swim on the American 800 freestyle relay, but the relay finished fourth, and he had not been fast enough for the 400 freestyle relay.

In 1999, his income and business ventures were growing very favorably. The Davis family had bought their first house, but his swimming continued to plateau. In August, he finished fifth place at the Pan Pacific Games in Sydney. His 200 time was only 1:48.9, representing no improvement at all over the past three years.

Suddenly it was the fall of 1999 and the Olympic year. Josh was no closer to winning an individual medal at the Games than he had been four years before. In reality, if you aren't improving in the sport of swimming you tend to be losing ground simply because of the rest of world is getting better. The 200-meter freestyle was a great example. Pieter van den Hoogenband from the Netherlands, two young Australian sensations, Ian Thorpe and Grant Hackett, as well the Aussie's standard-bearer Michael Klim were all lowering the world record and moving further out of reach for Josh.

2000 OLYMPIC YEAR

There is a productive tension that exists in nearly any sport between a coach and an athlete. When a young swimmer starts out they may need a coach who displays the characteristics of a cheerleader. When they mature they may need a coach who functions more as a consultant. There are moments when if an athlete holds even a small degree of fear for their coach, it can motivate them to push themselves further than they would if left alone.

Eddie Reese had been patient with Josh's entrepreneurial enterprises, knowing that he had responsibilities to his family. He loved Josh Davis and liked to say, "There are some swimmers where you earn your income coaching because they are challenging. Josh Davis is special. I would coach him for free." But the relationship had become too comfortable to bring out the best in Josh. Eddie believed in "shocking the body" with different kinds of work in practices during each season, and even from one season to the next. What happened next shocked Josh.

Eddie called Josh into his office. He knew a change was necessary in order for Josh to meet his potential and help the United States Olympic Team in 2000.

"Josh, my brother Randy is moving to Austin in January. I think you should go swim with him."

Josh couldn't believe what he was hearing. Leave Eddie? Leave Kris? Leave the University of Texas brethren he trained with? Leave the beautiful Texas Swimming Center that had been home to his greatest high school feats for four years and another nine years as a Longhorn and then a post-grad? One-half of his life and nearly all of his swimming success had been prepared, built, and achieved in this environment. He was more than shocked; he was stunned. But he knew in his heart that as usual, Eddie was right.

On February 1, 2000, Josh Davis began training with Randy Reese at the Circle C Swim Club. Randy had a well-earned reputation for success with innovative and a no-nonsense approach to coaching. Just like the Harmony Hills Cabana Club had been, Circle C was located only two blocks from Josh's new house and he was swimming outdoors. He could walk or ride his bike, but there would be no more missed practices. Randy had been creative and effective for many years in Florida, innovating different training modalities. He utilized everything from wheelchair races, to the rope climb, to swimming up and down rivers to train swimmers.

Since leaving the University of Florida in 1990 he had taken a break from coaching. But he returned with the same expectations and optimism for the success of his swimmers that he'd had at Florida.

Josh and Randy sat down by the pool in their first days together to discuss where they were going.

"I don't understand why no one has gone 1:43 [in the 200 freestyle]," Randy said to Josh. "1:43!" Josh laughed. "That's fast! No one can do that."

But Randy was matter of fact in his belief in Josh and his capacity to improve. "Of course it is," the coach told him.

Dr. Ron Karnaugh joined the group with his own goals for an individual Olympic medal. Ron had made the 1992 Olympic Team, graduated from the New Jersey Medical School in 1999, been the oldest male swimmer ever on the US National team at age 31, and in 1998 finished third at the World Championships. He had trained in various locations over the years, finding the program he believed could help him most effectively. For nine years Josh had trained with his teammates at Texas and didn't like getting beat in practice. But now he had someone to compete with each day who wasn't a teammate in a traditional sense. A part of his daily mission was to win every training set and beat Dr. Ron in practice.

Randy's program was intense. Warm-up for the long course practice in the morning was a mere 200 swim, 200 kick, 200 pull. Afterward they swam fast until the two hour time frame was complete. The evening practice was short course or the width of the pool, and consisted of a five minute warm-up, 30 minutes of kicking while wearing shoes and then "baskets."

The baskets were essentially buckets linked to a pulley system that extended to a bar and pulley 40 feet in the air. A belt around Josh and Ron's waists hooked on to the rope and to the pulley system. Randy loaded an appropriate progression of weight into the basket for each swimmer. Swimming across the pool with the rope connecting them with the movable basket of weights could be very difficult but prompted them to hold onto and control the water to move across the pool. With a descending weighted basket assisting their return to the starting side of the pool, sometimes they worked on perfect technique and other times they were instructed to swim as fast as they possibly could.

The training in the pool was the entire program. Josh never did a push-up or ran. He also never missed practice. By the March nationals he was adapting to the new type of work and swam his best time of 1:47.9 in the 200-meter freestyle. Four weeks prior to the Olympic Trials, however, he was exhausted. After 300 meters of warm-up he got out of the pool.

"I'm done," he said to Randy.

Randy had told him he was one of his hardest workers ever, but this was the first time Josh felt Randy was disappointed in him.

Josh said, "I'm 27 years old and I just can't keep training this hard."

Josh had always trusted his coaches and Randy had brought him to a new level of conditioning, but his intuition told him he had to rest. Over the next few weeks he followed his long-developed plan during taper. This included lots of "pretty swimming" with occasional strong or paced efforts. He made sure he was getting a maximum amount of sleep and visualized every detail of his races. He had also learned to double his intake of water, vegetables and fruit, and avoided anything with saturated fat. He may have missed some training sessions over the past four years, but his daily living habits and knowledge of how to prepare himself for peak performance was superb.

The Olympic Trials were August 9–16 in Indianapolis. The 200-meter freestyle preliminaries and semi-finals were swum on the second day. Josh won both stages of the team selection. In the finals on the third night he was nervous. But when he put his hands on the edge of the starting block the nervousness disappeared; a sense of calm came over him. When the horn released him on the start he took off on the first 100, put his feet on the 100 wall and recorded the fastest 100 split during a 200-meter freestyle in the history of swimming of 50.9. He tired on the final 50 but touched the timing pad in 1:47.2, breaking Matt Biondi's 12-year-old American record—the same record he admired so much when he saw it in on television when he was 15 years old. His 100 freestyle was also his best time of 49.4 and earned him a spot in at least the preliminaries for the 400 free relay in Sydney. The hope for an individual medal was alive.

2000 OLYMPIC GAMES – Sydney, Australia (Team Captain)

The team training camp was at the Rose Bowl Aquatic Center in Pasadena, California. Josh was elected team captain again. He trained in the middle-distance group under Coach Mark Schubert, with Lenny Krayzelburg, Scott Goldblatt and a 15-year-old named Michael Phelps. The youngster was tremendous on butterfly sets, but Josh enjoyed beating him on all the freestyle sets and the other strokes. Michael generally stayed in the water for an additional 15 minutes after the older men finished their training.

When the team was about to fly to Sydney, Josh had an unusual request. His third child was about to be born. If he flew home to Austin, it was possible to induce labor and he could meet his child before flying to Australia. The coaching staff reluctantly agreed. Josh flew to Austin and the team flew to Sydney. After a quick hello to his new baby, the father of three was back on a plane to rejoin his team for the Olympics.

The interest and enthusiasm for the sport of swimming in Australia is unlike any other country in the world. It is the smallest continent on earth, but also a country and an island. The population is most dense on its eastern and southern coasts. Swimming makes sense for safety and there are swim schools everywhere. Being a swim star in Australia is akin to starring in European football (soccer) in or being a basketball or baseball star in the United States. The country was pulsating with the excitement of hosting the Olympics and especially the sport of swimming.

The Olympic order of events was the same as the US Trials. The 200-meter freestyle finals were on the third day and Josh was competing with Australia's most sensational young swimmer, 17-year-old Ian Thorpe. He stood 6' 5" tall, had size 17 feet and had opened the swimming competition by trouncing the field in the 400 freestyle and setting a new world record (30:40.59).

Ian qualified second for the finals behind the Netherlands' Pieter van den Hoogenband and Josh Davis qualified fourth. They sat in the ready room of the natatorium with the other four finalists. When called, they walked single file into a dark hallway and then through a doorway onto the pool deck. Lane one went first, then two, three, four, then Ian and then Josh out onto the pool deck. As the first swimmer passed through the doorway to the pool the crowd stood and clapped. When Ian Thorpe entered the room the better part of 18,000 hometown fans roared a deafening sound.

Josh Davis got off to a quick start and turned first at the 50 with a time of 24.4. Halfway through the race it was van den Hoogenband 50.8, Thorpe 50.9, Davis 51.0 and Massi Rosolino from Italy 52.0. Josh was still a strong third at the 150 turn. But on the last length, Rosolino just edged by him and out-touched him at the finish for the bronze medal with a time of 1:46.65 to 1:46.72. Even though Josh had bettered his American record, he was seven-hundredths of a second short of the goal that he had worked so hard for. Giorgio Lamberti had been right: Josh Davis could swim as fast as he did—or just about. The swimmers exited the pool and the media swarmed the three medal winners. Josh walked by himself to the warm-down pool. He cried like a baby.

The Australians were on fire in Sydney. Josh earned a silver medal by swimming the preliminaries of the 400-meter freestyle relay. Ian Thorpe passed Gary Hall at the finish in the finals and the Australians broke the world record (3:13.67 to 3:13.87). The Aussies ran away with 800-meter freestyle relay when Thorpe (1:46.03), Klim (1:46.40), Todd Pearson (1:47.36) and William Kirby (1:47.26) destroyed the global standard with a blistering effort (7:07.05). Even with Josh's superb split, the American team of Scott Goldblatt (1:49.66), Davis (1:46.49), Jamie Rausch (1:48.74) and Klete Keller (1:47.75) was a distant second (7:12.64).

The last day of the Olympic swimming program consisted of only the 50 freestyle, 1500 freestyle and 400 medley relay. Most swimmers have completed their swimming by that day and their four years of extreme commitment and preparation is over. Many swimmers look forward to watching athletes in other sports compete over the second half of the 16–18 day festival and are beginning a week-long party. But on the last day of the 2000 swimming events Josh wasn't thinking about partying; he looked forward to flying home to Austin to be with Shantel and their three children.

During warm-up for the men's 1500 freestyle finals, the otter went back into the pool for one last Olympic swim. American Chris Thompson was warming up. When the US team was paired for roommates in the Olympic Village Chris didn't have one, so Josh and roommate Neil Walker invited him to join them. Thompson was finishing a tremendous year, having made the US team at the Olympic Trials with a time of 15:09. Chris qualified sixth for the finals the previous day with a time of 15:11.21. Warm-up wasn't going well. His coach Jon Urbanchek was giving him times for his pace 100s and they were slow. Chris was upset and cussing. Josh was watching. The coach was trying to calm Chris, but nothing was working. It was an impending disaster.

As a leader there are times to speak up and times to keep quiet. Josh Davis considered the merits of his choices. He caught Coach Urbanchek's eye, sensed his frustration and agreement to intercede. Josh interrupted warm-up. "Chris stop; come here a minute," Josh said. Chris complied. "Chris, you've come 10,000 miles here to swim. This is your moment. Your parents have flown around the world to watch you. They believe in you. Your teammates are up there in the stands getting ready to cheer for you. They believe in you. There are thousands of kids across America that would give anything to have earned the opportunity you have in front of you." Josh went on, "Go show the Aussies what you've got! You can do this!"

Josh and Jon stood by the media area and watched the 1500 race. Chris Thompson improved his time to 14:56.81, broke the American record and beat Alexei Filipets of Russia by seven-hundredths of a second to win the bronze medal, the exact difference in time that Josh needed to win a bronze medal for himself. Chris pulled himself from the pool and walked to Josh and Jon. He wore a huge smile. "Thank you both. I never could have done that without either one of you." Of all the moments and all the medals in his swimming career Josh Davis liked that one the best. His mother and his father had laid a foundation for him to lead. His coaches provided the mentors when he needed them. But eventually he followed his faith and American swimmers followed him.

Following the Olympics, Josh Davis continued to swim and attempted to balance his family, business ventures and training. He had visions of continuing to swim at an elite level at least through the 2004 Athens Olympics. But by 2003 he had gradually traded the priorities of earning a living and taking care of his growing family for the daily time to train to perform at a world-class level. At the 2004 Olympic Trials, he did move through the preliminaries and into the semifinals of the 200-meter freestyle. But in the finals Michael Phelps lowered his American record in the 200 freestyle and took over the reins as America's new standard-bearer in the event. Josh stood with his mother and father and watched this passing of the torch. Along with him was his wife Shantel. Josh was positioned in his most important leadership roll—to that of his five children beside him.

Josh Davis and his family live in San Antonio, Texas. He networks with other Olympians and conducts masterful clinics around the United States, inspiring and giving young swimmers leadership and motivational skills to help them reach their potential. He continues to give to swimming and be one of America's greatest leaders in the sport.

LENNY KRAYZELBURG

September 28, 1975

THE SURVIVOR

(lane 1) Lenny Krayzelburg 1988, (Rt) Baby Leonid in Ukraine

Living in communist Russia at the peak of the Cold War in 1975 was challenging. The "war" wasn't a military conflict but an economic standoff between the West (Japan, Western Europe and the United States) and the Soviet Union and several other Communist countries in Eastern Europe commonly called the "Soviet bloc." The soaring economic success of countries in the West underscored the stagnant economic growth of these communist countries in the Soviet bloc. War had broken out between the Soviet Union and Afghanistan. Families formerly concerned for their economic survival became increasingly worried about the survival of their sons who were sent to fight in the Afghan war. This is the story of a boy who survived—and became one of the greatest swimmers on the planet.

* * *

"Bileti!" (Beel-YET-ee!)

The usher at the stadium gate called, "Bileti!" ("tickets" in Russian)

"Bileti!"

Oleg Krayzelburg shifted his nine-month-old son Leonid into his left hand and reached his right hand into his pocket for his ticket.

"Bileti."

Soccer was the king of sports in the Soviet Union. Oleg Krayzelburg loved the FC Chernomorets, their local team in Odessa, a seaport on the Black Sea in southern Ukraine. He carried Leonid into the city soccer stadium.

The crowd roared as the players dashed onto the field to begin the game. That roar has the same sound in Russian, in English or in any language around the world. The 4,000-seat venue overlooked the commercial shipping docks. Oleg loved the escape of being a soccer fan and longed for his son Leonid to be an athlete. He looked across the green field, at the faces of adoring fans, and hoped he might be watching his boy play in a stadium like this one day.

Ukraine was one small part of the massive Soviet Union, slightly smaller than Texas, and the government controlled most aspects of life. The Soviet central administration was so powerful that political dissidents were regularly harassed, persecuted, or sent to prison by the KGB, or secret police.

1979 EARLY YEARS – Ukraine, USSR

In 1979, the government opened a window of opportunity for citizens to apply to leave the country and Oleg seriously considered it, but he wasn't ready yet. Much of the Krayzelburgs' family lived in Odessa, and that family life was very important to them. Odessa had a pleasant climate with very little snow in the winter months. People came to vacation on its southern coastline along the Black Sea, and it was considered by many to be the "French Riviera" of the Soviet Union.

Free enterprise and capitalism didn't exist in these Soviet states. Sports programs were run by the government. The two programs were called Dynamo, conducted by the GPU (The State Political Directorate) and later the KGB, the Soviet internal security and secret police, and the other was the Red Army program. The infamous East German sports system that gained notoriety during the Cold War was modeled after the Soviet system. If a child showed talent at nine or ten years old, they were invited to go to a boarding school for athletes. At the school they had professional coaching and the opportunity to train daily with other talented young athletes.

Oleg Krayzelburg operated a government-owned coffee shop; his wife

Yelena worked as an accountant in a shoe factory. Leonid was their first child, followed by sister Marsha who was born three years later. Soccer programs began for children at age seven. While the Krayzelburgs waited for the soccer programs to start, they put their five-year-old son in swimming lessons. Leonid attended classes a few times per week for 30 minutes each. He quickly began to show some talent in swimming, so his father abandoned thoughts of his son becoming a soccer player and supported the development of his swimming skills. By the age of nine he showed enough ability to be selected for an Army sports school located right in Odessa. That allowed him to live at home and still receive excellent coaching.

By fourth grade, Yelena walked Leonid to the trolley at 5:45 in the morning to ride to the sports facility where he trained with a group of 35 boys and girls at 6:30 a.m. After running, they swam for about an hour and then went to class at the school across the street, which started at 9:00 a.m. At 2:00 p.m. Leonid and his training group walked back across the street and trained for another two to three hours.

Lenny Krayzelburg Developmental Progression:

8 and under: 3 x week,
                 30 minutes, basic skills
9-12 years old: 5 x week
                 1 hour swim, 1 hour dry-land, mix of skill and conditioning
                 6 x week
                 2 hour swim, :30 minutes dry-land, mix of skill and conditioning
13-14 years old: 6 x week
                 1:45 minutes, 4,500 yards mix of skill and conditioning
15-16 years old: 3-4 x week
                 1:30 minutes, 4,000 yards

The Krayzelburgs were Jewish. Most of the time, making friends with other boys and girls in his swim group made the long training hours enjoyable. But lingering resentment and continuing persecution of Soviet Jews, although not carried to the horrendous extremes seen in Europe during World War II, could still make life difficult and painful. At times Leonid's classmates insulted him with ethnic slurs that they had likely heard at home. Leonid's instinct was to defend his honor and that of his family and fight. Many citizens of Jewish heritage had migrated out of the Soviet Union to Israel when given the opportunity, but the Krayzelburgs stayed.

The world of sports, and swimming in particular, was one in which Leonid felt at home. His athletic ability earned him respect among his peers. At age 10 he and the other swimmers were taken to the second-floor gym for instruction in lifting free weights, plyometrics, stretching and a full land program to strengthen their bodies and improve their swimming. At the pool his coach Vitaly Ovakymian was considered an expert. He had a history of success with swimmers at the European Junior Championships and Red Army National Championships, so when Oleg was told his son was "born to be a backstroker," the optimism grew for his son's future as a swimmer. Oleg attended practices whenever he could and followed Leonid's progress in earnest.

Leonid was meticulous in tracking his progress. At the age of 11 and 12 he kept a log book of his practice times. Coach Vitaly Ovakymian reviewed it with him each week, observing his improvements in practice and meets. At the end of the season the group traveled by train to the Red Army National Age-Group Championships in Kiev. Oleg made his way there to watch. Leonid was improving and eventually winning silver medals in backstroke. Other swimmers weren't so successful. The long days with early mornings took their toll, overtaking their desire to improve, and they stopped swimming. By 13, about 85 percent of the group Leonid had started with was no longer swimming.

On October 1, 1988, Mikhail Gorbachev became the Head of State of the Soviet Union. He acknowledged the unhappiness of many Jewish families with life inside the country and offered them the opportunity to make their exodus. Oleg and Yelena Krayzelburg yearned for freedom and the opportunity they had heard about in the United States. They also recognized that the war between the Soviet Union and Afghanistan had been at a stalemate since 1979. It was likely that their son eventually would be drafted and sent to fight, so leaving Ukraine might mean the difference in his survival. The Krayzelburgs had never traveled far from home, but they decided that emigrating was worth the risk. They found a needed sponsor in New York and Los Angeles and began making preparations for moving to California.

The "Cold War" wasn't a physical war; it was a war of policy and economics and emotion. For the Krayzelburgs leaving their home and extended family was not easy. In the summer of 1988 Leonid Krayzelburg was about to enter seventh grade. He needed to tell his coach he was leaving but didn't know how. Finally he summoned the courage two weeks before the family departed. Coach Vitaly had an Armenian heritage and could empathize with the desire to be free of the tight-fisted rule of the Soviet Union. He understood the Krayzelburgs' desire for a better life for their family and children and supported them in their adventure.

1988 COMING TO AMERICA

In the fall of 1988 they left the Ukraine. Other Soviet Jews were moving to Israel, but not the Krayzelburgs. They wanted America for their family, but the process required to do so made the journey more difficult. First they stayed three weeks in Austria, then two months in Rome. Oleg asked and received from Coach Vitaly a dry-land program for Leonid to do while they traveled so he wouldn't miss training. Even if a pool wasn't available during their entire travel period he made sure his son did the required number of stretch cord pulls, ran, and stayed in generally good condition.

In March of 1989 the Krayzelburgs finally arrived in Los Angeles and into a life that was completely foreign to them. Other families from the Soviet Union had moved to West Hollywood and so did the Krayzelburgs. Unable to speak English yet, they could easily communicate and make friends in that neighborhood. They needed many things: Social Security numbers, a home, and Oleg and Yelena needed work. That would take time, but within 10 days Leonid's father made certain he was on a swim team.

Oleg had asked the Jewish Federation to help them find a good swimming program in the area where they lived. Several teams were closer to where they had moved, but Team Santa Monica had been developing swimmers at a Junior and Senior National level and therefore was the one that had the most appeal. Head Coach John Apgar had an impressive résumé, having worked for legendary USC Coach Peter Daland early in his career. Coach Apgar and the club agreed to allow Leonid to swim without any fees since his parents had no income.

The Krayzelburgs didn't own a car and could not speak English. But Leonid's parents showed him the bus stop nearest to their home and the route to swim practice. He got on the bus at Wilshire Boulevard and rode it to Westwood. Then he transferred and rode another bus to Pico Boulevard, ending with an eight-block walk to the pool. The daily trip took up to an hour in each direction. Leonid never missed practice.

Team Santa Monica – 1989-1990 – Coach John Apgar

M-W-F 6-7:30 pm, T & Th 7-8:30 pm, Sat 8-10:00 am

        4-5,000 yards per practice

        Warm-up with stroke drills

Weekly Pattern:

Monday: Short rest endurance, plus speed set

        10 x 300s on 4:30

        Each 300 faster, each 100 within each 300 faster

Tuesday: Endurance/Threshold Set 2400-3200 yards

Wednesday: Speed - 8 x 50s on 3 minutes

Thursday: Test set with pace element

        5 x 100s best 100 plus 20 seconds on 1:20, 500 descend 100s on 6:00

        5 x 100s best 100 plus 20 seconds on 1:20, 500 negative split on 6:00

        5 x 100s descend to as fast as possible on 1:20

Friday: Aerobic

Saturday: Speed or Competition

Coach Apgar designed his practices to force the athletes to think. They always began with a warm-up of drills working on perfect technique. Leonid had an unusually high head position when swimming backstroke. They worked to try and balance out his body and let his head sink back in the water more. John used single-arm drills and asked him to stay on his side for six kicks and keep his core firm and slide on his side. Another regular drill series of 100s John called "wig-wag." They swam a length with their arms always moving opposite each other; then they kicked a length and then swam a length with hands touching above their eyes; then they kicked another length. After warm-up, they swam a major series. Leonid was amazed at how fast his times were compared to in the Ukraine. Then it was explained to his chagrin that he was swimming in a yard-pool, not a meter-pool like in Odessa.

Coach Apgar or Theresa Poscuso, the assistant coach, drove him to the weekend swimming competitions. In the early morning hours in his neighborhood the previous evening's nightlife was finally tapering off when he was picked up in front of his apartment at about 6:30 a.m. Leonid tried to understand the English of his drivers. He gradually learned the language, modified his first name to a more American-sounding "Lenny," and in about nine months his parents were also speaking English.

In the summer of 1989 he qualified for the Southern California Junior Olympics. This wasn't a great feat for a boy so highly ranked in Russia. But at almost 14, he was only 5' 6" tall and weighed about 135 pounds. He was becoming frustrated with how fast the swimmers were at Team Santa Monica and getting tired of the long trip to swim practice. Plus he didn't seem to be getting faster. He loved to follow sports on television and especially the Los Angeles Lakers basketball team. By the middle of the winter of 1990, Lenny started to think about giving up swimming to become a basketball player.

There were new opportunities in America for the Krayzelburgs, but there were also challenges. They didn't realize how incomes could be so meager for people who weren't highly trained. Oleg found work as a cook for $2.50 per hour, Yelena worked as a pharmacy assistant. Their income was small but steady, and life seemed to be settling down in their new country. Like many of the swimmers in the Ukraine who participated in the long hours of swim training at their sports school, Lenny was getting worn down from the extensive hours devoted to swimming and especially the commute to practice. It appeared that he would be another victim of burnout.

During dinner one night Lenny told his mother and father, "Swimming isn't fun anymore."

Dismayed, his father replied, "But you spent all that time developing your swimming skills in Odessa, Son."

Lenny was firm in his feelings. "The Santa Monica kids are so much faster than me. I'm not getting anywhere."

Oleg restrained his emotions and forced himself to listen to his son.

Lenny went on, "I'm really enjoying basketball. I practice whenever I have free time. I want to be a basketball player."

His father didn't say much, but the dream of his son becoming a prominent athlete seemed to be over.

"I want to stop swimming," Lenny insisted.

Two weeks passed without Lenny swimming. Yelena Krayzelburg talked with her son. "Lenny, your father can't sleep at night," she said. "He won't say it but he's very disappointed that you stopped swimming."

Lenny understood the sacrifice his parents made to bring their family to America. He loved and respected his dad tremendously and wanted to find a solution. He agreed to swim a few days a week in a very low-key program near their home called the Westside Jewish Community Center (JCC) Swim Team. This gave him time to play basketball and he also picked up some jobs. He worked in the local library and then for the City of West Hollywood Recreation Department when he turned 16. In the summer he worked as much as 30 hours a week lifeguarding and doing odd jobs. His 100-yard backstroke time was only 1:00. When he went to the Far Western Championships with the team, his times reminded him how far he was from being competitive with the swimmers in the area.

The local high school, Fairfax, didn't have a swim team. Lenny joined the junior varsity basketball team, which gave him a greater social connection in the school. At the same time he swam four to six hours a week at the JCC. He started his senior year in high school in the fall of 1992. He had grown and now stood nearly six feet tall. Despite his small amount of training, he swam very respectable times of :54 and 1:55 in the short course backstroke events. It wasn't fast enough to attract the interest of college coaches, but for the little work he had invested he showed potential.

1993 SANTA MONICA CITY COLLEGE

His parents hadn't realized how expensive a college education was in America. He wrote letters to various college programs looking for scholarship help from swimming. Each day he looked in the mail, but there wasn't any correspondence from any schools. In January of 1993, his search for a path to college continued. There is an extensive junior or "community" college (JC) system in California. Each JC affords students in the local community a way to attend the first two years of college at minimal expense, after which they usually enter a four-year college or university. Lenny and a friend went to Santa Monica City College to get an application. They decided to take a look at the pool and stopped at the pool office.

Coach Stu Blumkin was sitting at his desk. "Hi, Coach, my name is Lenny Krayzelburg. I'm a swimmer and go to Fairfax High School." Stu thought a friend was playing a practical joke, since Fairfax had no swim team. But when Lenny told the coach his times the coach's interest grew. Lenny's enrollment in a class at SMCC, while still a high school senior, allowed him to attend the "community workout" in the morning.

The morning swim session at SMCC was a mix of college swimmers, Masters swimmers, tri-athletes and lifeguards. Lenny was inspired by the positive attitudes displayed there. They loved the crisp morning air, the steam floating off the water, the sun rising, and devoting time to improving their health and fitness. One of the Masters swimmers and coaches, Gerry Rodriguez, took a great interest in Lenny. Every day Gerry gave Lenny a tip about his backstroke technique. For the first time since he left the Ukraine, he was back training twice a day. Lenny finally felt like his swimming was improving.

In the morning he trained at Santa Monica City College and after school

at the JCC, along with lifting weights on his own. By summer he was working during the day and didn't have enough time to attend the JCC practices.
He competed in the Los Angeles Invitational (now known as the Janet Evans
Invitational) near his home and was reminded again of how much of a difference there was between him and the top swimmers in the area. His times were
1:05 and 2:15 in the 100-meter and 200-meter long course backstrokes. He sat
in the stands with his coach during finals and watched the swimmers in the
finals turn in times of :57 and 2:02. *They seem to be in another world, both in
their times but also in their skill development,* he thought. When UCLA coach
Ron Ballatore walked by, Lenny watched with reverence.

In the fall of 1993 Lenny took more classes at Santa Monica Community
College. The athletic program included water polo in the fall but no swimming until February, so Lenny joined the water polo team. They did swim
training in the morning and water polo in the afternoon. Oleg Krayzelburg
made it clear to Coach Blumkin that Lenny shouldn't be wasting time with
water polo. But the coach argued that Lenny needed to enjoy himself at the
pool and this was a great way to do that. His basketball skills helped him
adapt quickly to water polo and he was voted onto the all-conference team.

By the spring of 1994 he had been training twice a day for much of the
year and it showed in his level of condition. Bruno Diederichs became a
regular training partner and the two challenged each other. Coach Blumkin
was so excited about the pair that he shared his enthusiasm with his coaching
colleagues at SMCC. The baseball coach stopped in to watch part of practice
one day.

He asked Stu, "Where is your kid that's going to be so good?"

Stu pointed to Lenny and said, "He's going to be the best in the world."

On a series of 5 x 200 yards backstrokes leaving every 4:00, Lenny swam
short course yard times from 2:01 on the first one to 1:52 on the last one. Clearly
he had the ability to adapt to Stu's training quickly and swim fast in practice.
The coach wrote his prediction as "the best in the world" on a piece of paper,
put it in an envelope and sealed it.

SMCC TRAINING - Coach Stu Blumkin

Training Season February through May Championships

Mon-Friday: 6-7:30 am –3,500-4,500 yards per practice

               M, W, F 30 minutes of weights, 1 hour of swimming

               T-Th 1.5 hours of swimming

Mon-Friday: 1:30-3:30 – Water training 5,500 yards per practice

Saturday: 8 -10:00 am

Saturday 2/5/1994

Warm-up: 300 swim, 200 IM SD, K 3 x 300

Main Set: 8 x 100s 10 seconds rest (3 back, 5 free), 200 easy

               2 x 300s back on 4:30

               5 x 150s free on 2:00

Speed Set: 12 x 100s broken on 1:45 (10 seconds rest at the 50, 5 seconds rest at the 25s)

               Goal is both to work on proper pace and to go fast

               Lenny 6 free (50 at 28, 25s 11.8), 6 back (50 at 28, 25s at 12.5)

               5,000 yards

Monday Morning 2/7/1994

Warm-up: 400 swim, 400 choice, 300 kick

Pull: 6 x 150s on 2:10

Kick: 6 x 150s on 2:40

Main Set: 3 x 300s on 6 min (1 free, 1 back)

Loosen up: 200 easy

Sprint Set: 2 Fast 75s on coaches watch Lenny (39, 38)

               4,300

Wednesday Morning 3/30/1994

               400 free, 300 IM Reverse Order Stroke Drill, P – 800

Kick: 4 x 200s on 3:15

Swim: 600 Build Swim (start 60% effort, finish 80%)

Speed Set: 5 x 100s on 2:00 (Lenny free times: 56, 55, 54, 53, 53)

Loosen Up: 6 x 75s easy on 1:45

Speed Set: 2 x 200s back broken (First set: 4 x 50s on 1:00 28s, Second set: 4 x 50s on 1:15 27s)

               4,150

Provided by Coach Stu Blumkin

The Junior College Championships were held the first week of May at Cypress Community College. A German citizen named Matthias Otte was one of the top swimmers and attended Orange Coast College. On the first day of the three-day championship he won the 200-yard individual medley (1:54.24) and on the second day the 100-yard butterfly (50.13). He appeared to be on his way to being named "Swimmer of the Meet." But Lenny won the 100 back in 50.71 and the stage was set for the two to face off in the 200 backstroke on the final day of the meet. Lenny loved to race. He touched the wall first at 1:47.9, establishing a new national record just ahead of Otte at 1:48.3. Lenny Krayzelburg was named "Swimmer of the Meet."

Ron Ballatore at UCLA had sent Coach Blumkin an international swimmer before when he wasn't ready for the UCLA academics. Stu looked forward to returning the favor and the campus was close to the Krayzelburgs' home. In Russian culture, parents don't like having their children go far from home, so the proximity of UCLA was perfect for them. But in the spring of 1994 UCLA suddenly and inexplicably dropped their men's swimming program. The school Lenny seemed destined for hadn't survived the creativity of the UCLA administration and commitment of its athletic director.

Stu wanted Lenny to be able to continue to train in the summer and since UCLA wasn't an option, he called Coach Mark Schubert at USC to see if Lenny could train there. "Our summer program is open to anyone that can keep up," Mark told Lenny. Lenny explained that he needed to work in the afternoons but that he could attend the morning practices. They agreed to give it a try.

Lenny was unaware that his coach for these morning sessions was one of the most successful coaches in the history of American swimming. Mark Schubert's legacy at the Mission Viejo Nadadores included 44 National Club Championships as well as two NCAA championships at the University of Texas with the women's teams. His swimmers had achieved extraordinary success on the world stage, including the grandest arena of all, the Olympic Games.

Lenny may not have appreciated who was coaching him but he did notice the swimmers: Janet Evans was world record-holder in the 400 and 800 meter freestyle events, Kristine Quance was one of the premiere American women swimmers, and Jim Wells was a top American middle-distance swimmer and backstroker. All were part of the training group at the Trojan Swim Club. Lenny liked to chase people in the pool and now he had some of the best in the world to go after.

Lenny raced to keep up in warm-up and as long as he could through each session. Since he was swimming only the morning practice, while his training group became more tired during the afternoon session, Lenny recovered and came back ready to chase them the next morning. It didn't take long for many of the swimmers to start asking, "Who is this guy?"

He may have been annoying to them, but the coaches noticed his attitude and ability. Assistant coach Don Wagner told him, "Lenny, you can be one of the best backstrokers in the world." That was great to hear but far from any sort of reality in Lenny's mind. Right now he was the local Junior College champion, trying to figure out how to go to a four-year university.

During the first week of July, the Trojan Swim Club, including Lenny, drove up to Santa Clara for one of the major competitions leading up to the US Nationals. In the 200-meter backstroke he finished second to 100-meter world record-holder Jeff Rouse, swimming a time of 2:03.9. He was amazed. It was the 16th fastest time by any American in the event in 1994. The previous summer he had watched the same swimmers in awe, and now he was competing with them.

One the reasons for Mark Schubert's enormous success as a swimming coach was his belief in his system of training and the capacity for most athletes to succeed in it. His record of success dated back to the 1976 Olympics and the accomplishments of swimmers such as Shirley Babashoff and Brian Goodell who won Olympic gold medals. There was proof in his confident and laser-focused approach with athletes. When they returned to USC after the Santa Clara International meet, Coach Schubert looked Lenny squarely in the eye and told him, "Lenny, you can be the best backstroker in the world." To back it up he told him, "I'd like to offer you a full scholarship (grant in aid) to USC."

The Krayzelburg family was thrilled at the offer of an opportunity for Lenny to attend a prestigious private school like USC. However, there were still many complicated NCAA rules to comply with for Lenny to be eligible to compete in swimming and earn financial assistance at USC. He needed the credits necessary to compete in the NCAA system from SMCC. Lenny and Coach Schubert agreed that during the following year he would forgo college competition while enrolled in the junior college system. That would allow him three years of eligibility for swimming representing the Trojans.

During the school year of 1994–95 Lenny trained in the afternoon with Santa Monica and then went to his job with the West Hollywood Recreation Department. In the mornings he swam at USC but not with the team. Because the NCAA rules prohibited him practicing with the team before he enrolled at USC, he swam in the diving well by himself. On some of the days his friend Gerry Rodriguez kept him company. They were lonely practices and without the chasing opportunity that he longed for, but it was a temporary inconvenience that he happily put up with.

1994-1995 USC – Sophomore Year

In March of 1995, the five-year wait for citizenship ended and Lenny Krayzelburg became an American citizen. When school let out in the spring he was able to train full-time at USC with Schubert's Trojan Swim Club. Brad Bridgewater, one of the top backstrokers in the country, had transferred to USC from Texas and he and Lenny could now push each other in practice day in and day out.

At the summer nationals at the Rose Bowl Aquatic Center in Pasadena, Lenny earned "Rookie of the Meet" honors when he finished 14th in the 100-meter backstroke (57.1) and 10th in 200 (2:02.5). There were three USA National teams picked for international competition based on performance at the nationals. Lenny just missed qualifying for the World University Games Team by a few tenths of a second. Suddenly Oleg and Yelena Krayzelburg's dreams of their son becoming a world-class swimmer were alive again!

1995-1996 USC – Junior Year

In the fall of 1995, school was about to start and Lenny was excited to be a USC student. He had an apartment and a roommate. Coach Schubert called him to his office. "I've got bad news, Lenny. Our compliance office has determined that you're still a few credits short of being eligible to swim at USC this semester." Lenny had to go back to SMCC to get the credits. USC didn't have the backstroker they thought they would have for the first semester. Lenny had to wait to be a Trojan. He had survived much worse circumstances and he would survive this one. When the school semester ended in December he was finally able to train full-time with the college team and Brad Bridgewater.

The 1996 Olympic Trials were held in Indianapolis the second week of March. Lenny was quickly thrust into the most pressure-packed competition in the United States for the most elite swimmers. But he was so new to national level swimming he didn't have great expectations.

On the third day Lenny improved his best time to 56.1 and finished 11th, just behind Bridgewater. The pair of USC-trained swimmers had more endurance than speed. They had kept up in practice with many of the USC freestyle swimmers while swimming backstroke. Two days after the 100, Brad qualified first (2:00.16) and Lenny second in the heats (2:00.49). The final heat was going to be introduced before the finals, but Lenny had a problem.

"Lenny, USA Swimming has no information for a bio for you," Coach Schubert told him. No one had ever considered that detail in Lenny's amazing progress into the upper echelons of the swimming world. With the help of the USC Sports Information team, they quickly put something together.

Brad Bridgewater handled the immense pressure of the final race to qualify for the Olympic Team nicely when he dropped his time to 1:59.1 and won. Lenny, however, did not perform as well. Oleg Krayzelburg was disappointed. His evening swim was slower than the preliminaries (2:00.7) and he finished fifth. Despite the results, the fact that just the previous year he was taking courses at SMCC and not competing and now was in the finals of the Olympic Trials was remarkable. He left Indianapolis with growing confidence that his rise to the top of the swimming world in backstroke was not a matter of "if" but "when."

Two weeks later the NCAA Championships were held in Austin, Texas. Lenny succumbed to the flu and finished last in the 100-yard backstroke (50.2). In the 200 he beat only two swimmers (1:48.8). His distress at not performing well for his team was tempered by the great support that his teammates and coaches showed him. He survived the terrible disappointment.

An Olympic summer was starting and his teammate Brad Bridgewater was after a gold medal while Lenny set his sights on winning his first USA National Championship. They took a three-day break and then began training. Their normal routine was 10 practices per week, with Wednesday mornings, Saturday nights and Sundays off. The morning sessions were from 6–8 a.m. and the evenings 2–4 p.m. They did an hour of dry-land or weights after the evening practice.

Coach Schubert planned the sessions so that two were dominated by pull sets of 3-5,000 meters, two on kicking, two on race-pace speed, and two on quality repeats alternating easy/fast swimming. When it came to long course performance on swim sets, Lenny and Brad were quickly becoming the strongest backstroke training tandem in history. They pushed each other constantly. If one of them saw the other speeding up, the other one speeded up, too.

USC Training Bridgewater/Krayzelburg 1996 – Coach Mark Schubert

M, T, Th, F, S 5:45-8:00 am – First 15 minutes stretch, then 2 hrs water training
M-Fri 2-4:00 pm -   Water training
M-W-F 4-5:00 pm –   Dryland Circuit: Sit-ups, Legs (squats, lunges,
                               froggies, etc), Med Balls, Surgical Tubing
T-Th 4-5:00 pm, Sat 8-9:00 am – Weight Training

Long Course Training Sets:
Two Major Pull Sets/wk: 4 x 100 free on 1:20, 400 Back on 5:00
                            4 x 100 free on 1:20, 2 x 400 back on 4:55
                            4 x 100 free on 1:20, 3 x 400 back on 4:50
Two Speed Sets/Wk:

                            3,000 Mixed Warm-up
                            150 easy
                            50 fast (:28 or better), 2 x 100 easy
                            100 fast (1:00 or better), 3 x 50 easy
                            150 fast (1:31 or better)
                            Repeat 4 times

Two Quality-Descend Sets/wk:
                            9 x 200 back
                            3 on 2:40, descend to 2:10
                            3 on 2:50, descend to 2:08
                            3 on 3:00, descend to 2:05
Two Major Kicking Sets/wk:
Short course yards: 50 easy, 25 underwater, 50 easy, 50 underwater
                            50 easy, 75 underwater, 50 easy, 100 underwater
                            (one breath before each turn)
                            Repeat 4 times

Reprinted with permission *Swimming World Magazine*

"I have always respected my coaches," Lenny explained later. "They give their best to conduct practice and I should do the same as a swimmer. My respect for Coach Schubert was so great because every day he came ready for practice. Every day he was focused and giving his best, so how could we give any less?" Lenny's way of showing his coach respect was through his effort and performance in practice.

The Olympics were in Atlanta the last week of July and the US Nationals in Ft. Lauderdale the second week of August. On July 26th Lenny sat at home watching the finals of the 200-meter backstroke on television. Brad Bridgewater won the gold medal (1:58.54). Lenny's phone rang immediately. The sound of a crowd cheering was in the background.

Mark Schubert's voice came through the phone, "Lenny, in four years this could be you."

Lenny responded, "Mark, I will do everything possible to make that happen."

Mark Schubert was solidifying an Olympic dream and already looking ahead four years in the hope of coaching another swimmer to a gold medal.

On August 13th, Oleg Krayzelburg received his first close-up glimpse of an American gold medal when Lenny won the national championship in 1:59.3. Two days later he followed up with his best-ever 100 of 55.9 in preliminaries and captured another gold medal in the finals (56.1). It seemed that every time he swam he got faster. But even though he was a champion he was also a student of the sport. He was constantly scanning the competition, looking for ways to improve. His stroke technique was developing beautifully but he was still far behind the leaders in short course swimming when it came to the use of the underwater dolphin kick.

Lenny Krayzelburg's Backstroke Technique in His Words:

I establish my body position with head back, chin up high and strive for a "dry chest." There is no slow tempo in backstroke. I want my hips rotating so that I'm never flat on my back. My hand enters pinky first and scoops wide from my body. When I'm at my best, it feels as though I'm holding onto the rung of a ladder and moving my body down the pool.

When USC started school in September, Olympic 200 Champion Brad Bridgewater was taking a break and a hungry Lenny Krayzelburg started training for his junior year of NCAA swimming. Brad returned to training and they both competed at the US Open, swum in short course meters, the first week of December. Lenny was victorious over his teammate in both the 100 (53.6 to 54.5) and 200 (1:55.1 to 1:56.5). "If it weren't for training with Brad, I don't think I would have made it to this level," Krayzelburg said. "We have a real friendly rivalry. We always laugh and smile before a race. It's only two minutes or 55 seconds (long course) when we really want to beat each other; otherwise we're friends" (SW February 1997).

As the college season progressed, it became apparent that Lenny's improvement was on a collision course with the great Texas backstroker Neil Walker. Neil was very proficient at underwater dolphin kicking. Lenny studied videos over and over of his competitor's kicking to try and improve his own. He concluded that Neil Walker had less amplitude (wasn't as wide in its up and down motion) and was flatter on his kicks. He worked at improving the quickness of his kick and keeping it in a narrower sphere. His dual meet times of 1:43 and 1:44 were indicative of his adaptation to training even in the midst of the hard work. At the Pac 10 Championships in February, his time of 1:40.5 just missed Brian Retterer's American record.

At the NCAA Championships in March Lenny's underwater dolphin kicking was still no match for Neil Walker's. Neil won the 100-yard event easily (45.6 to 46.5) although Lenny's time was nearly a four-second improvement from his previous best the year before. Perhaps most impressive was that he had shrugged off the previous year's eighth-place finish to move up to second in the event. The much anticipated battle in the 200 evaporated when Neil broke his hand touching the wall in the 200 medley relay. Lenny won easily in 1:41.10 and was surprised to hear from Coach Schubert, "Thanks for being the first male NCAA Champion I've ever coached!" Mark's résumé of Olympic medalists and NCAA women's champions were many, but this was a first for him.

1998 - PROFESSIONAL SWIMMING

The year following an Olympics is frequently a year in swimming when Olympic stars take a significant break or retire. Lenny Krayzelburg was quickly moving in precisely the opposite direction. His improvement was so dramatic and the possibilities so great that he hungered for more. Fortunately he had a training partner in Brad Bridgewater who was intensely ambitious as well. They talked openly with Coach Schubert about breaking Tripp Schwenk's American record (1:58.3) in the 200-meter backstroke at the US Nationals in Nashville. This would also be the trials for the US Pan Pacific Team scheduled to compete in Fukuoka, Japan, two weeks later and the World Championships scheduled for Perth, Australia, in January of 1998.

At both local and international meets they both competed in, Brad and Lenny roomed together. While they basked in each other's friendship and the confidence that their preparation was superb, the subject of racing was never brought up. Lenny had more speed than Brad. On July 29th, he also had more than Neil Walker when he beat both him and Brad in the 100-meter backstroke 54.69 to Neil's 54.77 and Brad's 55.56. Three days later in the 200 the two Trojan teammates were far ahead of the field and the only two swimmers under two minutes. Lenny won handily in the finals with a new record of 1:58.04. Brad's preliminary time of 1:58.9 was the second-fastest time in the world to Lenny's.

The new American record-holder was asked about his Russian heritage by *Swimming World Magazine*. "I'm totally changed right now," Krayzelburg said. "I'm definitely an American. Michael Jordan is my idol." Always present was his attitude of gratitude; this time for his training partner, "Day-in, day-out, twice a day ... we're just going at it. It's amazing, and it's fortunate for me. He's definitely helped me out." On the cover of *Swimming World Magazine* for September 1997 was the face of a swimmer racing backstroke. The caption read "Special K, Lenny Krayzelburg, New American Record Holder." The picture was of Brad Bridgewater—a mistake?

After the nationals, the US National Team quickly departed for Fukuoka, Japan. The summer before Lenny had watched these swimmers on television, but now he was traveling as a teammate. His first indoctrination had come in the fall at a national team camp. Now he was wearing USA National team apparel and treated not only as a part of the team but also as an important contributor. This was a role he earned with his performances, as well as through his humble and respectful attitude to those around him. He was floating on a cloud enjoying this experience as a USA National Team member.

On August 10th, he swam even faster when he won the 100-meter backstroke in his best time of 54.4. The next day it was more of the same when he dropped his own American record in the 200 to 1:57.87. Lenny's energy distribution was precise with his even splitting of 58.26 and 59.5. Those performances earned him a spot on the World Championship team for 1998.

The World Championships were held in January of 1998 in Perth, Australia. The traditional swimming year is divided in half with training building to two peaks. For Lenny Krayzelburg the year was divided into thirds with a peak for the World Championships, another for the March NCAA Championships and a third for the summer nationals. Lenny and Brad trained well through the fall, but they were not as fast in Australia as they had been the previous summer. Lenny won the 200-meter backstroke in a close race (1:58.8). For the first time since his amazing progress began during his freshman year at Santa Monica, he had not swum his best time in a major meet. When he saw his winning time on the scoreboard he slapped the water in disappointment.

Coach Schubert gave him a stern education about his behavior when they had time alone. "In 1984 Rick Carey won the 200-meter backstroke at the Olympics and reacted the way you did, Lenny," the coach told him. "There are hundreds of thousands of kids who would give anything to win a world championship or an Olympics. When Rick did that he gave the impression to millions of viewers that he was a sore winner. I don't want to ever see you show that type of emotion after a race."

The coach's stern lecture was a huge learning opportunity for Lenny, pointing out that his behavior was now seen in a public way and he would be accountable for it. When he barely won the 100 (55.00), he showed no negative emotion in missing a best time. He led off the American medley relay and the US lost in a close race to the Australians. There was no hiding that bitter feeling but it served to fuel his motivation to make amends in the future.

The 1998 NCAA Championships were another disappointment for Lenny Krayzelburg. He was beaten in the 100-yard and 200 backstrokes both by Neil Walker and Tate Blanhik. They each possessed an excellent underwater dolphin kick that Lenny still lacked. The 200 was a close race, but Tate kicked past Lenny on the last turn and the pool simply was not long enough for him to overtake Tate before the finish. This ended any significant racing in the short pools for Lenny's career. He understood long course was his strength and it was time to turn his sport into his profession.

TROJAN SWIM CLUB PRACTICE 1998 – Coach Mark Schubert

SATURDAY May 30, 1998 A.M.

Warm-up:	1 x 400 on 6:00 free
	Swim 2 x 200 on 3:10 back
	4 x 100 on 1:45 (drill/swim) stroke
	1 x 400 on 6:00 (free)
Swim:	1 x 300 on 4:25 (50 free/50 back drill/50 free)
	1 x 200 on 2:50 (50 back/50 breast/50 breast drill—2 kicks, 1 putt/50 back)
Loosen up:	1 x 100 on 1:20 choice
Rest:	2:00
Firestone Drill:	16 x 1:00 Kick (Done in 15-meter diving well. Kick all-out, holding onto wall for one minute, then sprint to the other side of the well.
Odds:	Underwater fly kick; evens—fly, no breathing)
Pull:	4 x 100 on 1:35 free or stroke
	4 x 100 on 1:30 free or stroke
	4 x 100 on 1:25 free or stroke
Rest:	2:00
Quality Set:	Swim 4 x 200 on 8:00 best stroke or IM—or 4 x 150 for sprinters (Lenny did backstroke in 2:07, 2:05, 2:03, 2:01)
Rest:	2:00
Swim:	4 x 50 on 4:00 choice of strokes: (Lenny did free in 25.8, 25.4, 25.1, 24.6)
Rest	2:00
Warm-down:	Swim 1 x 250 on 3:00
Total:	3,450 meters (plus Firestone Drill)

Reprinted from *Swimming World Magazine* July 1998

Professional swimming was beginning to be recognized in 1998 but there were still limited opportunities. However, looking ahead to the 2000 Olympics Lenny Krayzelburg was both a rising star and seemed like a real possibility to win three gold medals in Sydney. This made him more attractive to sponsors than nearly any other swimmer in America. He signed a contract with Advantage International to represent his interests. Gerry Rodriguez helped him work out the details of a contract with Speedo and through some local friends he found a reputable attorney to review his contracts.

With the help of Speedo and a couple of other deals, he was now earning more than $100,000 annually with incentives to boost that income in the future with bonus money for world records and world rankings. One of the most important provisions of his Speedo contract was that the company would pay all travel expenses for his family to his major international competitions. The Krayzelburg family adventure continued.

Lenny was professional in his approach to his sport and thorough in his preparation. In order to improve his strength, he worked with USC assistant coach Jim Montrella to devise a customized dry-land program. He progressed from doing an exercise 20 times at a difficult weight for two weeks, to 30 repetitions for two weeks, then 40 repetitions so that he was performing the exercise for about one minute and 55 seconds. This replicated the same amount of time to establish a new world record in the 200-meter backstroke.

Coach Schubert's training program was extremely difficult, particularly in the volume of work performed each week. Four hours of pool training and one hour of dry-land training most days of the week was typical. While there was also an early morning running group several days a week, which included Coach Schubert, Lenny's unnatural, heavy-footed running style often hurt his lower back, and when that occurred he would substitute stationary bike riding before afternoon practice.

Monday, May 25, 1998 (Long Course) – Trojan Swim Club – Coach Mark Schubert

Warm-up:	1 x 600 on 9:30 (200 free/200 stroke/200 free,)
	6 x 100 on 1:45 (50 kick/50 swim—stroke)
	6 x 100 on 1:30 (50 free/50 fly)
Rest:	2:00
Swim:	12 x 50 on 1:05 (15 race/35 easy); get partner,
	alternate racing 2 underwater/2 surface
Rest:	2:00
Kick:	6 x 150 on 2:15 w/fins—best stroke: 25m underwater/25 surface
Rest:	2:00
Mains Set:	1 x 800 free on 10:00 – negative-split
	2 x 400 free on 5:00 – descend and negative-split
	4 x 200 back on 2:30 – descend and negative-split
	8 x 100 free on back on 1:15 – descend and negative-split
	16 x 50 back on :40 – descend and negative-split (Lenny did 31s)
Warm-down:	400 easy

Swimming World Magazine July 1998

Lenny trained hard but also prided himself in leaving his swimming at the pool and enjoying life away from it. On weekends he always went home to his parents' apartment and enjoyed spending time with his family. His father would prepare and pack up some of his favorite Russian meals with lots of meat and carbohydrates to take back to his apartment. That gave Lenny meals to heat up for dinner the following week. He also loved the feeling of flopping on the couch and feeling not able to move. That was proof to him that he had given everything he had during that day's training.

The summer championship season of 1998 included the Goodwill Games in New York and then 10 days later the US Nationals in Clovis, California. The Goodwill Games format was an unusual one with a round-robin of races in an innovative dual-meet format. He completed the competition with the second-best time in the 100-meter backstroke (55.1) and best in the 200 (1:58.1). At the Nationals, Brad Bridgewater swam an outstanding swim in the heats (1:58.24) and Lenny felt he needed to do something different to win the race at night. He changed his race strategy to assert himself much more aggressively in the first half of the race with a 57.1 split, gaining a commanding lead over his friend, teammate and rival—in an effort to break his will. The plan seemed to work and he set a new American record (1:57.3) with Brad finishing a distant second (1:59.5). (A 15-year-old named Aaron Peirsol was third with 2:01.39!)

In 1999 it was important to take advantage of the World Cup in Europe to spice up the year of competition without the NCAA program. In January, Lenny's back was aching from his running and the travel. The USC medical staff advised him to spend two weeks doing very light work to let it heal. Used to training very hard, not liking missing a workout, and panicking over the loss of training, he realized that a break could help him. Because of that, he had an exceptional March Nationals without shaving down. His 200-meter time of 1:56.95 improved his American record and his 100 of 54.77 was outstanding as well.

At about this time Brad Bridgewater had become increasingly uncomfortable with his overall training situation working with Coach Schubert, so he made a personal decision to move to Irvine and spend the rest of that year training under Coach Dave Salo.

Despite the loss of his training partner, Lenny's training remained superb. He often swam backstroke as fast—or faster—than freestyle and raced against the freestylers in practice. The summer training plan was to take only a short rest for the US Nationals in Minneapolis and rest and shave for the Pan Pacific Games at the end of August three weeks later. When he swam a 1:56.35 in the

200-meter backstroke in Minneapolis, he just missed Martin Zubero's long-standing world record. His 100 of 54.00 was close to Jeff Rouse's world record as well. His approach to the next competition was one of positive expectation. It wasn't a question of whether or not he was going to break the world record; it was only a matter of *when*. In the training camp prior to the Pan Pacs he swam 4 x 50s backstroke with 10 seconds rest and added up the times to 1:53.8. He used these training sets to build his confidence, which reached a peak when he went "Down Under."

"When" came on August 24, 1999. Swimming at the Olympic pool in Sydney, Lenny Krayzelburg swam the 100-meter backstroke faster than any other human in history (53.60). Three days later he took off on the front half of the 200 with no worries that anyone could compete with him. This carefree sense of dominance and creation put his feet on the wall at the 100 turn in a time of 56.1; at the 150 he was timed in 1:15.6. He struggled on the last length but touched the wall in 1:55.87 to smash the 200 record as well. Lenny had learned an important lesson in public relations in Perth the previous year. Affable by nature, he made sure he demonstrated that quality to the great swimming fans in Australia and became a tremendous crowd favorite.

He was swimming so fast that Coach Schubert helped arrange a time trial for a 50-meter backstroke to try to break the world record. Lenny took advantage of the opportunity. In what he looked back on as one of the best swims of his life he swam a 24.99 and new world record. "I felt like I was swimming in air with my hands holding water with perfect traction."

Australia loves the sport of swimming and that national passion helped generate 12 world records during the competition. The Aussie men's team was strengthened by the development of young stars Ian Thorpe and Grant Hackett, who combined with established veterans like Michael Klim to give Team USA all they could handle in the team point competition. The US needed a win on the 400 medley relay to close out the meet and hang on to the mantle of the reigning team champion of world swimming. Lenny led off in 53.67 (the second fastest 100 backstroke ever) and the US held on to win the race and the team competition.

Lenny Krayzelburg was the only triple gold medal winner for the United States men's team during the Pan Pacific Games. He now held three world records. He had established himself as one of the most reliable performers on the US team, someone who handled himself full of confidence, demonstrating respect for his peers, his competitors, all coaches and for the sport itself. Surviving the pressures of Olympic expectations, however, is an entirely different matter.

The Reebok shoe company produced an ad campaign in 1992 that followed the progress of decathlete players Dean and Dan toward the Olympic Games in Barcelona. Lenny was a huge sports fan and followed the series of commercials. The finale was to be the outcome at the Games themselves, but then something unexpected happened: Dan didn't qualify for the US team. That made a big impact on Lenny. Despite his standing in the world of swimming, he took nothing for granted in the Olympic year. He made it his mission to excel in every practice, every set and on every swim. Brad Bridgewater was back to train with him, too, and Coach Schubert increased the length of their main sets so they were training at the highest level of their careers.

When Lenny sliced his toe on a touch pad at the short course World Championships in March it was a bump in the road. He already had outstanding times (1:57.7 and 54.62) at the US Open in December and was training well. With a stitched and taped toe he continued to train. There were more flops down on his couch after practice than ever before. The training plan was to rest just slightly for the Olympic Trials and be at a peak for the Olympics themselves about five weeks later.

At the Janet Evans Meet three weeks before the Olympic Trials, the smooth road of the last four years to swimming prominence developed a huge pothole. It came in part because of the great progress of 17year-old backstroke phenom Aaron Peirsol. Aaron was making huge improvements throughout the year. He swam for the Irvine Novas with Dave Salo where they trained in a low-volume and very-high-intensity program. They swam relatively fast in nearly every meet.

At the US Nationals in March Aaron had swum the fastest 200-meter backstroke of anyone in the world thus far that year. His time was 1:57.0. Three-quarters of the way through the 200 backstroke on July 14th, Lenny seemed to be in full control of the race when he virtually collapsed. His final 50 split was 32.2 and slow enough that Aaron went right by him to win (1:59.0 to 1:59.3). The feeling of exhaustion for the final 50 was something Lenny had never felt before and it shook his confidence deeply.

Assistant coaches tend to be less of a disciplinarian than the head coach. One of Mark Schubert's outstanding assistants at the time was Larry Leibowitz.

After conferring with Mark about his race, Lenny unloaded on Larry. "That was horrible, Larry! I think we may have overdone our training. I can't get through the Trials this way."

"Hey, calm down," Larry reassured him. "You're just tired."

"I feel terrible," Lenny said.

"You'll be fine," Larry countered. "You've been doing a lot of work."

So it was some consolation two days later when Lenny easily won the 100 in 54.6. But the experience in the 200 convinced him and Coach Schubert to change their approach to the Olympic Trials so that Lenny would get a short rest before them.

The study of the human mind tells us that our experiences can't be replaced. It is the accumulation of our experiences, colored by our emotions, that makes up our attitudes, the collection of which forms our self-image. Lenny Krayzelburg's confidence was so shaken that he needed to muster and consolidate every positive aspect of his self-image over the remaining three weeks until the Trials in order to survive the pressure. He knew exactly how to do it. Whatever he did in practice he knew he could improve on in competition. He claimed ownership of every single repeat or time that he swam in his training that was good. He focused on it. He colored it with positive emotion. He took it home with him. He was in the process of rebuilding his belief in himself.

The Olympic Trials were August 9–16 in Indianapolis. The event format for selection to the team was the same format as the Olympic Games. In the 50, 100 and 200-meter events there were preliminaries in the morning, semi-finals the same evening, and finals the next night.

In order to strengthen his level of expectation through the event series, Lenny developed a progressive method of reducing his friction in each race. In the preliminary heats of the 100-meter backstroke he swam what he described as a "smooth effort," recording a time of 54.3 wearing just his swim briefs and without a cap. In semi-finals he still went without the cap and swam in a brief, just missing his world record with a 53.67.

In the finals he sensed a close race with Neil Walker who was always out fast, but then couldn't keep up with Lenny in the final 25 meters. Lenny decided to try and stay with Neil, with poor results. He forced his speed early, slipping as he went, tiring earlier than normal and although he won, his time was a disappointing 53.8. His public response was that everything was great; he was on the Olympic Team. "This is a tremendous honor," said Krayzelburg. "First of all, I feel so lucky to have come to the US, and I want to thank my parents for that. Now I have the monkey off my back, and I can go down to Sydney and swim fast."

The 200 worried him and rightfully so. He kept a slight lead over Aaron Peirsol throughout the race, extending it just a bit on the last length to win in a time of 1:57.3 to Aaron's 1:57.9. The time was far off his world record. Again, he spoke with confidence.

"I promise you I'll be better in Sydney. I'm definitely excited with my swims this week. Now it's time to go to Sydney and win a couple of golds. I tell you, our team looks great right now. I guarantee we're going to be awesome in Sydney."

But when he saw Coach Schubert, he expressed his concern. "That didn't feel right," he told his coach.

Mark reassured him. "Hey, this was a short taper; you'll be fine in Sydney."

2000 OLYMPIC GAMES – Sydney, Australia

Lenny trusted Coach Schubert and set out to reinforce his confidence during the training camp by performing in practice, acknowledging it and dwelling on the positive results in training. The initial camp was at the Rose Bowl Aquatic Center in Pasadena. It was at the same pool as Lenny's first nationals. That was enough for him to stop and appreciate how far he had come in the last five years. The seed of Mark Schubert's phone call from Atlanta four years before had grown, and Lenny was in position to win an Olympic gold medal.

The pressure built on Lenny from expectations as America's greatest hope for a male to win multiple gold medals. Television, newspapers, sponsors, and his family were all certain he was going to succeed. His picture was on the cover of *TV Guide* as an image to draw viewers to Olympic swimming. He could not get out of his mind the importance of winning gold medals for the throngs of people that sponsored and supported him. History seldom recognizes how good a swimmer you *had* been in the time leading up to the Games—or whether you held a world record. It only mattered how you performed at the Olympic Games themselves. Lenny's opportunity was transformed into an obligation, and to make matters worse he simply still didn't feel at his best in the water.

Brad Bridgewater didn't make the team and Lenny and Tom Dolan were matched up as roommates in the Olympic Village. They had become friends during the World Cup competition and Tom was a light personality to be around, something Lenny welcomed. He skipped the opening ceremonies to rest his legs.

He was relatively calm when he swam the heats and semi-finals. But the night before the finals, it hit him that he didn't possess his accustomed expectation for success, and he struggled with the unwelcome intrusion and distraction of self-doubt. He thought to himself, *If I'm not good for 53 seconds, I may never have this chance again.* He shared his emotions with Tom Dolan. Tom had won the 400 individual medley already and tried to lighten his mood. Normally that might have succeeded, but Lenny tossed and turned through the night.

When the sun came up he couldn't eat. After warm-up for the finals he went to the ready room. Normally he felt as though his competitors noticed his confidence, but tonight he was certain they sensed his fear; self-doubt nagged at him. The walk to the starting blocks seemed to take forever. The Australian favorite, Matt Welsh, walked behind him and the ovation from the hometown crowd of 18,000 spectators when he appeared on the pool deck was enormous.

Welsh had improved to 54.0 at the Aussie Trials and was the leading challenger for the gold medal. *I can't wait to get this over with,* Lenny thought. Finally they were instructed to enter the water. Lenny leaped into a familiar world and the water silenced more than the noise of the crowd; it had quieted the negative inner voice that had been plaguing him. He was in his element. With a few seconds to start the race he finally became poised. Submerging himself in the familiar environment had washed away his unsure feelings. *Focus and swim your race,* Lenny thought to himself.

For the first 75 meters the field was together. Lenny could see Matt Welsh in the next lane was right with him. But Lenny was a great finisher and he surged toward the wall. He reached for the touch pad and as he did glanced toward Matt. Lenny was ahead and knew it. A sense of relief overcame him. He had won the gold medal in the 100-meter backstroke. He leaped from the pool and gave the obligatory winner's interview; then a quick change and on to the award stand. Finally, he was able to dive into the warm-down pool and cry. Tears of joy filled his goggles as he swam.

After he warmed down, he made his way up to the spectator seats to see his family. He had never seen his father cry before. Oleg Krayzelburg was overcome with emotion and collapsed, his eyes welling with tears of pride and relief. Lenny tried to lighten the moment with a joke. It didn't work. From Odessa in the Ukraine they had come through Austria to Rome to Los Angeles. And finally, in Australia in front of 18,000 swimming fans applauding him, Lenny Krayzelburg and his family struck gold.

The heats and semi-finals of the 200 backstroke were a formality. When Lenny walked onto the pool deck for the finals he was nervous but found a calming influence in front of the huge crowd of people. The human mind can only consciously think of one thing at a time and Lenny focused on the majesty of the grand event he was a part of. He scanned the sea of humanity tucked into this facility for the evening to honor his sport and the athletes in it. He became at peace with his opportunity to give his best effort toward victory.

In Olympic history only Roland Matthes (1968), John Naber (1976) and Rick Carey (1984) had been able to win gold medals in both backstrokes. The development of pace and varying strategies in his amicable rivalry with Brad Bridgewater gave Lenny an edge, and one that he made use of. He held a slight lead over Aaron Peirsol at the midway point, and then with 25 meters remaining on his third length he quickly increased his speed and tempo. By the time he turned at the 150 he was a body length in front. Pain hit him hard on the last 25 meters, but Lenny held on to become the fourth double Olympic backstroke champion, edging Aaron Peirsol 1:56.7 to 1:57.3.

The euphoria of being Olympic champion twice and fulfilling the expectations of so many sponsors and supporters didn't wear off quickly. It endured into the night, through waiting and drug testing. Shortly before midnight Lenny found himself sitting at a McDonald's in the Olympic Village talking on his cell phone with a friend in the United States. Although the medley relay still remained, he now felt relieved of enough pressure to enjoy his teammates, cheer for them and help the USA close out these Games in the strongest way possible.

The final event of the Olympics in swimming was the 400 medley relay. Lenny handed Ed Moses a slight advantage after the backstroke leg on the medley relay. Ed opened a big lead in his breaststroke leg, Ian Crocker maintained it in butterfly and Gary Hall anchored against the 100-meter freestyle world record-holder Michael Klim for Australia. Lenny couldn't watch. He had turned away and did not see Ed or Ian swim. He hadn't wanted to witness ever again an American defeat such as the one they had suffered at the hands of the Australians at the World Championships the year before. But with about 15 seconds remaining in the race, he anxiously looked up and saw that Gary was in a great position to win—and he did.

Lenny Krayzelburg became one of the most highly decorated swimmers at these Olympics with a third gold medal and in world-record time. His success came so suddenly that the sky seemed like the limit for him for the next four years. But his left shoulder had bothered him a little bit before that relay swim.

2000 OLYMPIC AFTERMATH

The window of opportunity for successful Olympians can be small, particularly in the sports that are not driven by long-term media contracts like soccer, basketball, American baseball and American football. Lenny Krayzelburg delivered on the media buildup and was now in a position to reap the rewards. He had a great story to tell and did so as a guest on "Late Night with David Letterman." He was a judge for the Miss America pageant and appeared on "Hollywood Squares." He was a celebrity participant on "Who Wants to Be a Millionaire?" When he won $32,000 on the "Millionaire" show, he donated half to a cystic fibrosis charity. After a three-week whirlwind media tour he stopped at home.

His father asked him, "Why aren't you training?" Lenny knew and accepted that his father always wanted more success for him.

He politely answered, "Well, I just won three gold medals. I've been training nearly non-stop for four years and thought I would enjoy the results."

Lenny's plan for the 2004 Athens Centennial Olympics was to take a two-month break and then have a low-key year in 2001. A part of that plan was to go to Israel for the Maccabi Games, rather than compete in the World Championships. He really wanted to explore his Jewish heritage and by competing in their major international competition he could do that.

By November he was back in the pool training and all was going well. Great swimmers listen to their bodies. Despite a huge capacity for training with pain, they know the difference between a dull overall pain that comes with lactic acid buildup or muscle fatigue and a sharp pain that indicates an injury or the potential for one. It was nearing spring and each time he lifted his left arm or began to pull, his shoulder bothered him.

Lenny was officially a volunteer assistant coach at USC. That gave him full use of their excellent medical and training staff. An x-ray didn't show any damage, but an MRI showed a tear in the labrum (cartilage) that creates a cup to hold the head of the humerus (upper arm bone). Lenny had never had a significant injury before and was stunned. He and Coach Schubert decided to put off the surgery until late August, after the Maccabi Games. With that timing he would have two to four months to recover and hope to recover to train well by winter.

The Maccabi Games were an even greater experience than he had imagined. Not only was he able to see the Holy Land that he always read about, he was also stunned by the welcome he received from the Israelis. His Olympic victories and television appearances were broadcast there and he was treated as a huge celebrity. Because of his shoulder injury he didn't swim the 200-meter backstroke, but won gold medals in the 100-meter backstroke and 400 medley relay. The highlight for Lenny, however, was being chosen to carry the American flag in the opening ceremonies.

Afterward, there were two months of rehab after surgery, and Lenny knew that someone was always out trying to beat him. He was eager to train and the shoulder was feeling good. He worked harder and harder into 2002. Then he developed a constant cough, which led him to see a sinus specialist. Surgery was necessary to control the drip that was causing the cough. He missed a few weeks of training but quickly returned to good condition.

In a mid-season meet in New York he swam times of 55 and 1:59 that put him on target for the August Trials in Ft. Lauderdale for the 2003 World Championships. On the morning of his flight back to Los Angeles he wanted to get in some type of workout. There wasn't time to get to a pool, so he went down to the hotel fitness center to use the treadmill and do some running. After warming up and doing a long relaxed jog, he turned the speed up to work as hard as he could on a sprint. He tripped and fell. His knee hurt when he walked, but he made it back to Los Angeles.

The doctors in LA told Lenny that he had torn his ACL and would need surgery. He and Coach Schubert consulted again on the timing. They elected to train with the tear and compete in Ft. Lauderdale, then have the surgery and prepare for the summer World Championships. Lenny succeeded in making the World Championship team, finishing second to Aaron Peirsol in both backstrokes although his injuries slowed his times to 54.0 for 100-meters and 1:58.6 for the 200.

Lenny always treated his coaches with great respect and encouraged having complete and open communication with them. He was 27 years old and felt as though the training hadn't changed much since he came to USC when he was 19. He wanted to do more speed-work in the hope of improving the final 50 of his 200 backstroke. An extremely conscientious worker, it was never enough for him to simply complete a set. Although he liked racing the freestylers (ex: 6 x 300s backstroke long course on 3:40) and prided himself on swimming fast in practice (ex: 20 x 100-yard backstroke on 1:00), he didn't feel his training program had adjusted to account for his age.

In May of 2003, he began to feel the same ache in his left shoulder. He and Coach Schubert went to the USC doctors and they scheduled another MRI. His labrum was torn again. They were devastated. There were 14 months until the Olympic Trials and they had to make a choice between going to the World Championships in August or having surgery now. They elected to do the surgery immediately in hopes of resuming training in the fall for the Olympic year. With surgery and time to rehab, Lenny thought about his training more than ever. His talks with Coach Schubert didn't give him a sense that anything would change in the Olympic year.

OLYMPIC YEAR 2004

Four years earlier in 1999, Brad Bridgewater had spent time training with Dave Salo at the Irvine Novas and shared the differences with Lenny. Dave was extremely innovative. He believed in molding his training around the mind of an MTV viewer. He gave his swimmers something hard, fast and generally unusual for about 20 minutes and then they started a new "20-minute training experience."

If Lenny wanted a change, this concept represented a dramatic difference from Mark Schubert's successful program based on building a strong endurance foundation with 45-minute to one hour main sets. Lenny called Dave Salo to ask his permission to join the Novas. He told the coach that he wanted to have Aaron Peirsol's permission to join his club. Aaron was training in Texas, but it was a statement about Lenny's respect for the coach-swimmer relationship to want Aaron's approval.

Dave gave Lenny his consent to join the Novas. Lenny and Mark finally talked. It was an emotional exchange. Lenny knew that he owed more than he could ever repay to Mark for the opportunity he had been given over the previous nine years at USC. He was hurt by Schubert's words but knew that he was hurting his coach too. Time would pass and this relationship would be repaired. But now he was going to train an hour south in Irvine. The news went viral in the swimming community and Mark Schubert was gracious. "Anything Lenny Krayzelburg feels he needs to do I support. He is a special athlete and a special person."

IRVINE NOVAS

Practices were fun! Each day Lenny walked into the William Wollett, Jr. Aquatic Center not knowing what was going to happen. There was no pattern. The only expectation was that it would be hard and fast. Coach Salo loved paddles and fins and seeing his swimmers go fast. He believed in the precision of getting details correct in training to prepare for the fastest possible racing. A swimmer once said to the coach, "You could conduct a practice in a bucket." The next day buckets lined the pool deck and were used in training. Despite all the "toys" and innovations, Lenny admired Dave's absolute confidence in his method and how it reflected supreme preparation for world-class swimming.

In October Lenny's shoulder ached again. He and Dave consulted with Olympic Team doctor and former swimmer Scott Rodeo, who had a proven reputation as one of the very best shoulder surgeons in the world. His professional opinion was that optimal recovery from shoulder surgery for a swimmer could take up to a year. Lenny had been trying to do it in a few months. There were eight months until the Olympic Trials.

They created a plan to attempt to have the shoulder survive through the Trials—and if Lenny could make the team, through the Olympics. For four months they would train around the shoulder. Then for 100 days before the Trials Lenny would swim with the team and deal with the pain. The injury indicated that he could not do the endurance training for the 200 and his opportunity for a return to the Olympics in Athens would all come down to the 100.

Training around the shoulder meant more innovation. Lenny generated lactate riding a stationary bike at the pool while the swimmers built lactate in the pool. It wasn't easy riding. It was sprint riding in an effort to mimic the oxygen uptake that occurred in the pool and usually lasted a full hour. On some swimming sets he worked out of the water; then, at the precise moment that Dave planned, he jumped in and swam a short fast series. When he did drills in the pool they were all single-arm drills, using his right arm to protect the injured shoulder from more inflammation.

Research has shown some cross-body effect in training. This means that despite the effort to keep the left shoulder from being stressed with exercise by not swimming with it, blood still circulated through it and the unused shoulder received a mild training effect. Over the four months, Lenny improved his kicking and maintained a rigid cross-training routine. Then the first week of April the 100 days of water training began. Dave and Lenny attempted to lessen the pressure on his shoulders by moving his hand in toward his body on his pull. This weakened one of his strengths as a backstroker but it was a tradeoff for less trauma to the shoulder joint when he swam. He sprinted and sharpened his swimming with combinations of kicking and swimming to minimize further tearing of the shoulder.

The American system of selecting an Olympic Swimming Team is objective. Some people might judge it merciless. There were no positions held for world record-holders or those who had achieved greatness in years past or held promise for the future. The only criterion for earning a place on the team was swimming fast enough in the right race.

Nearly every quadrennial, the field of prospective Olympians improves and therefore the demand to be faster to make the team becomes more and more demanding and the results are separated by less and less time. Lenny made it through the heats and into the semi-finals of the 100- meter backstroke. In the semi-finals he posted the fifth fastest time of 55.05. It was well off his world record but close enough to Aaron Peirsol (54.22), Peter Marshall (54.40), Dan Westcott (54.50) and Randall Bal (54.89) to have a chance to finish in the top two and make the Olympic Team.

On July 9, 2004, all the expectations that surrounded the Trials and Games four years before were gone. Lenny summoned one great effort in the finals to put himself onto the team and back into the Olympic arena. His time of 54.06 wasn't fast enough to beat Aaron Peirsol's winning time (53.64), but it was enough to edge out Peter Marshall (54.10) and Randall Bal (54.20) and make the team.

Winning a swimming race can be a matter of circumstance. The time that wins in one race may be last in another. In Athens, Aaron Peirsol won the gold medal in the 100-meter backstroke in 54.06, exactly the same time that Lenny Krayzelburg swam at the Trials. When Lenny reached for the wall in Athens he was a little farther away than he realized. He stopped the clock at precisely 54.38 seconds. It was a time fast enough to beat Matt Welsh (54.52), but not quite good enough to beat Japan's Tomomi Morita (54.36) and Austria's Markus Rogan (54.35). Oleg Krayzelburg was disappointed that Lenny didn't win a medal, although he did earn his fourth Olympic gold medal by swimming the preliminaries of the USA 400 medley relay that won in the finals.

In the four years leading up to the 2000 Olympics everything seemed to go right for Lenny Krayzelburg, and in the four leading up to 2004 everything seemed to go wrong, including another shoulder surgery after the Olympics. But the shoulder had survived long enough to allow him to battle his way back to the Olympics. He had faced and successfully fought many obstacles: the journey from the Ukraine to the United States, almost leaving the sport of swimming completely, the series of competitive hurdles that comprise the United States Swimming program, Olympic pressure, and several injuries requiring surgery. He had survived.

There would be no game shows or television guest spots after Athens, but there were two more honors for Lenny before and after the 2004 Olympics in Athens, one that he received, and one that he gave.

The received honor was bestowed by his teammates, naming him co-captain of the USA Men's Olympic Swimming Team.

The one he gave was donating $100,000 to the West Hollywood JCC for repairs to their pool. This contribution enabled him to start the Lenny Krayzelburg Swim School there in order to teach children to swim and prevent them from drowning and perhaps, just perhaps, discovering another Olympic swimmer. The school blossomed into a franchise and has spread since to other JCCs around the United States.

Lenny Krayzelburg was inducted into the International Swimming Hall of Fame in 2011.

IAN CROCKER

August 31, 1982

THE UNDERDOG

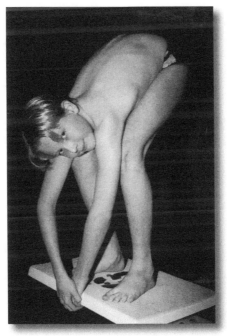

1992

Up until now the stories of our swimmers' journeys to winning Olympic gold medals have for the most part been set in environments quite conducive to an individual pursuing and achieving swimming excellence. Portland, Maine, however, has never been known as a hot spot for swimmer development. Pools designed for competitive swimming training, much less competing, are rare in Maine. In fact, as recently as the 1990s there weren't any 50-meter pools in the entire state—none indoors, none outdoors. The summer outdoor-pool season is short in Maine, not at all ideal for the summer swim leagues that feed young prospects into USA Swimming club teams. Swim coaches who aspire to gain the best resources and build a fine competitive swimming program do not even consider Maine, let alone flock to it.

No wonder that in the 100-year history of the modern Olympic Games there had never been an Olympic swimmer that had grown up in the state of Maine.

* * *

"Ian!"

No response other than the customary "noise."

"Ian!" Gail Crocker yelled louder from the living room of their home.

Ian's time after school and before swim practice was dominated by his diligent approach to learning how to play the guitar. He had taken some lessons in eighth grade, but they were hard to sustain with his swim schedule. Fortunately, Ian's teacher taught him how to learn notes by ear. As a result he was developing the ability to quickly connect the music from the radio to the guitar strings, the strings to his fingers and his fingers to his brain. Ian had fantastic concentration—when the activity was something he enjoyed. More often than not, hours of guitar practice would pass before his mother called him for dinner while to Ian it had felt like he had just arrived home a few minutes before.

"Dinner already?" Ian yelled. He heard his mother walk up the stairs and down the hall toward his room. She knocked on his bedroom door.

Gail opened Ian's door and stuck her head inside his room. Ian stopped playing the guitar, leaned back in his bed and waited. "Sharon just called. There's fecal matter in the pool. Practice is canceled tonight."

"Fecal matter?" Ian questioned. "Mom, you mean someone pooped in the pool again."

"Well, yes."

Every few weeks a child in the preschool program seemed to have an "accident" in the Reiche Pool, and by regulation it had to be shut down for at least 24 hours.

"We've missed three practices in the last three weeks," Ian complained.

"Make it four, dear; they won't get it sanitized until tomorrow afternoon. So you guys are out of there tomorrow morning too."

"Really?"

"We're supposed to have 12 inches of snow tonight, so at least it saves your dad another 4 a.m. bout of shoveling the driveway."

"Can't we go to the Riverton Pool and practice there tonight?" Ian asked.

"You know we can't use that pool anymore, at least not until the school programs end in the spring. Sorry, son."

The four-lane Reiche Pool was used all day long, first by preschool programs and school programs, then by some high school teams and then eventually by the Portland Porpoise Swim Club. PPSC didn't have use of the pool until 6:30 p.m., and often by that time the pool was dirty at best and un-swimmable at worst.

Gail Crocker closed her son's bedroom door. She didn't know much about swimming beyond the fact that Ian loved the sport, and to her that's what mat-tered most. She also knew that he had a dream of swimming in the Olympics one day. To her that dream seemed pretty far-fetched for a lot of reasons, not the least of which was the constant problems the team faced in getting adequate hours to train. As she walked back down the hall, she mumbled to herself, "There are times I wonder if we shouldn't have just stayed at the Y."

It was at the Portland YMCA, back in 1989, where Ian took his first swim lessons. There wasn't as much snow that year and the winter had been rela-tively warm by Portland standards—there had been only nine days that the temperature was below zero (-18 Celsius). The YMCA had a small instruc-tional pool with warm water, which was wonderful for getting the little ones started. Ian took his swimming lessons there with his nine-year-old sister Amy, and while she was progressing nicely six-year-old Ian was failing in the guppy group. Simple reason ... he couldn't figure out how to float.

Gail and her husband Rick Crocker did not at that time hold aspirations for their children to be competitive swimmers. They did, however, want them to be water-safe. Rick worked as a lab technician for Bath Iron Works in the ship-building business. Gail was trained as a nurse, and she had expanded on her certification as an RN and moved to managing The Turning Point, a car-diac rehab center. While their careers kept them busy, they felt it important that their children have an activity that provided exercise, recreation and a social outlet.

PORTLAND YMCA – The Early Years

There wasn't a great deal of choice regarding youth-oriented activities during the cold Portland winters, so Ian continued with his swim classes at the Y. By the time Ian turned eight he had learned to float and hold his breath so, with his parents' approval, he joined his sister Amy on the Y's swim team. Ian's first coach was Dee St. Cross. She had earned her WSI certification and was actively learning about competitive swimming from Don Murphy, the team's head coach.

Don had stumbled into swimming because of his love for his wife. They were living in New York City, and when Don would come home from his job in the flooring business, his wife would still be at the pool working with a small girls' swim team. Don missed his wife at night, so he decided to go to the pool and get involved. Some years later, after his wife passed away, Don moved first to Massachusetts and then eventually to Maine where he became the swim coach at the Pine Tree Swim Club (PTSC), an affiliate of the Portland YMCA.

In order to be an effective coach, Don educated himself about the sport. He became a regular participant in the annual ASCA World Swim Coaching Clinics and closely followed the research and work of famous swim coach Jim "Doc" Counsilman. Don took all that he learned about the skill of swimming and passed it on to Coach St. Cross.

Dee taught her young swimmers how to better balance their bodies in the water and how to streamline properly off the walls. She also helped them refine their arm and leg movements. In doing so she liked to use word pictures in her instruction. For example she described the freestyle kick as "quick and tight," and the breaststroke arm movement as "cleaning the inside of a bowl of frosting." She used a hesitation drill in backstroke in which the swimmers looked at their arms above their eyes, paused, and then continued the flow of movement forward and down into their arm and hand entry.

For young Ian the swim team quickly became the center of his social life. Dee's son was also in the eight-and-younger practice group and sleepovers at the St. Cross house became a regular occurrence. Before long, buoyed by the strength of the youngsters' social connection, PTSC's eight-and under relays broke a couple of Maine's YMCA Swimming relay records. Due to the boys' quick success, they earned themselves a travel-meet to Rhode Island where they were to swim against the best YMCA teams in the northeast. While Ian and his friends didn't break any records at the meet, they did enjoy the excitement of hiding in the hotel parking lot and running away from the Rhode Island State Police, who had been called to the hotel to investigate a commotion—a commotion that the *boys themselves* were causing. Don't take me wrong: They weren't troublesome kids; it was just hard for them to sit still.

When Ian turned nine he moved up a training group and was to be coached directly by Coach Murphy. The upward move increased Ian's practice schedule from two to three nights per week and added Saturday mornings.

Coach Murphy had locked on to Doc Counsilman's teaching, "Scull water first, then move to still water and, at every angle, there is still water to be found." Don taught that very principle with vigor. Though 70 years old, Don never stayed put at one end of the pool. He was always on the move, walking up and down the pool deck in order to see hand pitch, elbow positioning and underwater sweeping patterns, and then he signaled instructions to his swimmers. For example, he would shout, "Extend! Extend!" while at the same time he extended his arms forward and behind to visually remind his swimmers to reach forward and finish through even when they were highly fatigued.

During the winter months in Maine it was a common activity for folks to watch sports on television, but that wasn't for Ian. He just wasn't a sports fan. As a youngster he tried out for basketball even though he'd never seen a game and didn't know the rules. No surprise that he didn't do well. A few years later he tried track and field, again without success. There was also a failed attempt at karate. Truth be told, no other sport or activity came nearly as easily to him as did swimming. In the summer of 1992, as a nine-year-old, Ian made a point to watch the Olympic swimming events on television. He was thrilled at the racing and the American success. *I want to do that* he thought to himself.

Coach Murphy liked to say, "No deposit, no return." He educated his swimmers—even at nine and ten years old—that practice was an investment in their upcoming performances at meets. While Don increased the stress of training sets when Ian was nine and ten, his priority was teaching correct movements. "Head, hip, feet!" Coach Murphy yelled. Those were his cue words for butterfly. They meant head dips, hips rise up, and feet kick down. "Ian! Make believe there's a rod through you neck. I want to see your head move forward not up and down."

By the time he turned 12, Ian was tall and lanky. When he extended his hands out in front of him while swimming he felt the water easily and quickly. He didn't pull it backward. Instead, Ian wrapped his hands around still water, anchored himself and then moved his body forward. He had a gift to swim efficiently. And always at PTSC he was coached to improve that skill, rather than forced into working only to survive practice. Don made the sport more interesting to Ian by writing times or splits on cards to use as a visual cue to teach him how to distribute his effort evenly in the longer 100 (yard or meter) races.

The top group at PTSC swam six practices per week, an hour and 45 minutes per practice. They covered about 6,500 yards in each session. There were 60 swimmers in the squad and 10 swimmers in each lane. Ian moved into the top group at age 12, which meant that he was much younger than most of his training mates. At first he struggled to keep up with the older swimmers, but Coach Murphy wasn't worried; he felt that Ian needed the challenge. From time to time Don would allow Ian to stop and rest for a short period in practice. A minute or so later, he was back swimming and racing with his older teammates. On some nights the coach pushed the swimmers to swim fast regardless of their fatigue. Other nights he felt they needed some time to recover and he emphasized technique.

Developmental Progression - Portland Y/Pine Tree Swim Club – Head Coach Don Murphy

8 & Under – 5:45-6:30 pm
       3 x week 45 minutes
       Streamline, balance and kicking
       Skills & Drills

9-10 – 6:30-8:00 pm
       3-4 x week 90 minutes – 8 swimmers per lane
Warm-up: Technique & Skills: 15 minutes
Main Set: 20 x 50s on 1:00 (1 swim, 1 kick, 1 pull, 1 swim)
Total: 2,400-3,600 yards

11-12 – 6:30-8:45 pm
       5-6 x week 2:15 – 10 swimmers per lane
Warm-up: 2,000
Main Set 1:   5 x 200 on 2:45 (once a week on 2:30)
Kick & Drills: 1,500
Main Set 2:   10 x 100s free, 6 on 1:30, 2 on 1:20, 2 on 1:10
Sprint: 3 x (5 x 50s on 1:00)
Warm-down
Total: 6,500-6,800 yards

        Provided by Coach Don Murphy and Dee St. Cross

Coach Murphy taught the Crockers and all of the team parents that a swimmer could only have one coach, and that was not the swimmer's parent(s). Gail and Rick readily agreed with Coach Murphy's philosophy, but at the same time they recognized that the club needed support and gave it happily. They served as timers and worked on committees, and they also recognized how important it was for coaches to hear "Thank you" from the parents. They said it often. They truly appreciated all the PTSC coaches had done for Ian.

At swim meets Ian shined, but he was puzzled about something. He loved to race and to feel the affirmation that his harder practices were paying dividends. His parents modeled hard work and service. But as he turned 12 he felt increasing resentment from the older swimmers at the Y and some of their parents in regard to his ability and his achievements. In fact it became common for his older teammates to taunt and tease him.

At the New England Championships in March of 1995, 12-year-old Ian Crocker swam his best time of 24.07 in the 50-yard freestyle. He and Coach Murphy were sitting together waiting for the next race and Ian revealed his secret dream from when he was nine years old.

"Coach, I want to go to the Olympics."

"There's a cost to whatever you want to do in life, Ian. If you want to go the Olympics, you've got to pay the cost."

Ian didn't say anything; he just listened.

Coach Murphy continued. "Each day there are tens of thousands of swimmers all over the United States working hard at swim practice. To be on the Olympic Team you have to be willing to work harder than just about anyone else. Only you know when you're giving your very best effort. But, if you, Ian Crocker, are willing to pay the cost, then I think you can do it."

A significant number of Olympic swimmers started in the YMCAs across America, but very few continued in those programs up to the point when they reached the pinnacle of the sport. Portland Y didn't offer much of a summer program for either training or competition. When the spring thaw arrived Ian needed a place to train. There was a US Swimming (USS) club in town called the Portland Porpoises, and they offered a solid summer program. And when Nate and John Stevens, who swam with Ian at the Y, decided to move over to the Porpoises in the spring of 1995, Ian and the Crockers decided to follow—though with heavy hearts. Fortunately Coach Murphy understood the move and they parted on good terms.

1995 PORTLAND PORPOISES

Training with the Portland Porpoises in the summer of 1995 overwhelmed Ian. They did far more endurance work than Ian was accustomed to, and for the first time he truly began to understand that sustaining pain was an important part of training.

With some regularity a group of the Porpoise swimmers drove the two and a half hours each way to Dover, New Hampshire, to do some long-course training in the Jenny Thompson Pool. It was a brand-new experience and Ian began to learn the differences between swimming in short-course (25-yard) and long-course (50-meter) pools. And in the summer of 1995, Ian raced his first 100-meter butterfly in competition.

By the end of the following summer (1996) Ian saw that the increased training load was really paying off. He swam his first 1500-meter freestyle (short-course meter pool) that year, and as he did, Coach Tim and Coach Bridget watched the beginning of his race and thought, *He's going out too fast!* But Ian showed he could swim the long races well. He sustained his pace nicely and surprised his coaches by finishing strong. Although the pain building in his stomach wasn't something Ian enjoyed, he preferred the shorter races. That summer Ian's long-course times improved to 2:06.8 in the 200-meter freestyle and 1:04 flat in the 100-meter butterfly.

At the end of the summer of 1996, Coach Mark and Coach Bridget left the Porpoises, leaving the team in need of a new coach. The club hired Sharon Power who was from north of the border in Nova Scotia, Canada. Sharon's mentor was Gary McDonald, a silver medalist in the 1976 Olympics, and her swim coaching education was based upon a Canadian system that was very much detail-oriented. Sharon longed to succeed as a swimming coach and once told a Canadian male colleague, "I want to have an Olympian." The coach responded, "Have a baby."

Note: *Though acceptance of senior-level female swim coaches in the US was less than it should have been in 1996, upon her move south Sharon immediately sensed that gender bias wasn't nearly as prevalent in US swim coaching circles as it was in Canada.*

1996–1997 PORTLAND PORPOISES – Ninth Grade

In September of 1996, at the beginning of her first season with Portland, Coach Power conducted a meeting with each of her new swimmers. From the outset she established a system where each swimmer was responsible to set short and the long-term goals. When Sharon first met with Ian she told him, "I'd like you to assess your summer season based on four areas: your technical, tactical, physical and mental development." Ian had just turned 14 and didn't fully comprehend what his new coach was saying. If he and Coach Power were dancing he wasn't keeping up, but he was certainly dazzled by her footwork. Sharon seemed to know more about swimming than anyone he'd ever met.

In their 30-minute meeting Sharon was also struck by Ian's swimming intelligence. He described the feeling of the water bubbles moving over his hand when it entered the water and he pitched it just the right way. And when they discussed Ian's long-term goals, he said matter-of-factly, "Swimming at the Olympics."

Maybe Sharon Power didn't need to have a baby after all.

Coach Power designed a program that provided Ian and his teammates with their best opportunity to meet their goals. When Sharon began her tenure at the Porpoises, she had at her disposal the use of a six-lane 25-meter pool. Her weekly training plan rotated three areas of emphasis: The first day was long aerobic work to prepare their bodies for the week and it included a lot of kicking. The second day was endurance-oriented and focused on a long, difficult series of swims. The third day was speed-oriented. Ian and his teammates went through this training cycle twice over the six single-workout practice week. She included "Mental training" twice per week as well. During those sessions the squad discussed goals and practiced visualization. Even though opportunities for facilities and training time in Maine had many restrictions, Sharon still believed in teaching her swimmers to dream.

At first Sharon liked the idea of her swimmers (in the USA) participating on their high school teams along with their club teams. But she discovered how much training they missed because of high school meets and practices. Maine's 12-week high school swim season lasted from mid-November to late February. The rules for participation were as restrictive as any state in the country: Swimmers could not miss a high school practice (or meet) for any reason other than illness and remain on the high school team. Conversely, the level of expectation for training and performance in Maine high school programs was dismal. In a two-hour high school practice Ian's workout might cover 2-3,000 yards of low intensity work. And the competitive results weren't any better. The boys' 1996 100-yard butterfly state champion's winning time was 55. Ian had achieved that time the previous winter at age 13.

In ninth grade Ian swam for his high school, Cheverus Jesuit School. The high school used the same pool as the Porpoises after school, then the club age-groupers swam from 6:30 to 7:30 and the older swimmers practiced from 7:30–9:00. Coach Power asked Ian's high school to grant him permission to miss the high school practices. She was denied. As a result, Ian's schedule dictated that he attend high school practice in the afternoon, go home and do his homework, have dinner and then go back to the pool for club practice at night. There were high school dual meets most Tuesday and Friday nights, and with travel time that meant Ian wouldn't get to practice at all on those days. Nonetheless, in his high school division championships in his freshman year, Ian swam to a meet record in the 100-yard freestyle (47.34) that still stands as of this writing.

Through the winter months of 1997 Coach Power battled for better pool hours, a battle that she flat out lost. The winter hours that the Porpoises utilized in the Riverton six-lane pool were taken away when school was in session. Most of their training would have to be done in the Reiche four-lane 25-yard pool, a facility that didn't even have lane markers painted on the bottom. On the upside, the youngest Porpoise swimmers became accustomed to it and didn't know there were pools with lines on the bottom. On the downside, when they went to their first swim meet they were scared. The lines on the bottom appeared to move and looked like snakes! Beyond the lack of lane markers, the Reiche pool didn't have starting blocks (it was only three and a half feet deep). Only on occasion were they allowed to use lane-lines to divide the pool's surface into four lanes, and lane-lines or not the training groups were jammed into tightly packed lanes of circle swimming.

The limitations of the Reiche facility only increased Ian's challenge of becoming a national level swimmer from Maine. Undeterred, Ian exploded onto the national scene anyway. As a 14-year-old he posted amazing times such as 1:39.2 in the 200-yard freestyle, 46.24 in the 100 freestyle and 50.7 in the 100 butterfly. Simply stated, Ian showed great strides in his first season with his new coach, not to mention his immense natural ability.

Sharon challenged her swimmers in their pool workouts. When there was a heavy dose of long endurance sets, Ian pleaded with her. "I'm a sprinter."

Her response was, "You don't know what you are." Ian swam all distances in meets, and Sharon trained him as a distance swimmer. Regardless of his occasional complaint about the endurance regimen, he accepted that it was a small price to pay for swimming fast in meets.

By the summer of 1997 Ian had grown quite a bit and stood well over six feet. He had also grown accustomed to Coach Power's challenges in practice and was showing wonderful improvements in meets. It was rare for any swimmer in Maine to qualify for the Junior Nationals, yet as a 14-year-old Ian did. Ian's first Junior National trip to Miami University of Ohio was the first of many costly travel trips funded by the Crockers as traveling from Portland, Maine, to pretty much anywhere was quite expensive. It also put a strain on the Porpoise small coaching staff. Fortunately, when Coach Power traveled with Ian, she was able to enlist the help of volunteer coach Don Caton to cover the remainder of the team.

Ian's first Junior National meet that summer was the highest level of competition he had ever faced, yet the 14-year-old handled it beautifully. On the first day Ian swam his best time (53.01) in the 100-meter freestyle and placed 10th. The next day he won the 200 freestyle in a time of 1:53.8. Following finals and a quick dinner, Ian and Sharon went to the hotel where Sharon found her copy of the most recent world rankings. Ian's 200 time that night fell just short of being ranked in the top 150 in the world.

"Do you think I'll ever make that list?" Ian asked.

The next day was the preliminaries of the 100-meter butterfly. Ian swam the race without utilizing any kind of breathing pattern but still posted the 23rd fastest time in the meet, which snuck him into the bonus finals. After the race he went over to talk with Coach Power.

"You know what I say to someone who swims like that?" Sharon asked.

Ian's eyes widened beneath his blond hair.

"Two words, pal: Breathing Pattern!"

In warm-up for finals the coach had Ian practice one stroke with a breath, one without a breath. Using his new breathing pattern Ian won the bonus final in a time of 57.6, the third fastest time of all 24 swimmers in the finals of the 100 fly.

1997–1998 PORTLAND PORPOISES – Tenth Grade

Entering his sophomore year in high school the possibility that Ian might become the first Olympic swimmer from Maine seemed real. But so were the conflicts with high school swimming. Ian recognized the relationship between the increased workload with Coach Power's practices and the significant improvement in his times. He wanted even more of that success and knew that in order to continue to progress toward his Olympic goal he needed to practice twice a day at least once or twice per week. He was no longer willing to miss his club team practices to attend high school dual meets and try to fit his schedule around attending high school practices. Even though high school athletes received the bulk of the local publicity, Ian decided to stop swimming for Cheverus.

A fog of ignorance hung thick in the halls of Cheverus High School regarding Ian's decision to forego high school swimming. Many of the students, coaches and even teachers, derided Ian's decision and treated him terribly. Cheverus was a small school, with only 100 students in Ian's class. They offered Advanced Placement classes for students with exceptional academic ability. Yet the appreciation for talent and a commitment to excellence was not extended to someone excelling in a non-school-related individual sport. In fact one of Ian's teachers had the gall to deride him as an "Olympic wannabe" right in front of his classmates. It was that very comment that fueled a pressure campaign designed to get Ian to change his mind. The verbal assaults came not only from his former high school teammates but from many of his classmates as well. Ian was shy to begin with and the ostracism at school hit him hard.

As tough as it was, Ian stuck to both his beliefs and his dream.

Winter days in Maine are cold and short, and the lack of sunlight always bothered Ian. His mom or dad would wake him at 4:30 a.m. for swim practice, and when he left the pool for school at 7:15, the sun was just beginning to appear. When school was over at 2:45 p.m., the sun was already disappearing behind the trees, and by 4:00 p.m. it was pitch black. At this time of year Ian yearned for the physical outlet that his swim training brought him each day.

For Ian, another great relief from the stress of school and the bleak winters was playing his guitar. Each afternoon when he came home from school he'd go up to his room, position himself on his bed, adjust the strap and take hold of his guitar. He would then find a song he liked on his radio and concentrate on playing along with it.

"Oh, where have you been my blue-eyed son?" Dylan squealed over the radio.

"Ian, time for dinner!" his mom called.

Ian was in the middle of learning "Hard Rain" by Bob Dylan. He heard his mom, but remained focused on moving his fingers correctly to the melody.

"Ian, come on! Time for dinner!" his mom called again.

"OK, Mom, I'll be right there!" the tenth-grader yelled back.

Ian sung the lyrics quietly. He was getting it. "I saw 10,000 talkers whose tongues were all broken."

"Ian!"

"What did you hear my blue-eyed son? I heard the roar of a wave that could drown the whole world. I hear 10,000 people talking and no one listening," Ian sang with Dylan.

Ian dropped his guitar on his bed and raced down for dinner.

"Sorry, Mom! What a great songwriter Bob Dylan is. Amazing." Nourished by his musical escape, Ian gobbled up his food and readied for swim practice.

Due to his performance at Junior Nationals the previous summer, and in particular his 200 free, Ian was presented with a wonderful opportunity. USA Swimming was taking the best 18-year-old and younger boys, and the best 16-and-younger girls to England in January for a competition. The trip was both a reward for their performances and an education in training and competing internationally. Ian's initial reaction was that school was challenging enough, and he liked being home and with his friends on his new swim team. The farthest he'd ever traveled from Maine was to Ohio the previous summer to attend the Junior Nationals. Ian told Coach Power that he didn't want to go to England, and Sharon wondered, *If he's unwilling to leave the country, how's he going to go to the Olympics?*

Sharon and Gail gently encouraged Ian to accept the trip to England, the first step of which was to attend a training camp at the US Olympic Training Center in Colorado Springs, Colorado. After quite a bit of soul-searching, Ian agreed to go.

Speaking at the Junior Team camp was Olympic great Matt Biondi. Matt articulated how introverted and out-of-place he felt when he was 14 and 15 years old. Ian thought to himself, *Wow! Just like me ... maybe I'm OK.* Typically, Ian had a very difficult time adjusting to a new group of people, but Matt's comments had such an impact on him that after his talk was over, Ian went to Matt and thanked him. Buoyed in large part by Matt's speech, Ian reluctantly agreed to go to England in May with the team.

Coach Power believed that you "train up and race down." In other words, train for a distance longer than the event you will compete in. During the normal school week the pool sessions were limited to 90 minutes and the volume of practice was restricted accordingly. When school was on a break, however, the team acquired extra pool time and Sharon piled on massive amounts of volume (yardage).

During the holidays in December of 1997, a Canadian team came down for a short training camp with the Porpoise team's older swimmers. The combined group was able to use the Riverton pool, which meant 25-meter training as well as the use of starting blocks and six lanes with lane-lines! It was a glorious upgrade from the Reiche pool. For an extra challenge, the group tackled 100 x 100s. After the long and difficult set there remained 40 minutes in the extended three-hour practice.

"Good job everyone!" Coach Power affirmed. "We have 40 minutes remaining and we're going to do some easy swimming as a recovery from that great set."

"Sharon, how about if I do a 'get out' swim?" Ian proposed.

Sharon consulted with the visiting coach. Then she asked Ian, "What do you have in mind?"

"How 'bout we cut that warm-down in half if I better a certain time?" Ian asked.

Sharon consulted again with the visiting coach. "Under 53 for 100 meters."

"But that's like 47 in a 100-yard free!" Ian argued.

The coaches stood their ground. The team moved out of the center lane and began slapping kick boards on the water and cheering in support of

Ian. He got out of the pool and shook his hands to loosen up his forearms. He adjusted his goggles. The coaches cleared their watches. Ian stepped up on the block.

"Take your mark!" Sharon commanded. "Go!"

With the prospect of getting out of practice 20 minutes early, the two teams cheered madly. Ian raced against time. He loved this sort of challenge. When he touched the wall every swimmer was silent in anticipation. Did he make it?

The Canadian coach and Sharon compared watches. The Canadian coach yelled, "51.6!" The teams went crazy. It may have been a dark, cold December day in Maine, but in that moment Ian Crocker was a hero in the swimming pool.

Winter Break "Monster Sets"1997

Short Course Meters
Warm-up: 1000 easy swim
Main Set: (Endurance 1- Endurance 3 energy systems):

        20 x 100s Free on 1:30
        20 x 100s Free on 1:25
        20 x 100s Free on 1:20
        20 x 100s Free on 1:25
        20 x 100s Free on 1:30
        Ian "get out" swim of 51.6 100 meter free.
        20 minute warm-down

Short Course Meters
Warm-up: 800 easy swim
           800 IM Drill/Pull/Kick/Swim x 50
           Swim 4 x 100s IM descend on 1:40
           Swim 4 x 50s sprint on 1:15
           200 easy swim
Main Set: 24 x 200 Butterfly (4 sets of 6) on 3:00
           Holding breathing pattern for 6 then add 10 seconds to the interval Ian declined adding 10 seconds to the interval, did the breathing pattern and all on 3 min
Warm-down: 800 double arm back/breaststroke x 100
           5,000 meter freestyle for time

           Reprinted with permission ASCA Clinic Book 2000

The increase in Ian's training volume began to cause difficulty with his shoulders. His mother and coach took him to an orthopedic doctor who advised him that while his swimming benefited by his having loose shoulders it was also causing them to become irritated with the long training. As a result, Ian started a shoulder-strengthening program, stopped using hand paddles and agreed with Coach Power to tell her when his shoulders hurt. If they did hurt, Ian would kick the remainder of practice. Regardless of how much endurance work Ian was able to complete, it was hard to keep him from going fast. Ian recorded his best times that winter of 1998 in the 100-yard freestyle of 45.6 and the 200 freestyle of 1:38.0.

1998 US SPRING NATIONALS – Minneapolis, Minnesota

His performance from the previous summer qualified Ian to attend his first US Long Course National Championship in March of 1998 in Minneapolis, Minnesota. It was another long trip from Maine and a large expense for his family. Ian was refining the way he paced his races and improving his times. The 200 was one of the most delicate races to pace, especially swimming long course. Too much effort too soon could create a disaster on the final length. Holding back too much on the first half of the race could put you in a place from which you could not recover. In the preliminaries of his 200-meter freestyle, Ian split the two halves almost evenly with times of 56.5 and 56.0 (1:52.6) to qualify third.

Even though he was just 15 years old, Ian was unruffled in the midst of the competition with the older swimmers. At night he started even easier on the first 50 and lagged in last place, but he finished the last 50 in 27.9 to nearly run down the winner, Josh Davis (1:50.51 to 1:51.57). After warming down, Ian dipped into the hot tub near the warm-down pool. A few minutes later in plunked Josh wearing a warm smile. Josh introduced himself and complimented Ian on his swim. The gesture by the 24-year-old Olympian helped put Ian at ease and initiated a lifelong friendship.

Shortly after the nationals, the US National Junior Team flew to England. Ian was scared. He felt alone. He walked around with his headphones on continuously, locked in his self-made musical cocoon. He looked out at his adopted teammates and thought, *Everyone is so excited to be on this trip but me. What's wrong with me?* Even with his friend from New England swim meets, Erik Vendt, on the trip, Ian felt lost and homesick.

Over the first several days Ian never spoke unless he was absolutely forced to. He roomed with Brendan Hansen. Each night Ian lay in bed with tears running down his face. When his emotions became even more overwhelming he pressed his face into his pillow so Brendan wouldn't hear him and cried himself to sleep.

A "rookie talent show" is a part of each national team trip, and as this Junior Team trip was the first National Team trip for every swimmer, each of them was required to put on a skit of some sort. Ian was asked by a couple of teammates to be in a skit taken from "Saturday Night Live." The scene was meant to be in a living room in a middle class home with two parents telling their teenagers they're worried about them and that they hired a motivational speaker to talk with them. Ian's role was to play the part of Matt Foley (alias the immensely overweight comedian and late Chris Farley). Ian hid in a bathroom with a pillow under his shirt. His heart pounded as he waited for his cue to open the door, step out in front of the team and speak his lines. He heard his cue, opened the door and walked out to face his audience.

Ian used the same high squeaky voice that Chris Farley used when playing the character. He shouted as he entered the scene. "Hi, my name is Matt Foley and I'm a motivational speaker!" The team went wild. Ian was speaking!

Ian acted the part as though he had just drunk five cups of coffee. He moved and gyrated constantly just like Chris Farley had on television.

"I'm 35 years old. I am divorced and I live down by the river in a van."

His teammates and the staff were hysterical. Ian spoke earnestly to the swimmers who played the teenagers in the skit as he tugged on his pillow and made huge arm motions to make his point.

"I know you think you're going to go out into the world and take it by the throat and stick it in your pocket!" Ian blasted.

"But you're wrong!" he squealed, to the roaring group of high-achieving American athletes. "You're not going to amount to jaaack squat!" The team went crazy with joy.

Ian Crocker was a star! The skit connected him with the team. Finally at ease, Ian thoroughly enjoyed the remainder of his trip. Ian returned home feeling relieved that he had conquered the fear of traveling with a US Swim Team—at least for the time being.

After Ian's 200-freestyle performance at the '98 Spring Nationals in Minneapolis, Coach Power's dream of coaching an Olympian was moving more quickly toward fruition than she could have ever imagined. As a result she pushed Ian even more with sets as long as 7200 yards. But the person who pushed Ian the most was his teammate John Stevens. John had qualified for senior nationals in the distance races and was stronger than Ian on the long endurance sets. Ian was faster on sprint work. If Ian didn't keep up on the long sets John berated him, and there were days when John pushed him so hard that Ian's goggles filled with tears. Ian had so much respect for John that no matter how mad he got at him, he didn't yell back—he just worked harder.

In August of 1998, Sharon had Ian swim at the Junior Nationals in Buffalo as a part of his preparation for US Long Course Nationals ("Seniors"). Though over the course of Ian's career he hadn't raced very much long course, Sharon long had recognized Ian's speed and racing ability and she cultivated it. Ian added national qualifying times at that "Juniors,'" in the 100-meter butterfly (55.7) and the 50-meter freestyle (23.28).

In the eyes of many, Ian seemed to be on his way to stardom.

The 1998 US Long Course Summer Nationals were held soon after in Clovis, California, and it was to be the selection meet for several US National Teams that would be competing the following summer (1999). Even though he had grown two inches over the last year and now stood 6' 2" tall, Ian was still just 15 years old. Many of the college swimmers had skipped the Spring Nationals because of NCAA competition, and most of the post-graduate swimmers had skipped Spring Nationals because they had participated in the World Championships in January. In August in Clovis, all of the best swimmers in America were in attendance.

The Quadrennial Plan developed by National Team Director Dennis Pursley was to select two different groups of swimmers for the two major international competitions that would be held in the pre-Olympic year of 1999. This would give twice as many elite American swimmers international experience competing in various parts of the world. It would also inspire them to prepare for the 2000 Olympic Games that were to be held in Sydney, Australia. The highest level team selected, the "A" Team, would compete at the '99 Pan Pacific Games.

Ian's performance in Clovis changed his expectations from one of opportunity to obligation. He defied his youth and placed fourth in the 200-meter freestyle (1:49.48), which qualified him to be on the National "A" Team. His time also ranked him 14th in the world for 1998. Ian also turned in outstanding swims in the 100-meter freestyle (50.83) and the 100-meter butterfly (54.94). His fourth place swim in the 200 free meant that he would most likely swim the 800-meter freestyle relay along with his individual races at the "Pan Pacs," which were to be held at the Olympic pool in Australia. The American swimming community began to believe that Ian was going to be a very impactful swimmer on the 2000 US Olympic Team. Some even called him the next Mark Spitz, who won seven Olympic gold medals in the 1972 Olympics.

It's one thing for a young kid to watch a swimmer perform in the Olympic Games and *dream* about being him. It's quite another when that dream starts to become about *you*. The reality of how close Ian was to becoming that Olympian created tremendous problems as he now felt a tremendous obligation to succeed, not just for himself but for everyone around him. What if he failed?

1999 – PAN PACS – Eleventh Grade

Coach Power may have been more welcome in the US than in Canada as a female coach, but her gender still left her in the huge minority since American "senior" swim coaching remained a male-dominated profession. Despite the success of Ian and her team, she was overlooked when voting took place in Maine Swimming for coach of the year. Her voice in supporting Maine swimmers with national and international aspirations still didn't carry much weight in local swimming politics. Ian sensed this, and he deeply wanted to succeed for her, just as much as he did for himself.

Several coaches in the nearby New England LSC (Local Swimming Committee) saw Ian developing and offered Sharon their advice and resources. Mike Paratto in Dover, New Hampshire, had coached Olympic legend Jenny Thompson and offered the Porpoises long-course training opportunities. Josh Stern and Don Lemieux were coaching young Olympic hopefuls of their own in Erik Vendt and Samantha Arsenault. They all shared their experiences with Sharon and offered encouragement. USA Swimming saw Ian's potential and sent video and stroke drills to try and correct an imbalance in his freestyle. Support seemed to be coming from everywhere ... except from Maine.

Ian felt caught between two opposing forces. At school his accomplishments in national swimming were well-known but never recognized. Instead, he was still being ostracized by his classmates for giving up high school swimming.

Ian was uncomfortable accepting a role on the USA Swimming National A Team. He had watched swimmers like Gary Hall and Josh Davis on television as they competed in the 1996 Olympics. In Ian's eyes they and others were heroes; how could they be his teammates? While Ian signed the papers of commitment to accept the trip to the Pan Pacific Games, he once again did so with great reluctance. As a matter of fact he insisted he did not want to go. He thought, *How much fun could it be to travel with a group of older swimmers that were already close friends?*

As the autumn leaves changed color and fell from the trees, the pressure on Coach Power and Ian to perform for the American Swimming Team mounted. They launched back into the fall season with additional early morning practices. They worked on the suggestions from US Swimming on balancing his freestyle. At first they seemed on their way to building on their success of the previous year of 1998.

Portland Porpoise School Training Schedule – Coach Sharon Power

AM Sessions:	5,000 yards
PM Sessions:	5-6,000 yards
Monday:	5:30-6:50 am – Aerobic (Long warm-up, Drills, Long kick set)
	7:30-9 pm – Endurance (24 x 200s on 2:40, then 2:30 – Descend 1-4 then hold 4 x 3)
Tuesday:	6-6:50 am – Dry-land & Weights (added 1999) –Yoga, Pilates, Light weights with tempo
	7:30-9 pm – Sprint (4 x (100 on 4 min, 7 on 3 min, 50 on 2min, 25 on 1 min)
Wednesday:	5:30-7:00 am – Aerobic
	7:30-9:00 pm – Endurance
Thursday:	6-6:50 am – Dry-land & Weights (added 1999) - Yoga, Pilates, Light weights with tempo
	7:30-9:00 pm – Sprint
Friday:	5:30-6:50 am – Aerobic
	7:30-9:00 pm – Endurance
Saturday:	8-9:30 am – Sprint or competition

The 1999 US Spring Nationals were held in Long Island, New York, the last week of March. The competition typically wasn't as challenging at the Spring Nationals as it was in the summer since most of the college swimmers were involved in the NCAA Championships and did not attend. Although Ian didn't feel sharp in the water, he finished fourth in the 100-meter freestyle with his best time of 50.38. The next day he swam the 200 freestyle—the event that loomed so important to the swimming community and to his chances of making the Olympic Team in 2000. He failed to make it into the championship finals. He won the consolation finals in the evening (1:51.9) but was 2.5 seconds away from the swim that had dazzled so many people in American Swimming the summer prior. He started grumbling to Coach Power about the possibility of quitting swimming.

On the last day of the meet Ian qualified for the consolation finals in the 100-meter butterfly. He won his heat at night finishing ninth place with his best time of 54.6.

Coach Power saw Ian's potential to make the 2000 Olympic Team and be a contributor at the Games. But she also witnessed the stress he felt over his perceived responsibility. She was afraid that he would quit swimming if she continued to ask him to do long grinding sets and marathon sessions. She shifted the training to allow more time to be spent on technique. They experimented with the underwater dolphin kick on his side and other skills they had seen at the nationals. They also added more kicking to their program and created more variety by doing a significant amount of his kicking wearing shoes. The changes helped Ian enjoy practice and kept his mind on the task at hand rather than what might be in his future.

Ian was still saying he wasn't going to the Pan Pacific Games. Sharon and National Team Director Denny Pursley communicated regularly and Denny knew of the problem. At Denny's behest, Josh Davis called Ian and encouraged him to go. Finally all of the parties came to an agreeable solution. Gail and Rick Crocker would make the trip with their 16-year-old son and Ian could bring his guitar.

The Pan Pacs were to be held in Sydney, Australia, in large part to serve as a dress rehearsal for the aquatic facility that was to host the Olympic swimming events one year later. The long flight and the first few days of the trip overwhelmed Ian. His hero Gary Hall was on the trip. Ian admired Gary's swimming ability and also shared Gary's passion for guitars and classic cars. Ian did see some familiar faces, and he was already comfortable around Josh Davis and Erik Vendt.

Although Ian had performed his now famous Chris Farley skit during the Junior Team trip to England, Pan Pacs was his first "official" USA Swimming National Team trip and he was faced with performing before the team once again. His one request for the talent show was, "Please! Just don't make me dress up as a girl." After the talent show was over, Ian felt more at ease with his new teammates and started to have fun—even though they made him dress up as a girl.

The '99 Pan Pacs served as a battleground to determine world swimming supremacy between the USA and Australia. The crowds were massive and the meet was a prime television event for a country that loves swimming. The spectators would not be disappointed. Before the week was over 12 world records had been set.

Young Ian Crocker wanted to contribute to Team USA, but he just didn't understand how he could. He didn't want to be a part of the 800-meter freestyle relay because of the pressure attached to performing in such an important team event. His mind-set created reality.

On the second day Ian was only the seventh fastest American (1:53.04) in the 200-meter freestyle, finishing 23rd overall. His performance was so miserable that it ensured he wouldn't be on the relay. Ian fared no better on the third day of the meet as he finished last among the Americans in the 100-meter freestyle (51.2).

Mercifully, Ian had a day off before he was scheduled to race the 100-meter butterfly. His teammates, coaches and Denny Pursley all tried to encourage Ian, but he felt completely detached from his comfort zone. In the preliminaries on the final day of the meet he was last again with a time of 55.8, over a second slower than his best from the Spring Nationals. Pan Pacs was shaping up as one of the worst swim meets of his life.

Only four swimmers from any given country were permitted to swim again in the finals, and in the 100 fly the Americans had five. But Ugur Tanner, who was fourth, didn't feel well and decided to scratch from the finals.

Ian would have one more chance to perform.

Ian had an established pattern of performing better in finals than in the preliminaries. In the 100 fly his pattern held to form. He won the consolation finals and swam his best time ever of 54.31. The fastest American was Dod Wales, who swam just a little faster with a time of 53.7. "Ian, you could be good at that!" coaches said. "Hey Ian, nice swim," teammates said. He was surrounded by a team that encouraged him. He really didn't know what a good 100 butterfly time was because all he had focused on was the 200 freestyle.

Ultimately the trip with the US National Team affected Ian in a positive way. By the time the team flew back to the USA he had decided that traveling with America's best swimmers and representing his country was something he wanted to do again.

OLYMPIC YEAR 2000 – Twelfth Grade

The US Olympic Swim Teams were getting older each quadrennial. This happened because more college graduates were continuing their swimming careers and taking advantage of the physical and emotional maturity that accompany most people as they move into their mid and late twenties. The average age of the 1996 Men's Olympic Swim Team was 24.9 years. The youngest team member was 19. Given these facts, the possibility of Ian Crocker making the 2000 team at age 17 seemed extraordinary, even if he was able to train in a perfect environment. So Ian's parents got together with Sharon and they brainstormed different ways to best help Ian succeed. Eventually they arrived at a somewhat radical idea: Why doesn't Ian put off his senior year of high school for a year in order to eat better, sleep better and train without distraction in his effort to make the 2000 US Olympic Swim Team?

Ian Crocker wanted no part of staying in cold, dark Portland for another year and putting off his final year at Cheverus High School. He wanted to find a college to attend and, if possible, in a warm, sunny climate. Ian was considered a blue-chip prospect by virtually every college coach in the country. The phone rang constantly with calls from coaches. The NCAA rules dictated that he was allowed five official college visits. The recruiting process takes a toll on many high school seniors because of the long weekends, late nights and travel time to and from their school visits. Five times during September and October Ian made the flight from Portland to Boston, then to Michigan, Auburn, USC, Arizona or Texas. The trips themselves were 48 hours of non-stop activity, followed by the long trip home.

Coach Power planned Ian's fall competition schedule in such a way as to best prepare him for Olympic Trials in August. Sharon wanted him to race against quality competition and in long-course pools, so she entered him in the US Open and World Cup meets. His performances were awful. Her support network of coaches noted to Sharon how exhausted and depressed Ian looked. Sharon guessed that showing Ian what really hard work looked like might motivate him, so she arranged for the two of them to go down to Germantown Academy in Philadelphia to train over a weekend. Coach Dick Shoulberg's group included Olympic hopeful and endurance specialist Maddi Crippen (400 IM). Unfortunately the experience backfired, as Maddi swam all over Ian during the workouts. Ian traveled home wondering more than ever if he had what it took to be a great swimmer.

Sharon and Ian canceled the trip to the US Open.

It was difficult for Ian to make his college choice, but the worst part was saying "no" to four coaches who had been extremely nice to him in the recruiting process. Ultimately, he decided to attend the University of Texas. He liked the warm weather and the team members, but he especially liked the coaches. Ian thought Head Coach Eddie Reese and his assistant Kris Kubik would help him swim faster while at the same time helping him grow into the man he wanted to be.

In November Gail Crocker and Coach Power agreed to enlist the assistance of an energetic trainer named Joanne Arnold in an effort to add to Ian's physical and mental training program. Joanne suggested that they get back to focusing on the present and let go of any discussion of the Trials in August. They worked with Ian on listening to his body and helping him to better understand the process of training. They decided that any conversation about Olympic Trials would be focused five years ahead to 2004.

USA Swimming had given Ian some money for travel and competition expenses leading up to the Trials. The funds made it easier financially for Ian to fly to Federal Way, Washington, in the last week of March for the US Spring Nationals. It was another nationals without most of the college swimmers; nevertheless Ian's expectations were low. He even refused to compete in the 200-meter freestyle. Somehow, on the first day of the meet Ian swam his best time in the 100-meter freestyle. Two days later he swam his best time in the 100-meter butterfly of 53.61. When he looked through the names on the results, his was the fastest of all of the Americans.

During the first two years that Ian had trained with Coach Power his 200 freestyle had developed quickly under a heavy load of endurance work. The change in his training program over the past year may have been made with the intention of keeping Ian in the sport, but it also allowed him to show his speed potential in the 100-meter butterfly, the 100 free, and the 50 free.

On the car ride home from the airport in Maine, Ian said to Coach Power, "Maybe we should think more about Olympic Trials this summer."

Sharon replied, "There's still time to consider it. You still have a chance."

"It would be really stupid if I didn't make the Olympic Team."

Sharon stared straight ahead and drove, working hard to contain her excitement.

Five months before the 2000 Trials Ian's natural speed was developing noticeably. There was no longer anyone in the Porpoises program who could push Ian or challenge him in practice. Some of the swimmers in his training group were as slow as 1:14 in the 100-yard freestyle. They practiced with 10 swimmers per lane and Ian's wide arm span limited most of his butterfly training to using one arm. Coach Power had tried various ways to get him to put more effort into his training over the past six months but without success. So she decided that the best way to get Ian to work hard was to enter him in as many competitions as possible and let him race.

To say the least, Coach Power's plan for Ian Crocker was unconventional, but so was Ian's approach to his daily countdown toward Trials. In June there was a training camp in Colorado Springs for the National Team that provided a great opportunity for both athlete testing and building camarade-rie among the potential members of the Olympic Team. Ian declined the trip, and instead went to his high school graduation and the various events before and afterward. Sharon arranged for a long-course training camp with Mike Paratto's Seacoast Team down in Dover, New Hampshire. It would be the only long-course opportunity available to Ian prior to Trials. Ian declined that trip too, and instead went to a concert with his girlfriend.

Sharon felt some frustration, but she soldiered on. During the week she had Ian do as much aerobic work as he could take, then on the weekends they traveled and he raced. He raced from Nova Scotia to Long Island. Some results were good. He won the 100-meter freestyle in mid-July at the Long Island Open in 51.6. Some results were bad. He didn't place in the top three in any other event at the same meet.

As they neared the Trials many of Ian's workouts consisted of an easy 1500–2500 meters for his entire practice. Other days he performed race-pace swims. The formula was simple: race and rest, race and rest. Eight days prior to the start of the Olympic Trials Ian went to the US Junior Nationals in Miami, Ohio. The Junior Meet ended August 5th; Olympic Trials was scheduled to begin on August 9th.

2000 US OLYMPIC TRIALS

At the Olympic Trials in Indianapolis, the 200-meter freestyle was Ian's first event. The fastest six swimmers would qualify for the Olympic Team—the first two as individual competitors, the next two as relay swimmers, and the next two as relay alternates. Ian finished 65th. His time of 1:54.32 was about five seconds off his best. The Portland newspaper published an article the next morning that said he had "blown his opportunity to make the Olympic Team." But after the race, Coach Power was undaunted. Sharon sensed that Ian believed his best chance to make the team was in the 100 freestyle, while she believed it was in the 100 butterfly. When Ian came to see her after his terrible 200 free performance, she calmly told him, "Shrug it off. You've got more opportunities in the next few days. Go warm down and let's go get some food."

Two days later Ian swam fast enough in the preliminaries of the 100-meter freestyle to qualify for the semi-finals. Later that night Ian turned in his best time (50.04), but he placed 11th leaving him three spots short of the finals. He was very disappointed. Each night he watched as many of his friends from the Pan Pac team were introduced as qualifying members of the 2000 Olympic Team. Each night he confided in Coach Power, "Those are my teammates! I'm as good as they are. Why am I not on their team?" The obligation that Ian once felt to swim the 200 freestyle and the 800 freestyle relay had dissolved, and what surfaced to take its place was a desire to join his friends and go back to Sydney as an Olympian.

Ian lay in bed in his hotel room and thought about how he was going to swim the 100 butterfly. *A controlled stroke on the first 50 meters. Head down, hips up* [in the same way that Coach Murphy taught him]. *Caress the water out front with my hands.* [If he rushed his "anchor point" out front he slipped.] *Wrap my hands around the water. On the second length build speed. The last 25 meters snap the kick and finish.*

In the preliminaries of the 100-meter butterfly Ian remained calm and that was reflected in his result. Ian swam to a best time of 52.82, which narrowly missed Neil Walker's American record of 52.7 and seeded him first going into the semi-finals. Ian was thrilled! He knew he had more in him. He thought he could have started faster and worked harder at the beginning of the race. Coach Power didn't agree but analyzed the times of all the swimmers in semi-finals. Ian was well ahead of the eighth-place swimmer. The coach supported his experiment of starting the semis with more effort. Ian tried his adjusted race-plan that night, and while he remained the leading qualifier coming out of the semi's he had slowed a little bit to a 53.0.

The last night of the Trials was August 15th, and one of the last events on the finals schedule was the men's 100-meter butterfly. As with the other events, the top two performers in the 100 fly would earn spots on the Olympic Team. The eight fastest swimmers in America sat in the ready room waiting to be introduced to the packed crowd of 4,000 spectators and the 1,000 or more athletes on the pool deck. Some of the men in that room knew that if they finished anything lower than second, this would be the last swim of their career.

Ian was nervous, but he focused on performing well rather than being afraid of failing. He also received an important boost from the fourth-place qualifier for the finals, Tommy Hannan. Ian had met the University of Texas swimmer during his recruiting trip to Austin. Tommy was a big strong athlete who intimidated Ian outside the pool. Tommy approached Ian in the ready room and offered quietly, "Swim your own race and you'll be fine." Did Ian just hear that right? One of his competitors for making the Olympic Team just gave him constructive advice?

Ian swam his own race. He was relaxed at first, fierce at the finish and won (52.78). With justice served for noble acts, Tommy Hannan improved tremendously and finished second in 52.81. Ian felt like he was in a dream.

Two days prior he was down and out, and now suddenly he was on top of the world. He had always thought of himself as a freestyler, yet now he was the best sprint butterfly swimmer in America.

Coach Power was elated ... and relieved.

Following finals Ian was kept busy, first by the award ceremony for making the Olympic Team and then by a mandatory drug-testing procedure that seemed to take forever. Later on Ian told the press, "I just wanted to come here and experience it, take it all in and see what happened. It turned out good." A reporter mumbled, "Now there's the classic understatement."

Finally, Ian was able to see his parents and witness how proud they were. The great state of Maine finally had its first Olympic swimmer.

2000 OLYMPIC GAMES – Sydney, Australia

After two days at home Ian flew off to Los Angeles for a training camp. From there he and his "teammates" flew to Sydney, Australia. The experience he had gained at Pan Pacs the previous summer had helped him mature tremendously as a swimmer and as a person. This time around he felt at home with his friends on the National Team. Adding to his comfort level were two swimmers even younger than him on the team. They were Aaron Peirsol, who had just turned 17, and Michael Phelps who was just 15.

Coach Power suggested to the Olympic Team coaches that Ian's training be built on a high concentration of speed work.

Coach Power Olympic Training Camp Guidelines:

Warm-up:	2-2,500 meters
	Technique Work: 3-500 yards or meters
Kick set:	500-1,000 yards or meter, approximately 200 of it quality on alternate days
Speed work:	At the Los Angeles Camp: 100s on 5:00 on alternate days
	At the Brisbane Camp 50s on 5:00 on alternate days
	Get at Time Trial in 100 free once the Games have started 2 to 3 days before the 100 fly
	Swim down 400-600 after every workout

Reprinted with permission ASCA Clinic Book 2000

It wasn't until the seventh day of the Olympic swimming program that the men's 100-meter butterfly was to be contested. When Ian walked out on the pool deck for the preliminaries he was nervous, but he was so impressed with the crowd noise that a smile creased his face from ear to ear. He was embracing the experience. The 18,000 roaring fans from Australia were even louder than the concert he'd attended with his girlfriend not so many months ago. Ian looked up into the stands and spotted Coach Power who watched eagerly from the seat she had moved to near the pool deck.

In the preliminaries Ian rushed his stroke and placed ninth (53.45). Afterward he found Sharon and he immediately blurted out, "What a stupid swim!"

Sharon agreed, "Yes it was!" But then reassured him, "But you know you did just what you needed to. You're back in semi-finals. Now just settle down and do the job. You know how to swim that race." She finished with, "Like Nike says, 'Just Do It!'"

In the semi-finals that evening, Ian kept calm on the first length and made sure to hold onto the water on his first two strokes following his breakout from the turn. Ian finished strong. His time of 52.82 earned him the third seed in the next evening's finals.

Ian focused on achieving two goals in the finals: One was to overtake Neil Walker's 100 butterfly American record, and the second was to place in the top three and win an individual medal. He came away from the race having achieved one of his goals. His time of 52.44 was the fastest time ever swum by an American swimmer, yet he finished fourth, narrowly missing the bronze medal.

The final event of the Sydney Olympics was the Men's 400-meter medley relay. The USA had never been beaten in the event in Olympic history. In each of those Olympic gold medal performances, the USA had set a new world record. Earlier in the week Australia had won both the 400 and 800 freestyle relays, each in world-record times. Two years earlier, at the 1998 World Championships, Australia had handed the US men a stinging defeat in the medley relay. The expectation for the finals was that the Aussies had an advantage in butterfly and the US had an advantage in breaststroke.

In the first leg of the race backstroker Lenny Krayzelburg gave the Americans a slight lead. In the breaststroke leg, while turning in the first sub-minute split (59.8) in history, Ed Moses extended that lead to 1.8 seconds. The two freestylers—Gary Hall for the United States and Michael Klim for Australia—were considered about equal, so if Ian Crocker could maintain at least some of that lead during his butterfly leg, then the USA had an outstanding chance to win the gold medal.

During the butterfly leg Krayzelburg, who had been so upset by the medley relay loss at the World Championships, couldn't even watch. The crowd roared as Australia's Glen Huegill blitzed to the fastest butterfly relay split in history (51.3). Yet with all this and more, Ian kept his cool and swam his race. He extended his arms to anchor his hands, he allowed his hips to rise, and made sure his stroke flowed through the first 50 meters.

As he pushed off the wall at the turn Ian started to pick up his kick, more and more as he progressed through the second 50. His hands snapped through while he concentrated on holding his stroke length. He extended his fingers toward the wall and handed Gary Hall a large lead. Despite Michael Klim's great effort, he didn't gain an inch on the American team. When Hall touched the timing pad at the finish, the Americans had once again established a new world record (3:33.73) in the Olympic Games. Seventeen-year-old Ian Crocker had recorded the fastest butterfly split ever turned in by an American (52.10). Not only was Ian the first swimmer from Maine to ever make an Olympic swimming team, he had just held his own against the best swimmers in the world.

"The Star-Spangled Banner" was the final anthem played in the 2000 Olympic swimming program. Ian stood shoulder-to-shoulder with his idol Gary Hall to his right and Ed Moses to his left. A gold medal hung around his neck. With his right palm placed squarely over his heart he quietly sang the anthem while his eyes locked onto the rising American flag. Coach Don Murphy sat in Maine and watched on television. His heart pounded with pride and excitement. One could only wonder if that flag would be rising and if that anthem would be playing were it not for the contributions and sacrifices made by Don Murphy, Sharon Power and the Crocker family.

After the awards ceremony Ian greeted his coaches and family, then he went to the locker room and changed into his clothes. When he exited the locker room he walked back out onto to the pool deck. The lights were dimmed and it was eerily quiet. The competition pool was being re-staged for water polo. The lane lines had already been pulled out. His mind flashed to Portland, Maine, and their four-lane pool with no lane lines. The water in the Olympic pool was clear and vast without structure or division. The Olympic swimming program was over and Ian's 2000 Olympic swimming experience concluded. From announcing his Olympic dream to Don Murphy while swimming at the Portland Y, to pronouncing his quitting of the sport of swimming to Sharon Power, some would say his journey was impossible; others might concede just improbable. Ian reached into his pocket, wrapped his fingers around his Olympic gold medal and pressed it into his palm. He couldn't help but smile.

In Portland, Maine, on the front lawn of Cheverus Jesuit High School, the school administration hoisted an Olympic flag up their school flag pole.

2000–2001 THE UNIVERSITY OF TEXAS – Freshman Year

The Olympics ended the last week of September, so when Ian arrived in Austin the first week of October it was too late to take fall semester classes. For a shy young man from Maine, it was difficult to connect with the other freshman who had been in school for more than a month. He roomed with Brendan Hansen, who liked spending his free time outdoors hunting and fishing. Ian liked to sit in his room and play his guitar. Without much to do, Ian trained with the team and waited for classes to begin in January of 2001.

At the 2001 NCAA Championships held at Texas A&M in March, the Texas Longhorns stampeded the country rolling up one of the highest point totals in meet history while defeating a strong Stanford team. For the first time, other than at the Olympics, Ian swam on relays that were crucial to his team's success. His tremendous freestyle anchor leg of 41.9 on the 400-yard medley relay the first night of competition was the first taste of the many contributions Ian made to his team over the course of the meet. He finished 13th in the 50-yard freestyle (19.9), fifth in the 100-yard freestyle (43.1) and won the 100-yard butterfly in 45.9. It had been years since he'd swum short-course times that meant much to him. His improvements and the team environment were great reassurances that he had made an excellent choice of where to attend college.

In the summer of 2001 Ian stayed in Austin to train. For the first time he enjoyed practicing in a 50-meter pool and being surrounded by athletes with world-class ability and world-class goals. At the Summer Nationals Ian won the 100-meter butterfly, though his time of 52.46 was no faster than he had swum in Sydney. Michael Phelps didn't swim the 100 fly at this meet, but he did draw the attention of the swimming world when he set the world record in the 200-meter butterfly (1:54.9). After the nationals, Ian traveled with the National Team to Fukuoka, Japan, for the World Championships. Ian had a great race in the 100-meter fly and was just nipped at the finish by Australia's Geoff Hugeill (52.22 to 52.25). Ian lowered his own American record in earning the silver medal.

2001-2002 THE UNIVERSITY OF TEXAS – Sophomore Year

Ian had been challenged by the long dark days in Maine, but he also found long dark emotional days in Austin, Texas. Most young ladies and young men that go away to college have times when they struggle to find comfort in their independence and self-reliance. It was no different for Ian. He became close to a girl and tried to please her, but his efforts were never enough. He made friends, but struggled to develop an identity other than that of an Olympic swimmer. He sunk himself into playing the guitar, but all too often the music brought him deeper into himself rather than revealing his inner joy. His personal struggles negatively affected his swimming, and his swimming affected his personal struggles.

The NCAA Championships highlighted each winter season for Texas. In 2002, Ian finished fifth in the 50 (19.8), ninth in the 100 (43.0) and won the 100-yard butterfly in a new NCAA record of 45.4. The team won a narrow victory over Stanford, but Ian had improved little since the year before. His search for his swimming potential and his search for his maturity as a young man started him questioning everything around him. He asked himself, *Have I already reached my peak in swimming? Should I stop? Would I feel more comfortable at some other school? Should I transfer?*

By summer his mood that had been going downhill was now entrenched in a valley. Going to the mall scared him, and bad traffic ruined his day. Fights with his girlfriend continued. Training was a bore. Finally Gail Crocker boarded a plane and flew to Austin to see him. She was alarmed at Ian's state of mind. She recalled her son as a young boy asking, "How can I make the world a better place?" Gail wondered where that goodwill had gone and how he could be in such a depressed mental state. Her professional background told her there were diagnostic tests that could help them discern Ian's mood and how to help him. Ian agreed to take the tests.

It was determined that Ian was clinically depressed. He began taking medication and seeing a doctor weekly. He also sought to make positive changes in his life that started with finding a roommate for the fall who was an engineer and knew nothing about swimming.

The 2002 US Long Course Summer Nationals were in Ft. Lauderdale and served as the selection meet for the Pan Pacific Games to be held again in Fukuoka a few weeks later. This time Michael Phelps entered the 100-meter butterfly. Michael was having a "coming-out party," breaking world records with a performance so dominating that it demanded that the world of swimming sit up and take notice. Michael won the 100-meter butterfly in 51.88, breaking Ian's American record by beating Ian by nearly half a second.

Michael didn't swim the 100 fly at Pan Pacs, and Ian edged Geoff Hugeill with a time of 52.4.

2002-2003 THE UNIVERSITY OF TEXAS – Junior Year

Neither Eddie Reese nor Ian Crocker could accept being beaten by Michael Phelps, especially since Ian hadn't improved significantly in the last two years. Coach Reese built his career helping underdogs find their potential. From Gary Shatz at Auburn to Shaun Jordan at Texas there were dozens of young men with little background and lots of hope that Eddie helped develop into world-class swimmers. Diagnosing the missing ingredient that separated a swimmer from his potential was, and is, a critical part of Eddie's genius.

Furthermore, the coach's first world record-holder was William Paulus in the 100-meter butterfly in 1981 (53.81). Texas swimmer Neil Walker was the American record-holder (52.8) when Ian broke it. Eddie had been very successful helping his swimmers excel in the event. In Ian's first two and a half years with Sharon Power he had survived many of her "monster sets," and if endurance helped him then perhaps it would help him now. Eddie put Ian in the Texas distance lanes with Matt McGinnis, Ricky Berens and occasionally freshman Aaron Peirsol every Monday, Wednesday and Friday during the fall semester of 2002.

Ian always preferred racing to training, but he remembered and accepted Coach Murphy's edict that everything of value in life has a cost. He willingly accepted the challenge to build his endurance. The afternoon water sessions were conducted immediately after hard work in the weight room. When Ian attempted 20 x 100 yard freestyles on 1:00 and completed 17 of them he was proud to be one of the few team members to make it that far. After a few months of distance work he moved into the middle-distance group, and by February he was a sprinter again.

Little by little he began to make positive changes in his life. His music interests moved from Pink Floyd to more optimistic artists like Dylan and the Allman Brothers. He was moving closer to finding himself as a person, rather than a swimmer obligated to perform. Beer became boring in Ian's junior year. He stopped drinking alcohol, starting fishing, and dated a girl that accepted him for who he was. He took his guitar to clubs some nights to play. He finally found that at the pool he could be an athlete, but away from it he could be a person.

Life was improving wonderfully. Ian's investment of endurance work gave him more reasons than ever to perform well at the 2003 NCAA Championships. He did win the 100 butterfly in 45.67, but didn't score in any other individual event. Auburn ran away with the meet despite Texas swimming in their home pool and adding freshman world record holder Aaron

Peirsol to their team. Ian was qualified to swim on the US Team at the World Championships in Barcelona in July. But he was so disappointed in his continued stagnant swimming performances that he confided in his teammate Neil Walker that he saw his swimming career coming to an end.

"I think this may be it for me."

"What?"

"This may be the last long-course meet of my life," Ian said.

"Really?" Neil asked. "What do you mean?"

"It's been three years now and I haven't improved my 100 fly at all. I'm going to be a senior, and I'm thinking about finishing up with the NCAAs and calling it a career."

The search for speed had been a part of Ian Crocker's psyche since he was a small boy feeling his hands in the water to maximize his control of it. The distance work he'd invested in during the fall hadn't seemed to help him find speed for the NCAAs. But when Ian tapered for the 2000 Trials, Coach Power let him float easily through as little as 1500–2500 yards of swimming two or three days per week. He asked Eddie Reese if he could try approaching the World Championships that way. He was a college junior now and fully grown to nearly 6' 5". Eddie complied with his request.

Ian arrived in Barcelona having rested over the last four weeks more than he ever had before. He felt speed. In the semi-finals of the 100-meter butterfly he swam a 52.21. It was just a little better than his best time, but it felt easy. In the following heat Michael Phelps broke the world record with a time of 51.47. But Ian was about to shake up the world.

In the finals Ian swam his race by staying in rhythm on the first 50. He put his hands on the wall and turned in the time of 23.99. Michael turned in 25.1. On his first two strokes after he exploded to the surface Ian held water and gradually increased his effort. Michael had more endurance than any butterfly swimmer in the world and was catching up—but not much. On the last 25 meters Michael closed the gap on Ian, closer, closer, but Ian had too big a lead. Ian Crocker finished, looked at the scoreboard and his time was 50.98! A new world record! Michael had swum the second-best time in history, but not quite good enough at 51.10.

The next month *Swimming World Magazine* pictured Ian Crocker on the cover strumming his guitar in front of his classic old car.

2004 OLYMPIC YEAR – THE UNIVERSITY OF TEXAS – Senior Year

The 2004 NCAA Championships were held in Long Island and the pool was set for short-course meters. The purpose was to draw attention to swimming before the Olympics began by giving the participants the chance to break world records that were only kept in 25-meter courses. When the championships were over one report started with a headline: "IAN THE GREAT." This is why:

On the first night of finals Ian split an astonishing 48.62 100-meter butterfly on the Texas 400 medley relay that broke Australia's world record by nearly three seconds. He was also second in the 50 freestyle in 21.53. On the second night he split 21.8 on the butterfly leg of the 200 medley relay. Then he uncorked a 22.76 50 split on his way out in his 100-meter butterfly and ripped through the distance in 49.07, shattering the world record.

Ian's final individual swim of his collegiate career may have been the most impressive of all. The year prior he had not scored a point in the 100-yard freestyle. This time he was swimming to win. He trailed Cal's winner of the 50 freestyle, Duje Draganja, at the halfway point, but then flew by him. When he stuck his fingers into the finish he broke Russian legend Alexander Popov's 10-year-old world record by a half a second (46.25).

Ian summed up his amazing performance: "Since I began swimming, there have always been dreams of records and gold medals. But the big goal has been going to a separate level, like Phelps and Thorpe. It's a disease that I won't be satisfied with until I get there" (SW April 2004).

Ian Crocker had a gift for swimming speed. Perhaps an even better example was when the UT team held long-course Time Trials after the Big 12 Championships at the swim center for team members that had yet to qualify for the Olympic Trials. Ian and the swimmers that weren't performing in the time trials came to cheer for their teammates.

"Ian, why don't you put on a suit and swim a 50 and see what you can do?" Coach Reese asked.

"You want me to?"

"Sure, swim the 50 fly."

Ian went in the locker room and pulled on a full-body racing suit. He came out about 20 minutes later.

"Eddie, when am I up?" he asked.

"Three more heats, about 10 minutes."

Ian Crocker swam the 50-meter butterfly, touched the wall and the officials and the staff went into a frenzy. They began calling people who did drug testing for USA Swimming that were in the local area. They needed to verify all the standards necessary to make it official: Ian Crocker broke the world record with a time of 23.30.

Mark Spitz established an Olympic record of winning seven gold medals at the 1972 Olympic Games. In the entire history of the Games, only Matt Biondi in 1988 approached Spitz's feat. But talk was growing that Michael Phelps might be able to equal the record at the 2004 Athens Games. He could do it by being on three winning relays, win both individual medleys, both butterfly events, and possibly upset Ian Thorpe and Pieter van den Hoogenband and win the 200 freestyle. The Speedo Company made the possibility more interesting by offering him $1 million if he was successful. Beating Ian Crocker in the 100-meter butterfly was a major hurdle to overcome, and the whole world knew it.

The 2004 Olympic Trials were held in Long Beach, California, in a parking lot, but it was a spectacular setting. An above-ground pool was constructed and bleachers were built for 9,000 spectators. Ian's dreams that he disclosed at the NCAAs of "getting to another level" were buoyed by a second-place finish in the 100-meter freestyle (49.06). That swim earned him the opportunity to swim the event individually at the Games, as well as made him a likely member of the 400 freestyle relay. In the finals of the 100-meter butterfly he lowered his world record to 50.76, beating Michael Phelps who swam the time of 51.10.

2004 OLYMPIC GAMES – Athens, Greece

The centennial Athens Olympics seemed to be the perfect setting for Ian Crocker to show the world his gift to swim fast and how he had transformed it into a reality. He had the potential for two relay gold medals, another for the 100 butterfly and the possibility of medaling in the 100 freestyle. The format at the 2004 Olympics placed the 400 freestyle relay before the individual event of the 100 freestyle. Tradition in America is that the first two finishers from the Trials are placed on the relay but only in the evening finals. This is done to reduce their workload during the competition and with the knowledge that American depth is so great that the very best swimmers are not required for the qualification of the relay into the finals that consist of eight teams. Ian rested in the preliminaries. But he wasn't feeling well. His throat was sore and he felt bad enough that antibiotics were considered, although not used.

Gabe Woodward led off the morning relay in 49.9, Nate Dusing swam second (49.), Neil Walker swam third (48.1) and Gary Hall anchored in 48.7.

Neil's performance clearly earned him a position on the evening relay. The question for the USA coaching staff was whether Michael Phelps should be added to the relay or whether Gary Hall should swim on it. The 100-meter freestyle was not one of Michael's strongest events. But he had swum the event well enough during the year to merit consideration. It was also impossible to ignore the fact that he had the chance to rewrite the record books by winning seven or eight gold medals at the Athens Games, but he needed the relay swim to begin the herculean feat.

Gary Hall was a strong consideration. He had a legacy of great relay swims at the Olympics. He had finished third at the Trials (49.16), just a tenth of a second behind Ian Crocker. He wanted to redeem the USA loss in the 2000 Games to the Australians in an event that the USA had never lost until that occasion. On the other hand Gary was 29 years old and many swimming experts questioned the background of work he carried with him into the Olympics. Coach Reese was the head coach for the Men's Olympic Team and chose Michael Phelps to join Crocker, Walker and Jason Lezak for the relay.

Ian led off the relay in 50.05, the slowest lead-off leg of any team in the finals. The Americans were in eighth place and never recovered. Michael Phelps (48.74), Neil Walker (47.97) and Jason Lezak (47.86) could not make up all of the distance they were behind. South Africa won the relay with the American team 1.45 seconds behind, winning a bronze medal. Ian was devastated. From his perspective, he had not only cost his teammates gold medals, he had also taken away Michael Phelps' opportunity to win eight gold medals and earn $1 million. The press wanted to know why Gary Hall wasn't on the relay. Eddie Reese told them, "Ian Crocker can't swim that slow." He simply couldn't believe that regardless of health that Ian could have such a poor swim.

The next day was the individual event of the 100-meter freestyle. Ian's time of 49.72 was well off his time from the Trials. There was one day to rest before the preliminaries of the 100-meter butterfly. His throat was still hurting and he wasn't well. He managed to get through the preliminaries and semi-finals with the fastest time (52.0)—still much slower than his best time.

In the finals of the 100-meter butterfly he shot off the start like never before. He turned in 23.5, and by the time he took his first two strokes at 65 meters he led Michael Phelps by nearly a full body length. Ian held onto the lead all the way under the flags with five meters remaining. But Michael has an uncanny way of getting his hands to the wall. He stopped the clock .04 sooner than Ian did to win the gold medal in a time of 51.25 to Ian's 51.29.

Ian Crocker had overcome so much over his life to get to the Olympics and then get here again. He knew the definitiveness of finishing second. There would be no swim for the gold medal on the medley relay. As hard as he had tried to rebound from his devastating lead-off leg on the 400 freestyle relay, during these Olympics he had come up just short of a gold medal in the 100-meter butterfly and the potential for a great relay experience to close out the swimming events at these Olympics just as he had four years prior.

While Ian pondered his disappointments a press conference was being held. Ian was in the training room when Eddie Reese came in and told him the results.

"Ian, we want you on the medley relay tomorrow night," Eddie said.

"What? What do you mean?"

"We feel as though you have the most experience swimming relays and starting off of Brendan (Hansen, his teammate at Texas). You're on the relay."

"But Michael earned that spot," Ian protested meekly.

"Michael wants it that way too," Eddie finished. "Get ready to swim the relay tomorrow night."

Ian thought to himself, *This is a gift way too big to accept.* But he didn't have a choice.

Michael Phelps had won a record four individual gold medals at the Athens Olympics, but his decision to ask for Ian Crocker to take his place on the final relay won the respect and admiration of the public everywhere. At the press conference he explained that he had a poster of Ian on his bedroom wall to motivate him to train to beat him. But he had more to say than that. "For me, doing that, it's tough," Phelps said. "But Ian is one of the greatest relay swimmers on the US team. He wasn't feeling too well in the 400 freestyle relay, but I'm willing to give him a chance to step up tomorrow night and hopefully win the relay. I'm proud of giving someone like Ian another chance," he said. "We came in as a team," he added. "We will leave as a team" (ESPN 8/21/04).

Aaron Peirsol led off the 400 medley relay in a world-record backstroke leg of 53.45 and the Americans never looked back. Peirsol and Brendan Hansen (59.37) handed Ian Crocker a lead. Ian swam the fastest butterfly relay leg in history of 50.28 while Michael Phelps cheered from the spectator area. Jason Lezak brought the gold medal home (47.58) and the Americans set a new world record in a time of 3:30.68.

Ian Crocker stood proudly on the award podium with his teammates and friends as the American flag was raised and the national anthem played. Then he went and found Michael Phelps. They hugged with gratitude. Ian had given Michael competition. Michael had given Ian his respect. They both gained from the other.

Ian Crocker continued to swim for four more years until the age of 26. He represented the United States in his third Olympics in 2008 in Beijing. This time Ian swam the preliminaries of the 400 medley relay and Michael swam the finals. They both won gold medals—again. The world record Ian set in the 100-meter butterfly in 2003 stood a full six years until broken by Michael Phelps in 2009.

Not everyone can be an Olympic swimming champion, but Olympic champions come from everywhere. Once upon a time that couldn't be said about Portland, or *anywhere* in Maine, but because of Ian Crocker it can be said now. Ian Crocker ignored his underdog status and found coaches and friends who loved and supported him in the exploration of his gift to swim fast. When one pool closed in Portland, Maine, they found Ian another pool to train. After he cried himself to sleep in England, he found the courage to get on the plane and go to Sydney, Australia. His 200 freestyle flopped at the first Olympic Trials, but he recovered to make his first Olympic Team in the 100 butterfly. When he encountered a plateau, he worked harder. Whenever a door closed, he and his support team found another door to open. He had parents who provided every opportunity they could conceive of to help him overcome the challenges of swimming in Maine.

Most of all, Ian Crocker relied on his courage to overcome any geographical, physical or emotional obstacle in order to see how fast he could be. And he did just that.

Ian Crocker resides in Austin, Texas. He works with his friend and Longhorn teammate Josh Davis conducting marvelous swim clinics around the United States. If you peek into one of them you might see a child that's struggling to keep up riding down the pool on Ian's shoulders. Ian likes underdogs.

GRANT HACKETT

May 9, 1980

THE GREATEST TRAINER IN THE WORLD

After World War II swimmers in Eastern Europe traditionally were given a boost and direction in their development from an early age in specialized sports schools run by the government (primarily the former USSR and the GDR). In the United States, summer swim leagues were the launching ground for the careers of most American swimmers. In Australia, however, the special characteristics of that unique island/continent/nation provided a genesis for swimming that was unique as well. Swimming makes sense for safety in Australia, but it is also a source of national pride. Eighty percent of its population of over 22 million people lives less than 30 miles from a 16,000-mile coastline that includes over 10,000 sandy beaches, almost all of it awash and glistening in rolling surf.

All the Aussies have ever needed to get started in competition is the ocean. There are contests on the beach and in the surf that draw great attention from the nation, including (but not limited to) beach volleyball, surf riding, surf lifesaving, open-water swimming, and Ironman. The favorites are almost always the ones that are the most grueling. The longest race in pool swimming is the 1500-meter freestyle and to be the best at it, you must become the greatest trainer in the world. In the sport of swimming, that means Grant Hackett. This is his story.

* * *

A sliver of sun sent a blaze of light across the ocean that reflected off the windows of the homes along the shoreline of Southport. It was daybreak on the Gold Coast of Australia. The waves crashed on the beach and sounded like thunder to the surf fisherman. Seagulls swept across the water surface and along the beach in search of breakfast. In a week's time those on their morning walk would have to find another favorite spot to look for shells. This golden beach would be transformed into a sports venue filled with bleachers seating a mass of spectators to witness the heroics of hundreds of contestants competing in the famous "Uncle Toby Super-Series."

The Super-Series began in the 1980s. Its original format included a 22 km ski leg (kayak), a 2.2 km mile run, a 2.3 km swim, another 2.2 km run, another swim and another 10 km run. This race lasted over four and half hours. The series expanded its sites so that thousands entered under the umbrella name of "Uncle Toby's" each summer. These athletes battled the riptides and steep wave walls while facing the sweltering humidity and baking temperatures under the Australian sun. The event was so popular in Australia that in 1998 the prize money was nearly $1 million.

Many athletes who competed in these events became professionals and earned a living performing in it. In the early 1990s its popularity was so widespread it was recognized as a major sporting event and was carried on Network 10 television in Australia. The sight of the competition on ski boats traversing 10-foot surf was a demonstration of the fortitude of these Australian athletes, and the grueling competition whetted the appetites of the millions of countrymen tuning in. In 1996, 20 of the top performers were flown to the US to appear as part of the television series "Baywatch." The coach of some of the most successful triathletes in both the Uncle Toby and other international competitions was Denis Cotterell, also a coach for competitive pool swimming.

It was Sunday January 18, 1998. The Challenge Swim Stadium in Perth, on the west coast of Australia, played host to the seventh and final day of the FINA Long Course World Swimming Championships. The Australians had battled the Americans race after race in a great show of strength, building their prospects toward the Olympics they would host in Sydney in 2000. Although most of the pool events lasted a few minutes or even as little as 22 seconds, the Aussies loved the long races.

The home fans were chanting "Aussie, Aussie, Aussie—Oy! Oy!" They were trying to inspire their entrants in an event known in some parts of the world as the "mile" but which in Australia was most commonly known as the "fifteen-hundred" (1500-meter freestyle). It sounded longer when stated that way. Kieren Perkins had won the 1500 at the last two Olympics but had not competed over the 18 months since the 1996 Games. The crowd offered their best vocal effort to help their beloved Aussie men succeed in this, the last individual race of the World Championships.

In lane seven, 17-year-old Grant Hackett opened a commanding two-body length lead over the field on the first 300 meters. His friend and Aussie teammate Dan Kowalski trailed in fourth in lane five. Hackett held each 100 split at 59 seconds for the first 600 meters and then settled down to 60 seconds per 100 and maintained a large lead throughout the race. On the final 100 meters the crowd leapt to their feet, urging Hackett and Kowalski on. While Hackett seemed to have an insurmountable lead, Kowalski was in a battle for second with the Ukraine's Igor Snitko. Grant poured on the speed on his final 100, recording a 56.4 split, and touched the wall with a winning time of 14:51.70. Dan flew through the final 50 meters making up more than a second and narrowly grabbed the bronze medal from Snitko in a time of 15:03.94 to 15:04.30. America's top performer Tyler Painter was left more than a pool length behind, finishing in a time of 15:23.40.

The crowd loved the finish and so did the Australian television commentators. They broadcast the conclusion of the race and the celebration afterward over national television.

"The Australians are back in business! Grant Hackett is now the second fastest Australian 1500 swimmer of all time and the third fastest in the history of the world!"

Grant climbed from the pool and raised his arms over his head in celebration.

The announcers narrated the scene over the air waves: "He's a great bloke! He's a great Australian!"

Grant marched victoriously around the pool deck to Coach Cotterell and the two clamped a handshake.

"There he is with his coach Denis Cotterell. He makes you proud to wear the green and gold."

The interviewer on the pool deck stopped Grant and asked him, "What were you thinking about during the race?"

Grant responded, "That I was going to be a world champion! I didn't want to over-swim the first part like I did in the 400 against Ian (Thorpe), but I thought I was holding up well."

"What has been the influence of Denis Cotterell?" the interviewer asked.

"Oh, he's been huge; he's a fantastic coach. He's been there since I was seven years old. And I've also got to thank my parents, my brother, his girlfriend, all my mates: Chris, Branch, Hadley, Matt, and of course Joel and all the people at the Bond School." Grant continued later, "Everyone wants to be a part of the Australian team for the Sydney Olympics. It will be a tough team to make."

Grant was euphoric, but Australian National Team Director Don Talbot was cautious about his future in the 1500 at the Sydney Olympics when he said, "Don't count out Kieren Perkins."

Kieren Perkins stood at poolside commentating for television. He had earned his legendary status throughout the competitive swimming world. Each of his two 1500 Olympic victory swims was the highest rated sporting event of the year that the Australians watched on television. The national tradition of success in the mile dated back to the 1920s and included the names of swimmers such as Frank Beaurepaire and Andrew "Boy" Charlton on through a lineage that included Murray Rose, Jon Konrads and Stephen Holland. Perkins had his sights set on being the first man to ever win the 1500 at three consecutive Olympics.

Perkins' life and development with Coach Jon Carew was well documented, but Grant Hackett had burst onto the swimming scene in just the past 18 months. Therefore, most of the swimming world didn't know much about him.

THE EARLY YEARS

Grant Hackett grew up on the southern coast of Australia in Southport, a suburb of Gold Coast City. The name "Southport" was taken from its British heritage as a seaside resort. It was located at the most southern port of the State of Queensland in Brisbane, Australia. Once a timber mill town, over time it became a center for tourism. The temperate climate ranged from 83 degrees Fahrenheit (28 Celsius) in the summers in January to 70 degrees (21 Celsius) in the coldest winter months of June. An American might think that living in Southport was like living in southern California.

Grant came from a very athletic family. Both his parents had been runners at a national level. Nev, Grant's dad, was a towering man. He had been a national level football player and Margaret, his mum, had played at a similar level in tennis. "Played" was actually an understatement in explaining their participation. The Hackett brothers were competitive like their parents; it was a trait inherited by Grant and brother Craig, his elder by six and one-half years. Nev and Margaret took a strong interest in their boys' athletic activities, but also impressed upon them that a good education was important to their future. Margaret worked as a hairdresser. Nev's career as a police officer suggested a strong role model of right and wrong.

One of the popular activities along the Gold Coast was the "Surf Lifesaving Program." This was a program in water safety that the city organized and conducted. It had evolved into competitive races. The races included combinations of running, swimming and paddle board. There were competitions for all ages, and Craig started when he was 10 years old. Much to his chagrin he was beaten by a girl. Her main advantage in the contest was in the swim portion. He asked his mother and father if he could get some swimming lessons to help him. They complied and four-year-old Grant went with him.

After learning the basics in a swim school, Craig and Grant joined the Miami Swim Club under the direction of Coach Denis Cotterell. Grant had tried other sports, including rugby, but he and Craig loved the water and embraced the Surf Lifesaving training and competitions with much enthusiasm. During the week, they practiced their swimming skills at the pool. On the weekends they participated in the Surf Lifesaving Program. Nev Hackett was an ardent supporter of the boys' swimming and often stayed at the pool or on the beach to watch them practice.

Coach Cotterell was very well-trained to coach swimming. He had a degree in physical education and served an apprenticeship under Coach Gordon Petersen at the famed Valley pool in Brisbane. While working under Petersen, Denis was exposed to the race preparation of Olympic Champion Shane Gould and began learning about how to treat and train athletes who wanted to be the best in the world. In 1976, when Denis was just 23 years old, he helped form the Miami Swim Club in Southport. His interest in the Surf Lifesaving racing made him not only a successful pool coach but also a budding expert in training for the surf races.

SKILL ACQUISITION

Hard training is a key to success in swimming, but not the only key. As Denis developed his coaching methodology, he strengthened his belief that the most successful swimmers in the world weren't just those that did a high volume of hard training. He believed that skill development was also necessary to realize a swimmer's potential. With this in mind, he set up his swim program with the first step to teach the young swimmers to increase the "range" or distance per stroke. He used a mantra of "Quick Connection – Long Use." This meant that he wanted his swimmers to anchor themselves with their hands in the water as quickly as possible when they began a stroke and then continue to "hold on to the water" for a long time. He believed that the practice of mediocre swimmers was "Long Connection – Short Use." He worked to educate his coaching staff and swimmers that he wanted a quick—but not rushed—catch out front of the body and wanted the hand and forearm to keep in contact with the water as long as possible.

Coach Cotterell subscribed to many of the theories about skill acquisition advocated in Daniel Coyle's marvelous book *The Talent Code*. For example, it made sense to Denis that it takes 10,000 hours, or 10 years at 1,000 hours per year, to truly ingrain a skill. With that in mind, he formulated his method of technical development based upon repetition of perfection that began when children first entered his program at a very young age. He devised a system in an attempt to isolate the correct swimming movements and then strive to repeat them over and over.

To develop these skills he adopted the utilization of four training facets that other swim coaches might label as drills. They were fingernail drag, fist drill, wrist drill and "EO." He used these drills specifically for freestyle and they were the basis for Grant Hackett's skill development. The fingernail drag was achieved by lightly dragging the fingertips across the surface of the water. This forced a high elbow and low hand recovery. With the elbow and the hand in this position, it reduced the distance of radius of the hand to the shoulder. This increased the likelihood of the body maintaining a straight body line through the water. In doing so it discouraged the body from wiggling and creating more resistance.

The fist drill was done by entering the water with a closed fist and pulling with a closed fist. This movement forced more sensitivity to the wrist and underside of the forearm to achieve and maintain traction in the water. In order to accomplish this, the forearm must be pressed to a position in which it is perpendicular to the bottom of the pool and the elbow stays higher—toward the water's surface.

Wrist drill was done similar to fingertip drag but with the hand dragging through the water. This created some resistance to the recovering arm and produced "reciprocal inhibition" of the muscles in the recovering arm. In other words, the resistance of the water against the hand and back of the wrist would force the shoulder muscles to contract to recover the arm and drive the impulse from Grant's brain to his forearm to create proper arm location. It also encouraged appropriate relaxation when the elbow was raised slightly to recover clear of the water surface. With the hand underneath the water surface, it's easier to feel the "quick connection" with the hand in catching water.

"EO" or "Elliptical Overstroke" was Denis' name for lifting the arm in the air and recovering it over the body with nearly a straight arm. The reason for using the EO facet was to produce a more ballistic recovery. This was done by increasing one's shoulder rotation by swinging the arm up and over the shoulders. By rotating the body, the larger oblique muscles are engaged for use following the quick connection of the hand when it's extended out front of the body. This rotation increased the efficiency of Grant, Craig and the other swimmers in two ways. They could apply more leverage on the water and they could slide through the water with less resistance on their sides than they would otherwise do when they were flat on their trunk.

Denis believed that a swimmer's key developmental ages to produce what Coyle reported as "myelin-wrapped skill circuits" are before they reach their teenage years. Furthermore, the facets themselves were not enough to produce good skills. It was the athlete and coach's attention to the detail of doing them exactly right that was the essential ingredient. The squad utilized kick boards for many drills but not just to isolate the legs. By placing one hand on the board and doing a drill with the other arm Grant and his teammates increased their core stability and body balance while isolating a single limb's movement.

Craig Hackett demonstrated exceptional talent as a young swimmer. He had an athletic physique, seemed to have the natural athletic gift of coordination and was a very successful age-group swimmer. In 1992, he just missed the Australian Olympic swim team when he placed sixth in the 200-meter freestyle. He was so disappointed about this result of his efforts that he turned his attention to competition in the ocean.

Each morning, Coach Cotterell combined his workouts with aspiring competitors in the Uncle Toby Super Series as well as some of the best triathletes in the world. After 30 to 45 minutes of general work, Denis drew a squiggled line down his chalkboard and divided his training sets for the pool swimmers from the triathletes. Craig trained with the group as a pool swimmer. When he switched to concentrating on the Uncle Toby's Series he continued training with Coach Cotterell but moved to the triathlon group. Craig became runner-up in the marathon race of Uncle Toby's in 1992 and 1996.

Grant watched the attention and fame his brother gained from his success. He became eager for his own. But one of the things he noticed about the ocean races was that no matter how well prepared a competitor was, the wrong wave at the wrong time could change the outcome of the competition. In the pool, there were the same conditions of the water and of the course swum for all the competitors.

In the age-group program, Coach Cotterell tried to minimize parent trips to the pool by having the 10-year-old swimmers only attend a few practices each week but practice for a relatively lengthy period of time when they were there. When Grant was nine and ten years old he practiced three to four times per week for two hours each practice. When he was 11, he continued to develop his skills by attending six sessions per week. Each of those practices covered a total volume of 4-5,000 m in two hours. Denis and his staff walked the pool deck and reminded his young charges over and over "Quick Connection – Long Use." Grant's skills were becoming excellent at this age.

Grant Hackett Developmental Program Summary

Skill Emphasis Using Four Facets of Freestyle:
          1) Wrist Drag, 2) Fingertip Drag, 3) Fist Drill, 4) EO

9-10 Years Old: 3-4 Sessions per Week - 2 hours per session, 2-4,000 meters day or 12,000 meters per week

11 Years Old: 6 Sessions per Week - 2 hours per session, 4-5,000 meter per session or 26,000 meters per week

12 Years Old: Joined senior training group
          7 Sessions per Week - 2 hours per session, 6-7,000 meters per session or 45,000 meters per week

Grant began to train with the older swimmers when he was 12, although only attending seven practices per week. Each day at practice he had outstanding swimmers to compete with, the best of whom was Dan Kowalski. At the 1994 World Championships Dan was part of the Australian world record-setting 800-meter freestyle relay and won a bronze medal in the 200-meter freestyle. By 1995 Dan was the short course world champion in the 1500 (14:48) and 400 (3:45) freestyles.

Australians labeled Kieren Perkins "a living treasure" and Grant idolized him. As Grant competed in the age-group program he kept his sights on outperforming the Australian super-star's National Age-Group records for the 13-14-year-old age group in the 100, 200 and 400-meter freestyle events.

Perkins had been so dominating since 1992 that the task to stay on target to outperform him was daunting. At the 1992 Barcelona Olympics, Perkins demolished the 1500 world record in a time far ahead of the world of 14 minutes and 43 seconds. At the 1994 Commonwealth Games he broke the 400, 800, and 1500-meter freestyle world records and was named Male Swimmer of the Year by *Swimming World Magazine*. During his career he broke world records 12 times. Perkins represented great success as well as presenting a clean cut, well-spoken young man to Australians. He served as spokesman for many products that included the line of Uncle Toby's cereals.

Coach Cotterell could see the enormous potential in Grant as he came through his program but especially when Grant was 14. He had posted respectable times of 16:07.5 for the 1500 meters, a 4:06.7 in the 400, and a 1:57.3 in the 200 freestyle. Grant was still an adolescent and had his own moments of mischief, including driving his father's car without a license. The coach knew that the decision to be great had to be made by the boy himself, and on his own timetable. The coach watched and waited patiently.

1996 A DECISION OF COMMITMENT

The 1996 Australian Olympic Trials scheduled for April were a great target for Denis to use to coax Grant into increasing his preparation commitment. He trained eight practices a week in the eight months leading up to competition. The results at the Trials of his increased commitment were striking. He swam a swift time of 15:30.6 in the 1500, broke Kieran Perkins National Age-Group record and finished fifth. His teammate, Dan Kowalski won the 1500-meters (15:10.4), the 400 (3:50.6), and was second in the 200 freestyle (1:49.0). Grant recognized how much his increased commitment had contributed to his improvement, as well as the success of his training mate Kowalski. The "light turned on" in Grant with a powerful surge and stayed lit. He could see that he had great potential in swimming and that it could be realized with an effective coach like Denis Cotterell.

He came home and told his coach, "I want to do this." Denis was thrilled to hear those words, but what followed was even more impressive. "If I expect to be the best in the world then I've got to do the best work in the world, be the hardest worker and be the best trainer."

After the 1996 Olympics in Atlanta, it seemed that Kieren Perkins might decide to retire before Grant Hackett ever had the chance to catch up to him. Perkins seemed to be struggling. He had missed the team in the 400-meter freestyle in which he held the world record and only qualified to swim the 1500. But Kieren was a champion and showed his exceptional will in Atlanta. His time in the heats of the mile qualified him into the eighth and last position for the finals by a mere 24-hundredths of a second, putting him in the outside lane. Even so he won the gold medal and in the process added to his legendary status in Australia.

Dan Kowalski didn't win a gold medal in Atlanta but he still offered proof that Denis Cotterell's training program incorporated a blend of speed and endurance that could prepare a swimmer to compete with the world's elite at a wide variety of distances. Dan was the first swimmer at the Olympics in 92 years who won a medal in all three events—the 200 (bronze), 400 (bronze) and 1500-meter freestyle (silver). This type of versatility was so rare that in the history of competitive swimming only Australia's Jon Konrads in 1956 and the USA's Tim Shaw in 1974 had ever held world records at all three distances at one time.

Coach Cotterell believed Grant had a chance to overtake Perkins and break his world records. Grant was tall, had an excellent natural feel for the water, had refined his skills very well in the Miami developmental program, and adapted well to work. His range (distance per stroke) was tremendous. Perkins used about 38 strokes to traverse the length of a 50-meter pool while Grant needed only about 33.

Denis also studied the best distance swimmers over many years and noticed the difference that a six-beat kick (per stroke cycle) made. He took note that in 1976 the 1500 Olympic Champion Brian Goodell could turn on a ferocious finishing kick when he finished races that proved lethal to his competition. The coach decided that the way to set new world records in the 1500 and beat Kieren Perkins was for Grant to have a strong kick through the entire race, and if possible, that it be a six-beat kick.

TRAINING DESIGN

Coach Cotterell was comfortable with tweaking the training program he had used with Dan Kowalski for Grant Hackett. It had proven to be extremely effective. But it is the willingness to work every day, twice per day, that can make or break such a program. Dan was special in his application of effort and Denis could now see that Grant Hackett might actually be even better.

The training year at the Miami Swim Club was from May of one year to April of the next. Coach Cotterell thought of his training in blocks of stress and adaptation that lasted weeks, and as they accumulated, years at a time. With that in mind he devised a three-week rotation of training blocks or mesocycles. Each mesocycle included training at or near Grant's race pace at least twice per week. During the three-week block of training, the coach slightly increased the quality, and then over the final few days of the cycle incorporated an evaluation of how Grant had progressed. If necessary, the mesocycle ended with a time to recover and adapt to the training load.

MESOCYCLE PLAN

Week/Micro 1

Mon.   am: AT (10 x 300s or 5 x 500s)
        pm: Short Interval Rest (AT-> Max Vo2, 400-200s)
Tues.   am: A I-II – Technique, Kick 2000 meters, Alactic Sprints
        pm: Heart Rate Set 2.4-3,000 meters
Wed   am: off
        pm: Quality (50s-150s), A I (2-3000 meters)
Thurs   am: AI-II-Tech, Kick 1.5 meters quality
        pm: Short Interval Rest (50-150s)
Fri.   am: Total Recovery AI-AII (skills), Alactic Sprints
        pm: Mixed Pace, Set (K 50, P25-50) or over distance (800-2000)
Sat   am: Pace Set or Alternative Heart Rate

Week/Micro 2

Mon   am: same as Micro 1
        pm: Heart Rate Set (2.4-3,000 meters in 100s)
Tues   am: same as Micro 1
        pm: Short Interval Rest (200-400s)
Wed   am: Off
        pm: Quality (50s-150s) alternate by weeks
Thurs   am: same as Micro 1
        pm: Short Interval rest (50-200s) OR O'Dist (800-2000)
Fri   am: same as Micro 1
        pm: Heart Rate Set (2,400-3,000, 50-200s)
Sat   am: Pace (200-400s) by 100s or 50s

Week 3/Micro 3

Consisted of (3 days) work + (3 days) adaptation
Can be interchangeable, using the first half of the of Micro 1 or Micro 2
depending upon adaptation

Reprinted with permission from the ASCA Magazine 2002

The total volume of meters per week that Denis Cotterell planned for Grant was not nearly as much as what some swimmers were covering in other parts of the world. Each of the Miami training sessions was no more than 7,000 meters. But in the full program, there were consistently 10 training sessions each week for about 49 weeks of the year. After a five to six month training segment, Grant took one or two weeks off, and then he began training again. The short breaks provided just enough time for him to repair some of the trauma to his body from training. Because of Grant's commitment to becoming the best trainer in the world, he could then capitalize on the conditioning he had gained over a five or six-month training block by resuming his training routine. Each year he built a progressively better conditioned body.

The art of coaching was essential to Denis Cotterell's success with Grant, Dan Kowalski and others. He constantly evaluated the progress of his swimmers and gradually shortened the intervals of the repeats over the course of several mesocycles. He made sure that Grant swam fast times, held his range and sustained his kick. He subtly decreased his intervals to swim repeats. For example, he might assign a set of 12 x 400s and early in the season the sendoff for the series would be a larger interval of 5:00 on number one, 4:50 on number two, 4:40 on number three and 4:30 on number four. They would complete the 12 x 400s by repeating that sequence three times. But after several mesocycles, that training day became 2 x 400s on 4:30 and 2 x 400s on 4:20 repeated three times to create 12 x 400s. If Grant could hold the same fast training times with less rest, his endurance had significantly improved.

There were three parts to creating the optimum weekly training plan for Grant. First, the total training load had to have enough stress to create a training effect or stress. Second, the stress had to be specific to his races, including proper stroke count and six-beat kicking. The third necessity was that the athlete had to be willing to experience and learn to tolerate the pain necessary to hold the proper training paces every time it was physically possible to do so.

If the weekly training load was appropriate, Grant finished the week in a very fatigued state but still performing good training times. Most of the swim sets during the week were designed so he had enough time to quickly recover in 20 to 30 seconds and perform well on the next swim. Denis used his art and intuition to adjust the load throughout the week to achieve a balance to the various training system stresses and bring the microcycle to a successful close.

Coach Cotterell knew the split times for every world record and geared Grant's training toward them with the goal of eventually bettering them. Even in the early season he expected Grant to be able to perform training times that were as fast as his personal best splits and gradually move closer to those of Perkins or the other world records that they targeted. For example, the average 50 meter time for Italy's Georgio Lamberti's world record in the 200 meter (long course) freestyle was 27 (on his last three 50s). The coach would regularly give Grant a set of 12 x 100 easy on 1:20 and then ask him to swim a 50 fast on :50 seconds. The pace for Grant's best time was 28.5 per 50, for a 1:52, but over a number of years they aimed to progress toward swimming 26s. It was essential to keep stroke range and sustain a six-beat kick during these race pace sets.

Dealing with pain was one of Grant's strengths. He laughed at it. He recognized the "pain barrier" as the fictitious overall dull pain that comes on with the onset of lactic acid, muscle fatigue, as well as lungs that scream for more air. He saw breaking through the pain barrier as his path to his goals and realizing the type of notoriety that both his brother and Dan Kowalski had achieved.

1997

The first developmental step in Coach Cotterell's plan was to increase Grant's basic endurance by increasing his overall volume. Speed was not as important at this stage. Following the Trials, Grant added a session or two per week to increase his practices to nine or ten per week, as well as adding dry-land sessions twice per week and a third land session of a 30-station circuit without weights.

The increase in training time, coupled with school, made for long days. Most mornings Nev said good-bye for the day by opening the garage at 4:45 a.m. Grant drove himself to swimming then to school. He wasn't a great student but he was a good one. After school he drove back to training and usually arrived home around 8:00 p.m. His mum would often look at him in amazement when he came in the door and say, "I don't know how you do it."

The free-spirited and competitive nature of Australian culture embraced and enthusiastically celebrated sport and sporting successes. Grant Hackett wanted to be part of that, but he wasn't there yet.

Grant's early morning training and long days eliminated late nights during the week and some of the social events at school. Most of his friends respected his commitment to swimming and didn't try to distract him with temptations that would interfere with his determined journey. The few that were jealous fell by the wayside as he unintentionally built a support system for himself. If there wasn't a swim meet on the weekend his Saturday night might be spent playing music or having a night at the movies. "Braveheart," starring fellow Australian Mel Gibson, was playing at the time and was one of his all-time favorites.

Sacrificing social time with his mates along with the increase in practices per week paid off for Grant in the course of just a few months' time. Much of the Australian Olympic Team passed up the Winter Short Course Nationals in September of 1996. That left the door open for Grant to win the 1500-meters (14:58.06) and earn the right to swim it and the 400 freestyle (3:50.6) at the short course World Championships in Gothenburg, Sweden, in April of 1997.

For six more months, Denis challenged Grant with his recipe of endurance and speed work in preparation for the Long Course Pan Pacific Trials in March of 1997. The fastest Australians would earn the right to compete against the Americans, Japanese, Canadians and other Pacific Rim countries in August. Notably absent was Kieren Perkins, who was getting married and becoming a family man. As a result, there was discussion in the Australian swimming community that perhaps he would retire.

News of Grant's improvements due to changes in training spread quickly in Australia after the Trials, where he lowered his best times dramatically and finished third in the 200-meter freestyle (1:51.7), first in the 400 (3:51.6) and won the 1500 (15:03.6). The press began to suggest that Grant might be the next Australian star and perhaps even surpass Perkins as the greatest 1500 swimmer in the world. When asked about the 16-year-old's success, Perkins said, "Until he goes under 15 minutes, he's no competition." Although he needed no additional motivation, Grant was perturbed by Perkins' comment, which served only to stoke the fires of his determination further.

Two weeks later the 1997 World Short Course Championships were held in Gothenburg, Sweden. His first international competition was a huge success when he won the 1500 (14:39.5) and finished third in the 400 (3:43.8). Following the competition he had a week off, although Coach Cotterell recommended toward the end of it that he swim three to six practices of 3-4,000 meters. The easy swimming would help loosen his body in preparation for the next step of training toward the Pan Pacific Games in August.

One of the advantages of being a world-class swimmer is the opportunity for international travel. The Pan Pacific Championships in Fukuoka, Japan, in August of 1997 was one of those. Exposure to life and customs in other countries is often an eye-opener, and the Japanese culture and hospitality was quite a thrill for everyone. However, another benefit of travel to international meets is making friends with other swimmers, especially fellow countrymen with whom you travel and share a room. Grant was just 17; his younger roommate on the trip was 14-year-old Ian Thorpe. They hit it off, one moment relaxing in their room, the next moment engaging in a series of friendly competitions. One of them started when young Ian tossed a piece of fruit at the ceiling fan. It landed in perfect halves on the table in the room. That initiated additional fruit-launching and other contests of skill and chance.

At the pool in Fukuoka, Grant Hackett was spectacular. Kieren Perkins' average splits per 100 for his world record 1500 was 58.7. The 800-meter free-style was on the first day, August 10th and Grant averaged 58.8 to swim a time of 7:50.3 and earn a decisive win over American Chad Carvin who trailed by more than seven seconds. The same night Grant also won the consolation heat of the 200 freestyle in a best time of 1:49.5. On the second day, he beat his fruit-flinging countryman Ian Thorpe in the 400-meter freestyle (3:47.2 to 3:49.2). He also swam on the second place Aussie 800 freestyle relay. Two days later he won the 1500, but the cumulative fatigue from all the previous racing had a significant effect on him as he could only manage a time of 15:13.2. It was likely that Kieren Perkins was still of the opinion that Hackett was no competition until he bettered 15 minutes.

At only 17, Grant was rapidly moving toward the top of the swimming world. But he didn't just want to win, he wanted to realize his potential and see how fast he could swim. The World Championships scheduled for January in Perth gave him just four months to prepare. He was a great student in Coach Cotterell's "swimming class." All Denis had to do to get Grant to improve was suggest he raise his elbow slightly or strengthen his kick and Grant made every effort to integrate the instruction into his swimming. The coach joked about his athlete's intense personal responsibility for his swimming when he said, "Grant is a very hard taskmaster" (SW July 1999).

Each practice began with 2–3,000 meters of drills and warm-up sets. The weekly pattern was rather consistent, although Denis tried to disguise sets with slight variations to avoid boredom in the group. The morning session was filled with all the surf athletes and triathletes, bringing the six-lane pool to capacity with about 60 swimmers. They included Australian Ironman surf lifesaving champion and world 5k open water silver medalist Ky Hurst, surf legend Trevor Hendy and world triathlon champion Jackie Gallagher.

Some of the training times and sets for Kieren Perkins were published and Denis understood that for Grant Hackett to beat Perkins in competition, he needed to outperform him in training.

KIEREN PERKINS – LONG COURSE 1996

Heart Rate Set: 30 x 100s – 10 on 1:40, 10 on 1:35, 10 on 1:30

Time HR	Time HR	Time HR
58.1 160	59.3 130	57.8 157
58.5 167	58.8 143	58.2 155
58.9 167	58.2 153	57.9 164
58.2 167	58.5 150	58.5 157
58.0 168	58.3 159	58.4 162
58.2 166	58.0 155	58.4 163
58.5 163	58.0 145	58.4 160
58.1 167	58.4 159	58.8 166
58.4 168	58.2 164	58.8 161
57.6 171	57.6 162	

Reprinted with permission 1997 ASCA World Clinic Book

After their most difficult and challenging sets, Grant wanted more. "Coach! [gasp] Denis! [gasp]." Trying to catch his breath and talk at the same time Grant Hackett sputtered, "Coach, hey, next time can we make that set harder by ...?" Grant was the first swimmer Denis had coached that at times was thinking of harder challenges before he was.

Long Course 1998 – HEART RATE FOCUSED PRACTICE

Warm-up:	800 meters (150 free/50 form stroke x 4)
	8 x 150s on 2:15
	2, (breath, 3, 5, 7), 2 (fr/water polo drill/fr), 2,
	(fr/fly/fr), 2, (fr, bk, fr)
	8 x 50s on 1:00 (2 drills, 2 stroke count, 2 drills, 2 build)
Main Series:	30 x 100s on 1:40 (10 at 30 beats below max heart rate, 10 at 20, 10 at 10)
Swim-off:	2 x (3 x 100s/4 x 50s on 45)
Fins:	3 x (200 kick/scull/drill/stroke) 4 x 50s explosion with 25 meter sprint on 1:00
Warm-down:	200 meters

Reprinted with permission ASCA Magazine 2002

1998

At the 1998 World Championships the Aussie swimmers rocked the crowd at The Challenge Swim Stadium. They dominated the American men who only won five gold medals in the entire competition. A great example was on the second night the Aussies brought the home country crowd to rousing sustained applause with their victory in the 800 freestyle relay. Michael Klim (1:47.67) and Ian Thorpe (1:47.6) gave Grant Hackett (1:48.4) a lead, which he handed over to Dan Kowalski (1:48.73). Dan easily held onto it for the win and nearly a new world record (7:12.48).

The fourth day of competition was the 400-meter freestyle. Grant used his speed and stretched out to a huge lead at 300 meters of nearly 2.5 seconds over the second swimmer, Ian Thorpe. His early pace had brought him to within 38-one-hundredths of a second of Kieren Perkins' world-record pace, while Perkins watched. But Thorpe was in the process of earning the nickname the "Thorpedo" and he looked like one on the last 100. "Each time I breathed," remembered Hackett, "I could see him catching me ... but I couldn't do anything about it" (SW March 1998).

Thorpe swam faster than Hackett on the final 100 by an amazing 2.44 seconds, as he finished the race with a final split of 55.4. Grant led through 399 meters but was beat at the finish 3:46.24 to 3:46.44 by 15-year-old Ian Thorpe, who became the youngest world swimming champion in history (by one week) over countryman Stephen Holland (in 1973).

The poise of world-class athletes is always scrutinized and judged by the careful eye of the spectators. It's not unusual for athletes in their 20s or even 30s to say things in the midst of disappointment they later regret. But at 17, Grant Hackett kept his cool after the loss. "Maybe I could go out a little slower ... but it's good to know that I'm holding up at world-record pace for three 100s. Maybe someday it'll be four." Grant went on, "But all the credit goes to the guy [Thorpe]. He swam his race. He came on strong, and I had nothing left. I spent my pennies."

Grant won the final event of the world championship, the 1500. The victory and celebration poolside with Coach Cotterell and broadcast on national television brought him opportunities for sponsorships and endorsements. The Holden car company became a sponsor and that fit his love of cars perfectly. For the first time, his training would be compromised for his commitments to those sponsors.

Grant wasn't just becoming the best trainer in the world, he also was a model of persistence and consistency. His determination to improve was relentless, and his one- or two-week breaks between seasons were long enough to recharge his system, let his body recover and his mind gear up for another 25-week training regimen. He was building layers of conditioning, one upon the other, and performing more consistently through the training week, completely committed to his training regimen.

One morning at 5:00 a.m., he went to drive his $50,000 Black Holden HSV Commodore sports car to practice and it was gone. Some brave thieves had stolen it from police inspector Nev Hackett's garage in the middle of the night. Fortunately it didn't slow him down or cost Grant any training. He just borrowed the family car temporarily and Holden dropped off a silver version of the sleek wheels for him shortly thereafter.

Coach Cotterell's training program required a commitment of 25 hours or more of intense training each week. In training each day, he kept in mind Kieren Perkins' world-record 100 average of 58.7 for the 1500 and of 55.6 for the 400. When his squad needed some perspective on how much of a challenge a swimmer was capable of meeting, he occasionally turned to the recently published book, *Four Champions, One Gold Medal.* It was devoted solely to the years building up to the 1500-meter race at the 1976 Montreal Olympics between Australian Stephen Holland and the Americans Brian Goodell and Bobby Hackett.

One of Denis' favorite stories from the book was about the "other" Hackett, the American with the first name Bobby. It started with Bobby swimming 100 x 100s yards freestyle on 1:00, an iconic demonstration of endurance that few swimmers in the world have ever been able to achieve. Practice seemed over and a party was taking place. Then the story continues from the text of the book:

"The party was held in a room adjoining the pool. It was fun and everyone wished Bobby and his teammates good luck at the nationals. Then Coach Bernal told Bob, 'Come on, we're going back to the pool to finish practice.'

"Bobby was caught by surprise. He was not happy and protested. The coach explained that he expected Hackett to be able to do 'anything, at any time for him to be completely ready for the Olympic Trials and Games.'

"Back to the pool they went. The next training set was two 1650s. The first was backstroke, the second one was butterfly, which Bobby swam in under 17:30. Although immensely fatigued from the day's training, Bobby was ecstatic to have swum so well." (*Four Champions, One Gold Medal*)

The Commonwealth Games were held in March of 1998. Grant finished second to Ian Thorpe in the 400 (3:47.1) and won the mile (14:56.2). In

September, the Trials were held for the Short Course World Championships scheduled for April. Grant set his first world record with a time of 14:19.5 in the short course 1500-meters. He also finished second again to Ian in the 400 (3:40.04). There was still no sign of Kieren Perkins.

1999

Grant was nearly 6' 6" tall but thin. He showed great progress toward his goal of becoming the greatest distance swimmer in the world when he established a new global standard in the short course mile. But his 200-meter freestyle was not fast enough to compete with the top swimmers of the world and not fast enough to swim on the Australian 800 freestyle relay. Coach Cotterell decided to add weights to his dry-land circuit in late September of 1999.

The amount of weight he could push up on the bench-press exercise was 90 pounds. Science tells us that in the first two months of weight training most of the improvements in strength training are due to neural stimulation. This helps explain his improvement in his first three months of strength training, when his bench press increased to 180 pounds. He was recruiting the use of explosive muscle fiber that had never been stimulated.

The last week of March 1999, Australia held their trials for the Long Course Pan Pacific Games. It was also one week prior to the Short Course World Championships in Hong Kong. The logic of the scheduling stems from the fact that there is more stamina required for long course competition than for short course competition. Therefore the Aussies selected their best long course team the first week and expected them to perform well in an extended taper (rest period) in a short course pool the next week.

A major goal of the season was for Grant to get on the Australian 800 freestyle relay. Coach Cotterell had made that public when he said, "If I don't get him on that relay, he'll kill me." The second and third week of March was taper time, or a period of reduced work, for Grant. His strength development was helping his speed work be the best it had ever been.

TAPER Practice 1999 – RACE PACE FOCUS

Warm-up:	400 meters (150 free/50 form stroke x 2)
	4 x 150s (kick/drill/stroke count) on 2:40
	Pull – 16 x 50s (paddles optional) on :40
Main Series:	40 x 50s:
	16 on: 45 (every fourth at 200 meter race pace)
	12 on: 50 (every third at 200 meter race pace)
	8 on: 55 (every second at 200 meter race pace)
	4 on 1:00 (all at 200 meter race pace)
Loosen:	500 meters (50 free out/50 backstroke back)
Second Series:	10 x 50s On: 50 (all at 1500 meter pace)
Warm-down:	5 x 100s on 1:30
Total:	5,300 meters

Reprinted with permission ASCA Magazine 2002

In the first week of long course Trials, he swam his best time in the 400 meters (3:45.5) but finished second to Ian Thorpe yet again. He won the 1500, also in his best time of 14:48.6. But, with the added strength, his 200 freestyle showed spectacular improvement. He won the event in the time of 1:46.99. He had finally beaten Ian Thorpe in a race, as well as one of Australia's reigning stars, Michael Klim. Grant was so close to Georgio Lamberti's world record that Coach Cotterell put him in the lead-off position on their club's 800 freestyle relay, in order for him to get an official time. Grant swam with no fear or consequence of falling apart in the race, since there really was nothing to lose. He swam the first 100 a half-second faster than Lamberti (51.99). Even at that fast pace, he still finished strong and set a new world record of 1:46.67.

When they arrived for the 1999 Short Course World Championships in Hong Kong, Grant went in the pool to loosen up. Coach Cotterell's eyes widened when Grant told him, "I feel better than the Trials" (SW June 1999). Only one swimmer had ever been faster than 3:40 seconds for the 400 in short course meters. It was Ian Thorpe. Ian swam four seconds faster than his world record with an incredible effort of 3:35.6. Unexpectedly, and unfortunately for him, he was beaten by Grant Hackett. Grant had learned that allowing Thorpe to stay close to him at the end of a race was athletically lethal. He described Ian's finishing kick with his size 17 feet as looking like a waterfall. Others explained the feeling of being in the next lane when he swam by you as being "in the surf." So Grant started the 400 so fast that Ian couldn't keep up and never caught up.

Hackett's first 100 split was 52.4 and he pushed off the 200 wall in the time of 1:47.1. Ian was trying to stay close but was a full second behind with a 1:48.1. At the 300 turn Grant split 3:42.0. He held off Ian on the last 100 for a new world record by nearly four seconds of 3:35.01. "I'm learning to focus on myself and executing the perfect swim," Hackett said afterward. His 200 splits of 1:47.1 and 1:47.9 were about as even a distribution of effort as a swimmer could have (52.4-54.7-54.9-53.0).

The aftermath of the Short Course Worlds left the swimming community buzzing about the Australian team and the prowess of its rising stars Hackett and Thorpe. Ian set a new world record in the 200 (1:43.2) and Grant was victorious in the 1500 (14:32.8). In 18 months Australia would host the Olympics in Sydney and the future and fortunes of its beloved water sport appeared to be in perfect hands.

The Pan Pacific Games in August 1999 were a mere stopover on the way to the quadrennial Olympic celebration to come. Grant was sick at the beginning of Pan Pacs but still swam on the world record-setting 800 free relay while they tested out the Olympic pool. Three days later he won the mile in 14:45.67. Grant Hackett had done so much hard work and was so well-trained that he was better than the rest of the world in the endurance event even when he wasn't at his best.

In September of 1999 the training for the Olympic year was at its peak. There was little change in Grant's program; it was just a matter of doing it better than ever before. His dry-land was tweaked to include two days of weight training and running, two days of exercise circuits and one day of medicine balls with stretching. Dan Kowalski had battled a series of shoulder problems but was making a bid to return to the Olympics. Grant was so fast and so consistent in practice that Dan and his other training mates nicknamed him "The Machine."

2000 OLYMPIC YEAR

In the last week of April 2000, three weeks prior to the Australian Olympic Trials, Grant Hackett became sick. His glands were swollen, he was coughing and he had a cold. Denis Cotterell was a master at both challenging his athletes and knowing when to allow them to recover. He had known Grant for 12 years and had coached him every day for the last eight. He knew it was time to let him recover for a few days to get well, so Denis reduced his training load.

IAN THORPE DEVELOPMENT

Coached By Jenni Ashpole and Chris Meyers in Doug Frost's age-group program

8-10 Years Old: Gradually increased from 2 to 3 to 4 sessions per week of 60 minutes
Stroke Drill emphasis: Single arm with kickboard
Crane image of lifting hand as far forward for entry as possible

11 Years Old: 5 sessions per week
Used school vacations to gradually increase the number of sessions per week
Gradually increased this year to add Saturday, then Tuesday and Thursday a.m.
6 x 300s on 6:00 in 25-meter pool, descended to 3:30

Coached By Doug Frost
13 Years Old: Moved into "national group"
Training as many as eight sessions per week
6 feet tall
Kick – 50 meter (short course) with board 29+ seconds

14 Years Old: 10 sessions per week
2 hours each session
3 dry-land sessions per week

AEROBIC MESOCYCLE OF WORK

(Coach Frost continued to carefully increase quality swimming each succeeding mesocycle)

MON	AM:	A2 (aerobic level 2)
	PM:	Lactate Tolerance
TUES	AM:	A1 (aerobic level 1)
	PM:	AT (anaerobic threshold)
WED	AM:	Off
	PM:	A2
THURS	AM:	AI
	PM:	AT
FRI	AM:	A2
	PM:	AT
SAT	AM:	A1

Aerobic phase: Microcycle I: 60,000 km/week
Microcycle II: 70,000 km/week
Microcycle III: 80,000 km/week

Example of AT: 10 x 200s on 2:30 (LCM) – hold 2:10s with Heart Rate 40 beats below maximum (213)

2002-2004 Coached By Tracey Menzies
Source: *Ian Thorpe: The Biography* – Greg Hunter
See *The Swim Coaching Bible I* for a detailed program

After the recovery days Denis gave Grant a test set and he had a tremendous performance. But then he relapsed to a state even worse than before. Medical personnel drew blood from Grant 10 days prior to the Trials and a series of tests were conducted. The medical team revealed to the coach that Grant had Epstein-Barr virus. In 35–50 percent of cases it leads to mononucleosis.

Grant had devoted himself to training for four years and the biggest prize—the "brass ring"—would be success at the Olympics in Sydney. But if he couldn't perform well enough at the Trials he would never get the chance to reap the rewards of his considerable investment. Coach Cotterell decided that if he told Grant he had the virus it would put doubt in his mind and affect his physical readiness, which would make it even more difficult to qualify for the Australian Olympic Team. He made a decision to keep the diagnosis to himself.

There were 10,000 spectators for his first event at Trials, the 400-meter freestyle. Ian Thorpe sped out front and stayed there to set a new world record (3:41.33) while Grant helplessly lingered behind. His time of 3:51.05 was his worst in major competition in four years but was still good enough for second which enabled him to swim it at the Olympics.

Two days later he swam the 200 freestyle. He was well off his world-record time, which was wiped out by Thorpe (1:45.51). He finished third (1:47.81), enabling him to be on the Australian 800 freestyle relay. Later his mate Michael Klim announced that he was relinquishing his second-place position to concentrate on his shorter events, the 100 freestyle and 100 butterfly. Because Hackett's time would now be the second fastest for the Australians, Klim's decision allowed Grant to swim the 200 at the Games.

The 1500 freestyle was on the final day of the Trials. Kieren Perkins was there. Although he had hardly competed for four years, for the last decade Kieren Perkins had ruled the world of distance swimming and won gold medals at both the 1992 and 1996 Olympics, and he was ready to have a go at it again. For him, the Australian Trials were just the preliminaries. His swim of 15:01 was his best since the Atlanta Games and earned him the second spot on the Olympic Team behind Hackett. Grant's time of 14:56 was well off his best, but he was on the team in three events and there were three months to the Olympics. Coach Cotterell's presentation of his condition to the public was that they had simply missed their taper for Trials. The coach said that experience would be useful information in preparation for the Olympics. But recovering from Epstein-Barr requires absolute rest and there wasn't time to do that and do the training necessary to be the best distance swimmer in the world.

2000 OLYMPIC GAMES – Sydney, Australia

The atmosphere in the Olympic Aquatic Centre in Sydney, Australia, was electric. The 18,000 spectators in the venue were also highly educated swimming fans. Mothers talked with their children right through dinner-making preparations explaining the disciplines and the distances. The check-out clerks at grocery stores traded stories and predictions about their favorite Australian swimmers from Susie O'Neil to Ian Thorpe. Teenagers scrambled for tickets to see and cheer their favorite swimming stars. Swimming mania was rampant in Australia. The most anticipated event was the 1500 on the final day of the competition and it would feature their beloved sports hero Kieren Perkins.

On opening night, however, the first event was the 400-meter freestyle and the Aussies couldn't ask for a better beginning than to have Thorpe and Hackett going head-to-head for the gold medal. In the preliminaries, Grant was better than he had been at Trials, but he was only the eighth qualifier (3:48.9) and well off of his best time. Ian glided out to an early lead of 52.4 with Grant charging through the same distance in second place (53.6). At the 200 Ian turned in 1:48.8 and Grant was fading badly. While Ian Thorpe finished in a new world record of 3:40.59, Grant Hackett limped into the finish, forgotten by many, in seventh place (3:48.2).

The next day, September 17, was the 200 freestyle. In the preliminaries Grant Hackett finished ninth (1:49.2). The swim was so poor that he not only failed to earn a swim in the finals, he was also taken off the Australian 800 free relay. The following night he watched Thorpe, Michael Klim, Todd Pearson and William Kirby wallop the Americans and the world record in the 800 freestyle relay. Just one year before Grant was the world record-holder in the 200 freestyle and now he was swimming 2.5 seconds slower that his best time. He was just one of the thousands in the home crowd watching the celebration of the great victory by the 800 freestyle relay. How could things get worse?

Four days later Kieren Perkins qualified first in the preliminaries of the 1500-meter freestyle (14:58.3). Grant was nine seconds slower (15:07). Children talked on their school buses in Australia about whether or not Kieren would become the first swimmer in Olympic history to win three gold medals in the grueling 1500 meters. Waiters handicapped the race on a slip of paper to their guests. On September 23rd, 18,000 spectators took their seats, wondering if they would bear witness to swimming history. Grant Hackett was still unaware that he had the Epstein-Barr virus in his system. It had been four days since the preliminaries of the 1500, but would the additional days to recover be enough time for someone, even as highly trained as Grant Hackett, to have a chance to be close to his best?

Kieren Perkins was paraded out to the starting blocks wearing a black full bodysuit of the same style that Ian Thorpe had made famous. The black fabric compressed his body from ankles to wrists and neck. Was he a super-hero or was he a villain that stood in the way of the greatest trainer in the world being anointed a champion? Grant wore his customary suit that hugged his hips and stretched to his ankles. He looked like a kid in jeans standing next to the elegantly adorned Perkins. Over the past four years all but eight of the best male distance swimmers in the world had dropped aside in the competition for the 1500 title. Perkins, Hackett and six others mounted their starting blocks.

The horn sounded and the swimmers blasted off the starting blocks. Grant Hackett immediately swam to the lead. He had done this a few days earlier but struggled to finish in the 400. He had made a habit of seeing Ian Thorpe whiz by him in the closing meters. After 100 meters he turned first and heard his inner voice urging him on saying, *I can do this!* By the 300 he was ahead and Perkins trailed him by two seconds. The voice again urged him, *You can do this!* Kieren was still in second place and trying to hold the distance constant between them in the hope that he would gain as Hackett tired. He would close in like a fisherman slowly reeling in his prized catch.

When Grant pushed off the wall at 400 meters, the clock read 3:52.11, nearly as fast as his 400 time from the Olympic Trials. Just like he had done in training he pounded away at 59.9 100s, holding Kieren Perkins at bay. As Grant made his "Quick Connections – Long Use," he swooped through each length with 33 long strokes. His kick was steady as he produced the living image of what Coach Cotterell had envisioned in how to beat Kieren Perkins.

As they approached 800 meters the defending champion was churning away at 38 strokes each length and closed the gap to 1.8 seconds. There was a mere five meters between the two of them. But the surge had cost Perkins valuable energy. The world record-holder was the one that was tiring, not the challenger, and even his courage was not enough to beat Grant Hackett today. Grant kicked away from Perkins, leaving him in his wake. The enormously partisan Australian-dominated crowd rose to their feet, wildly applauding and cheering the imminent one-two finish by their countrymen. Grant held his lead, never sure of victory until his fingertips pressed into the touch pad after 1500 meters, stopping the clock at 14:48.33. Kieren Perkins touched five seconds later in at time of 14:53.59.

Grant Hackett leapt so high that half his body cleared the water and he triumphantly thrust his fist into the air! He had been counted out by nearly everyone except the one that counted most: himself. Just as he had pounded out tens of thousands of meters and endless hours of training, he pounded his fist repeatedly into the water and exulted in his hard-earned victory and the path he painfully endured to earn it. When he climbed from the pool, he spoke with reporters.

"This is the one you want to win." Grant said, glowing in victory. "This is the Olympics, in your own country, here in Sydney. I mean, it's everything you work for. It comes to this day, and I've done it and I'm very happy."

Perkins' image as a national treasure was intact as he demonstrated immense grace in being beaten by Hackett. "Grant has been on top for the past four years and deserves to win. I gave it everything I had," he smiled. "I prefer to be beaten by an Aussie over anyone else."

Kieren Perkins hadn't passed the torch as the greatest distance swimmer in the world to Grant Hackett. Grant had wrested it from him even when his health had been compromised. He was just beginning his own reign.

More business deals in the form of sponsorships and endorsements followed Grant's gold medal, and they gave him the opportunity to be a spokesman for charities and hospitals. He learned how to deliver long public service announcements flawlessly. That was the result of his meticulous attention to detail, which he had honed in his quest to reach his potential as an athlete. The hospitals and other charities benefited from his celebrity status.

Grant's life with filled with activity. Music was a passion for him. He listened to it and he made it, playing the drums and guitar. His celebrity status was elevated when the Varta Company took advantage of his energy and rhythm to sell their batteries on television. The commercial was shot without Grant speaking a word. The swimming star was filmed with his ears covered by headphones plugged into a portable CD player and dancing poolside in a full bodysuit with the brand stamped across his chest. All of a sudden the music stopped and so did Grant's dancing. He pulled the batteries from the CD player, threw the CD player in the trash, pulled a new one out of a tote bag filled with new CD players, popped in the same Varta batteries and resumed his dancing.

A short break from swimming was necessary to recover from the effects of the Epstein-Barr virus, but then he was back in training. The full extent of his potential was still unknown and he wanted to reach it. The weekly sequence of training gradually developed its own protocols and content based on Grant's past workout performances. The Monday morning main sets helped him and Coach Cotterell evaluate his adaptation from the previous week. On Monday night the training was focused on quality. The Tuesday morning emphasis on improving his kicking sought to strengthen the weakness of an essential attribute that separated Grant from the rest of the world's distance swimmers. Without a stronger and improved kick he was vulnerable to the swimmer who might be considered the "other" best freestyle swimmer on earth: Ian Thorpe.

KICKING PRACTICE EMPHASIS – Long Course

Tuesday Morning – Aerobic Emphasis on Kicking
      5 x 400s on 7:30,
OR,   10 x 200s (3 on 3:45, 3 on 3:40, 3 on 3:30) then an extra 60 seconds rest and one high quality

Thursday Morning – Some Quality Emphasis on Kicking
      4 x (300 on 5:40, the 100 Quality on 2:00),
OR,   2 x (16 x 50s steady on 1:15, 50 fast on 1:00)

2001

The first step toward the 2004 centennial Olympics in Athens was the Pan Pacific Games in Fukuoka, Japan, in July 2001. Ian Thorpe and Grant Hackett battled each other in the pool, pushing one another to time performances never seen before, and in some cases, not seen since (at the time of this writing). On July 22 the competition began with Grant lowering his personal best in the 400-meter freestyle to 3:42.5, only to be thwarted by Ian's world record-setting 3:40.17. The 200 freestyle was another record for Thorpe who clearly had more speed than Hackett when he swam a new standard of 1:44.06.

The following day, July 24th, Thorpe elected to swim the 800 freestyle in an attempt to test his versatility and see if he had the ability to go for multiple gold medals in Athens in 2004. Ian and Grant began the competition by swimming stroke for stroke for 700 meters. The "Thorpedo" kick on the final 100 meters was too much for Hackett to contend with. While he had swum faster than any human had ever swum the distance (7:40.5), it was second-best again to Ian Thorpe's 7:39.1—his third world record of the competition.

In the 1500 on July 26th, there was Grant Hackett and then there was everyone else. Ian Thorpe was not about to attempt the distance, opting for the 100 freestyle instead. All of Grant's training was geared toward excellence at the mile, but as the race was contested, it turned into less of a contest and more a display of his overpowering stamina. To put this performance in perspective it is necessary to note that while Graeme Smith established a new

British national record to finish second in 14:58.94, Grant Hackett touched the wall almost before Smith had taken his first stroke off the last turn. In the process, Grant ripped Kieren Perkins' world record from the books with an eye-popping 14:34.56.

Kieren Perkins was commentating for Australian television at the event. "[Grant's] mental strength was demonstrated by the way he got straight back into the pool after the Olympics. That's the hardest time to switch back into gear mentally." Grant Hackett added, "Fortunately, it's something I enjoy—the training and the challenge of improving. When I get over that feeling, it's probably time to go," he laughed. "I aim to get up and show my rivals I can still improve big chunks—that I'm not stopping at 14:34," he warned. Perkins complimentary nod to Hackett was proof to everyone that the former distance superstar realized Hackett had taken over the reins indeed.

2002

Hackett's strength development continued into 2002. His 6 6" frame had added functional strength and he weighed almost 200 lbs. His 100-meter freestyle relay split benefited from the additional muscle and was down to a 49.05. For a distance swimmer this showed an amazing amount of speed. When he recorded a time of 14:41.6 in his 1500 win at the Pan Pacific Games it was his 12th time of swimming under 15 minutes and was one of his six swims that were among the all-time top-ten 1500s.

2003

His versatility was demonstrated again at the 2003 Long Course World Championships when he finished third in the 200-meter freestyle (1:46.8), second in the 400 (3:45.1), first in the 800 (7:43.8), and first in the mile (14:43.1). His 1500 again dominated the field and was 18 seconds faster than second place. He seemed perfectly prepared and poised to enjoy the results of four years of focused training in front of the entire world at the Olympics in Athens.

Most people say that their greatest strength can also be their greatest weakness. Grant Hackett's greatest strength may well have been his unrelenting demand for training excellence from himself. He worked painstakingly to gain any improvement or change in stroke technique, tempo, or turning skill that he could turn to his advantage. He gauged the progress of his overall training by the times he performed and whether they were an improvement over his previous best. If they weren't satisfactory, he was angry and upset. His focus and determination pushed him to give more of himself to get to his training goals.

The popularity of swimming in Australia provided Grant Hackett a variety of opportunities for revenue in the form of sponsorships as well as being involved in community service. His non-training time was committed to earning a good living; he also was helping hospitals and charitable foundations raise money with his public service announcements. His life was not only that of a sportsman but also of a celebrity, and the attendant responsibilities kept him constantly busy. The hectic and tiring pace of these activities and the effort of trying to balance training against making a living was beginning to take its toll.

2004 OLYMPIC GAMES – Athens, Greece

By February of the late Australian summer of 2004, as a result of pushing himself relentlessly in preparation for the Athens Games, Hackett was suffering from breathing problems. He was hospitalized for a bronchial condition. The chronic problem did not abate and between February and the August Olympics he had been through 15 rounds of antibiotics but was still unable to shake the problem. By the time he had landed in Athens, fluid had entered one of his lungs. The lung was partially collapsed and functioning at 25 percent of its full capacity. He and Coach Cotterell kept the extent and severity of his condition secret from the Australian medical team for fear that to protect his health or even his life they might not let him swim in the Games.

On the first night of Olympic swimming, Grant Hackett showed his continued commitment to finding his ultimate swimming speed by appearing behind the starting blocks with his head completely shaved of hair. The 400-meter freestyle unfolded in much the way it had over the past six years. Ian Thorpe and Grant Hackett led the field. Once again, after they swam 200 meters Ian began to apply pressure and established a small lead.

Over the previous two years Ian had rejected his standard training method from his Coach Doug Frost that had included a substantial endurance component. Instead, he substituted a more speed-oriented regimen. Thorpe's reasoning was in part the desire to improve his 100-meter freestyle, but it was also based on the mental fatigue of training in a similar way each of the past six years. Grant Hackett was swimming with terribly compromised health, but he had never compromised when it came to training. He accepted and relished the fact that to be the greatest swimmer in the world, he also had to be the greatest trainer.

As Ian Thorpe began his fourth 100, he increased his kick. So did Hackett. Ian led, but Grant wouldn't let him get too far in front. On the final length Ian didn't have his usual extra finishing gear. Grant closed quickly on the final 50 meters, inching nearer and nearer to Thorpe. Ian Thorpe touched in the time of 3:43.1 and Grant Hackett 3:43.36. Anyone watching video of the last 100 of that race would easily conclude that if the pool had been just five meters longer, Hackett's crushing last length would have put him at the finish wall ahead of Thorpe.

After a day off, Thorpe won the 200 freestyle (1:44.71) with Peter van den Hoogenband second (1:45.23) and Michael Phelps third (1:45.32). Grant Hackett was fifth (1:46.56). The following day Hackett kept the Aussies close to Phelps on the opening leg of the 800 freestyle relay, but the lead slipped away to the Yanks. Even Ian Thorpe's furious finish couldn't catch Klete Keller and the USA won the 800 freestyle relay that had eluded them so often over the past five years.

Thus far in the Olympic Games there seemed to be little reason to doubt Grant Hackett's health status based on his performances. But the 1500 requires the greatest amount of aerobic capacity in any of the events in pool swimming and far more than a 400 or 200-meter freestyle. (The efficiency of one's lungs is critical to producing the energy necessary for success.) In the heats, he qualified third with a time of 15:01.89. There were two young guns, each six years Grant's junior, Larsen Jensen (15:03.75) from the USA, and David Davies (14:57.03) from Great Britain who swam well in the preliminaries. They saw the target on the champion's back, sighted on it, and were ready to attack. He would need to dig down deep to win the gold medal.

In an interview with *Swimming World Magazine* the previous year he had explained his mental toughness: "There is nothing better than practical experience to develop mental toughness—far better than reading about it in books ... I've had to deal with competitive pressures—in particular, having to perform at the Sydney Olympics with glandular fever along with the huge national expectations. I was considered the lowest odds to win the 1500, and I've dealt with that and come out successfully on the other side."

On August 14th, the 1500 was an intense race from start to finish. Afterward, reporters wrote of Grant Hackett: "It is the toughest race of his life, one that tears off the mystique enshrouding this event. Grant has to work for this one—hard. And the winner is in doubt until the final few strokes." The scoreboard read 1 – Grant Hackett 14:43.40 Olympic Record; 2 – Larsen Jensen 14:45.29; and 3 – David Davies 14:45.95.

Grant Hackett's emotional face at the finish was near tears. His body was wracked with pain. He was still the best in the world, even when he wasn't at his best. He never mentioned his illness until November.

2005–2007

In the fall of 2004 Grant took 12 weeks off, his longest training break since committing himself to pursue his ultimate swimming potential. He competed in the Long Course World Championships in the summer of 2005. He broke Ian Thorpe's four-year-old 800-meter freestyle world record with a time of 7:38.65. He won his fourth straight 1500. He also became the most decorated swimmer in the history of the World Championships by winning 17 (14 individual and 3 relay) medals. And his shoulder ached.

In November of 2005 he had shoulder surgery but believed he still had more to achieve. No one had ever won three 1500-meter Olympic gold medals, and he wanted to see if he could do it. In 2006 he battled back problems and exercise-induced asthma.

The year 2007 was a series of ups and downs. He was married to singer Carrie Alley, but it was just two weeks after the 11-year streak of winning every 1500 he competed in came to an end. He swam at the Long Course World Championships in Melbourne with a miserable result. He finished third in the 400 freestyle, seventh in the 800 and seventh in the 1500.

There were only 16 months to the 2008 Olympics in Beijing and the chance at a three-peat in the 1500. Grant decided he had to make a change in order to have a chance at the gold medal.

2008

Denis Cotterell may well be the finest distance swimming coach who has ever walked a pool deck, but sometimes even the combination of a great coach and great swimmer isn't a strong enough chemistry to become the best in the world. Grant packed up his belongings and moved to Melbourne to swim with Coach Ian Pope.

Coach Pope knew Grant from a training visit that he made with him during 2007. He believed that Grant had become committed to so many sponsors, charities and business enterprises that it was compromising his swimming training. If he was going to give himself a chance to extend his reign as the greatest distance-swimmer in the world, he would need every ounce of energy every day to train and recover. To avert sickness, he avoided crowds and when he did go out in public, he didn't touch handrails. When he went on an airplane, he wore a mask to keep germs at bay. He only drank from sealed water bottles. He contacted all of his business interests and let them know that he was going to devote himself to swimming through the Beijing Olympics and was only going to make one appearance per month for his sponsors. He told the public, "I just want to have no regrets. That's all you can finish with. You can't control other people's performances."

Coach Pope's training program had similarities to Denis Cotterell's at the Miami Swim Club. The total volume of training was similar to Grant's past program of about 65,000 meters per week, although occasionally they might reach 75,000 meters. But some significant changes were included to adapt training for an athlete who was 27 years old. Wednesday was a day of complete recovery, swimming at a low intensity. That training was followed with a massage and at his coach's insistence Grant spent the rest of the day in full rest mode away from the pool. Tuesday and Friday mornings had always been his easier sessions of the week but they lowered the intensity further at those practices. The goal was to train fast but have more time for adaptation.

2007-08 TRAINING MICROCYCLE - Coach Ian Pope

Mon   am: Aerobic, Pull-kick
       pm: 1,500 Race Pace training, Main Set: 3,000k
Tues   am: Aerobic easy recovery
       pm: 400-200 Race Pace training, primarily 50s, occasionally 100s
Wed   am: off
       pm: Recovery, very low intensity, massage
Thurs   am: Aerobic, Pull-kick
       pm: 1,500 Race Pace training, Main Set: 3,000k
Fri   am: Aerobic easy recovery or off
       pm: Depending upon fatigue level, this could be quality.
Sat am: Quality

Coach Pope took him through a series of strength tests and together they determined that more core strength would help him, so routines to improve that aspect of his training were added to his program.

Grant was still his severest critic and relentlessly drove himself. If he couldn't perform the times he wanted in practice, he would become infuriated with himself. But Ian Pope was a calming influence and acted to save Grant from his own frustration. At his age, the missing ingredient to training faster, and being the best trainer in the world, was for Grant to give his work *time* to work; he needed to extend the recovery time between bouts of heavy lactate-transport training or race-pace efforts.

At the 2008 Victorian Short Course Swimming Championships in July, his final Australian meet before departing for the Olympics, Grant Hackett proved he was back in top form. On July 19th he lowered his short course 800-meter world record set seven years earlier in 2001 to 7:23.42. With four weeks to go until the 1500 he seemed to be back in top form.

Suit technology contributed greatly to the lowering of nearly every world record leading up to 2008. How much did it contribute? It's impossible to say. Multiple swimsuit companies designed and manufactured suits that added buoyancy. There had also been the long-standing practice of using compression to streamline and stabilize the body parts, which helped swimmers get faster and faster. A few years later the swimming community established new restrictions on body-part coverage and material content and properties in order to place more value on a swimmer's training than on the choice and makeup of their racing suit. It was strongly felt, and advocated for, that races should be based on the ability of the swimmer, not the properties of the suit they chose to wear.

DATE	7/23/2008						
TIME	1245 15 x 100s on 1:05						
VENUE	Singapore Island Country Club						
LAP	50M	100M	SR 0-50	SR 50-100	SC 50-100		LA
1	26.9	56.3	39.0	37.5	32		
2		58.0	36.5	36.5	32		
3		58.3	35.5	36.5	32		
4		58.7	35.7	35.2	32		
5		58.8	37.0	36.5	32		5.9
6		58.0	38.0	37.0	32		
7		58.3	37.8	36.4	32		
8		58.4	37.0	36.5	32		
9		58.6	37.8	36.1	32		
10		58.5	37.0	36.5	33		6.4
11	27.8	57.2	37.7	37.2	33		
12		58.8	37.5	37.0	33		
13		58.0	36.3	37.0	33		
14	29.1	58.7	37.0	36.2	33		
15	28.1	54.9	37.0	39.0	34		9.2
1500M TIME		14:29.5					3 MINS
AVE (2 - 14)		58.3					10.3
							600M
							4.2
							400M
							1.7

LAP	50M	100M	SR 0-50	SR 50-100	SC 50-100	LA
DATE	7/25/2008					
TIME	0945 - 10 x 100s on 1:05, 5 x 100s on 1:00					
VENUE	Singapore Island Country Club					
1	26.7	55.3	40.0	37.5	32	
2	28.7	57.3	37.5	37.5	32	
3		57.0	37.7	37.7	32	
4		57.4	37.9	37.0	32	
5		57.5	37.4	36.5	32	5.1
6		56.3	39.0	36.5	32	
7		57.5	36.5	37.1	32	
8		57.6	37.1	37.1	32	
9		57.7	37.4	37.4	32	
10		57.8	37.8	36.6	33	6.7
11		56.2	39.0	37.9	32	
12		58.4	37.1	34.9	32	
13		58.6	37.1	37.1	32	
14		58.4	37.4	36.7	33	
15	28.2	55.6	37.7	38.5	34	8.6
1500M TIME		14:18.6				3 MINS
AVE (2 - 14)		57.5				9.3
						600M
						3.4
						400M
						2.2

2008 OLYMPICS – Beijing, China

The preliminaries of the 1500 were fast. Eighth place was a 14:49.5 by Larsen Jensen of the USA. In the final heat of prelims, Grant Hackett swam a time of 14:38.92, a new Olympic record. "That was the easiest 1500 I ever swam," he confided to Coach Pope following the race. The expectations for the three-peat were high.

In the finals two days later, Grant swam in lane four and the second-seeded Ryan Cochrane from Canada swam in lane five. The two of them cruised out to a slight lead in a packed field. As the race unfolded Grant was in control. Cochrane led slightly at 800 meters with a split of 7:51.0. The champion had Cochrane in his sights and was very comfortable. But when he pushed off the wall at 1100 meters Ous Mellouli, swimming over in lane seven, inched ahead. Ryan Cochrane in lane five was blocking Grant's view of him. Ous Mellouli had traveled from Tunisia to the University of Southern California in 2004 to train with Coach Mark Schubert in a high-mileage distance program. Since 2006, he had had been coached by Dave Salo in a program based less on mileage and more on speed. Mellouli continued to lead and Grant Hackett still didn't see him.

Mellouli held the lead through 1300 meters and then began to push forward. As Grant moved ahead of Ryan Cochrane he saw Ous. Grant had always been at his best establishing and maintaining speed, not at accelerating and gaining speed. Grant increased his kick, but so did Ous. With 50 meters remaining, Ous was still in command. Grant Hackett was closing in, kicking harder and summoning every ounce of energy possible to get to the wall first. His final 50 was 27.9. Ous Mellouli's was 28.4. But the scoreboard gleamed in lights 1 – Mellouli 14:40.84; 2 – Hackett 14:41.53; 3 – Cochrane 14:42.69.

Grant Hackett had set out to become the greatest distance swimmer in the world. For 11 years he won every 1500 race he entered. On August 14, 2008, he held the world records at both short and long course meters for the 1500 and 800 freestyles. His announced method to reach his performance goals was to work the hardest and be the greatest trainer in the world. Perhaps he best assessed the result when right after the conclusion of the mile in Beijing he said to his coach Ian Pope, "I left no stone unturned."

Grant Hackett's 1500 world record of 14:34.56, set on July 29, 2001, was the only record that survived the "techsuit wars" of 2008–2009. By 2011 it was the oldest men's record in the books. On July 31, 2011, it was broken by Sun Yang of China with a time of 14:34.14. Yang exhibited incredible efficiency, taking only 27 strokes each length and the amazing speed to swim 25.9 seconds on the final 50. Yang's coach much of the year is Denis Cotterell.

Grant Hackett is married to Carrie Alley and the father of twin girls Charlize and Jagger. He has hinted at a career in politics. Grant is also an Ambassador for Uncle Toby's.

AARON PEIRSOL

July 23, 1983

THE BELIEVER

(L-R) Aaron, Brian Pajer, Hayley Peirsol Circa 1994

The plethora of outdoor training pools in southern California has been offered as a reason for the region being the birthplace of many great pool swimmers. The climate to utilize those facilities 12 months of the year has provided the opportunity for clubs, coaches and athletes to explore and develop their full potential without the many training time limitations faced in other climates around the world. To be one of the very best athletes on earth, however, requires several personal qualities that separate them from the millions of others that train and race. The most powerful quality athletes can have is the ability to control and direct their intentions: focus their mental energy on their desired physical reality. In order to accomplish this, an athlete must consistently direct their thoughts to their vision of their future achievement of athletic excellence. This is the story of such a person. Aaron Peirsol is a believer.

* * *

THE EARLY YEARS

The moist, salt air pressed against Wella Peirsol's face as she jogged the bike path that provided her a hard surface along Newport Beach. She was plugged in. Not to a musical device, but to the sound of waves crashing on the sand and the sight of bouncing white water sprinkling the air. The fog was thick on this 55 degree September morning. It blocked the view of Catalina Island off shore and challenged the seagulls that chattered loudly in their hunt for breakfast. Wella breathed deeply and felt her heart pound.

Once she had exercised through dance, but in recent years she had picked up running and swimming. She loved pushing herself physically on long runs and sighed silently in gratitude for her visiting parents at home with her two young children. She hadn't had enough of these days, she thought. How could she organize her life around the dental office and being a single mother to get to the beach and ocean more often?

"Gifts!" Wella blurted out as she came in the house carrying two large boxes.

Hayley and Aaron dropped what they were doing and raced to their mother. They ripped open the boxes.

"Rollerblades?" Aaron asked his mom.

"You betcha, Baby!" Wella chirped. "We're going Rollerblading!"

The Peirsols lived in a tract of homes in a neighborhood in Corona del Mar, a section of Newport Beach, California. Wella took Hayley and Aaron out the front door to the cul-de-sac and showed them how to pull on knee pads, lace up their new gifts, and slide on elbow and hand padding. They started their new adventure slowly, holding their mom's hands and walking with their skates.

"Push-glide and then enjoy the ride on the blade, Aaron!" Wella instructed.

Within minutes Aaron was coordinating his movements on his own. At seven, it came to him much easier than his sister who was three years younger. Hayley did her best to walk with the skates on. Wella had a plan. She would teach her kids to Rollerblade and they could skate while she ran. Wella was molding her children's life around her active lifestyle.

When Aaron was five years old their pediatrician had told Wella to try swimming to help him with his asthma. A few times each week he took his inhaler with him into the Newport YMCA pool that was covered by a bubble in the winter months for swim practice. The warm humid air inside the bubble was a perfect environment to help clear his breathing. Wella looked for each chance she could swim and run, while Aaron swam.

Wella signed Aaron up for the swim team at the Y in 1988. His coach was Stacy Zapolski. She was just 23 years old, but a loving teacher. Stacy taught Aaron how to swim the four competitive strokes and introduced him to the concept of being timed for a length of the pool. She showed her group of eight-and-younger swimmers the camaraderie involved in being on a relay. She introduced the idea of attending swim meets as being invited to a party with other teams. The Peirsols and Stacy enjoyed their shared experience in the sport of swimming so much that after Hayley joined the group, the coach eventually named her daughter Hayley.

The Peirsols were a family of three and they liked being in motion. It wasn't long before Hayley and Aaron were smoothly gliding through six miles of Rollerblading along the Newport Beach bike path while Wella ran. A stop for a treat at their favorite bakery was a just reward. Aaron's favorite was a cinnamon roll, a choice that initially was made after much consideration of all his options. The YMCA was a place for Aaron and Hayley to play racquetball and basketball while their mom swam or exercised. It was also where she met Tim Hartig.

Tim worked as a mortgage broker, was single and had two children of his own. His oldest daughter Erin was 11. His son Greg was eight, the same as Aaron. Wella and Tim fell in love. They moved into the Piersol home in Corona del Mar. They joked that they were "the Brady Bunch," characters in a popular television show chronicling the adventures of a blended family. Bunk beds were set up in Hayley and Aaron's rooms and they each enjoyed having a stepbrother and stepsister.

The Peirsol family members were inseparable. With Wella's inspiration, Tim became a very good runner and the kids became exceptional on Rollerblades. The cul-de-sac functioned as a roller hockey rink much of the time. Everyone swam on the swim team, enjoyed the swim meets together and rollicked in a busy home in 1991.

They loved being at the beach. The family exercise outings along the bike paths and boardwalk of Newport Beach were a part of their regular routine. By age 9, Aaron and Greg were old enough to try out for the Junior Lifeguarding Program at Newport Beach. The purpose of the program was to teach children to respect the hazards of the ocean and to learn how to care for it. The boys easily passed the three-minute test for treading water and the 100-yard swim test.

Beginning in the summer of 1992, each morning from late June to the beginning of August they spent three hours on the beach in the program. When spoken to, "yes" was the only accepted response from the boys. Responding "yeah" earned you 10 push-ups. They learned about weather, surf reports, beach safety, ocean safety and boating safety. They ran, practiced ocean safety maneuvers and swam. They participated in the "Marathon Mile" race the first week of August around the Newport Pier most summers. Aaron was showing little remnants of his asthma and within a few years it would be completely gone.

Aaron loved the water in whatever form he could find. The family spent even more time at the Corona Del Mar pool in 1992, and Aaron joined the water polo program. He had increasing success in the pool races and worked hard at practice. Occasionally, a foot cramp at practice stopped him from finishing. He was thin and lanky, and when he wanted a hot shower, on occasion pretended he had a foot cramp to get one.

One of Aaron's favorite non-water pastimes was reading a record book that Coach Zapolski made available to the swimmers each year. Inside there were various time standards and records for each age group in southern California and nationally. Aaron insisted that he had to have one and eventually Wella splurged to buy him one. He studied the book like some studied the Bible. It served him in swimming in a similar way as it serves some in the Spirit. He looked to see what the standard was for swimming fast, at what distance and in what stroke. He scanned to see what an AA time was or an AAA time was. He especially looked at the name of the person who held the record. He highlighted all the records.

Coach Zapolski's squad accepted several invitations to southern California US Swimming competitions. On the car ride to the meets, Aaron often studied his record book. He asked his mom one day, "How do you get to be a really great swimmer, Mom?"

Wella didn't know much about competitive swimming but she logically told him, "It's a long process, Aaron. If you really want to be great, you work hard and go to the Olympics. But it takes many, many years of practice to get there, Aaron."

Aaron, Hayley and their teammates enjoyed racing and improving at the meets. But there seemed to be one team that stood out with the performance of swimmers Aaron's age: The Irvine Novas.

1993 AGE-GROUP AT NOVAS

In the fall of 1993, the Peirsols made the decision to change swim clubs and join the Irvine Novas. Their head coach, Dave Salo, had taken over the position three years earlier and the team had made remarkable progress under his direction. As a swimmer, Dave had enjoyed the coaching of the great

John Urbanchek at Long Beach State College. Dave began his coaching career while working on his doctorate in exercise physiology at USC. He had trained his swimmers at the Downey Dolphins the way he had been trained, with volume as a critical measure of hard work.

One day a USC professor asked him, "Why do you place so much value on volume as a measure of work?" Dave seriously considered the professor's point and eventually created a program based on skill and intensity. In the program Dave developed, swimming at race pace was a part of every practice, all season long. This approach would have a lasting impact on Aaron's success as a world-class swimmer.

During the previous summer of 1992, Dave was looking for a new head age-group coach. He wanted someone who shared his value for excellent stroke, start and turn technique. He selected one of his swimmers who had just completed his swimming career at the US Olympic Trials. His name was Brian Pajer. Brian's background was unique. He had been injured for most of his high school years and therefore didn't swim. But he attended UC Irvine where he resumed his swimming career with considerable success. Each summer he trained in different programs that were excellent. They included swimming with Jozsef Nagy and Mike Barrowman at the Curl-Burke Swim Club and Mitch Ivey and Pablo Morales at Concord-Pleasant Hill, as well as at the Novas with Coach Salo. Brian progressively synthesized all of these experiences and developed his own unique coaching style.

Coach Pajer based his technical program on perfect stroke technique and his personal development program on each swimmer being accountable for their actions. He held great expectations for his young age-groupers that typically stayed with him between the ages of 10 and 12. If they were accomplished enough at 13, they could move to the senior group with Coach Salo. When Aaron joined the team as a 10-year-old, he was humbled by the many good young swimmers on the team. Aaron practiced for a few weeks and then he talked to his new coach.

"What are your goals for this season, Aaron?" Brian asked.

"I want to break Chas Morton's national record in the 50-yard freestyle," Aaron answered confidently. Chas Morton had dominated the national records for 9–10-year-old swimmers. Aaron thought of Chas as someone with fire coming out of his eyes and lightning from his rear quarters. (Well, he thought of Chas as something special.)

The coach responded with an impressed smile. "That might be tough, Aaron, but we'll see what we can do. I really like your backstroke. "

"Yes, coach," Aaron responded respectfully. He had no doubt he could achieve his goal.

The culture for fast age-group swimming with the Novas was demanding. Expectations were high. The Novas set local and national relay records. At the same time, Aaron noticed the intense pressure *some* kids swam under, even being cursed by their parents for not swimming fast enough. He saw how physically developed some of them were at such a young age. Aaron expressed to his parents that swimming was his sport and he would be responsible for his success—a remarkable statement for a 10-year-old. He was making real progress with the Novas. Uncharacteristically for someone his age, he remembered his mother telling him that swimming was going to be a long-term sport to meet his goals.

Aaron's parents supported him completely in pursuing his dreams. However, if you walked into Wella and Tim's home there were no swimming medals or trophies on display. Their home was for loving and supporting their children. It was a sanctuary for getting away from the busy day and the demanding tasks often associated with it.

1993 IRVINE NOVAS Age-Group Training – Coach Brian Pajer

2.5 hours, six days per week
Typical practice structure was:
10-15 minutes active & static stretching
20-25 minutes medicine ball/stretch cords/body weight core exercises
1.75 hours swimming (short course yards)
Note: All of these drills weren't done every day, but most were.
An example of a backstroke progression series that Aaron would have done:

 4 x 25 on :40 kick on back, arms at side, inhale 3 kicks, exhale 3 kicks
 4 x 25 on :40 kick arms at side, 9 kicks right side, 9 kicks left side
 10 x 25 on :35 backstroke odd-right arm, even-left arm
 6 x 25 on :35 backstroke 9 kicks, 3 strokes, 9 kicks

All of these were focused on body position, rotation, and timing
 8 x 25 on :35 6 underwater fly kicks, 6 strokes backstroke, then easy free
 8 x 25 on :35 6 underwater fly kicks, backstroke swim
 3 x (4 x 50) on 1:00 backstroke swim by 50's: 1-smooth, 1-build,
 1-smooth, 1-fast
 4 x 25 backstroke fast from a racing start

   Courtesy of Brian Pajer, currently Head Coach Irvine AquaZots

When Aaron looked at his "record book Bible," he believed he could achieve whatever he wanted if he was willing to practice hard enough. He followed Coach Pajer's suggestion and turned his attention to the southern California and national age-group records in the backstroke. Because of his long thin frame and the way he swam backstroke technically, long course (50-meters) achievement came easier to him than short course (25-meters or yards).

His birthday of July 23rd also meant that he was physically mature during the summer for his age. In the long course season of 1994 he bettered the southern California record for 10-and-under boys in the 100-meter backstroke just before he turned 11. Aaron didn't break Chas Morton's record in the 50 freestyle but he did break the national record with a time of 1:12.13. He thought to himself, *I just joined the Novas last fall; that happened pretty quickly. I wonder what I can do next?*

1993 IRVINE NOVAS September 14th – (short course yards)

Stretching & Dry-land (30 minutes)
Warm-up: Snake (300)
Warm-up: (3x25) x 4 scull 1-forward, 1-backward, 1-boat on :40, :40, 1:00
Drill: 8x75 free odd-25 rt, 25 lt, 25 swim, even-25 advanced timing, 50 swim on 1:20
Swim: 8x75 free on 1:10 odd-build, even-50 fast, 25 smooth perfect stroke
Kick: 10x25 fly w/zoomers odd-arms at side, even-arms in front on :35
Drill: 4x50 fly w/zooms 25 rt, 25 lft on 1:05
Swim: 6x50 fly on 1:00 odd-smooth, even-fast
Swim: 8x25 fly on :40 fast 1 breath only
Kick: 8x50 25 free, 25 fly on 1:00 or 1:10
200 wd w/dive every 50

Courtesy of Brian Pajer, currently Head Coach Irvine AquaZots

IRVINE NOVAS AGE-GROUP PRACTICE - September 15th:
(short course yards)

Stretching & dry-land (30 minutes)

Warm-up:	300 choice
Drills:	Breaststroke progressions:
	6 x base position pushoffs
	6 x base pushoff & 5 kicks
	5 x (4x25) By round: scull, flat pull, flat pull, uw pull, full pull @ :40
Main Set:	4x50 brst (25 2klp, 25 swim) on 1:05
	4x50 brst (25 uw swim :20 rest, 25 swim) on 1:30
	6x50 brst swim on 1:05 odd-smooth, even-fast
	20 minutes of starts

Backstroke progressions:

        4 x (4x25) - By round: kick on back, rt/lft, 9-3-9, swim on :40

        8 x 50 backstroke swim w/6 kicks off each wall on 1:00

        8 x 25 back w/zooms 6 kicks + flat breakout off each wall on :35

Warm-down: 200 (25 1 breath, 25 regular)

Courtesy of Brian Pajer, currently Head Coach Irvine AquaZot

Many swimmers view their birthday into an older age-group as an intimidating challenge. Aaron saw it as a wonderful opportunity to retool and refocus to improve and swim faster times. When he turned 11, he used what he closely observed in his teammates to learn everything he could to get faster. He carefully thought through his practice habits, his skills and the way he paced races to review all the opportunities he had to improve to catch up to the older kids. Then, he pressed forward to achieve the top times in the new age group with confidence.

Coach Brian had strict standards for practice performance. He expected correct stroke mechanics or the group would start over. If someone wasn't making the assigned repeat interval or was falling behind the group, the coach might give them a 1000-yard butterfly to do. If he wasn't pleased with how fast Aaron or a teammate was swimming in practice, they might be dismissed for the night. Brian was gentle when correcting personal character but more abrupt when eliminating swimming mistakes. If he didn't feel their swimming was at the level he expected he would usually say, "Let's try this again tomorrow."

"I got kicked out again," were words that Aaron's mom and dad heard on the phone regularly. Making it through a week of practice without being kicked out was very challenging with Brian as coach. Sometimes Aaron and his friends looked at each other and asked, "Do you think something's wrong; we haven't been kicked out yet this week?"

At 11, occasionally Aaron would even resort to claiming a foot cramp to get to the warm showers on a cold night. The swimmers in the group loved Coach Pajer's honesty and trusted him. If the coach told Aaron he could do something, he believed him. Coach Pajer's challenges toughened Aaron and his teammates, including future Olympians Amanda Beard, Michael Cavic and Kristen Caverly.

A side benefit of practicing in such a competitive environment with the Novas was that no one needed to go to a high school football game on a Friday night to have fun. Everyone looked forward to "Friday Fun-Day." The huge park adjoining the swimming complex was the site of Ultimate Frisbee and soccer. There was a series of basketball games on the courts by the pool. On Friday nights, Aaron and his teammates had lots of fun on land and then did a short swim practice to recharge for Saturday morning practice.

Swim meets were intense learning experiences. Aaron and his friends Gonny Shimura, Jeff Sutherland and Quinn Fitzgerald raced with each other and learned from each other. They had goals of national relay records. They helped each other with their relay starts, goggle adjustments, and refining close race strategy. In between races, they played cards and talked, sometimes with teammates but also with coaches and swimmers from other teams.

The summer long course season was always a highlight for Aaron. When Aaron was 12 he established the national age-group record for the 100-meter backstroke of 1:03.59. He, his friends and his family were excited. But in his mind he always thought, *You've got a long way to go.*

1996 NOVA SENIOR GROUP

One of the common goals of the younger swimmers was to move into Coach Salo's "training group" consisting of those 13 and above. It was where the big kids were—where their heroes on the team trained. Aaron moved into Dave's group in the fall of 1996 when he was in the seventh grade. He was 13 years old. Since Aaron had a late summer birthday, Wella had elected to start him a year later in school than a lot of children.

He knew he had a lot to learn from the older swimmers and was going to benefit from trying to keep up with swimmers that were high school and even college age. Bobby Brewer was a world-class backstroker and became both a training partner and teacher for Aaron. He was 12 years older than Aaron and spent time teaching him how to perfect a backstroke start and to develop his underwater dolphin kicking. At first Bobby beat Aaron badly on everything they did in practice, but over the period of many months, Aaron pushed himself to where he could regularly keep up with him at practice.

Notably, Dave Salo didn't write his practices down. He relied on his intuition to assess his swimmers' physical and mental state during the first few minutes of each session. Then he used his innovative abilities to create swim series that were usually only 20 minutes long and they were complex in detail. For example, he might ask them to swim two lengths but with 12 vertical dolphin kicks and six push-ups at the other end of the pool. Aaron was determined to be more committed to swimming now that he was in Coach Salo's group, but he still had maturing to do. Often before Coach Salo finished explaining a set, Aaron was beginning to experiment on his own to determine which way to position his hands to create the best water pistol to the back of the head of a teammate two lanes over. Eventually Aaron developed his ability to concentrate and remember auditory direction. But initially he followed his teammates and asked quietly, "What are we doing?"

Once a swimmer is 13, their competitions can be open to all athletes that are of equivalent age or higher. Aaron had always used the age-group standards and records to guide him toward his next goal. Even though he was only 13, since he was now in the senior training group, he needed to zero in on new targets. He never had a great deal of strength and pure speed; therefore, he was really excited to begin competing in the 200 backstroke. At a meeting with Coach Salo that fall to discuss his goals, Dave gave Aaron a new target.

"Aaron," Dave explained confidently. "As a country, we are not very strong in the 200-meter backstroke right now. Lenny Krayzelburg is developing and may soon become the new kingpin, but after Lenny the field is wide open. You have a real chance to make the Olympic Team in 2000."

For some swimmers the goal might have been too grand to believe. Aaron simply thought to himself, *I think I can do that. The fact that Dave believes it must mean it's very possible. I'm sure there will be ups and downs along this long path.* What Dave had told him was in the privacy of their coach-swimmer relationship and a new goal that Aaron kept to himself.

On a dark, cold night at practice that season the senior group had trained for two hours and Aaron was exhausted. They had just completed a test set of 3 x 300s on 5:00. Everyone was dismissed except for Aaron. Coach Salo asked him to stay in the water. Dave was clearly unhappy with Aaron's performance.

"Aaron, I want you to do another." Dave told him.

"I'll do my best," Aaron responded respectfully. Aaron swam again. Dave wasn't satisfied.

"Let's do another," Dave ordered. Aaron swam another 300, but it wasn't faster.

"Let's do another," Dave said again.

Aaron thought to himself, *What do you want from me?* But he swam another and it was no faster. Aaron touched the wall and Dave knelt down at the side of the pool in front of him.

"Listen," Dave said to him. "You have the ability over the next four years to do something really special. Our goal is for you to make an Olympic Team. In order to do that you have to train like Jeff Rouse and Brad Bridgewater [former world record holders] did when they were here." Aaron knew those names and respected them greatly. He fed off his coach's belief in him and the excitement over the prospect of being able to reach his special goal. He intensified his training to get there.

In addition to demanding daily intensity from his swimmers, Dave constantly emphasized performing the last half of their races correctly. He gave Aaron a "Tempo Trainer" to put under his goggle strap. It beeped at the correct tempo for him to keep in his backstroke. They used the device particularly on long repeats of 200 and 300 distances. The beeping was annoying at first but helped build Aaron's growing capacity to concentrate on details of training and race perfection.

Dave's workouts were always designed to simulate race conditions and race pace. He loved for the swimmers to use fins because it allowed them to perform technique and skills at race speed. For example Aaron wore a pair of fins for a set of 3-5 x (3 x 50s on :50, then 200 fast on 3 min). The goal of the 50s was to swim at 200 pace, which was not difficult with the fins on. On the 200 he was instructed to swim as fast as possible. As the set would progress, Aaron felt himself warm up and train with a similar rhythm and pain that he had at the end of the 200 backstroke.

Up and down the pool deck the coach walked. He looked for appropriate skill adjustments and race tempo (arm speed) and then communicated corrections to Aaron and the other swimmers during their rest period or with voice or hand signals while they swam. After a 20-minute set, Dave explained a new training experience for the next 20 minutes.

The overall season plan didn't account for much of a change in training. Coach Salo wanted the swimmers to experience the physiological training process specific to their races from early season to the end of it. As their conditioning improved so did their meet performances.

1998 NOVA Senior Practice – Coach Dave Salo

Warm-up: 400 on 5:30, 4 x 100s on 1:30, 4 x 50s on :45

Drills: 12 x 25s on : 30
(Odd, head up, catch-up strong kick/Even, 25 catch-up or breathe 3rd, 200 pace-time: 12.5s)
5 x (2 x 25 + 50) on 30 and 55
Odd 25s Catch-up/Evens 25s catch-up, breathe every 3rd, 200 pace-time :12.5s
50s – Dolphin kick on back to 15 meters, then sprint swim remainder – time 200 pace +1=27.5s

Swim: 4 x (3 x 25s + 75) on :30/1:10
25s are kick, pull, catch-up with no breath
75s are 200 pace plus 3 seconds (Aaron's best time 1:46 yards, so 42.7)

Swim: 3 x (4 x 25s + 100) on :30/1:40
25s are holding 200 pace
100s are holding 200 pace + 5 sec – work on good stroke technique)
4 x (2 x 25s + 50 + broken 100) on :35/1:10/1:45
25s are 10 seconds kick against wall, 2 flips, streamline kick to 15 meters, sit-scull rest of 25
50s are V-sit Scull first lap, sit kick second lap
100s are 25 fast kick, 50s of 200 pace, 25 sprint
3 x 50s on :50 stretch out
3 x (300 at 1,650 pace + 2 x 100s at 1,000 Pace/500 + 4 x 50s (descend from 500 pace) + 8 x 25s sprint backstroke on 3:30/1:30/:50/:35 - :45 seconds rest between rounds – last round backstroke)

Warm-down: 4 x 50s on :50

Reprinted with permission from *Swimming World Magazine*

Dave understood that building Aaron's endurance at this age was critical to his long-term success. Aaron was a willing accomplice. At the 1997 Long Course Junior Nationals in Clovis he had just turned 14. Coach Salo had him swim the 400, 800 and 1500-meter freestyle and the 400 individual medley. He also swam the backstrokes, finishing sixth in the 100 (59.3) and winning the 200 in 2:05.4. During the winter short course season he improved his 1650 to 15:59.

At home, Wella and Tim shared many conversations behind their closed bedroom door about how to best parent their children. Wella watched over their children diligently and guarded their self-esteem. Tim balanced Wella's primary concern for Aaron's joy in living with pointing out the opportunities available in exploring his athletic potential. They understood that the time would soon come for Aaron to choose to invest more time in his competitive swim training, but they were cautious about that investment transpiring when he was this young.

The club offered two morning practices per week in the summer of 1998 to 14-year-olds. That year, Aaron was enrolled in his fifth year in the Junior Lifeguarding Program at Newport Beach. He loved the experience by the ocean each morning and the competition events that were increasingly demanding. The August "Marathon Runs" lasted up to seven miles. Aaron trained at the beach each morning and in the pool each afternoon. His mother was happy with this regimen as long as Aaron was happy.

During the summer months before Aaron's freshman year in high school, Wella and Tim followed through on a difficult decision. Coach Salo had asked Aaron to begin training twice a day, several days per week. In order to do this, it would be easier on the family to live in Irvine in order to shorten the drive to practice at 5:30 a.m. Aaron, who had just turned 15, wanted to attend Newport High School to be with his lifetime friends, many of whom were from the Junior Guard program. Aaron's siblings also wanted to go to Newport High School.

The family solution was to move their home to Irvine, less than a mile from the pool they trained at, and Wella or Tim would drive their kids to Newport for high school each day. Each day he was wakened by one of his parents before dawn. An English muffin or bowl of cereal was always waiting for him. After practice in the morning, Tim or Wella drove Aaron, Greg and eventually Hayley to Newport High School. Then they went to work and afterwards one of them picked up the kids and brought them back to Irvine for the evening practice.

Aaron found Coach Salo's confidence in his training inspirational. Each day Aaron saw Dave surveying him and his teammates during the early sets in practice, knowing that he was going to provide them with a new challenge, but one that was specific to their needs and physical state that day. Then the coach would assign a 20-minute period of work. If a swimmer didn't understand how to do a set or had a question about the set, Dave pulled him out of the water and explained what the purpose of the set or training emphasis was and how it applied to his races. Aaron knew that the training at the Novas was unconventional in its low volume and fast swimming in practice.

He continued to believe, however, that if he came to practice every day and worked as hard as he could, he was going to reach his goals.

Dave and Aaron worked a great deal on pace for the 200-meter backstroke. Dave entered him in several 1650s or 1500s in the local senior meets that were normally meant for freestyle and Aaron swam them backstroke. Gradually, and through trial and error, he learned exactly when to increase his effort over 200 meters. When he was 15, Aaron became the youngest swimmer ever to swim faster than two minutes in the 200-meter backstroke (1:59.8). To Aaron it wasn't a "big deal." He was focused on becoming a part of the 2000 Olympic Team. His new age-record time was just one small step along the way.

Even though Aaron had the expectation to be on the 2000 Olympic Team, he was at his core a boy from the beach in Newport, California. He looked the part with his T-shirt hanging out over his shorts or suit. After winning a race or establishing a new record he could quickly be found chatting with a friend about a great surfing spot. The only disturbing moments he had in the pool were after an occasional loss. Those would not sit well with him and might take him a few hours to digest and learn from them before moving on.

At the Clovis Nationals (long course) in the summer of 1998 Aaron advanced into competition with the best swimmers in the country. In the preliminaries of the 200-meter backstroke he placed sixth (2:01.7), but in the finals he moved up to third (2:01.3) with only Lenny Krayzelburg and Brad Bridgewater in front of him. The development of pace that he had learned through racing 1500s backstroke, as well as in training sets, was impressive when he split 28.7 – 30.8 – 30.9 – 30.7 at night. That swim earned him a spot on the 1999 Pan American Team.

His inaugural international competition came the first week of August of 1999 in Winnipeg, Canada, at the Pan American Games. It was a great experience with the opening ceremonies, the multi-sport competitions and the sense that he was at a smaller version of the Olympics.

Aaron was easily impressed but seldom intimidated. He respected the competition but believed he would excel even in such illustrious company. He nearly won the 200-meter backstroke when he posted his best time of 1:59.77. He completed the summer competition season at the Minneapolis Summer Long Course Nationals the following week. Since he had swum the 200 in Canada, he only swam the 100 at the nationals. He made it into the finals (56.8) and placed eighth, his most accomplished finish to date at that distance.

2000 OLYMPIC YEAR

At the end of 1999 Aaron wasn't ranked in the top 25 in the world in the 100-meter backstroke. In the 200-meter backstroke he was four seconds slower than Lenny Krayzelburg's world record time of 1:55.8. But he was now ranked 10th in the world in the 200 and just .5 seconds behind the second-ranked Brad Bridgewater. Aaron had grown to 6' 2" and weighed 155 pounds. He was getting stronger every day and was excited for the dawning of the Olympic year.

By the winter of 2000 Aaron was one of the best trainers in Dave Salo's group even though he was only 16 and a high school sophomore. It was his fourth year in the senior group and the US Nationals were held that winter in Federal Way, Washington. Aaron won the 200-meter backstroke in the fifth fastest time ever swum of 1:57.03. He had just separated himself from all the other backstrokers in the United States in the event, except Lenny Krayzelburg.

Seldom did Aaron become exuberant after a win or a great time, but he knew the swim was a tremendous breakthrough in his swimming career. He was excited and hurried to see Coach Salo.

Aaron gave him a big bear hug and said in his ear, "Now that was f***g fast!!"

Dave told him, "This summer you're going to get to race Lenny every chance you can get. Everyone else races for second place when they swim with Lenny. Not you!"

Over that summer of 2000 Aaron did get to race Lenny Krayzelburg. At the Janet Evans Meet in Los Angeles he beat him in the 200-meter backstroke, coming from behind on the last length. This surprised both Lenny and Aaron. Aaron simply thought the world record holder was having an off day.

The Olympic Trials began August 9th in Indianapolis. Aaron was much younger than most of the male swimmers and he was nervous. His 200 backstroke was at the end of a week of swimming. Each day he watched swimmers race and celebrate qualifying for the Olympic Team. He also saw the large number of disappointments. There were many athletes at the end of their careers and upset over failing to make the Olympic Team. It reminded him that his opportunity would not be available for another four years.

It helped Aaron to know that his best time was quite a bit faster than the third fastest American in the 200. His first event was the 100-meter backstroke (55.97) and he placed ninth. Some swimmers might have dwelled on finishing only ninth and missing the final eight by one place, but not Aaron.

The Believer was instantly focused on the 200.

When he felt tense just hours before the 200 race, he controlled and focused his thoughts on his desired outcome. He reminded himself, *I've swum this race thousands of times*. He reassured himself that he had worked very hard and felt as prepared as he could possibly be. When he felt a rush of doubt pushing itself into his mind, he went where he felt most comfortable—into the water. It was a habit he continued throughout his career: 15 to 20 minutes before his race he swam and calmed his nerves. He said to himself, *This is just like practice ... just race like it's practice*. Then he went to the ready room for the finals.

Aaron trailed by just three-tenths of a second behind Lenny Krayzelburg the entire race and finished second in the 200-meter backstroke with a time of 1:57.9. He was nearly two seconds ahead of the third-place finisher. Aaron's earlier time from the winter nationals of 1:57.03 still stood as the number-one time in the world for the year. He was going to be the top-seeded swimmer for the event in Sydney. He was excited to be on the Olympic Team and his mental mantra of "you have a long way to go" steadied his forward focus and resolve.

2000 OLYMPIC GAMES – Sydney, Australia

In order to perform at the top of the world as an athlete, a swimmer must find a comfort zone in that arena. Aaron sensed that this was an opportunity to learn more about the Olympic experience. His personal sense of self-worth served him well as he moved easily through the travel and training with the team and staff. He varied his time with the different workout groups. No one else trained quite like he did. The fact that Dave Salo was allowed to spend time at the training camp was comforting to him. He saw that Dave was communicating well with the Olympic staff. It was clear that his training was in the best possible set of hands.

His roommate assignment for the Olympic Village was Michael Phelps. Michael, at 15, was two years younger than Aaron. He qualified for the team in the 200-meter butterfly. Both he and Michael approached the fantastic Sydney setting—with 18,000 fans and the enormous love their country had for competitive swimming—as something they would never take for granted. They were taking one step forward in their swimming careers. Aaron tried to accept that he belonged there, but he had no expectations for a gold medal.

The racing experience was very similar to Olympic Trials. Aaron was nervous but controlled his self-talk, reminded himself of his preparation and used his calming ritual of getting in the water before his race. He swam faster than Trials and again trailed right behind Lenny Krayzelburg throughout the race and won the silver medal (1:57.3). "I got the silver medal but I still get to stand up there for the US national anthem" (SW Sept 2000). As he received his award and the national anthem played, he felt an enormous sense of fulfillment.

Even more emotional for him was greeting his family afterward. Aaron's grandfather had been in poor health and there were questions about how long he might live. He, however, made the trip to Sydney to watch his grandson swim. Wella was overwhelmed with pride for her son. All the support that Tim, Hayley, Greg and Erin had given him was felt in his heart. They all had forged his success together. From Junior Guards, and Rollerblading at the beach, Aaron was on the top of the world. He quietly reminded himself that he had a long way to go.

Aaron came home and began his junior year of high school. Coach Salo gave him a month off from swimming. Aaron enjoyed each day without his normal routine. He loved the option of laying at home staring at the ceiling. After 30 days of physical and emotional rest, he was ready to go back to work.

WORLD RECORDS

With the silver medal in hand, it was now time for a new goal. For four years his overarching goal was on making the 2000 Olympic Team. He decided it was time to break the world record in the 200-meter backstroke. He trained exceptionally hard, with times in practice like never before. However, becoming the world record holder required much more than even Aaron first contemplated.

The 2001 Spring Nationals were held long course in the super-fast pool at the University of Texas in Austin in March. They also served as the Trials for the World Championships scheduled for July in Fukuoka, Japan. Aaron saw his Olympic roommate Michael Phelps on the pool deck and they shared their ambitions about each breaking a world record in Austin. Michael soon achieved the goal in the 200-meter butterfly. Phelps said when he looked at the scoreboard and realized what he had done, "I was so excited, I felt like my whole body stopped" (SW April 2001).

Aaron won the 200 backstroke by four seconds in his best time ever of 1:56.56, seven-tenths off Lenny Krayzelburg's world record. "I wish Lenny had been here," Aaron said of his southern California rival. "It's always better to compete against the best" (SW April 2001). Aaron was victorious in the 100 in a close race with Randal Bal and Peter Marshall, lowering his best time to 54.82.

Deep inside, Aaron felt that being a world record holder was a big responsibility and one that he found he wasn't quite ready for. Holding the world record would mean he no longer had anyone else's performance or time to shoot for. It meant becoming the hunted rather than being the hunter.

The 2001 World Championships were held (long course) in July in Fukuoka, Japan. Aaron's performance at the winter nationals earned him a spot on the team. His first swim was the 100-meter backstroke. As soon as Wella Peirsol saw the results from her home in Irvine, Dave Salo's phone rang.

A concerned Wella Peirsol's voice asked, "Dave, is Aaron all right?"

"What do you mean, Wella?"

"I saw how poorly he did in the 100 back and am just concerned."

Dave reassured her. "He's fine, Wella. He's fine. It's his first race in his first world championship. It's a new experience but he will be fine." As always, Wella wasn't concerned for his achievements, only that her son was safe and happy.

Aaron swam a 55.8 in the semi-finals of the 100 backstroke and that time failed to move him into the championship finals. Five days later he won the 200 backstroke (1:57.1) and his first world championship. Aaron was safe and happy and his mother, on the other side of the Pacific Ocean, knew it.

2001-2002 NEWPORT HARBOR HIGH SCHOOL – Senior Year

Several young swimmers in the United States during those years had elected to accept money as a professional for swimming and forego their college eligibility. Dave Salo met with Aaron's parents to discuss his options for his future. The swimsuit companies followed Aaron's progress and were interested in signing him to a contract that would likely pay for college and a lot more. The coach explained some of Aaron's options. He could stay in Irvine and train while attending college; he could also become a professional and go to college somewhere else; or he could follow the normal college scholarship path without being a professional. Wella Peirsol insisted, "Aaron is going to college and get his degree. Aaron is going to Stanford."

Aaron agreed with his mother that he was going to college. He wanted that experience both in the classroom and on a team. The social aspect of swimming was always important to Aaron and he valued his relationships with the swimmers and coaches he met through the sport. During the Sydney Olympics he first met Texas coach Eddie Reese. The recruiting process helped him get to know him better. The success of the Texas program in winning NCAA team championships, the friends he had made on that team and the quality of Eddie as a man were enough for him to decide to attend the University of Texas.

During his senior year of high school in 2002, Aaron realized he was ready to fully and calmly accept the responsibility of becoming a world record holder. The Spring Nationals were held long course in Minneapolis, Minnesota, the third week of March. In the preliminaries he swam a 1:57.1 200-meter backstroke and it wasn't a full effort.

Prior to the finals, Coach Salo told his team to be ready for the 200 back-stroke because something special was going to happen. His Nova team was improving rapidly at the national level with a new mix of young and older swimmers. They were positioned to win their first national championship and quite possibly have their first world record-setting swim. Cameras read-ied to record the performance for posterity. Computers were booted up and ready to send the pictures to media outlets around the world. What a great night for the "Nova" brand.

The announcer introduced the parade of finalists as they exited the ready room. Aaron walked down the pool deck with his headphones on and Led Zeppelin's song "Heartbreaker"' playing in his ears. The Novas cheered for Aaron.

One of the Nova swimmers said, "Dave, he's got his cap on inside out."The N-O-V-A was on the inside of the cap and the outside was all black.

Dave told them, "Quiet, quiet. Don't say anything." He knew Aaron was in the right mental place and noting such an indiscretion was something more than he was willing to do.

Aaron's splits were 27.7, 56.6, and 1:26.0. He lowered Lenny Krayzelburg's world record by seven-tenths of a second to 1:55.15. Hayley Peirsol cried tears of joy. She had been having her own great swim meet at these Nationals, fin-ishing second in the 800 freestyle and lowering her best time by eight seconds to 8:34.9. Aaron's teammates were thrilled by his achievements.

"To get right down to it, I knew it was my time," Aaron said afterward. "I was just confident before the race that everything was going to go as planned" (SW April 2002). Dave Salo added, "He's a great kid. He's been after this since he was 13, and it's good to see the things you talk to your athletes about come to fruition" (SW April 2002). Aaron continued the meet, swimming every team relay and winning the 100 backstroke in 54.4.

Just as Aaron had anticipated after setting the world record, there were more eyes watching him swim. After the nationals he flew to Moscow to the Short Course World Championships held at the Olympiisky Pool that were conducted in early April. More swimming experts wanted to examine his stroke technique, some assuming it must be the best method of swimming backstroke. Others wanted to see his body type, concluding it must be ideal for backstroke. He took the whole experience with good humor. He didn't disappoint anyone with his performance either. He broke the short course meter world record in the 200 backstroke (1:51.17) and led off the 400 medley relay world record team (Peirsol, Denniston, Marshall, Lezak) that set a new global standard (3:29.35) as well.

Visitors came to Irvine to watch him train. Aaron began to learn that coaches can have a tendency to "show off" or at least put on a good demonstration when there are guest coaches present to learn. A group from Japan was observing one Saturday morning. Aaron was tired and ready to go home for a two-hour nap when Dave Salo gave him his final training set.

"Aaron, I want you to put your fins on and swim 6 x 100 (yards) back on 1:00. On each 25, stay under water for 15 meters and hold all six of them under 50 seconds."

Aaron thought, *Are you nuts! I can't do that.* He tried, of course, and he succeeded. After the set was over, Dave flashed a quick smile his way reminding him that he was the best in the world.

At the summer nationals in Ft. Lauderdale, he won both backstrokes (54.0/1:56.2) beating injured Lenny Krayzelburg. Then he flew with the US National Team to Fukuoka, Japan, won the two backstroke events and was a part of the world record-setting 400 medley relay. By the time he arrived at the University of Texas for his freshman year of college he was a seasoned veteran of international competition and the dominant long course backstroker in the world.

2002–2003 THE UNIVERSITY OF TEXAS – Freshman Year

There were differences in the Texas swimming program and Aaron would come to welcome the changes. He had been in Coach Salo's program for six years and flourished in it. He understood, however, that there was much he could learn from Coach Reese and his fellow swimmers in Austin.

The Texas strength program was an important contributor to applying more pressure on the water and Coach Reese loved the prospect of Aaron building some muscle on his tall, thin frame. At the same time the coach knew that initiating such a strength program had the potential for wearing out a swimmer quickly. Unlike some college coaches, he personally designed the weight program, evaluated it and was in the weight room nearly every day monitoring it. Aaron and the freshmen lifted progressively for two to three weeks and then there was a week of testing and evaluating their progress. Eddie was looking for strength gains without his athletes experiencing a large bulk difference. He measured the results of their work to ensure forward progress and was always looking to avoid failing adaptation.

The swimming program's dry-land workouts were conducted on Tuesday and Thursday afternoons alternating with the weight program on Monday, Wednesday and Fridays. One of the critical exercises was "wheels." They were lawn mower wheels on an axle with a board fixed across the axle. The board was placed just below the knees and they crawled up the ramps of the football stadium. This strengthened their core and enhanced the stabilization of their shoulders. They also added push-ups and abdominal work and ran stadium steps.

THE UNIVERSITY OF TEXAS PROGRAM

Monday:	6:30 -8:00 am swim,
	2-2:45 weights, 3-5 pm swim
Tuesday:	off (or make up option am),
	2-2:45 Dry-land, 3-5 pm swim
Wednesday:	6:30-8:00 am swim, 2-2:45 weights,
	3-5 pm swim
Thursday:	off (or make-up option am),
	2-2:45 dry-land, 3-5 pm swim
Friday:	6:30-8:00 am,
	2-2:45 weights, 3 -5 pm swim
Saturday:	8-10:00 am swim

Day to day Coach Reese delivered his practice plans verbally and his swimmers listened carefully. "All right. We're going [to do] a 200 IM on 2:45, a 300 free on 3:45 and a 100 stroke on 1:30. I want the first round easy, fast, easy by swims and then continue that pattern so it becomes fast, easy, fast on the even rounds." Eddie held up four fingers. "We're going through it six times." Most of the freshmen laughed at the conflict in the number of four fingers indicating six rounds. The juniors and seniors chuckled at the freshmen getting their indoctrination into the coach's humor and a joke that had been used for several years.

On the first 200 IM that was supposed be easy, Aaron swam a 1:56. He beat everyone in the pool by a wide margin. He of course had learned from Coach Salo to swim fast in practice every day and every set. His teammates had swum easy as instructed. Assistant coach Kris Kubik walked over to Aaron and said, "Did you know that one was supposed to be easy?"

"I know." Kris acknowledged that it was how Aaron had learned to train. Aaron also had a goal to motivate his new teammates to swim faster in practice.

Just as there were visitors to Nova practices, there were often ones at the University of Texas. On a Saturday morning there was a coaches' clinic hosted at UT. Over time Aaron learned that these days were something to watch out for because practice was going to be especially hard. The main set was 6 x 200s (yards) on 6:00. Aaron thought to himself, *Now there's something I can do well on.* His first swim was 1:48, then he gradually progressed down to 1:45 on the last one.

Aaron grew to understand that in the Texas program Eddie trained people for the end of the season or the end of the summer. There was a larger and longer progression and evolution of training loads and type of work over the course of a five or six-month season than Aaron had experienced with the Novas. Although he tried to challenge his teammates to keep up with him in practice, he also gradually accepted that there were times he didn't have to swim at 100 percent effort. The end result of the training progression was that during the season an athlete was likely to be very fatigued and not swim nearly as fast as when he was rested at the end of the season for their championships.

By late January the team and Aaron were tired from hard training. They took the bus four hours to Dallas to swim SMU in a tri-meet with Arizona. Aaron loved the experience of college swimming, the dual meets and the team camaraderie. But he also loved targets, goals and the thrill of achievements. When they arrived at the pool he stood under the pool record board and studied the times.

Eddie Reese walked up and stood next to him. "What are you looking at?"

Aaron answered, "That 1:43.8, 200 back." Ryan Berube had set the record. He was the 1996 NCAA Swimmer of the Year and an Olympic gold medal winner. He was also a fantastic underwater dolphin kicker, making him a great short course swimmer.

Eddie told him, "You can't do that now [this time of the season]."

Aaron smiled. "I don't know about that."

When the 200-yard backstroke event came, Aaron ripped through the distance. As he approached the finish, he reached for the wall with his right arm and extended his left pinky and index finger into the "Hook 'em Horns" sign. He looked at the time on the board and aimed the "Hook 'em Horns" gesture at Eddie and the team. The time: 1:42.8. Aaron Peirsol was officially a proud Longhorn.

The Texas program had a long-standing tradition of representing the University in as first-class a manner as possible. The team members wore coats and ties to their away meets. They posed for many NCAA Championship team pictures with shirts tucked in and/or warm-ups neatly in place. Over the course of years there were challenges to these traditions, but the traditions were maintained.

The 2003 NCAA Championships were held in March, in Austin. Aaron Peirsol won the 100-yard backstroke in 45.71 and set a new American record in the 200 backstroke of 1:39.16. He always had difficulty coordinating his kick with his arms on freestyle, but he still managed a 4:18 500 and was a part of the NCAA record-setting 800-yard freestyle relay, splitting 1:34.57. When the awards ceremony was about to begin, he wore his T-shirt hanging out the same as he would have on the beach in Newport.

Kris Kubik thought to himself, *How do I get this world record holding and NCAA Champion to uphold our tradition of shirts tucked in?*

Kris leaned over to Aaron and said quietly, "Aaron, why don't you tuck your shirt in. If you do it, everyone else will follow along."

Aaron was quick to comply, "Oh sure." And he tucked in his shirt.

The announcer's voice came over the microphone. "Ladies and gentle-man!" it blared. "Our first award is for the Swimmer of the Meet, from the University of Texas, Aaron Peirsol!"

Amid the raucous applause, Aaron (out of long habit) quickly pulled his shirt out of his warm-up pants and went up on the awards stand to receive his award. He didn't mean any disrespect to the team or the program. He was just being himself. He was an unassuming beach kid from southern California.

Backstroke Technique Tips:

Aaron Peirsol, in his own words: "I could kick and pull at the same time."

Aaron's comment may seem incredibly trite, but he has a unique ability to drive his legs with a kick, while pulling at the same time. This was not something that Aaron could achieve in freestyle over a very long distance.

Aaron's Backstroke Turn: Neil Walker taught Aaron how to attack the wall without looking for it on his backstroke turn. He sighted his position with the backstroke flags and then at the appropriate moment rolled to his stomach and dove into the somersault of his turn. He did this in a unique way, with tremendous speed and usually outperforming all his competitors.

2003–2004 THE UNIVERSITY OF TEXAS – Sophomore Year

In the summer of 2003 the major competition was the World Championships in Barcelona, Spain. Aaron just missed the world record in the 100-meter backstroke by one-hundredth of a second swimming the second fastest time ever of 53.61. He also won the 200 in 1:55.92, swam on the 800 freestyle American record-setting relay (1:48.88) and the world record-setting 400 medley relay. All of a sudden it was the Olympic year.

The 2004 NCAA Championship was the last one for Aaron. It was swum in an unusual (for the USA) short course meters course in New York. He couldn't beat the assault of Peter Marshall's underwater dolphin kick in the 100 backstroke but broke his own world record in the 200 backstroke (1:50.64). He then announced that he was turning professional. "It took a lot of thinking, which started before college," Aaron said, in reference to his decision to turn pro. "I wanted two years in college, and it's been an important step in my career. It's about opportunity. I like the position where I am" (SW April 2004). Aaron had never swum for money, but the financial opportunities were too great to continue to pass them over. He had a window of time to take advantage of his success and after thoughtful discussions with his family, he made the decision.

Many swimmers work hard. Aaron Peirsol prided himself in working hard and smart. He had a personal culture that he learned in Irvine with Coach Salo and one that he grew with and contributed to at Texas. Training smart underscored the advantage gained by repetition in skill work and approaching all swimming at race pace. He understood the depth in America in an event like the 100-meter backstroke, which required preparing to be the best in the world to make the United States Olympic Team.

2004 OLYMPIC TRIALS

The setting for the 2004 Olympic Trials (long course) in Long Beach, California, was spectacular. The selection races were swum outdoors in front of 9,000 fans at the same time the sun was setting into the Pacific Ocean. The 100-meter backstroke field was deeper than any in history, including the past Olympic Games. The 200 backstroke presented a more interesting twist. Michael Phelps was trying to decide which events to swim at the Olympics and the 200 backstroke was a serious consideration for him. Aaron was clearly feeling being the hunted and wanted Michael to know and see that the only available Olympic medal in the event was silver.

The 100 backstroke was first. Aaron moved through the preliminaries and semi-finals without incident. He approached the 100 with the knowledge that a lot of swimmers had more speed than he did on the first 50. In the last 25 meters, however, he would close and win. His 53.64 was just off the world record but good enough to win, with Lenny Krayzelburg edging both Peter Marshall and Randall Bal to make the team.

The 200 backstroke had the Michael Phelps factor and Michael tended to bring out the best in Aaron when it came to racing. Aaron was first in the preliminaries and Michael second. In the semi-finals Aaron made a statement by putting the effort in to swim a 1:55.3 with Phelps two seconds behind. A new world record was the prize for a great finals race with Aaron winning in 1:54.74 to Michael's 1:55.8. Michael elected to drop his option to swim the 200 backstroke at the Olympics.

As Aaron had believed without a doubt, and Michael Phelps came to learn, only a silver medal was available.

2004 OLYMPIC GAMES – Athens, Greece

Winning an Olympic gold medal was one of the few things that the 21-year-old Aaron Peirsol had yet to accomplish in the sport. He understood that at the Olympics winning races is the priority over swimming a particular time.

On August 16th he swam the 100-meter backstroke faster than anyone else on earth that day and won in the time of 54.06. The race was remarkably close for second with 28-hundredths of a second separating second (54.35) from sixth (54.63). On another day the times would have had a different result. For example, Lenny Krayzelburg's time from the Olympic Trials was equal to Aaron's time that won at the Olympics. The Olympics were about racing and the measure of being the best was the gold medal—or so Aaron thought at the time.

When Aaron climbed from the Olympic pool after the 100, the press swarmed to talk with him, teammates congratulated him and coaches affirmed his achievement. He fulfilled his duties as respectfully and efficiently as he could, but he wanted and needed time to be alone. With only one real option he went to his favorite location—the water. He flopped into the warm-down pool and emotionally broke down. With tears flowing, his entire swimming career flashed through his mind. He thought about the missed nights out with friends, the early morning training sessions that he didn't always want to get out of bed for, the years of commitment and hard work. One striking realization came to him: It was worth it. It was worth all of it.

After the team was dismissed for the evening, he joined his family. A second flood of emotions ran through him. Winning an Olympic gold medal would never have happened without the love of his family. In addition to his family, his coaches and teammates all contributed to his sense of fulfillment.

Many people in the sport have an excellent swim, but Aaron Peirsol had achieved *swimming excellence*. He had developed his own ability to lock onto a goal and filter to himself those resources that could help him achieve it: the knowledge from his coaches, the competition from his teammates in training, the challenge of competitors in meets, and the support from his family and closest friends. He had learned how to train with skill and pain to create an artistic expression of human movement through water. His own internal resolve to triumph in goal achievement had developed over his years in competitive swimming as his single greatest resource. Aaron's capacity to filter out the distractions, the small failures and any hint of doubt was an essential part of his success and his development as a person. He was a believer in himself and in those he held close to him.

Two quick days passed before the preliminaries and semi-finals of the 200 backstroke. Aaron posted the top time in the semi-finals by two seconds. The finals looked to be a simple seal of approval on Aaron's domination of the world in the event. Tim and Wella looked forward to being a part of another special moment with their son. Wella had her hair done, dressed nicely and looked forward to the final "victory" swim for Aaron without the usual stress of a tight race.

The eight top competitors made up a field that had greatly improved from the four years prior and was the fastest in history. In the race for the gold, silver and bronze medals the second, third and fourth swimmers all swam times of 1:57. Aaron, however, was more than two seconds faster than the runner-up and swam the second fastest time in history of 1:54.95. (The fastest time in history was his personal best time.) Aaron felt good about his performance, but he looked at the timing board there was a "D" by his name.

Aaron shook his head in disbelief. For the first time since his childhood he had been disqualified. Disqualifications virtually never happened at the level of Olympic swimming because each athlete has had every nuance of their adherence to technical rules screened and polished over their swimming career.

He couldn't believe it. *Is this a joke?* he thought. *Are you kidding me?*

If doom has a sound that is what was heard in the groan of the fans in the swim stadium. Then a heavy silence fell over the natatorium. The officials quickly announced a delay of the awards ceremony and stopped all additional event preparation to address the nearly unthinkable action of a gold medal performance at the Olympics being summarily nullified.

Aaron climbed out of the pool. Eddie Reese was the head men's Olympic coach and he went to Aaron. The coach told him to stay calm and he would check into the disqualification. A thought went through Eddie's mind about what had happened four days earlier.

Kosuke Kitajima had beaten world record holder Brendan Hansen in the 100 breaststroke by a mere 17-hundredths of a second. Brendan was Aaron's USA and Texas teammate. In watching underwater video of that race afterward, it seemed apparent that Kosuke had used an illegal dolphin kick on his underwater pull-outs. (The rule has since been changed to allow swimmers to do this.) Aaron had said afterward to Eddie, "That gold medal is Brendan's." There was no disqualification. Aaron was a loyal friend and teammate. He went to the press and told them that the underwater video revealed a dolphin kick that might well have been the difference in Brendan winning the 100 breaststroke. Eddie worried that perhaps Aaron had been disqualified by an official retaliating over Aaron's complaint of the officiating in the 100 breaststroke.

Coach Reese walked to the video review room and Aaron walked into the warm-down area. Aaron found a place to sit alone and wait. He knew that there were others who would make every effort to see that justice was done.

The true goal of all right-minded officials is to establish a level playing field for athletes to earn their victories through their own preparation, consistent commitment and quality performance.

Shortly after the D appeared by Aaron's name, Wella and Tim popped out of their seats, traversed their row of spectators and descended the steps of the swim stadium. They needed to see their son and support him emotionally. Simultaneously, Jim Wood, the President of USA Swimming and its designated team leader, moved swiftly to the pool deck to investigate the disqualification. Jim was widely recognized as having a combination of a mastery of the technical rules, as well as an astute sense of diplomacy in stressful situations. He was also a person of extraordinary determination. He was the perfect person to represent Aaron's interests.

While it was not on Aaron's mind, a disqualification and loss of a gold medal affects not only an athlete but also affects institutions as well. USA Swimming measures its performance as a multimillion-dollar corporation, as well its success at the Olympics, by medals and in particular gold medals.

The United States Olympic Committee (USOC) paid an athlete $25,000 for winning a gold medal in Athens. Every silver medal was worth $15,000 and a bronze medal was worth $10,000. At the Sydney Games the USOC had paid a total of 2.95 million dollars to medal winners. Olympic medals are a definitive measure of success for both organizations.

Several minutes passed as Jim Wood found FINA Technical Chairman Carol Zaleski. He asked to see the documentation of Aaron's disqualification. The officials brought Jim the disqualification slip. The official was from France. Jim also thought to ask, "What did the official say?"

Aaron knew that he had performed his swim within the rules.

By now, Wella and Tim had confronted the Greek security guard who protected the competition area in the swim stadium. They insisted they be admitted to the pool deck area to see their son. The security guard could see their emotional state and let them pass. The guards at the next two checkpoints did the same.

Eddie Reese was told by one official that the disqualification was for Aaron making continual forward progress on his turn after he had rotated from his back to his stomach. He replayed the video over and over.

Aaron sat alone in thought.

While considering his situation, the swimsuit manufacturers considered theirs. They had invested millions of dollars to design and produce the fastest swimsuits. The more medals, and in particular the more gold medals, won by swimmers wearing their suits the greater their sales would be. In turn, those sales guided their investment into athlete sponsorships, bonuses and a variety of other monetary infusion into the sport.

When Wella and Tim appeared near the pool deck, photographers recognized them as Aaron's parents and began snapping pictures. To avoid them, Wella ducked into a restroom, closed the door while Tim searched for more information.

Aaron sat in thought and waited for the results of what he knew was a USA protest of the gold medal being taken away.

What ended up being a time vacuum of 25 minutes was a gift to Aaron. While the crowd waited in suspense, and Jim Wood worked intently, and his mother worried about her son, he was given time to consider more than ever before why he loved to swim competitively so much. He recognized that in addition to all the human relationships that were a part of his achievement of swimming excellence, he had an additional love: being in and around the water. Whether he was in the ocean or the pool, the flow of movement that he enjoyed as a boy in the surf provided a source of joy and personal expression to his core. His development of swimming excellence earned him the opportunity to work with non-profits and other public benefit organizations to promote the protection of and the respect for the water that he had learned in the Junior Guards. Earning a living while he swam was nothing more than a bonus. He realized that none of these things could be taken away from him. There was nothing more to be gained from a gold medal than he had already won.

Aaron felt a sense of calm come over him and embraced his transcendent experience.

Carol Zaleski and Jim Wood finally heard the rationale of the disqualifying judge: "Aaron had created continuous movement with kicking toward the wall after he had rolled onto his stomach going into a turn." Jim and Carol immediately knew that the infraction was not a disqualifying offense. The rule said that you couldn't make a continuous movement *after* pulling both arms down to your hips. The French judge was in error. There was also a translation problem with his French to English. Had he clearly written his remarks in English the immediate outcome might have been different. The disqualification was overturned by a panel of officials.

The US coaches went to Aaron and told him of the decision. Tim broke the good news to Wella. Aaron quickly prepared himself for the awards ceremony, walked to the podium and received his medal. He was still shaken from the surreal experience and experienced moments wondering if the officials might change their minds. He was comforted with his internal confirmation that medals weren't among the reasons he swam.

The final event of the Olympic swimming program was two nights later. It was the 400 medley relay. Aaron set a new standard on his backstroke leg when he swam the world record of 53.45. The US team won the gold medal.

2005–2008

Over the next three years Aaron ruled the backstroke events like no one had ever done in swimming history. He trained and raced with a target on his back but always looking forward with confidence. And he created his own goals for setting world standards. He believed in them and he achieved them.

In 2005 he swept the backstrokes at the short course and long course World Championships. He also led off the medley relays for USA victories in both competitions. At the Pan Pacific Games in 2006 he repeated the same sweep. He enjoyed the Pan Pacs even more because his sister Hayley earned a spot on the USA team. At the 2007 World Championships Ryan Lochte finally put an end to the streak when he slipped by Aaron on the final 50 of the 200-meter backstroke in Melbourne.

The Quadrennial pulsed to a close during the Olympic year of 2007–2008 at the University of Texas. Over the previous few years, swimmers had moved to Austin to be coached by Eddie Reese and train with Peirsol, Neil Walker, Brendan Hansen, Ian Crocker and other great competitors. They formed a training group that became the most prolific contributor to any Olympic Team dating back to the 1960s when George Haines' Santa Clara swimmers dominated the red, white and blue teams every four years.

The privilege of swimming in the Texas group was sustained in the minds of the athletes in Austin. Swimmers like David Cromwell from Harvard, Nick Thoman from the University of Arizona, Eric Shanteau from Auburn, all converged on Austin. Scott Spann transferred from Michigan. Aaron Peirsol sought to make them believers too. He, Neil, Brendan, Ian and the other team leaders believed that they would help each other become faster and rise to the top of the world standings by competing each day with one another.

As a group they also sensed that happiness was a choice. By focusing on their opportunity and empathizing with the varied financial situations they lived under, they valued each other's unique contribution to the environment they trained and lived in. They enjoyed a life dominated by carefree joy away from the pool and intense work in it. At the 2008 Olympic Trials, eight of them qualified to compete for the United States Olympic Team. Peirsol, Hansen, Shanteau and Spann were joined by Garrett Weber-Gale, Dave Walters, Ricky Berens and Ian Crocker as representatives of the total group in Beijing. All of the other teammates shared in an experience that they would always treasure.

In the Beijing Olympics 2008, Aaron was victorious again in the 100-meter backstroke and in the 400 medley relay. Ryan Lochte foiled his bid for a backstroke sweep when he beat him in the 200 1:53.94 to 1:54.33. Many athletes fill their life with disappointment that never actually happens. They have losses that are only a thought in their mind. Not Aaron. He always trained to win and believed he would win because of how he trained. Ryan's time broke Aaron's world record but it was the loss that brought a tear to Aaron. The conflict in the outcome wasn't acceptable, but he had no choice but to live with the results—for now.

LEAVING A STANDARD BEHIND

In the post-Olympic year of 2009, the swimsuit battles were at their peak. The suit technology continued to develop with little regulation until 2010 when the FINA Bureau was finally overruled by an overwhelming vote of its Congress to put a stop to it. At the same time more and more companies jumped into the contest for the outfit that provided the most buoyancy and compression. Deciding who was the best in the world seemed to be becoming as much about the advantages of the suit a swimmer wore as it was about superior physical preparation.

Some veteran swimmers took off the year after the Olympics from serious training and competition. Aaron Peirsol, however, prepared diligently for the World Championships in Rome. At the US Trials in July he had broken Ryan Lochte's world record, setting a new mark at 1:53.08. About four weeks later the USA team was at a training camp in Italy. Eddie Reese was enjoying his wife and family at home. Instead, Kris Kubik coached Aaron and traveled with the team.

At practice about one week prior to the 200-meter backstroke, Aaron strolled down the pool deck in his black competition suit.

"What are we doing today, Kris?" asked Aaron. He knew it was "show me day." That meant a day to do something fast and show what you could do.

Kris responded, "I've got in mind a 100 on 1:40, then 2 x 50s on :50 [seconds]." The intention was a broken 200-meter backstroke, practicing the speed and pace for the following week, as well as producing a physiological training load simulating a race.

"How bout we do it 2 x 50s on :50, then the 100?" Aaron posed.

"No problem. Sounds good."

National Team Director Mark Schubert and Michael Phelps' coach Bob Bowman pulled their watches from their pockets to time the short set, along with Kris. They all knew that the world record was in jeopardy the next week and the training set might be indicative of Aaron's performance.

Following warm-up, Kris walked the pool deck with Aaron and timed him.

"27.2!" Kris yelled on the first one.

"26.8!" after the second.

Then the 100 was going to be the major test. In the 2004 Olympics Aaron had won the event in 54.06. Aaron smoothly built his speed through the first 50, attacked the turn at the halfway mark and accelerated into the finish.

"54.1!" Kris told him after the 100. Coach Schubert and Coach Bowman's watches confirmed the times.

"1:48.2, added up," Kris said with goose bumps.

At the 2009 World Championships in Rome, Aaron Peirsol pulled his tech suit on and put the world records in a place that will likely challenge swimmers around the world for years to come: 1:51.92 for the 200 and 51.94 (achieved at World Trials) for the 100.

At this point, Aaron had won a total of 34 medals in major international competition spanning the Olympics, the Worlds, Pan Ams, and the Pan Pacific Championships. He owned 27 gold, six silver, and one bronze medal. Aaron had a deep and profound sense that he had achieved all that he had set out to do in the sport. Perhaps it was time to find other goals in other areas. He enjoyed his work as an ambassador for the Global Water Foundation, the Surfrider Foundation and as a spokesman for Oceana, which is the world's largest international ocean conservation and advocacy organization. Perhaps it was time to do more work with them? And, his mantra, "He still had a long way to go" in those areas still resonated in his mind and heart.

As fate would have it, the 2010 Pan Pacific Games were going to be swum at the William Woollett Jr. *Aquatics Center in Irvine,* California, where he moved as a 10-year-old to swim with the Novas. He decided to swim competitively through that competition. He didn't think about what a great opportunity it was for a community send-off, a grand media event, a parade or even a press conference. He won the 100-meter backstroke and swam on the winning 400 medley relay. Then he went into the showers, tucked his goggles under the lip of his suit and walked away from the sport.

There was no announcement or fanfare, just what he left behind: a standard for excellence and a legend—as The Believer.

Aaron Peirsol will be eligible for the International Swimming Hall of Fame in 2016. It is likely he will be admitted on the first ballot since he is widely regarded as the greatest backstroker in the history of competitive swimming.

AFTERWORD

The most important conclusions that are drawn from learning about these great athletes will be the ones the readers draw themselves. Below are some of the observations that came to the author in preparing this work that you might consider.

For most of these young men they seem to have drawn tremendous security from the support of their family and in particular from their mother. Perhaps in writing Volume II about young women we will find similar anecdotal support for them from their fathers. It seems as though the freedom to compete with the sense that your family supports you, regardless of the results, comes through in nearly every story.

Whether parents realize it or not, what they believe to be a gentle stick to prod their children may be received by their young ones as an electric cattle prod. In other words, their words and actions are extremely powerful. The most effective positive parenting seems to stem from being a great role model of we want our children to be. This model offers no stated expectation, but it may provide a child with an image to better guide the tiller of their life.

The next best advice for parents is to praise their children's efforts or process of achievement. Over and over we see in these stories parents coaching life, not swimming. As Coach Murphy said, each swimmer can only have one coach. The parent who focuses their praise on their child's results risks burdening their son or daughter with repeating them. The parent that praises the process of achieving those results affirms the personal qualities their child is developing through their athletic experience. Just as we see emphasized in the Matt Biondi story, a process for excellence is possible to duplicate in many other aspects of our lives.

Patience seems to be a worthy word to consider. With the benefit of hindsight, each athlete seemed to progress on their own emotional as well as physical timetable. Emotionally, some (Berkoff, Krayzelburg) weren't ready to explore their potential as early as others (Peirsol, Hackett, Crocker) but still had fantastic careers that continued well past their college years.

The patience for physical maturation was the only way that others (Biondi) could find their potential and develop solid motor skills. What happens to a tall lanky swimmer that is forced into "surviving practice"? The author's opinion is that the answer is in pools everywhere and it is quite ugly to watch. Perhaps there is a Biondi, or Davis, or Crocker, or Hackett out there that with patience and skill-work as a young swimmer will be prepared for the harder work to come when they reach their teen years.

Matt Biondi, at this writing, is the chairman of the math department for his school district. He set up the curriculum so that a student's placement in a math level is based on their current level of knowledge rather than their grade or age. He tells us the feedback from the students in their college years is enormously positive. Everyone isn't on the same timetable but they eventually can learn the math systems. This sounds like a good model for a swimming career.

Anyone interested in athletics can be easily fascinated by the "power of the mind." It comes through over and over in learning about great athletes. Many athletes lose before they ever compete by thinking about what they want to avoid instead of what they actually want to achieve. Thoughts are what make up each of our own realities, but thought patterns are begun before we know we are initiating them. For every negative child there is likely a history of negativity before a coach ever spoke to them. Those early life experiences and input can never be replaced, but they can be displaced by coaches, parents, teammates *and* the athlete's own self-talk that fill the person with positive, productive words and emotions. It is never too late to have a happy childhood.

Finally, the Pyramid of a Champion, from *Four Champions, One Gold Medal* seems to hold up beautifully. When we find competitive kids with some talent and give them opportunity (no matter how crude, Ian Crocker!) there is a strong likelihood of developing a very strong self-image. Once an individual sees themselves as a success, then—and only then—will they begin to work hard. And at that point, they are also much more likely to take responsibility for their success and failures.

Everyone can't be an Olympic champion but Olympic champions come from everywhere. For coaches and administrators, this fact might be most effectively translated into the knowledge that national-class athletes are in every club of 40 or more individuals. Within a club of 100 athletes there is almost surely someone with the ability to become world-class in their sport. Perhaps for parents it's good to know that one of those might be yours, but only when they've been appropriately nurtured and on their timetable.

Thanks for reading. Matt, Dave, Mike, Josh, Lenny, Ian, Grant and Aaron, thanks for sharing.

SOURCES

SWIMMING WORLD MAGAZINE, Sports Publications Inc., 228 Nevada Street, El Segundo, California

1980, 1981, 1982, 1983, 1984, 1985, 1986, 1987, 1988, 1989, 1990, 1991, 1992, 1993, 1994, 1995, 1996, 1997, 1998, 1999, 2000, 2001, 2002, 2003, 2004, 2005, 2006, 2007, 2008, 2009, 2010, 2011

AMERICAN SWIMMING COACHES ASSOCIATION CLINIC YEARBOOKS

> 2101 North Andrews Avenue, Suite 107, Fort Lauderdale, Florida
> 1989 Thornton and Biondi
> 1996 Volume 25 Nagy on Barrowman
> Volume 25 Carew on Perkins
> 2001 Sharon Power on Ian Crocker

2002 ASCA Magazine Volume 2 – Denis Cotterell on Grant Hackett
Ian Thorpe: The Biography – Hunter

INTERVIEW SOURCES

MATT BIONDI

Matt Biondi
Tom Jager
Stu Kahn
Nort Thornton
Richard Shoulberg

DAVID BERKOFF

David Berkoff
Joe Bernal
Bob Israel
Debbie Pollack
Jack Simon

MIKE BARROWMAN

Mike Barrowman
Mark Eldridge
Dave Green
Burt Hall
Jozsef Nagy
Kevin Thornton
Jim Williams

JOSH DAVIS

Josh Davis
Kris Kubik
Al Marks
Eddie Reese
Fletcher Watson
Jim Yates

LENNY KRAYZELBURG

John Apgar
Stu Blumkin
Lenny Krayzelburg
Dave Salo
Dee St. Cross

GRANT HACKETT

Denis Cotterell
Ian Pope

IAN CROCKER

Ian Crocker
Kris Kubik
Don Murphy
Sharon Power
Eddie Reese

AARON PEIRSOL,

Wella Peirsol Hartig
Kris Kubik
Brian Pajer
Aaron Peirsol
Eddie Reese
Dave Salo

ABOUT THE AUTHOR

Chuck Warner

Chuck Warner is the founder, President and CEO of ARETE Aquatic Services and the ARETE Swim Camp. His company focuses on assisting children and families through excellence and innovation in the world of aquatics. He has authored two books to this date. The first was published in 1997, called Four Champions, One Gold Medal and the second in June of 2012, ...And Then They Won Gold: Stepping Stones To Swimming Excellence."

Chuck grew up in the shadow of the great Bob Kiphuth at Yale University and the tradition of excellence that Kiphuth built at the school based in New Haven, Connecticut. He became hooked on coaching at age 13 and began full-time coaching while attending and graduating from the University of Redlands in Southern California. Shortly thereafter he proudly served as an assistant coach for Eddie Reese at the University of Texas where the art of being a good person and a great coach was on display every day.

In his coaching career he has helped swimmers reach the highest level of the sport in winning Olympic gold medals. He has been a USA National Team coach three times. His teams in Wilton and Sarasota won seven National Y Championships and at Cal State Bakersfield were runners-up at three NCAA Division II Championships. He was the Head Coach at Rutgers University for thirteen years where his women's teams moved from finishing eleventh in the Big East Conference when he started to being ranked twelfth in the nation.

Chuck has served the sport of swimming by authoring the first known code-of-ethics for any coaching organization in the world, when he did so for the American Swimming Coaches Association in 1986. He has served as President of the ASCA, is involved in directing their Fellows program and has served on USA Swimming's Olympic International Committee.

Coach Warner has been a popular speaker throughout the United States, in Europe and the Middle East. One of his favorite topics is "The American Swimming Team" a concept that USA Swimming has adopted for its marketing theme and acknowledged Coach Warner as its source. His passion for preparation and the benefit of the sporting experience has brought standing ovations on several occasions. He conducts regular seminars for swimmers and parents on the concepts of "The Intention of Arete" and "How to Make the Right College Choice."

The most important position that Chuck has ever enjoyed is to be the father of Annie Warner. Witnessing Annie's development as a dancer, as an actor, as a student, volunteer positions in church youth groups and coaching her championship softball teams have been some of the many joys it's brought. They live in Martinsville, New Jersey with their yellow lab Tissie – a heck of an outfielder in her own right.

You can order
...And Then They Won Gold and *Four Champions, One Gold Medal*
by going to www.areteswim.com and accessing the
Book * Media tab on the top left of the screen